Religion and Biography
in China and Tibet

Religion and Biography in China and Tibet

Edited by

Benjamin Penny

LONDON AND NEW YORK

First Published in 2002
by Routledge
2 Park Square, Milton Park, Abingdon, Oxon, OX14 4RN
711 Third Avenue, New York, NY 10017
Transferred to Digital Printing 2008

© 2002 Benjamin Penny

Typeset in Times by Graphicraft Limited, Hong Kong

All rights reserved. No part of this book may be reprinted or reproduced or utilised in any form or by any electronic, mechanical, or other means, now known or hereafter invented, including photocopying and recording, or in any information storage or retrieval system, without permission in writing from the publishers.

British Library Cataloguing in Publication Data
A catalogue record of this book is available from the British Library

Library of Congress Cataloguing in Publication Data
A catalogue record for this book has been requested

First issued in paperback 2013

Publisher's Note
The publisher has gone to great lengths to ensure the quality of this reprint but points out that some imperfections in the original may be apparent

ISBN 13: 978-0-700-71177-2 (hbk)
ISBN 13: 978-0-415-86158-8 (pbk)

In memory of
A.R. Davis
1924–1983

Contents

Acknowledgements	ix
Introduction T.H. Barrett	1
1. **Jiao Xian's Three Lives** Benjamin Penny	13
2. **The Virtue of Conformity** The Religious Re-Writing of Political Biography Barbara Hendrischke	30
3. **Everyday Miracles** A.J. Prince	49
4. **Representing Wŏnch'ŭk** Meditations on Medieval East Asian Buddhist Biographies John Jorgensen	74
5. **The Mirror of Life** The Structure of a 16th Century Tibetan Hagiography David Templeman	132
6. **Peng Shaosheng or Peng Jiqing?** Biographies of a Confucian Buddhist Colin Jeffcott	148
7. **The Epic and Nationalism in Tibet** Geoffrey Samuel	178
8. **Biography by Instalment** The Tibetan Periodicals *Sheja* and *Trunggö Böjong* on the Lives of Reincarnate Lamas Kevin Garratt	189

Contents

9. The Factor of Fate in Religious Biography   221
Scott Davis

Contributors   241
Chinese Character Glossary   244
Tibetan Glossary   250
Bibliography   255
Index   269

Acknowledgments

The inspiration for this volume came from a conference held at the Australian National University called "Biography in Asian Religions". Some of the papers in the collection were first delivered there, some were not; and, as is indicated by that conference's title, some of the papers given at that gathering did not fall into the parameters of this book as it became focused more specifically on China and Tibet. My thanks must first go to those who participated in the conference for their stimulating presentations and discussion, their intellectual generosity and their willingness to engage with work beyond their own fields of research. My thanks must also go to the authors of the papers in this volume who have shown forbearance and patience and humour.

In the preparation of this collection for publication I also wish to acknowledge the debt of gratitude I owe my friends Miriam Lang and Lewis Mayo for their encouragement, good sense and incisiveness. I also wish to thank Lewis, in particular, for the long hours he laboured on this book. Without them, this volume simply would never have appeared. I also acknowledge the Chiang Ching-kuo Foundation for International Scholarly Exchange and the Australian Research Council for financial assistance that has supported the venture and the Australian National University's publications fund for a publication subvention.

As ever, my deepest thanks go to my partner Gillian Russell who saw this project at its inception, has talked through it at every stage, and now, doubtless, feels the same satisfaction as I do that it is complete.

Introduction

T.H. Barrett

Ask anyone to name a good example of a religious leader today, and – especially if you specify a non-Western leader – the chances are that they will come up with the name of the Dalai Lama. There may be special geopolitical reasons for that, and for the vast amount that has been written on his current incarnation, and even on his family.[1] But even were we able to ignore the Dalai Lama, the image of the holy person has in any case scarcely faded from our awareness of the Sino-Tibetan world, not simply because of the activities of other lamas but also of Chinese Buddhist masters – who are at length beginning to vie with the Japanese, Koreans and Vietnamese who have hitherto served as the main representatives of Zen and other popular forms of Buddhism – to say nothing of Daoist teachers as well.[2] This has kept before historians of the area the importance of studying its traditions of hagiography, with the result that more and more attention is now being paid to the figure of the holy man – and holy woman, though in this collection, as elsewhere, materials on male figures tend to predominate, even if there are now studies and translations which seek to correct the usual bias of our sources.[3]

This particular volume, however, has somewhat different aims. By mapping the textual appearances of holy figures from different traditions over an extended canvas of time and space – and by adding an anthropological coda providing yet another dimension to the discussion – the contributions collected here raise a number of persistent problems concerning Sino-Tibetan religion and biography that would not readily become apparent within volumes following a more restricted approach. At the same time, the focus on culturally contiguous areas avoids the level of generalisation which is forced upon yet broader comparative studies – though there is obviously a place for such projects as well.[4]

The oldest materials treated here are Daoist, starting with Benjamin Penny's examination of the triple biography of Jiao Xian, which strikes with remarkable clarity a note of ambivalence that echoes through most of the subsequent chapters. In this particular case the ambivalence has much to do with the emergence of a new form of biography of a more religious sort into a culture that had hitherto been dominated by *vitae* structured either by bureaucratic values, as demonstrated a generation ago by E. Balazs and D.C. Twitchett, or by their inversion, as exhibited in the more recent work of Aat Vervoorn or Alan Berkowitz. If Daoism was to emerge as a coherent religion, then it needed to find a cultural space beyond these polarities, as Buddhism already appeared to have as part of its Indian heritage – though even there it can be argued that the logic of inversion was at work.[5] That Chinese Buddhists themselves had to work hard for their part to establish this space is suggested by the way in which they seized upon the term *fangwai* (originally introduced by an opponent), a phrase in the *Zhuangzi* used to describe the sage as 'beyond the bounds' of ordinary society.[6] As for Daoists, the achievements of Anna Seidel have brought home to us just how closely (albeit not completely) the structures and values of that religion followed those of the imperial bureaucracy.[7] The struggle to create space may therefore be seen as yet more difficult for them, as Barbara Hendrischke's ingenious study of a number of surviving examples of the rewriting of political biography in the Daoist mode would tend to suggest.

Perversely, however, the next two contributions, on Buddhism, depict a world in which Buddhism, having during the early sixth century become too divorced from the everyday, became as a result of subsequent crises later in that century (including the Northern Zhou persecution) urgently concerned to diminish the gap. An important essay by Stanley Weinstein already drew attention some time ago to the consequences of this in terms of the role of imperial patronage in the formation of new schools, in that 'usefulness to the state' became one obvious path towards reintegration into society.[8] But one shortcoming of such patronage was frequently to encourage competition for its benefits, and hence the generation of sectarian disputes. In the first instance these squabbles took place between Buddhism and Daoism, but they emerged also between and even within Buddhist schools, as notably in the case of the rift between Northern and Southern Chan. The battle lines might be drawn over spiritual legacies, but the prestige conveyed by the recognition of one's 'true' filiation could of course command at least some forms of material benefit. John Jorgensen shows what consequences rivalries intensified and perhaps even created by disciples of two fellow-students might have. But he shows as well one important consequence of the frequent closeness of religious biography to the realm of traditional, bureaucratic Chinese historiography: once the effort is made to apply sound scholarship and close reading to the surviving evidence, that historiographic tradition was meticulous enough that in some cases it is possible to re-read our texts so as to question the negative stereotypes which at first sight appear to be the only representations available to us.

Introduction

A more benign movement towards closing the gap between Buddhism and society can be seen in the study by A.J. Prince of Buddhist miracles in China, especially in the wake of the rise of Huayan Buddhism, with its highly 'immanentist' approach to spiritual power. In the new intellectual climate of the Tang period this power was no longer to be conceived of as 'out there' in some divisive way, separating the thaumaturge from the rest of society, but as of a piece with the whole of everyday reality. That this had consequences for Chan biography is amply demonstrated, for indeed the assertion of the spiritual value of the mundane has been taken at least during this century as one of the chief appeals of the Chan movement as against other religious traditions, including Western ones. It is perhaps no accident, for example, that the final words of the quotation that closes this essay were taken up by Jacques Gernet and adapted to form the epigraph of his celebrated study of China and Christianity.[9]

By the time, however, that Counter-Reformation Christianity appeared in China and Tibet, both those areas had evolved new modes of hagiography capable of spanning considerable periods of time. In the case of sixteenth century Tibetan traditions of the type explored by David Templeman this was surely at least in part a result of the Tibetan mode of establishing filiation through reincarnation. Yet, as he shows, such filiations served to guarantee the origin and continuity of teachings rather than to link separate personalities, a conclusion reinforced by the structural linkages he reveals within the biographies themselves, which essentially tie lives to doctrines. The Indian tradition by this period was capable of creating quite complex and sophisticated textual structures dedicated to the expression of doctrinal ideas through ostensibly linear, biographical narratives, so the closeness of the particular lineage that he treats to India (whither at one point it even reverted) may be of some significance: there some quite remarkable patterning of narrative in the interests of conveying religious meaning have recently been detected.[10]

By contrast Colin Jeffcott's account of the eighteenth century Chinese biographer and autobiographer Peng Shaosheng brings us back to a case of multiple textual personalities reminiscent of that explored by Benjamin Penny. Here, however, the ambivalent existence of Peng as a biographee in both Buddhist and Confucian worlds seems to affect modern scholarship as much as that of his contemporaries: the confusion over the date of his examination success is surely symptomatic, and the fact that he is officially listed as having passed eighteenth in the second class of the special session of 1761 may be of much lesser importance.[11] As to what was apparently important to Peng – his own struggle to reconcile religious and social roles – it would seem that there was no place in the biographical conventions of his day to do more than refer to his writings themselves. Yet we do know much more about a number of aspects of Peng's life than would be the case for many earlier figures. For example, as the denizen of a more modern world, it is in theory possible to treat Peng, like the Dalai Lama, within a family context, especially if his academically distinguished ancestors are counted as part of the group, together with the devout Buddhists amongst his female kin. And included in this latter group there were individuals whose poetry has been seen as revealing some sort of religious inner world.[12]

Gesar of Ling, by contrast, inhabits our modern world even today, but only after the fashion of King Arthur, as Geoffrey Samuel observes. The analogy, however, is particularly apt if it is made between the original Arthur, whoever he was, in the twilight of the ancient world, in relation to the Arthur of medieval times, and the original Gesar of medieval times and the Gesar of today. It is not simply that both were in life petty princelings living in the shadows of lost empires and fragmentary memories of larger views of the world.[13] Nor is their common involvement in ancient substrates of mythological lore concerning natural forces the end of their similarities.[14] The contemporary situation for Tibetans and Chinese as described by Samuel is remarkably like that for Welsh and English after the Plantagenet conquest as described by David Jones, namely, that "the tradition of Arthur . . . was, for the Welsh, an authentic part of their historical mythus, whereas for the English it was a literary convention . . .".[15] For Gesar, like Arthur, is *rex quondam rexque futurus*, a "Once and Future King", whose return has been rumoured well within living memory, if it is not still whispered even now.[16] There is no wonder, therefore, that in somewhat earlier days the Manchu rulers of China sought to identify him with Guandi, for Guandi was not simply God of War, but God of Loyalty besides.[17]

But such Tibetan figures of power are today faced with what is in a way a greater threat than being reduced to literature – that of being reduced, with the very best of intentions, to journalism, in the form of the periodical obituaries examined by Kevin Garratt. Yet the generally successful transfer of earlier biographical practices to a modern world, full of such formerly unimaginable events as death in Australia, suggests that so far autonomous Tibetan traditions in their new journalistic form are well able to cope with the rival products of China's mighty publishing industry, which he also examines. And even though the advance of a secularizing modernity is not being promoted by the Chinese regime with quite so much self-belief as before, the hitherto widely accepted notion of some sort of twentieth century East Asian retreat of the sacred in the face of the secular does give added interest to the final contribution of Scott Davis, taking as it does a starting point from the minimal determinants of the distinctively religious life.

For constructing a baseline for religious biography turns out to be no easy task, to the extent that the concept of 'fate' (*ming*), the ostensibly cut-and-dried criterion used to demarcate the religious calling, turns out to be no such thing. In fact, though the supporting illustrations are mainly from Zhu Xi and Mencius, we find ourselves in the philosophical world of the *Book*

Introduction

of Changes, where cut-and-dried causality yields to concurrence, a world in which, when the great man "precedes Heaven, Heaven is not contrary to him, and when he follows Heaven, he obeys the timing of its moments".[18] In this way some very different presuppositions concerning how life is lived are brought to the surface, in the light of which it becomes as important to approach the biographical texts we possess from Tibetan and Chinese traditions with as little in the way of "literary innocence" as we should when approaching the *Tale of Genji*.[19]

To go one step further, however, this anthropological approach to the lived holy life may serve as a key to unlock barriers imposed by other conventions, too. Up to this point, for example, we have allowed ourselves to follow convention in assuming the largely chronological approach to these biographical studies to be the most obviously productive – and, indeed, it has allowed us to discuss such matters as filiation and historical memory. Yet to what extent is this merely due to a cliché of our historiography – and much less so of our anthropology – that "history is about chaps, geography about maps"? Even in a modern secular context such a generalisation is patently not so at all, as a glance at the visitors' books in Dove Cottage, Grasmere, or Hardy's Cottage, Higher Bockhampton, will attest. Revered lives create memories drawing others across the landscape, and in English at any rate that process has given rise to a distinct genre in which biography is situated topographically, as for example the classic work *A Literary Pilgrim in England*.[20] By contrast the relationship between holy persons and holy places obtrudes only occasionally in the two excellent volumes on pilgrimage in China and in Tibet which have appeared to date.[21]

Nor does the importance of place obtrude too much here, though a close reading does provide some useful hints. Take, for example, Tankuang, who remained a supporter of Wŏnch'ŭk's scholastic legacy until a century after the latter's death. Surely it is his constant repetition of his links with the Ximingsi, the great monastery in the capital where he imbibed that legacy, even long after he had returned northeastwards to the Dunhuang area, which misled Paul Demiéville into thinking that he had remained there years later than he did.[22] Yet the predominant concern with sectarian filiations in recent scholarship on Chinese Buddhism (especially in Chan Buddhism, and especially in Japanese scholarship on that school) at the expense of studying figures within their landscapes has tended to devalue the strong sense of place that our sources often exhibit. The Sixth Patriarch of Chan for example, would surely look somewhat different as the inhabitant of a specific locale rather than as a number in a series, and indeed a doctoral study with this emphasis in mind is already under way in the Netherlands.[23] Admittedly the type of religious biography included in standard Chinese local histories tends to be extremely brief, but we also possess monastic, 'mountain' gazetteers and other spatially ordered approaches to the sacred (including sacred lives) in both Tibetan and Chinese.[24] Indeed, one might go so far as to suggest that it is in the very nature of holy persons within 'higher' religions to bring the broader perspectives of their traditions to societies which perceive religiosity in highly localised ways, and that it is in part a sense of the importance of this dual aspect of the holy life which lies behind the recent upsurge of scholarship in this area.[25] Just as much as the local officials of central government, they brought the outside world to the local community, so it is no surprise that in some respects the functions of the two groups appear to have overlapped.[26]

There was, however, a difference: bureaucrats represented the centre over the local, whereas holy figures stood not for the centre, but for the non-local, even the unlocalizable. This preference for no-place and for invisibility is already apparent in Laozi – who according to legend finally forsook the Middle Kingdom in a dramatic demonstration of the superiority of disappearance over centrality. And when religion eventually displaced politics on a more than individual level, in the late Han, its most successful (and, as it happens, most centrally placed) leader was Luo Yao, who unlike his contemporaries Zhang Jue of the Yellow Turbans and Zhang Xiu of the Five Bushels of Rice movements taught his followers how to vanish – hence the remarkable scale of his success is fully confirmed by the fact that we know nothing about him, his religion, or his adherents.[27] Note, too, one or two centuries later, the words of Liezi: "As for those sages who had the art of transforming the Empire, their way was employed in secret, their outward achievements were no different from other men's".[28] And consider, also, the many Tang poems on visiting hermits and finding them not at home – just like the ideal club of Groucho Marx, which would never have him as a member, so the ideal hermit, in the eyes of the Tang poet, was the one who was too choosy over his contacts with the secular world to allow himself to be found.[29] Finally, compare, much later, the verdict of Yuan Hongdao (1568–1610) on an old drunk whom he suspected of being a Daoist immortal in disguise: "I often see strange people in the cities and regret that I know nothing about their lives. And I regret that of the strange people holed up in the forests and mountains, probably only one out of ten appear in the cities! As for the strange people in the official records and unofficial books, surely they represent no more than one tenth of those who do appear in the cities" – so giving, once the concealment effect is factored in, a China fully one hundred per cent weirder than our all too conventional sources allow![30]

The quotation from Liezi in particular surely has a bearing on the conception of miracles, and suggests an intellectual lineage for Chan and its emphasis on the "secular as sacred" going back to Chinese origins. But one suspects that the originally Daoist notion of concealment is equally important for understanding the limitations of hagiography, about which several of the contributions below are refreshingly frank. As Barbara Hendriksche (following Benjamin Penny's doctoral work) suggests, the texts which she examines cannot be read as communicating much about Daoist practices – at best, they can be read as a form of advertisement, in other words as a prospectus for potential students. But it may be possible to take things further than that, for surely it is not just a late twentieth century mind that finds it possible to treat the very existence of text as a marker of absence. It is surely no accident that in our earliest source for Daoist biography, the *Liexan zhuan*, one of the figures whom she mentions, Lu Shang, leaves behind, as a token of his transformation into an immortal, a book. Objects such as a staff or sword were admittedly more common tokens, but we also hear of a written talisman performing the same function.[31] Even the omnipresence of the *Huayan Sūtra* in the structure of the cosmos, mentioned below by A.J. Prince, may perhaps be considered as one paradoxical form of the textualisation of absence, for it has been strongly argued that a rhetoric of absence forms a very important part of later Buddhist thought.[32]

But rather than venture into the magical wonderland of theory (and also because I hope to address the question of text as relic shortly in a study of the origins of printing), let us look rather at the way in which the original texts underlying the scholarship in this volume were regarded within the societies that produced them. The functions of the early Daoist sources must remain hypothetical, but as already pointed out, it seems likely that at least one purpose was to serve as a marker of exemplarity. Questions of readership are not extensively explored here, but elsewhere it has been observed that in Tang times the narrated lives of Buddhist monks did act to inspire others to emulate them.[33] This would appear to have remained a factor in later times also: one Daoist woman of the late nineteenth century lists for example Peng Shaosheng's biographies of devout Buddhist women, the *Shan nüren zhuan*, amongst the works on female religiosity which inspired her own career.[34] Such circularity – the production of biographies to stimulate the living of similar lives – remind one forcibly of the parallel world in China of martial prowess, with its careers progressing "from myth to myth".[35]

But, beyond the commemoration of the departed and the production of worthy successors, it is quite clear from the studies included in this volume that outside the community of readers that was in reality or potentially the same as that of the producers of these texts, the gaze of other, more hostile eyes was and is frequently envisaged. The servants of the state, it seems, also make their presence felt as implied readers of religious biography. In China this is generally covert – Barbara Hendrischke deduces from her comparative study the purpose of the rewriting which she analyses, but nowhere does any Daoist say "Please leave us alone – we are not interested in politics", in contrast to Chinese Buddhist apologetic of the type exemplified by such works as the *Hongming ji*, the *Guang Hongming ji*, and so forth, which repeat the point with dogged persistence. In Tibet, on the other hand, the whole conception of the state is not taken for granted, since as well as a certain awareness of the statecraft traditions of the Chinese empire, a marked influence from the looser 'galactic polity' model more common in South and Southeast Asia was also present, as Geoffrey Samuel shows, with the result that descriptions of the holy life and of the hero become sites of contestation between different political outlooks. As for Kevin Garratt's study of contemporary Tibetan religious biography, to describe that as politicised would be a considerable understatement. But even the worst vicissitudes of recent Chinese politics since the Cultural Revolution would not seem to have eliminated religious biography altogether, for in May 1989 we find that it was still possible, at least in Gansu, to publish the autobiography of a prominent Amdo Tibetan together with plenty of information (carefully vetted, no doubt) concerning Labrang Monastery and its fifth, twentieth-century "Living Buddha".[36]

At the same time, we should not underestimate the powers of resistance to the state that may still be embedded in religious biography. There are, after all, few more powerful images of bureaucracy subverted by complete irresponsibility in China than in the biography of the Monkey King that prefaces the *Journey to the West*, with its vivid depiction of his all too brief career in the courts of heaven.[37] It may be objected that the biography of a non-human should not be adduced as an example in the context of this volume, but we should remember that Gesar too, an equally ambivalent trickster figure, is linked with the Monkey King through his own penchant for appearing together with animal companions.[38] In any case the notion of religious biography in China too as being in a slightly different way a site of contestation between a number of different conceptions of the holy person is now well established by the work of Meir Shahar on Crazy Ji, a Buddhist figure of Southern Song origin whose exploits continue to be rewritten to this day by various strands in popular culture.[39] Admittedly "site of contestation" may be too narrowly late twentieth century a phrase to encompass the range of tensions on display over the span of this volume. But consider if you will the verdict of one of the very few properly trained Western sinologists to have observed imperial China in action, with regard to the *Strange Tales* of Pu Songling (1640–1715): "Alexeev saw the fantastic stories about foxes, monks, and other supernatural events as being a superb satire on the bureaucratic system".[40] To the extent, then, that the tensions that stimulate our interest in religious biography are linked to time-honoured patterns of bureaucracy in the region, since there seems little chance of the withering away of these patterns in the foreseeable future, the chances are, therefore, that neither will those tensions disappear.

For we may be fairly certain, after all, that narratives of the type surveyed in this volume will evolve, but there is indeed no sign that they are about to disappear. Whether we choose to read them historically, geographically, philosophically or politically, they will always remain, for all the constraints placed upon them, rich and rewarding materials. To be frank, on looking

Introduction

back at the foregoing introductory remarks, I feel yet more certain that their richness cannot be summed up in a few words. Some years ago my wife acted as teaching assistant on an introductory humanities course at a prestigious university in a country where the secondary education system stressed self-expression over analytic skills. She discovered therefore that the first assignment, on some such topic as "Aristotle's views on Literature", actually elicited a response for the most part on the theme "What I thought when I read Aristotle's views on Literature". I am all too conscious of having produced rather a similar type of response to this volume myself, and would accordingly urge readers not to dwell on my own off-the-cuff and purely personal remarks, but to read the studies that follow for themselves. They will certainly find a whole range of questions to occupy their attention, and will emerge with a much more acute sense of the problems raised by our records of holy lives in China and Tibet than can be conveyed in a brief introduction.

Notes

1 Mary Craig, *Kundun: A Biography of the Family of the Dalai Lama* (London: HarperCollins, 1997).
2 For Chinese Buddhism, a good example is Chi-Ying Fu and Ven. Master Hsing Yun, *Handing Down the Light: The Biography of Venerable Master Hsing Yun* (English title, Taipei: Commonwealth Publishing, 1995). Daoism has as yet produced no figures with such a high profile – that would be, after all, slightly un-Daoist, but for an impeccably modest biography of a humble Daoist layman, Norman S. Track, *Song of a Water Dragon* (Jamaica Plains: YMAA Publication Center, 1996) can be recommended.
3 For example, Miranda Shaw, *Passionate Enlightenment* (Princeton: Princeton University Press, 1994) for Tibet – but cf. J.W. de Jong in *Indo-Iranian Journal* 19.2 (1996), 184–187; Kathryn Ann Tsai, *Lives of the Nuns: Biographies of Chinese Buddhist Nuns from the Fourth to Sixth Centuries* (Honolulu: University of Hawaii Press, 1994), for Chinese Buddhism; and Catherine Despeux, *Immortelles de la Chine ancienne: Taoïsme et alchimie féminine* (Puiseaux: Pardes, 1990), for Daoism. I have not yet seen Hanna Havnevik, *Tibetan Buddhist Nuns: History, Cultural Norms and Social Reality* (Oslo: Norwegian University Press and Institute for Comparative Research in Human Culture, 1989).
4 For a pioneering example of such work, see Samuel N.C. Lieu, "The Holy Men and their Biographers in Early Byzantium and Medieval China", in Ann Moffat, ed., *Maistor: Classical Byzantine and Renaissance Studies for Robert Browning* (Canberra: The Australian Association for Byzantine Studies, 1984), 113–147.
5 See Daud Ali, "Technologies of the Self: Courtly Artifice and Monastic Discipline in Early India", *Journal of the Economic and Social History of the Orient* 41.2 (1998), 159–184.
6 An episode explored already in E. Zürcher, *The Buddhist Conquest of China* (Leiden: E.J. Brill, 1958), 161, "beyond this world"; 256 and 414, n.11.
7 The most thoroughgoing exploration of the connexion between bureaucracy and religion in China (written quite independently of Seidel's research) does quite

explicitly hesitate to suggest a complete identity of interests between Daoism and imperial bureaucracy: see Stephan Feuchtwang, *The Imperial Metaphor* (London: Routledge, 1992), 158–163, which is largely targeted at John Lagerwey's overstatement of the case.

8 Stanley Weinstein, "Imperial Patronage in the Formation of T'ang Buddhism", in A.F. Wright and D.C. Twitchett, *Perspectives on the T'ang* (New Haven: Yale University Press, 1973), 265–306.

9 Jacques Gernet, trans. Janet Lloyd, *China and the Christian Impact* (Cambridge: Cambridge University Press, 1985), [vii].

10 For a particularly complex example, see Simon Weightman, "Symbolism and Symmetry", forthcoming in Leonard Lewisohn, ed. *Proceedings of the Conference on Sufism in Safavid and Mughal Times* (provisional title).

11 Zhu Baojiong and Xie Peilin, *Ming-Qing jinshi timing beilu suoyin* (Shanghai: Shanghai guji, 1980), 2731.

12 Beata Grant, "Who is This I? Who is That other? The Poetry of an Eighteenth Century Buddhist Laywoman", *Late Imperial China* 15.1 (1994), 47–86, deals with the wife of a nephew, while other female kin are also mentioned in Peng's *Shan nüren zhuan*. For Peng and his great-grandfather, see T.H. Barrett, on pages 604–05 of "History Writing and Spirit Writing in Seventeenth-Century China", *Modern Asian Studies* 23.3 (1989), 597–608.

13 For Gesar, see R.A. Stein, *Tibetan Civilisation* (Stanford: Stanford University Press, 1972), 280, alluding to P. Pelliot, "La théorie des quatre fils du Ciel", *T'oung Pao* 22 (1923), 97–125, to which should perhaps be added as further background the schemes of eschatological warfare in Jan Nattier, *Once Upon a Future Time* (Berkeley: Asian Humanities Press, 1991), summarized 288–290.

14 Stein, *Tibetan Civilisation*, 223, 227, and cf. Squirrel Nutkin, as quoted by Beatrix Potter, *The Tale of Squirrel Nutkin* (London: Frederick Warne, 1903), 50:

> Arthur O'Bower has broken his band,
> He comes roaring up the land!
> The King of Scots with all his power,
> Cannot turn Arthur of the Bower!

15 David Jones, *Epoch and Artist* (London: Faber and Faber, 1959), 227.

16 Warren Smith, *Tibetan Nation: A History of Tibetan Nationalism and Sino-Tibetan Relations* (Boulder, Colorado: Westview, 1996), 550, n.20.

17 Stein, *Tibetan Civilisation*, 88; Prasenjit Duara, "Superscribing Symbols: The Myth of Guandi, Chinese God of War", *Journal of Asian Studies*, 47.4 (1988), 778–95, or *Culture, Power, and the State: Rural North China, 1900–1942* (Stanford: Stanford University Press, 1988), 139–148.

18 Richard John Lynn, *The Classic of Changes: A New Translation of the I Ching as Interpreted by Wang Bi* (New York: Columbia University Press, 1994), 138.

19 See page 304 of Mark Morris, "Desire and the Prince: New Work on *Genji monogatari* – A Review Article", *Journal of Asian Studies* 49.2 (May, 1990), 291–304, but note that if Genji is a Mills and Boon hero, he is still a Buddhist Mills and Boon hero.

20 Edward Thomas, *A Literary Pilgrim in England* (Oxford: Oxford University Press, 1980), originally published 1917. A more recent example would be Dorothy Eagle and Hilary Carnell, *The Oxford Literary Guide to the British Isles* (Oxford: Oxford University Press, 1977).

21 Susan Naquin and Chün-fang Yü, *Pilgrims and Sacred Sites in China* (Berkeley: University of California Press, 1992); Alex McKay, *Pilgrimage in Tibet* (Richmond, Surrey: Curzon, 1998).

Introduction

22 The actual situation emerges quite unambiguously from the latest version of Werner Pachow's study of Tanguang, *A Study of the Twenty-two Dialogues on Mahāyāna Buddhism* (Taipei: Tungchu Publishing, 1992), 145–149 (English text); cf. Jorgensen's n.275, below.
23 By Mr. Kees Kuiken, already the author of a monograph on policing in modern China.
24 Two topographical texts including biographical material are translated from Tibetan in the convenient textbook of Donald S. Lopez, Jr., ed., *Religions of Tibet in Practice* (Princeton: Princeton University Press, 1997), 103–134; note also pages 157–177 for biography as itinerary. For China, Raoul Birnbaum has devoted a number of studies to sacred geography, often making use of biographical sources, e.g. "The manifestation of a Monastery: Shen-ying's Experiences on Mount Wu-t'ai in T'ang Context", *Journal of the American Oriental Society* 106.1 (1986), 119–137. See also Franciscus Verellen, ed., *Culte des sites et culte des saints en Chine: Cahiers d'Extrême-Asie* 10 (1998), which gathers together over a dozen expert studies on the theme of religion and locality.
25 For example, Mu-chou Poo, "The Images of Immortals and Eminent Monks: Religious Mentality in Early Medieval China", *Numen* 42 (1995), 172–196; John Kieschnick, *The Eminent Monk: Buddhist Ideals in Medieval Chinese Hagiography* (Honolulu: University of Hawai'i Press, 1997); Stephen Eskildsen, *Asceticism in Early Taoist Religion* (Albany: State University of New York Press, 1998).
26 This case was first made by Jean Levi, *Les fonctionnaires divins: politique, despotisme et mystique en Chine ancienne* (Paris: Seuil, 1989); subsequent English-language scholarship has reinforced it.
27 Lu Bi, *Sanguo zhi jijie* 8 (Beijing: Zhonghua, 1982), 267, quoting the *Dianlue*.
28 A.C. Graham, *The Book of Lieh-tzu* (London: John Murray, 1960), 65–66.
29 This is readily revealed by concordances to the titles of poems, of which the only general one I have to hand is that printed with the *Tang wushijia shiji* (Shanghai: Guji chubanshe, 1989): see page 4 of this index, under *fang* (0062.7 in the four-corner system) for three typical titles by different poets; the same keyword reveals similarly formatted titles in individual concordances (in the series *Quan Tang shi suoyin*) to the works of others, e.g. in the poetry of Wang Wei.
30 Jonathan Chaves, *Pilgrim of the Clouds* (New York: Weatherhill, 1992, second ed.), 133–134.
31 See page 252a of the entry on 'Liberation of the Corpse' (*shijie*) in Sakade Yoshinobu, ed., *Dōkyō no daijiten* (Tokyo: Shin jinbutsu ōraisha, 1994), 249–253.
32 Malcom David Eckel, *To See the Buddha: A Philosopher's Quest for the Meaning of Emptiness* (Princeton: Princeton University Press, 1992), chapters three to six.
33 Kieschnik, *The Eminent Monk*, 12.
34 See the preface by Yan Zehuan to her *Nannü dangong yitong bian*, as included in He Longxiang, ed., *Nüdan hebian* (Chengdu: Erxianan, 1906).
35 Hellmut Wilhelm, "From Myth to Myth: The Case of Yueh Fei's Biography", in A.F. Wright and D.C. Twitchett, *Confucian Personalities* (Stanford: Stanford University Press, 1962), 146–161.
36 Meng Guofang, ed., *Huang Zhengqing yu Wushi Jiamuxiang* (Gansu wenshi ziliao xuanbian, vol.30; Lanzhou: Gansu renmin chubanshe, 1989): presumably this volume had been planned at a less politically sensitive stage, but at any rate its publication was not halted.
37 Memorably rendered into English by Arthur Waley in Chapters Four and Five of *Monkey: Folk Novel of China* (New York: Grove Press, 1958, paperback edition).

38 Glen Dudbridge, *The Hsi-yu chi: A Study of Antecedents to the Sixteenth-Century Chinese Novel* (Cambridge: CUP, 1970), 166.
39 Meir Shahar, *Crazy Ji: Chinese Religion and Popular Literature* (Cambridge, Mass.: Harvard University Asia center, 1998).
40 Helmut Martin, on page 192 of "Literature of the Ming and Ch'ing", in Gilbert Rozman, ed., *Soviet Studies of Premodern China* (Ann Arbor; Center for Chinese Studies, The University of Michigan, 1984), 183–195.

1
Jiao Xian's Three Lives

Benjamin Penny

Some time during the second half of the second century CE, a man called Jiao Xian was born in northern China near modern-day Sanmenxia. He seems to have led a quiet and uneventful life made remarkable by his selflessness, rejection of social convention and apparent supernatural powers. He may have lived into his late eighties, or to more than one hundred, or possibly he never died. He is remembered in particular, it would appear, for going out of his way not to be noticed. He had apparently no lasting influence and, as far as we know, quickly ceased to be of interest to those institutions which were responsible for producing what we now regard as historical materials: the court, great families, the organisations of scholarship and those of religion. We only know about him now from a few short biographical accounts and references that have survived, none of which attained the status of a formal biography in a dynastic history. This is not entirely surprising as Jiao seems to have been remembered precisely for living his life outside the expectations of his time.

The China of Jiao's recorded lifetime was in turmoil: there were local uprisings and empire-wide rebellions, a major dynasty fell and short-lived states were created and subsequently collapsed. These circumstances proved fertile ground for growing long-lasting reputations: some of the great heroes and villains of Chinese history, rendered as story, were active in this period, characters who became the subjects of historical debate, popular drama, religious veneration and novelistic invention. To a large extent, reputations such as these are granted by the institutions of later generations – choices are made as to who should or should not be remembered, commemorated, reinvented, celebrated or vilified. Jiao Xian appears not to have been favoured when these choices were made. In a few generations after his own time, this intriguing figure had been relegated to the backwaters of historical commentary – there remain no written records of him originating from after the second half of the third century.

Benjamin Penny

One biography of Jiao Xian appears in the collection of immortals' lives called *Shenxian zhuan* that was put together in the fourth century CE. Two other records survive in Pei Songzhi's fifth-century commentary to *Sanguo zhi*, the *History of the Three Kingdoms*, and there are one or two other references to Jiao in contemporary texts. These different writings are translated in this essay. They constitute different lives of Jiao Xian, not simply judging his conduct differently, but also differing in their assessment of his status of being.

One approach to divergent biographical materials such as these, in particular those concerned with an important religious figure, is to attempt to isolate a core of what is real and verifiable from what is mythic or simply erroneous. These later accretions are sometimes seen as deriving from devout adherents, revisionists or those promulgating sectarian positions. The most well-known of these projects is the "search for the historical Jesus," the goal of which is to isolate what in the gospels actually represents Jesus's true words and actions.[1] For scholars involved in discussions of the historical Jesus, the historical Buddha, or the historical Zhang Ling, verifiable data are at a premium. For other scholars the focus is rather on understanding how these differences in the biographies of a particular figure arose, setting aside the question of what is true and what is false.

Interpreting the differences in biographical records is by no means an unusual occupation for scholars of religious history. Biographies of religious figures have been written and rewritten for all kinds of purposes, the most common of which are promoting the interests of a certain cult or school or using the kudos of a famous religious figure to enhance the legitimacy of a dynasty or regime. These rewritings typically take place within an already established world of texts and are subject to the general constraints and possibilities of textual production at that time and place: audience expectation, stylistic convention, the conditions of book production and others. However, in each case, there was, at some stage, some version (or some versions – this process may have been multiple) of that biography in which a remembered life first became a written life. It is precisely this act, this moment of textualization, that is of concern in this essay as the entry into text necessarily means an entry into genre, and, in the case of Jiao Xian, entry into genre meant the constitution of three different Jiao Xians.

The argument of this essay is that the three biographical records of Jiao Xian that have survived constitute fundamentally different lives. These records may represent three independent iterations of a preexisting tradition which arose in commemoration of a local figure who was spiritually noteworthy. If they do, that preexisting tradition has been lost and is unrecoverable. In any case, what is important here is how three distinct generic traditions have organised that life. It is clear from the analysis below that each version of Jiao Xian's life stresses different things about him and each attempts to make use of his kudos for its own purposes, but this is only to be expected. What is perhaps more interesting is that as memories of an odd but noteworthy

Jiao Xian's Three Lives

man were constituted into three written texts the shape of Jiao's life, what made him noteworthy, indeed his very status as a being, was powerfully determined by each genre into which his life was written.

The Immortal's Life

The life of Jiao Xian from *Shenxian zhuan – Biographies of Immortals –* reads:

> Jiao Xian, courtesy name Xiaoran, was a native of Taiyang in Hedong. He was one hundred and seventy. Usually he ate white rocks which he divided up with other people. He heated them until they were like taro and then he ate them.
>
> Each day he went into the mountains to cut firewood to give to other people. He started out at the house at the end of the village and went around each in turn. Then he started again. He carried the firewood and laid it outside people's doors. If people saw him they spread out a mat and sat with him and set out food. He would sit but he never spoke with anyone. If he did not see anyone when he delivered the firewood, he set it in the doorway himself and then left. It was like this year after year.
>
> When the Wei succeeded [the Han] he was living on the banks of the Yellow River. He built a hut from grass and lived in it alone. He did not roll out bedding but used grass as a mattress and sat on that. His body was filthy, as muddy as a swamp. Sometimes he only had one meal every few days. He did not follow paths when he travelled and he had no social dealings with women. When his clothes wore out he sold firewood and bought old ones to wear. Winter and summer he wore an unlined robe. The prefect Dong Jing went to see him on this account but he refused to speak. This only made Jing consider him more worthy. When a scrub fire came through, his hut caught fire. People came to look for him and they saw him sitting formally in his hut not moving. When the fire had reduced it to ashes Xian arose with great dignity. None of his clothes or possessions were burnt. Then he rebuilt the hut.
>
> Many houses were damaged by a great and unexpected snowfall. Xian's hut toppled over. People came but could not see where he was. Worried that he might have frozen to death, together they dismantled it to find him. They saw Xian lying fast asleep under the snow; his skin glowed and he was snoring as if he had fallen into a drunken stupor.
>
> People knew of his marvellous powers and were keen to learn the Dao from him. Xian said "I do not have the Dao." Sometimes he grew older and sometimes younger. It was like this for more than two hundred years. Later he took leave of everybody and no-one knew where he went. Those who consulted him did not receive a word in reply.[2]

Shenxian zhuan is a collection of biographies of immortals or transcendents that was compiled in the fourth century. These were people who, through various disciplines – alchemical, gymnastic, meditational, sexual, medicinal, dietary – overcame death, some to take up a position in the celestial bureaucracy, some to live in the numinous places on, or under, this earth. The biographies in this collection, and in the tradition of immortals' biographies in general, tell us little of the details of the techniques aspirants used to attain the exalted state of immortality; rather they served as demonstrations that such a state existed and was indeed attainable. The attraction of these biographies was also partly in their depiction of the marvellous feats that immortals could perform such as flying, being in different places at the same time, healing, resurrection of the dead and what is usually termed transformation. The *Shenxian zhuan* biographies are part of a generic tradition of biographies of immortals that was extant at least two centuries before it was compiled and which continued for centuries afterwards.[3] The religious tradition from which the biographies came is conveniently labelled Daoist, though this designation is by no means an unproblematic one for Ge Hong (283–343) who is traditionally identified as the editor of *Shenxian zhuan*.[4]

In many ways the biography of Jiao Xian is a typical example of an immortal's life. Jiao is introduced in traditional Chinese biographical style with his courtesy name and place of origin. He is credited with an astonishing age – 170 – and his bizarre diet is noted,[5] in this case eating white rocks that are cooked to be like taro. These three pieces of information, and how they are presented, form the core of Jiao's biography. While the mode of identification used here is standard across all Chinese biography, secular as well as sacred, what is notable in this case is the absence of any other detail; Jiao's ancestry, education, any early signs of promise receive no attention and the biography provides no sense of a career or a development over time. Nor do we find other events in the biography located on specific days or in specific years – in the remainder of the biography there is a reference to only one date, the succession of the Wei dynasty in 220. Jiao is granted an age but no date or time of birth is given. In other words, the events in the biography are not located in time in the traditional Chinese way – a nominated year in a particular reign period of a certain emperor, or with a designation from the sixty year cycle. Thus, Jiao's life makes no reference to the measurement of time in days and years, it does not acknowledge the calendrical system of the court nor does it conform to the expected shape of a noteworthy career. These features place Jiao apart from his society, and his diet of white rocks not only reinforces that autonomy but it also directs the reader's attention to Jiao's body and its strangeness which will form a major theme of the life.

Jiao Xian dwelt on the edges of society where many others who followed this path also had, either literally or metaphorically. Each day, "year after year," he cut firewood for everyone in the village only accepting food when

Jiao Xian's Three Lives

it was offered and refusing to speak. This selfless performance of good deeds and refusal of personal interaction amounts to a rejection of the standards of normal behaviour. But the interest of the biographer in detailing the mundaneness of Jiao's rounds reflects a preoccupation with how Jiao lived his days, hour by hour. A similar sense of fine observation is apparent in the descriptions of his flimsy grass shelter, his grass mattress, his dirtiness, his eating very little, his lack of social interaction and his apparent imperviousness to cold. These are the things that are important in an immortal's life, that constitute and underpin the narrative. This history of Jiao Xian is, in important ways, the history of his body.[6]

In this record Dong Jing, the local prefect, (who will appear in the other biographies under discussion here) pays Jiao attention because of the particularity of his disciplines but Jiao disregards him.[7] Jiao did not so much rebel against government and its functionaries as pay them no heed. The bureaucracy here has no role in Jiao's life, its function in the narrative is simply to highlight his distinctiveness, respecting him but also revealing a fundamental lack of understanding of Jiao's nature. In this way, Dong Jing typifies the reaction of the society in general, and implicitly of the reader. Similarly, when Jiao was discovered to possess special powers, in this case his triumphing over fire and snow, "people" could only look on in wonder.[8] Jiao's incomprehensibility reaches its apogee in the final paragraph: he denied possessing the Dao, his body sometimes grew old, sometimes it became young, no-one knew where he went, he never answered questions.

No explanations are offered in this biography for the oddities in Jiao's behaviour, his body or his powers. This is, in a sense, its specific conclusion: the immortal's life is not subject to the same logic as that of normal people. We know he was special, the biographer implies, but we cannot know how, all we can do is to document the life in all its dirty, incomprehensible detail.

The features in Jiao Xian's biography that have been described above, and their commonality with other immortals' biographies, point to this record as one example of the genre and allow its inclusion in a collection of them. Thus, the way that this biography has been extracted from *Shenxian zhuan* for the purposes of this essay is clearly not the way it would normally have been read. Rather, Jiao's biography was one of many read in company with others, all mutually reinforcing the expectations of what an immortal was and how an immortal acted, and that immortals did, in fact, exist.

The Administrative Record

Jiao Xian's biography, as it appeared in a political history, *Weilüe*, the *Brief History of the Wei Dynasty*, reads:

Xian, courtesy name Xiaoran. At the end of the Zhongping reign period [189–190] there was an uprising in Baibo. At the time Xian was more than twenty and he kept company with Hou Wuyang of the same commandery. Wuyang was young and he [only] had his mother, so Xian had supported them. To avoid the Baibo rebels they moved east to live in Yangzhou where he took a wife. In the Jian'an period [196–220] they returned to the west and Wuyang moved to Dayang where he established a household. Xian stayed on the Shan side of the border. In the sixteenth year [211] there were troubles in Guanzhong. Xian lost his family and fled, alone, to an island in the Yellow River where he ate grass and drank water and had no clothes or shoes. At the time Zhu Nan, the chief of Dayang, caught sight of him and called him a "scholar-fugitive". He was about to dispatch a boat to arrest him when Wuyang said to the [head of the] prefecture, "He is a madman!" Xian was subsequently recorded on the register and was given a stipend of five *sheng* a day.

Later there was an epidemic in which a large number of people died. The [head of the] prefecture regularly ordered Xian to perform the burials and even children treated him with disrespect. Despite this he never took illicit paths but followed the orthodox tracks. When he went gleaning he did not take the large ears. When he was hungry he never gorged himself; when cold he never clothed himself excessively. He wove grass into a cloak and went barefoot and bareheaded. Each time he went out he would hide if he saw a woman, only to emerge a little later after she had gone. He built himself a snail shell hut,[9] sweeping the inside clean, making a bed out of wood and spreading grass on top as a mattress. When the weather turned cold he lit a fire to warm himself. He used to hum or drone and talk to himself. When he was hungry he took a job, simply eating his fill and not taking what he had earned. When he met anyone unexpectedly on the road he got down off it and hid. If someone asked him why he did this he always said, "Men of the grass and reeds associate with foxes and hares." He never spoke wildly.

Sometime during the Taihe [227–233] and Qinglong [233–237] reigns he took his staff, went south and crossed the Yellow River where it was shallow. He often said to himself, "The time is not yet right." After that people rather suspected he was not mad.

When the Grand Administrator Jia Mu first took up office in the Jiaping reign period [249–254], he deliberately passed Xian's hut. Xian bowed repeatedly on seeing Mu. Mu spoke to him but he did not reply. He set out food for him but Xian did not eat. Mu said to him, "The state has sent me to come to be your master. I have set out food for you, sir, but you have refused to eat it. I have spoken with you, sir, but you will not reply. This being so, I am in no position to govern you. It is right I leave." Xian then replied, "For what reason do you say that?" and said no more.

The next year a great number of soldiers was sent to attack Wu. Someone posed the question, "What do you make of this suppression of Wu?" Xian would not reply but intoned:

Zhunü, zhunü,[10]
Not fish, not meat.
One chases the other,
Intending to kill the ewe.
But the goat it was that died!

The people of the commandery did not know what he meant. After the armies were defeated in battle someone who was skilled in these things elucidated his meaning: the ewe was Wu, the goat was Wei. As a result all the people called him the hidden one.

The Gentleman Consultant Dong Jing of Hedong particularly admired exceptional behaviour. As he was not an old acquaintance of Xian he went to watch out for him in secret. When Jing arrived he tousled his white beard as if they went back a long way and said, "Ah Xian, it has been a long time. Do you remember the time we escaped from Baibo together?" Xian gave him a long look but did not speak. Jing obviously knew that he had received a kindness from Wuyang in the past because he said, "Do you remember Wuyang?" Xian said, "I have already repaid him." Jing again provoked Xian to get him to speak but he was unwilling to respond.

A little more than a year later, Xian caught a disease and died at the age of eighty nine.[11]

The *Weilüe* was an anonymous, privately compiled history of the Wei dating from the fourth century.[12] It is now lost, surviving only in fragments in other texts such as Pei Songzhi's (372–451) commentary to *Sanguo zhi*, the location of this biography. *Sanguo zhi* (composed by Chen Shou, 233–297) is the official history of the three states Wei, Wu and Shu that succeeded the Eastern Han dynasty after 220 CE. Pei introduces these records with the comment, "At the time there was an eremite called Jiao Xian who was a native of Hedong".

What is immediately clear in this account, and in complete contrast to the *Shenxian zhuan* biography, is the importance given to plotting Jiao Xian's life by date and location, that is by reference to the court calendar and official geography. That this life is "verifiable" by cross-reference to other texts deriving from the same institutions of official history is indicative of the structuring power of these concerns.

According to *Weilüe*, Jiao Xian grew up in very specific conditions, namely the turmoil surrounding the fall of the Eastern Han. Being more than twenty at the time of the troubles fomented by the bandits of the Baibo valley, means that Jiao would have been born in the late 160s. This uprising, which claimed to be connected with the famous Yellow Turbans, took place some 60 kilometres to the north of Hedong, his native place in the south of present-day Shanxi province.[13] He fled with his companions about 600 kilometres southeast to Yangzhou near present-day Huainan before returning some years later to settle on the Shan side of the river from Dayang, close to Hedong – Shan and Dayang faced each other over the Yellow River roughly on the site of the present-day city of Sanmenxia. In 211, in his mid-forties, he was forced to uproot himself again, losing his family in the rebellion led by Ma Chao and Han Sui against Cao Cao which took place at Tongguan about 50 kilometres west of Dayang on the confluence of the Wei and Yellow rivers.[14] It was at this point in his life, according to the *Weilüe* account, that he appears to have begun his eremitic existence, settling on an unnamed island in the river.

It is useful to pause here to note several distinctive features of this record: first, Jiao originally had a family and associates, and by supporting Hou Wuyang and his mother was participating in a social network based on accepting financial responsibility for the needy. Jiao's movements across the country are also thoroughly explicable – he and his family and friends fled from rebel uprisings. Similarly his decision to live as an eremite is explained by reference to his loss of family. Thus, it is implicit in the logic of official history – unlike immortal history – that explication is possible and can be provided. At the beginning of this record, Jiao is constructed as a normal, social being and his later descent into apparent madness and social exclusion are to be read as acts of volition.

Jiao Xian's decision to live as an eremite appears to have induced suspicion in the eyes of the officials. "Scholar-fugitive", the designation that Zhu Nan gives him, indicates that he was seen as potentially subversive, especially in the context of the local uprisings. Disenfranchised and disappointed scholars often acted as the leaders of such movements. Hou Wuyang's intervention – claiming Jiao as mad and thus giving him the status of official outcast – saves him by having his name entered on the population register of the district in which he now resided. This status in turn meant that Jiao was required to perform the most abject of tasks – burying plague victims – but rather than simply seeing him as reviled, the biography continues by stressing the same kinds of severe self-constraint we have seen in the *Shenxian zhuan* biography – not eating too much, wearing light clothes, never taking the large ears of grain, avoiding women. By associating Jiao's indifference to reputation with his conquering of worldly wants, the biography constructs him as unexpectedly pure. It should be noted in this context that in this record Jiao is said to have swept the inside of his hut clean, while in *Shenxian zhuan* it is his dirtiness that occasions comment.

When Jiao crosses the Yellow River the biography reveals its political nature explicitly. Jiao is presented as someone who is far from mad, and who, in

Jiao Xian's Three Lives

fact, possesses particular insights into politics. The visits of Jia Mu and then Dong Jing, apart from attempting to bring Jiao under bureaucratic control, both also seem to be aimed at ascertaining what knowledge he has. His mysterious verse is clear evidence of his predictive powers and his secret knowledge.[15] Soon after, according to this account, Jiao dies aged 89. If he was born in the late 160s, he would have died sometime in the 250s.

It is clear that this account and that of *Shenxian zhuan* concern the same person, yet they are very different. *Weilüe* is concerned with plotting Jiao Xian's life reign by reign and event by event: unlike the *Shenxian zhuan* record, there is sequence and historical specificity. Jiao Xian's life in the *Weilüe* account took place in public, under the purview of the state and adhering to its calendar, its geography and its bureaucracy.

Weilüe sees Jiao Xian through administrative eyes. It is about his movements, about his contacts and, most revealingly, about his encounters with the state. In his meetings with Zhu Nan, Jia Mu and Dong Jing, their titles are specified, and in one case the administrative result of the meeting is noted: his receipt of a stipend of five *sheng* a day. These details are not simply bureaucratic minutiae. The catalogue of Jiao's dealings with imperial authority grants the state an explicit regulatory role in his life, even if those attempts at regulation are rebuffed. If the *Shenxian zhuan* account is a record of Daoist transcendence, *Weilüe* is a record of bureaucratic management.

Moreover, when read in the context of contemporary discussions over the correct role talented scholars should play in society, where rejection of involvement with the state was regarded in some circles as the noblest option, there is possibly also an implicit criticism in *Weilüe* of the choice of withdrawal that Jiao made. It is clear that the narrator of this account regarded Jiao as perfectly sane, prescient about military affairs and morally upright. The correct place for such a man, it is implied, is in imperial service.

Finally, it should be noted that while *Shenxian zhuan* says that Jiao Xian's age at the time the biography was recorded as one hundred and seventy – and "later he took leave of everybody and no-one knew where he went" – *Weilüe* has him dying at eighty nine after an illness. In an administrative biography, unlike an immortal's, the subject has to die.

The Life of a Lofty Man

The life of Jiao Xian as a lofty man – from Huangfu Mi's *Gaoshi zhuan* – reads:

> No-one of that time knew where Jiao Xian came from. Some said he was born at the end of the Han. He moved from Shan to live in Dayang and had no father, mother, brothers, wife or children. When he saw

that the Han house was in decline he cut himself off from human contact and did not speak.

When the Wei succeeded [the Han] his practice was to build a hut from grass on the banks of the Yellow River and live in it alone. Winter and summer he wore no robe. He did not set out a mat to sleep and also had no grass mattress. He lay directly on the ground and his body was filthy, as muddy as a swamp. The five forms were all revealed to him and he did not walk among men. Sometimes he only had one meal every few days and when he wanted to eat he went to work as a hired hand. Others gave him clothes to wear and employed him to do a limited amount of work. He did enough to receive one meal and then he left. People wanted to give him more but he simply would not take it. There were also times he would not eat at all for several days. He never took illicit paths and he never met the glance of a woman. No words came from his mouth. Even when startled he never spoke with anyone. When food was left out for him, he never took it. The Grand Administrator of Hedong Du Shu[16] once went to see him with some clothes but Xian did not speak to him. King Jing of the Sima clan[17] heard about this and sent the Grand Administrator of Anding, Dong Jing, to go along and see him on some pretext. Xian would not speak and Jing considered him to be a great worthy.

After this a scrub fire burnt his hut so Xian then slept in the open. When heavy winter snows came, Xian lay naked in the snow and did not stir. People thought he was dead but when they saw that he was the same as before they did not consider him ill. Nobody was able to understand his intentions.

It is possible that when he died he was more than one hundred years old.

Somebody asked Huangfu Mi, "What kind of man was Jiao Xian?" He answered, "My knowledge is inadequate, but I can say a little from what anyone could see. What the world constantly hankers after is fame and gratification; what the human form cannot be stripped of is clothing; what the body can never be separated from is shelter; what the mouth can never be stopped from is talking; what the heart can never be cut off from is its affections. Now, Jiao Xian cast aside fame and gratification, stripped himself of clothes, left shelter, cut himself off from affections, shut his mouth and ceased speaking. Boundlessly he considered heaven and earth his house, in obscurity he merged with the forerunners of the utmost Dao. He emerged from the display of the crowd of forms and entered into the concealment of mysterious solitude. In all the world there was no man worthy to grasp his ideas; within the expanses of the four seas no-one could return his glance. He was as sublime as the ancestor of the Three Sovereigns. Since cords were knotted no-one has reached this apogee. How can the babel of voices describe him or the most constant mind attain his measure? He walked where no others could walk, suffered what no others could suffer. Laying himself open to cold and heat, he did not harm his essence; living in the wilds he had no fear for his human form. Being startled did not disturb his cogitations. Being separated from fame and love did not burden his mind. By abjuring what there was to see and hear he did not defile his eyes or ears. He placed his feet on earth that was not destroyed; he situated his body in a place where he stood alone. He extended his years beyond one hundred and his life was longer than a centenarian's. Even the most intelligent could not equal this. Since Fu Xi he is unique!"[18]

Huangfu Mi's (215–282) *Gaoshi zhuan*, or *Biographies of Lofty Men*, from which this biography derived, is now lost. The text of this life of Jiao Xian is included, like the *Weilüe* record discussed above, in Pei Songzhi's commentary to *Sanguo zhi*. *Gaoshi zhuan* collects records of those who chose to live their lives away from society for fundamentally political reasons avoiding involvement with the state and its functionaries.[19] The nobility of this goal had been recognised for centuries and indeed Huangfu's collection was not the first to have this title; the great literatus Ji Kang compiled a collection (also now lost) of this name. A text claiming to be Huangfu's is still extant but it would appear to be a late reconstitution from citations. A very truncated version of the preceding biography is included in it.[20]

The first part of Jiao Xian's biography from *Gaoshi zhuan* presents him as completely mysterious: it removes him from a definite native place and the date of his birth is unspecific hearsay. In this account he had no relatives at all and refused any social interaction, "cutting himself off from human contact" when he observed the declining state of the Han dynasty. In addition, Jiao's differences from normal humankind are extreme. He wears no robe, lies directly on the ground and sleeps in the open irrespective of the weather. As in the other records, Jiao is visited by the representatives of government: here he does not utter a word. In *Gaoshi zhuan* Jiao is not magical, the extremities he practises are simply extraordinary self-discipline. Nonetheless, the narrative part of the biography concludes, "nobody was able to understand his intentions."

Even Huangfu Mi claims to find himself at a loss to plumb Jiao's true nature, instead giving what may be termed an appreciation based on what, he says, anybody could have observed. Yet, while he claims explicitly not to understand Jiao, his appreciation leaves no doubt as to Jiao's status – according to Huangfu Mi, he had no parallel since Fu Xi the Sage King of high antiquity. Indeed, his incomprehension should probably be seen as a rhetorical device stressing his own modesty as the commentary on Jiao's life leaves no doubt that Huangfu himself thought the meaning of Jiao's life to be perfectly clear.

Benjamin Penny

What fundamentally distinguishes this account of Jiao Xian from the *Shenxian zhuan* account is the varieties of transcendence they promote. In *Gaoshi zhuan*, transcendence can be defined specifically as a series of negations of the standard human condition. This is made explicit in the rhetoric of Huangfu Mi's assessment where Jiao is credited with rejecting fame, clothing, shelter, speech and the affections; just those things that normal humankind cannot do without. Thus, while Jiao's biography as an immortal has him leading a life of simple but deep lack of concern for his social standing, his biography as a lofty man has him explicitly rejecting social life and all of its trappings in a way that could be characterised as consciously ascetic.

However, in that both *Shenxian zhuan* and *Gaoshi zhuan* are thematic collections of exemplary figures – in one immortals and in the other lofty men – the similarity of these two lives of Jiao Xian should come as no surprise; that the two collections are concerned with different categories of being does not affect their status as examples of thematic collections. These two lives are both examples of generic lives. It is here that the process of textualization is most clear: the differences in the presentation of this figure are generated by rendering his story as a biography of an immortal or a biography of a lofty man. Each of these genres is constituted not only by a set of narrative expectations, it also describes and constitutes a class of being. In the case of Jiao Xian, it is clear that memories of his life could be parlayed into both of these structures – his life was sufficiently malleable for both editors to be comfortable about claiming him as one of their own.

Some Fragments

There are several other fragments of text concerning Jiao Xian that point to the instability of the ascriptions of what kind of being he was. The first is from *Weishi chunqiu*, the *Springs and Autumns of Mr Wei*, which also survives in Pei Songzhi's commentary to *Sanguo zhi*:

> Thus, Geng Fu, the Inspector of Liangzhou, considered Xian to be an immortal and Fu Xuan of Beidi said his nature was the same as a beast. They both told his story but were unable to fathom him.[21]

Here Geng Fu, who is not identifiable beyond this citation, confirms the claims of *Shenxian zhuan* that Jiao Xian was an immortal while Fu Xuan (217–278), the author of the Confucian text known as *Fuzi*, takes perhaps the most negative view of him that we have encountered.[22]

The second is from *Xuefu*, *The Rhapsody on Snow*, written by Li Yong of the Jin, which clearly refers to him in one of its only two surviving fragments.

Jiao Xian's Three Lives

This reference indicates that soon after Jiao's time his remarkable abilities had become a standard literary reference point:

Jiao [Xian] slept in it yet he was not harmed,
Su [Wu] ate it and so lengthened his days.[23]

The third fragment is from *Bowu zhi*, a collection of anecdotes from the third century traditionally ascribed to Zhang Hua concerning strange occurrences, which says:

Recently in the time of Wei Mingdi (227–40) there was a Jiao Sheng in Hedong. He went naked and did not wear a robe. He sat in fire but was not burned. He entered water but did not freeze. All this was true – it was witnessed by Grand Administrator Du Shu.[24]

Here is the story pared back to the essential outward manifestations of Jiao's differences from normal humankind without regard for his motivations, his background, or the reasons for his attainments. This is standard for *Bowu zhi* which is concerned simply to take an anomaly, date it and provide an authority for it.

Conclusions

None of these accounts of Jiao Xian appear in newly-emergent genres. *Shenxian zhuan* is the second collection of immortals' biographies that survives, but there are references to another collection earlier than these two extant ones that has been lost. The *Weilüe* record follows the pattern of administrative biography set down as early as the first dynastic history, *Shiji*. Huangfu Mi's *Gaoshi zhuan* was the second collection of that name to have been compiled, and there are other collections of the same sort before that. Collections of anomalous occurrences had been known from early times and passing references to famous figures from the past are a commonplace in Chinese literary writing. In other words, the categories of text into which memories of Jiao Xian were written were all well established by the time the various records discussed in this essay appeared.

Jiao Xian's three generic lives are the lives of three different categories of being. That is, Jiao's story is constructed differently as it is written into each category of text by the expectations of that particular genre. On the one hand, the inclusion of a biography in a collection of similar biographies, be they records of immortals, lofty men or social outcasts, provides both a mutually reinforcing context in which that biography is read and a definition of that particular biography as an example of the genre. Thus, in the case of the *Shenxian zhuan* biography, simply by including a biography of

Jiao Xian in this collection the compiler makes the claim that Jiao Xian was an immortal even though this is not explicitly stated. In addition, the information provided about Jiao's life resonates with the information provided about the other figures in the collection. Similarly, the inclusion of Jiao Xian in *Gaoshi zhuan* makes the claim that Jiao Xian was a lofty man, no less a category of being than an immortal, but one in which a different quality of transcendence is elucidated. The lofty man demonstrates his loftiness by negating the mundane world, in particular the political world, rather than sully his high ideals. *Weilüe* on the other hand seeks to incorporate Jiao Xian into this very administrative world that is rejected in *Gaoshi zhuan*.

The period in which Jiao Xian lived saw ideas of conventional behaviour come under strong challenge and new religious movements take hold. The cult that came to be seen as the well-spring of the Daoist religion – the Five Pecks of Rice Sect, later the Celestial Masters – appeared as the Han fell and Buddhism strengthened and extended its position in China in the third century.[25] This period was a time of great turmoil when the stability of the united empire and its associated ideologies were all under threat.[26] The unified state that had been established under the Qin in 221 BCE had finally collapsed in 220 CE with the final decades seeing corrupt and unsatisfactory government. In the succeeding period three competing states, including the Wei, appeared but all three were, in turn, subsumed into the Jin by 280. Under these circumstances what kind of behaviour was correct for talented men was a genuinely open question. Should such men seek involvement with the state, reject the world by adopting a traditional model of eremitism, or seek an immortal existence? Thus, the claims made about Jiao Xian represented attempts to value or devalue certain kinds of behaviour and ideology, claims made by rendering particular and largely agreed biographical information into certain genres which represented different models of being. The fragments of text that have survived about him are evidence of attempts to co-opt Jiao's reputation by rendering him into an immortal, or a lofty man, or a mysterious hermit in need of regulation.

This essay has concentrated on the way that different genre produced different lives of Jiao Xian. A related question would ask about the reception of these texts and focus on the reading practices of early medieval Chinese people. Is it possible that readers could have had access to these three lives over their reading life and make comparisons between them as has been done here? To answer this question would require a knowledge of the material aspects of book production, the circumstances of book circulation and the prevalence and accessibility of libraries that is, at the present state of research, inadequate for these purposes. Of course, it would also be useful to know how many people could read at all, and perhaps most intriguingly, whether a reader in fourth- or fifth-century China would have been inclined to analyse biographical texts with their genre in mind.

Jiao Xian's Three Lives

Notes

1 The major recent version of this quest is represented by the work of the Jesus Seminar, see Robert W. Funk, Roy W. Hoover and the Jesus Seminar, *The Five Gospels: The Search for the Authentic Words of Jesus* (New York: Macmillan, 1993) and Robert W. Funk and the Jesus Seminar, *The Acts of Jesus: The Search for the Authentic Deeds of Jesus* (San Francisco: HarperSanFrancisco, 1998).
2 *Taiping guangji* (Beijing: Zhonghua shuju, 1961), 9:62–63. This biography is cited in *Yiwen leiju* (Shanghai: Shanghai guji chubanshe, 1965), 80:1377; *Sandong zhunang* (*Daozang*, HY 1131), 2:4a; *Taiping yulan* (Beijing: Zhonghua shuju, 1985), 477:3b, 669:6a (= *Yiwen leiju*), 849:7a; *Xianyuan bianzhu* (*Daozang*, HY 596), *xia*:2b (unascribed). The *Taiping Guangji* version of the biography has been corrected with reference to these citations.
3 On the Daoist biographical tradition see Benjamin Penny, "Immortality and Transcendence" in Livia Kohn, ed., *Handbook of Taoism* (Leiden: E.J. Brill, 2000).
4 See Nathan Sivin, "On the Word 'Taoist' as a Source of Perplexity", *History of Religions* 17:3&4 (1969), 303–30.
5 While not the favourite food of immortals, white stones are by no means unknown as foodstuffs in Chinese immortal lore. *Shenxian zhuan* also contains the life of the most famous exponent of this diet – Baishi xiansheng or Mr White Stone – from which he took his name. See *Taiping guangji*, 7:44.
6 It is true to say that Daoist biography as a whole is a kind of corporeal history, intent as it is on documenting the transformations of ordinary human bodies into extraordinary immortal ones.
7 Refusing to respond to the entreaties of the emperor or his servant is a common feature in these biographies. See, for instance, the biographies of Sun Deng (*Taiping guangji* 9:63), Liu Gen (*Taiping guangji* 10:67) and Wang Yuan (*Yunji qiqian*, *Daozang*, HY1026, 109:10a–15a. Volumes in the *Daozang* are identified by "HY" which precedes the number assigned to it in the index to Daoist literature in the Harvard-Yenching Institute Sinological Index Series).
8 Triumphing over fire and ice, or fire and water, are almost mandatory feats for an immortal. See the biographies of Li Gen (*Shenxian zhuan*, *Siku quanshu*, ed., 10:4b–5b), Ge Xuan (*Taiping guangji* 71:441) and Sun Bo (*Yunji qiqian*, 109:15b–16b). The locus classicus is the realised man in *Zhuangzi*, who could "enter water without getting wet and enter fire without getting burnt". See Guo Qingfan, ed., *Zhuangzi jishi* (Beijing: Zhonghua Shuju, 1985), 3 *shang*:226.
9 Pei Songzhi explains that "snail shell huts" were round like snails' shells.
10 The meaning of this line is obscure. The editors of the twelve-volume *Hanyu dacidian* (Shanghai: Hanyu dacidian chubanshe, 1986) explain the phrase *zhunü* as an incantation spoken when sacrificing a victim (vol.7, p.893). It may be coincidence but the only citation they give is this one.
11 *Sanguo zhi* (Beijing: Zhonghua shuju, 1985), 11:363–64.
12 This text is discussed in Aat Vervoorn, *Men of the Cliffs and Caves: The Development of the Chinese Eremitic Tradition to the End of the Han Dynasty* (Hong Kong: The Chinese University Press, 1990), 11–12. I am indebted to this book as a whole for its thorough and insightful discussion of the topic of eremitism in early China. For *Weilüe*, see Rafe de Crespigny, *The Records of the Three Kingdoms* (Canberra: Faculty of Asian Studies, 1970), 75–76; and Édouard Chavannes, "Les pays d'Occident d'après le Wei lio", *T'oung Pao* 6 (1905), 519. *Weilüe* appears to have followed the model of *Dianlüe* of Yu Huan which concerned the last part of the Han. Indeed, there is some confusion in the bibliographical record as to

whether *Weilüe* is a separate text from *Dianlüe* or not; however, it is likely that this confusion arose as the two appear to have circulated in combined form.

13 See Rafe de Crespigny, *Northern Frontier: The Policies and Strategies of the Later Han Empire* (Canberra, Faculty of Asian Studies, 1984), 346–51.

14 See de Crespigny, *Northern Frontier*, 163–165.

15 The episode in Jiao's life relating to his mysterious verse is quite datable. We know that the attack by the state of Wei on the state of Wu in which Wei suffered major losses must have happened a year later than one of the years of the Jiaping reign period, that is between 250 and 255. And indeed, in the eleventh month of the fourth year of the Jiaping reign period (December 252 – January 253) an attack by three routes on Wu was ordered by the Wei Emperor. In the twelfth month the Wei troops were routed and "the dead numbered tens of thousands". See Achilles Fang, *The Chronicle of the Three Kingdoms (220–265), Chapters 67–78 from the Tzu Chih T'ung Chien of Ssu-ma Kuang* (Cambridge, Ma.: Harvard University Press, 1965), 111–12.

16 Du Shu receives a biography in *Sanguo zhi*, 16:498–508; see 16:505 for his accession to this position.

17 Regent of Wei between 251–57, Sima Shi received the title Jingwang (of the Jin) posthumously when his son came to the throne in 265 as Jin Wudi.

18 *Sanguo zhi*, 11:364–65.

19 On eremitism in China, see Vervoorn, *Men of the Cliffs and Caves*; Alan Berkowitz, Patterns of Reclusion in Early Medieval China: A Study of the Formulation of the Practice of Reclusion in China and its Portrayal, unpublished PhD thesis, University of Washington, 1989; A.R. Davis, "The Narrow Lane: Some Observations on the Recluse in Traditional Chinese Society", *The Twelfth George Ernest Morrison Lecture in Ethnology* (Canberra: Australian National University, 1959); Wolfgang Bauer, "The Hermit's Temptation: Aspects of Eremitism in China and the West in the Third and Early Fourth Century A.D." in *Guoji Hanxue huiyi lunwenji* 9:1 (1981) and "The Hidden Hero: Creation and Disintegration of the Ideal of Eremitism" in Donald Munro, ed., *Individualism and Holism in Chinese Values* (Ann Arbor: Centre for Chinese Studies, University of Michigan, 1985), 157–98.

20 *Gaoshi zhuan* (Siku quanshu edition), *xia*, 17b. This biography is also cited in *Yiwen leiju*, 2:22, 64:1154, *Chuxue ji* (Beijing: Zhonghua shuju, 1962), 2:28; and *Beitang shuchao* (Tianjin: Tianjin guji chubanshe, 1988), 152:3a. On Huangfu Mi's *Gaoshi zhuan*, see Berkowitz, Patterns of Reclusion in Early Medieval China, 317–24.

21 *Sanguo zhi*, 11:365.

22 The surviving version of *Fuzi* does not mention Jiao Xian. On *Fuzi*, see Jordan C. Paper, *The Fu-tzu: A Post-Han Confucian Text*, Monographies du T'oung Pao 63, (Leiden: E.J. Brill, 1987).

23 These lines are cited at *Chuxue ji*, 2:28. *Quan shanggu sandai QinHan Sanguo Liuchao wen* (Beijing: Zhonghua shuju, 1958), 53:1767, has a different fragment which it cites from *Yiwen leiju*, 2:29. Su Wu (140–60 BCE) was sent as an envoy to the Xiongnu who detained him. The incident, in which he saves his own life by eating snow, can be found in his biography in *Hanshu* (Beijing: Zhonghua shuju, 1983), 54:2462–3.

24 Fan Ning, ed., *Bowu zhi jiaozheng* (Beijing, Zhonghua shuju, 1980), 5:63 (item 183).

25 On the Five Pecks of Rice Sect and the Celestial Masters, see Isabelle Robinet, *Histoire du Taoisme des Origines au XIVe Siecle* (Paris: Les Editions du Cerf, 1991), 61–83 and Stephen R. Bokenkamp, *Early Daoist Scriptures* (Berkeley: University of California Press, 1997), 1–6, 29–37. On the introduction of Buddhism to China see Erik Zürcher, *The Buddhist Conquest of China: The Spread and Adaptation of Buddhism in Early Medieval China* (Leiden: E.J. Brill, 1972).

26 For an overview of the political history of the period see B.J. Mansvelt-Beck, "The Fall of Han", in Denis Twitchett and Michael Loewe, eds, *The Cambridge History of China*, vol. 1, *The Ch'in and Han Empires 221 B.C.–A.D.220* (Cambridge: Cambridge University Press, 1986), 317–76. For intellectual and religious currents, see Ch'en Chi-yun "Confucian, Legalist and Taoist Thought in Later Han", in *The Cambridge History of China*, vol.1; Paul Demiéville, "Philosophy and religion from Han to Sui", in *The Cambridge History of China*, vol.1, 766–872; and Étienne Balazs (trans. H.M. Wright), "Political Philosophy and Social Crisis at the End of the Han Dynasty" and "Nihilistic Revolt or Mystical Escapism", in his *Chinese Civilization and Bureaucracy: Variations on a Theme* (New Haven: Yale University Press, 1964).

2

The Virtue of Conformity

The Religious Re-Writing of Political Biography

Barbara Hendrischke

Daoist biographies can be seen to have the purpose of advertising the religion to outsiders. This is outlined in the *Shenxian zhuan* preface, which explains the need for this collection of "Biographies of Immortals" by referring to the question of whether, in the past, there really were human beings who had become immortals. The preface then explains that knowledge of people who had turned into immortals is rare because they lived in seclusion and did not share the habits of their generation. Not one in a thousand, it claims, is known to the outside world.[1] From this one may conclude that the main purpose of Daoist biographies was to document the transformation of men or women into immortals; in Judith Boltz's[2] terms, their purpose was mainly commemorative. She adds the adjective "didactic", but they are clearly preparatory or introductory in nature. As Benjamin Penny has pointed out,[3] Daoist hagiography while telling its readers or listeners that they can become immortals does not go into detail regarding how this is to be achieved. Recipes, techniques and the other nitty-gritty aspects of everyday religious practice are left to another, no doubt more esoteric or interior, set of scriptures.

While it is clear that in concentrating on the invitational aspect of religious matters hagiographic material differs from other Daoist material, one could ask to what extent this concern also distinguishes the clearly eulogistic Daoist biographies from their secular counterparts, which are written from a variety of motives, changing with the differing intellectual approaches of the authors and their supervisors within officialdom. This paper is based on the assumption that within the period discussed – Yan Zhenqing (709–785) is the last figure dealt with – formal constraints in producing a 'biography', whether for secular or religious purposes, were of only minor concern to its authors, in that it is impossible to detect an overriding structural framework which dominated the literary composition of biography. The analysis presented here is purely contents-based and largely ignores the question of stylistic rules and patterns. This approach seems justified when one follows the structural analysis of *Shenxian zhuan* biographies undertaken by Penny[4]

The Virtue of Conformity

or the claim put forward by Durrant[5] that these so-called biographies, while amalgamating excerpts from historical biography also carry traits of the literary genre of *zhiguai* 'miraculous' stories.

Judith Boltz[6] has claimed that in Daoist biographies "there is seldom any insight into the development of the saintlike personality". This paper will provide some evidence for this claim, by documenting how limited were the traces of a human condition in accounts of those beings whose transformation resulted in immortality, and how little their concrete existence mattered in the realms of immortality. It has been argued that in all Chinese biography the particularities of individual lives were downplayed to intensify the role model which formed the basis of those accounts.[7] In this paper I will try to argue that this editing process was more rigid in Daoist biography than in the dynastic histories.

In order to create a model immortal the Daoist writer would in particular strip a concrete individual of ambiguous or controversial social and political involvement. I will give examples of this by comparing several biographies transmitted in the *Daozang* and in other material relating to immortality with biographies in the dynastic histories or in similar material. In order to simplify the comparison the figures chosen are known mainly as political personages. Here the differences are big and a rather coarse analysis is sufficient to point them out. The comparison of secular and religious biographies of religious personages would demand a more subtle approach to uncover the interrelations between the different layers of legend building. The scope of this paper is also limited by the one way direction of this comparison, which only attempts to establish some characteristic elements of religious biography.[8]

The material for this paper is further reduced by excluding cases where the two sets of biographies differ so widely in content that all that is shared by the two personages depicted in the realms of religious and political life are name and rank. For instance, this is the case in the *Han Wudi neizhuan*, which makes use of the emperor's name without any further link to the historical figure.[9] The interest of the story lies in the appearance of the Queen Mother of the West and in the search for immortality, not in the Han emperor himself, whose fame is used simply to create interest in Daoist magic and spirituality. Another pattern, which will not be of concern for this paper, is the reduction of a person's life to his death and afterlife. In the case of Lü Shang, who according to the *Shiji*, played a crucial role in King Wu's rebellion against the last Shang emperor, the *Liexian zhuan*[10] omits all details of his political involvement and instead informs us about what the sage ate and about the transformation of his corpse. Here the famous and slightly mysterious figure of the ancient sage is completely uprooted and transplanted into an environment of longevity techniques to help the Daoist cause.[11]

Other biographies which will be ignored are those which are strictly divided into two parts, separating the conventional curriculum vitae from the legends surrounding the end of a person's life. For instance, this is the case in the life story of Mei Fu (1st cent. BCE – 1st cent. CE) who entered history as an ardent propagator of the Confucianist cause, asking for stipends to be given to all of the Master's descendants.[12] The first part contains several pages of direct quotes from the *Hanshu*, including the text of two memorials. It also states that the hero retired, became interested in the nourishment of life,[13] left his wife and children and started a new career under a new name, adding that some people thought he had turned into an immortal. The other parts of this biography mention the geographical details of his ascension and present epigraphical and literary material on the subject. In this case, the religious biography shows too little concern for Mei Fu's career as a worldly person prior to his becoming an immortal to be of relevance for the comparative purposes of this paper.

The biographies which will be compared here are of personages who led political lives of some importance, aspects of which are preserved in their vita as Daoist immortals. It will be argued that although their political biographies were themselves subject to the ideological restrictions of official historiography,[14] they contain elements of existential struggle and intellectual as well as political confrontation which do not occur in the Daoist records. Hagiography seems to assume that to become an immortal involved an indifference to the fate of society to the extent that any controversial involvement in it had to be shunned. In order to protect his or her life the immortal would avoid risking conflict with the worldly authorities, and would avoid entering into worldly discussions so that he or she may save his or her mental energy for transworldly insights. A model immortal would make his or her career through a preoccupation with transworldly matters or immortality techniques. In this paper I wish to argue that as far as the model immortal could not avoid involvement in worldly affairs the manner of this participation was in harmony and agreement with the prevailing social forces, even when the political biography of the same person might present a situation of open disagreement.

Fan Li

One might consider the well-known Warring States politician Fan Li who helped King Gou Jian of Yue to conquer Wu and become hegemon as the prototype for this Daoist reduction of a person's life. There are a number of historiographic accounts of his life and deeds; these present a figure who was deeply involved first in the failure and then in the success of King Gou Jian. In addition, an appendix to the *Shiji* biography of Gou Jian contains an account of Fan Li's later years,[15] and the *Guoyu*[16] and *Wu Yue chunqiu*[17] as well as the more fictional *Yue jueshu*[18] contain abundant material. Fan Li's second life as a successful businessman also guaranteed him a passage in the *Shiji* and *Hanshu* chapters on the lives of the wealthy.[19]

The Virtue of Conformity

All later hagiographic accounts are based on the *Liexian zhuan*, which according to Max Kaltenmark contains material from the first centuries CE.[20] The complicated question of how far this text is Daoist need not concern us here. The *Shenxian zhuan* which undoubtedly is Daoist, mentioned the text as its competitor or predecessor in its preface. The *Liexian zhuan* text says:

> Fan Li, courtesy name Shabo, was a native of Xu [which was non-Chinese, Yi territory]. He served Taigong Wang [Lü Shang], teacher of the [first] King of the Zhou. He liked to eat cassia leaves and drink water. As prime minister of Yue he helped Gou Jian to defeat Wu. Later on he boarded a skiff and went to sea. He changed his name and when he arrived in Qi he had become Chiyi Zipi. More than a hundred years later he was seen in Tao, where he had become Mr. Zhu of Tao. His wealth accumulated ten thousand fold and he was then called Duke Zhu of Tao. Again, he gave everything up and went to Lanling to sell medicine. Later people, generation after generation, recognised him.[21]

This biography is extremely brief, as if to support the complaint put forward in the *Shenxian zhuan* preface that Liu Xiang's concise way of writing often led to the exclusion of interesting details. However, despite its brevity the vita adds some information to that put forward by the historical sources. It adds several layers to Fan Li's life: he was a great statesman with specific dietary habits many centuries before he entered the service of King Gou Jian, and after his success in business he gave everything up and became a dealer in herbs. In both respects the biography creates the aura proper to a Daoist immortal. The Daoist was characterized by a special diet, medicine or drugs and the ability to exist in this world for as long as he chose.

More telling, for the purpose of this paper, is what the *Liexian zhuan* account avoids dealing with. No mention is made of what caused Fan Li's move into private life, and no mention is made of the link between his official and business careers. The dialectical relationship between private and public life which was clearly manifest in Fan Li's secular biographies and which adds an archetypal touch to his life story is completely abandoned in the *Liexian zhuan* version. Fan Li's embarking on a boat is common to all the biographies but what were his reasons for this? The *Shiji* explains that he was full of distrust for Gou Jian, whom he had served for most of his life, and that he realized that "Gou Jian as a person was someone one could share dangers with, but difficult to live with in peace".[22] Another leading politician who remained in the service of Gou Jian was indeed put to death by his ruler.[23] The tension between politician and king is not referred to in the *Liexian zhuan*, where Fan Li is introduced as a loyal official, without further comment: his escape by boat is seen only as a demonstration of a Daoist quest for quietude.

Fan Li's second change of profession also invited varying commentary. The *Shiji* explains that he moved into business because he intended to make a commercial trial of the programme which had been developed for the economic strengthening of the state of Yue. The implementation of only five of the seven policies originally envisaged had been sufficient for Yue to achieve victory over a rich and powerful enemy. For the *Liexian zhuan*, Fan Li's commercial success is an aspect of the general superiority of his person, which makes it possible for him to succeed even in business, while the *Shiji* sees this move as proof of the great politician's enterprising spirit which extends into different sectors of life, transcending the border between political and commercial success, which at least in public was rarely crossed.

Among Daoist biographical works only the *Xuanpin lu*[24] attempts to establish connections between Fan Li's political, religious and commercial careers. It mentions a philosophical component in his political life, namely that he was said to have demanded harmony between human activities on the one hand and heaven and earth on the other. This agrees with Fan Li's image in the *Shiji* and *Guoyu*. It also mentions that in the resurrection of Yue not all newly available policies had been tried out. However, Zhang Tianyu's *Xuanpin lu* differs from other collections of religious biographies in that it explicitly aims not at depicting roads to immortality but rather at introducing the Daoist leanings of personages of general historical importance; Sima Tan, Wang Bi, Xie An and Li Bai are among the figures commemorated. In the *Lishi zhenxian tidao tongjian*[25] the *Liexian zhuan* passage is reprinted with no modification except for Zhao Daoyi's comment that according to a local account (the *Pengzhou ershisi hua zhi*), Fan Li had reached the stage of immortality on Mount Beimang in the Peng district of Sichuan, to the north-west of Chengdu. This approach is quite characteristic for Zhao Daoyi. If we accept the preface to his work, he attempted to produce a Daoist version of the *Zizhi tongjian* by selecting rather than re-writing earlier sources. Another branch of Fan Li's many lives reaches to Kong Anguo from Shandong, who according to the *Shenxian zhuan*,[26] learned the techniques of immortality from an old fisherman who was none other than Fan Li in yet another disguise. These additions do not change the gist of the old story; they only add detail to link the figure to specific localities.

The religious biographies cited in the above passage and throughout this paper stem from several collections of the lives of immortals, put together from the beginnings of religious Daoism in the second century CE until the Yuan Dynasty. Benjamin Penny[27] has attempted to define some guidelines which would link the differences in the contents and interpretative approach of some of these collections with the growth and maturing of the religion. The fact that it is possible to draw such a link is further proof of the central role played by hagiography in the representation of the religion. As the religion developed, the aim of immortality became the overriding goal of its believers, sidelining other social or spiritual aims laid out during Daoism's early stages. While Daoist biographies were mainly biographies of immortals, there was simultaneously a tendency for biographies of immortals to became specifically Daoist. The Daoist appropriation of a text such as the *Liexian zhuan* (marked for instance by the reference to it in the *Shenxian zhuan* preface, even if this stems from a later period than the *Shenxian zhuan* itself), which tradition had from early on linked to the scholarly non-Daoist figure of Liu Xiang, is proof of Daoism's increasing claim to the whole territory of immortality.

Friends and Foes of Han Emperor Wu

In setting up these images of immortals as role models and patterns of Daoist behaviour religious leaders outlined their own socio-political place. Thomas Smith has given a comprehensive overview of Emperor Wu's search for immortality as depicted in the *Han Wudi neizhuan* and other Six Dynasties literary sources, all of which are more or less closely linked to the Daoist cause. This material allows the conclusion that within the project of searching for immortality in some instances an alternative hierarchical structure was created, which differed slightly from the existing socio-political structure. According to these texts, Emperor Wu never succeeded in his search for longevity because in his hunt for the true recipe he was continuously obstructed by detrimental traits in his own personality and by the encumbrances of his position. Although he frequently received religious advice, and made some use of it, he failed. In these accounts of imperial failure, Smith sees public opinion at work. He extends the argument further by arguing that the emperor's spiritual or technical advisers in matters of immortality tended to become his victims, in that they all left the world as immortals only after the emperor had attempted to shorten their lives.[28] In this Smith sees the impact of social criticism, which in literature re-assigned the roles of winners and losers. In other words, Smith sees the Six Dynasties literary prose he deals with taking up the role of a vox populi and challenging the Imperial government's wrongdoings in the well documented *yuefu* tradition of Han times.[29] To establish religious merit as superior to political achievement certainly became an item on the agenda of some of the religious organizations which took shape in the post-Han centuries.

However, while Daoist sources downgraded certain powerful figures of the past and upgraded others who had failed in the realm of court politics, this upgrading did not include rebels. The price for hagiographic advancement was political disengagement. In stressing its heroes' political detachment Daoist hagiography transformed figures who had been political actors and who had proposed reforms or opposed policies into innocent victims of remote power struggles. According to Daoist hagiography the superiority of the immortal was based on spiritual power only, and hagiographic accounts streamlined individual lives for this purpose.

The highest ranking of Emperor Wu's supposed victims was Liu An, King of Huainan. Here the religious account harmonizes and smooths the picture which other sources paint of the king's life. The *Shenxian zhuan* hardly mentions any conflict in the relationship between Emperor Wu and Liu An. The text explains the historical events as if they had been the result of conflicts which arose between subordinates of the two men and then developed their own momentum, growing in scope until they led to Liu An's forced suicide as a supposed rebel, much regretted by the emperor. This picture is opposed to the account in the *Shiji* and the *Hanshu* which mentions several tokens of disloyalty in Liu An's actions: he sent his daughter as a lobbyist into the capital; he hoped for disorder at the imperial court and a lack of male children; he saw himself as a possible heir apparent; he planned military action; and he had a replica of the imperial seal manufactured for his own use.[30] None of these points is mentioned in the Daoist biography which moves in a very different direction, skilfully interweaving the king's career as a Daoist saint with his more worldly personality. According to this account, the essential elements of Liu An's life were his very high rank as the uncle of the ruling emperor, his well established literary fame and his successful acquisition of Daoist longevity techniques. In the *Shenxian zhuan*, the gradual process of learning to become a saint is the thread which runs through the whole biography just as the gradual transformation into a political rebel runs through the *Shiji* account. Both are well-written pieces of ancient prose. For the *Shiji*, Liu An's characteristic and fatal point of departure is clearly the capital punishment suffered by his father. The search for revenge is the main motive for his actions and is seen as having caused the friction with several high officials which in the end led to his downfall. In the *Shenxian zhuan*, the father's violent death is only briefly mentioned as if in passing, while Liu An's personality is seen as characterized by his erudition – details are taken from the *Hanshu*[31] – and his quest for Daoist insights. While suicide is the conclusion of Liu An's deeds in the official sources, in the *Shenxian zhuan* account they result in his ascent to heaven in broad daylight, accompanied by everything around him, including chickens and dogs, which feed on the leftovers of the potent immortality drug he had concocted. The biography also includes a description of the shock suffered by the imperial court when it is confronted with Liu An's ascent to the skies.[32] This is another topos of Daoist biographies: the shock, shame, regret or envy of those left behind in this world and this life when they observe the departure of others, in particular when they have caused or at least not prevented the death of those who gloriously rise into the skies.

Liu An's biography is remarkable in that the author of the *Shenxian zhuan* version openly accuses the standard historiographers, that is, Sima Qian and Ban Gu, of bias against Liu An's quest for immortality. The *Shenxian zhuan* author claimed that they had insisted on Liu An's rebellion and suicide in order to cover up his real merits as an immortal: "The Han officials kept it

The Virtue of Conformity

all secret. They did not mention that Liu An had found the Way to immortality, for fear that in later generations the rulers over men would discard all the 10,000 pursuits and compete with each other in search for the Way of Liu An. So they said that Liu An had performed a crime and had afterwards committed suicide without attaining immortality."[33] Liu An's Daoist biography includes a rare example of a hero's loss in status in comparison with his earthly life. After his ascent to Heaven he is said to have offended the heavenly authorities with haughty expressions and gestures. By way of punishment he is then sent to clean latrines and finally restricted to the position of a lowly immortal without any chance for further advancement. For this account the *Shenxian zhuan* deems it necessary to mention the testimony of a certain Zuo Wu, who also figures in the *Hanshu*[34] as a follower of Liu An. The *Shenxian zhuan* claims that, together with four others, he had been invited into the heavenly realms to pay Liu An a short visit in his new abode and on his return had reported what he had seen to Emperor Wu. Liu An's humiliation could well be interpreted as further proof of a certain 'law and order' mentality among the biographers of immortals. In order to warn against unruliness in the search for immortality, they let Liu An carry an anti-authoritarian attitude from this world into the afterlife and have the deities dish out an appropriate punishment. The fact that this unruliness was more typical of the behaviour seen in the dynastic history rather than in the Daoist tradition must be seen as a minor contradiction. The lesson of the incident is that a behaviour that is improper in the human realm is also improper in the divine realm, and that this applies even to kings.

As in the Fan Li biography, Liu An's personality was smoothed or streamlined by the Daoist biographer. The political and social aspects of his life were transformed to such an extent that they become hard to recognize. The Daoists stress the great admiration which the emperor felt for his uncle and also mention the many clients whom Liu An assembled as partakers in a longevity project rather than in the movement for a political restoration of the feudal, noncentralist system of Pre-Qin times.[35] Many deeds which could be seen as nonconformist, questionable or outright oppositionist were removed from this account of the king's actions. Here the religious biography remains aloof from the discourse of the profane historiographers who, although in agreement concerning the label of rebel, paint a slightly different picture by mentioning certain details or stressing certain nuances.

Sima Qian's *Shiji* account was necessarily more critical of Liu An's position than the one Ban Gu wrote several hundred years later when Emperor Wu was long dead. In contrast, the biography of Liu An as an immortal attempts to wipe out his role as a rebel. On the basis of the lives of Liu An and Li Shaojun, and in reference to earlier works by Kominami, Penny[36] argues that Daoist biography relies on local tradition for its sources; while Kominami's reference to chickens and dogs mentioned in the *Shenxian zhuan* as proof for the story's rural background is not particularly convincing, considering the life-style of ancient and medieval towns, the argument as such seems important. In Liu An's biography, the local flavour of religious sources might be more evident in the slightly different role these sources have laid out for the official Wu Bei, who in the *Shenxian zhuan* was one-sidedly depicted as an outright traitor while in his own *Hanshu* biography[37] and Liu An's *Shiji* biography his role was seen as more ambiguous, indicating that for a long period he acted as a loyal Huainan official. While he was not a native of Huainan but instead came from Chu, Wu Bei had been personally selected by the king to head the inside ranks of the royal government, unlike the centrally installed officials whom all sources saw as natural enemies of the king. However, the fact that Ban Gu honoured Wu Bei with a separate biography could itself be interpreted as a sign of certain services he did for the Han emperor rather than for the King of Huainan.

Whatever is the case for figures from the early periods, in hagiographical material from later centuries which contains frequent references to local practices, the argument concerning the influence of the local in Daoist biography is easy to sustain. To amalgamate aspects of a local hero with the standard traits of an immortal became common practice.[38] Daoism in the Han Dynasty and beyond consisted of more or less independent and isolated regional movements, the region of Huainan and Langye, the home of the *Taiping* group, among them. However, for the purposes of this paper, it must be kept in mind that the Daoist biography depicted the King of Huainan as a loyal subject of the Han emperor, rather than as an independent minded, if unsuccessful, politician.

The fashion for the search for immortality during the reign of Emperor Wu must be seen in conjunction with the emperor's personal interest in long life, which is documented by the dynastic histories as well as by Daoist sources. However, in Daoist material the emperor shares an image of fallibility with the King of Huainan. Shortcomings in the life-styles of both rulers were seen as obstructions on their roads to immortality. One could probably argue that the extent to which the emperor was superior in the realm of politics made him inferior to the King of Huainan in the alternative Daoist hierarchy, by the same rule which reduced the king to a lowly position in the world of immortals. In Daoist hagiography the emperor featured not as a model immortal but rather as a means to promote interest in the attractions of immortality and to document the achievements of those Daoist advisers who attempted to guide every step he undertook towards longevity. Dongfang Shuo was the most important Daoist personage in the emperor's entourage. Literary and religious sources alike depict him as a main source of inspiration for the emperor. The *Hanshu* points out how Dongfang Shuo's long career at the Han court resulted from his great verbal skills and from his masterly handling of the emperor's moods and fads. On both grounds he seems to have managed to uphold his position while at the same time severely and frankly reprimanding the emperor. However, Dongfang Shuo's behaviour and

The Virtue of Conformity

argumentative style were unorthodox and his influence rested on his personal influence over the emperor rather than on a secure position in the official hierarchy. Consequently, the historians' appraisal of him is multifaceted.[39] Zhu Shaosun, who completed Sima Qian's *Shiji*, expressed his critique by including Dongfang Shuo among the 'jesters'.[40] Ban Gu added intellectual weight to the figure of Dongfang Shuo by quoting from his writings and in particular by referring to the "Poem of Admonition to My Son" claiming that office for him is no more than a livelihood, and that he really leads the life of a recluse in the tradition of the *Zhuangzi*.[41] The poem shows all the frustration and arrogance of a maladjusted intellectual: "Taking the stance of the recluse, he pokes fun at the world; in a time of crisis, he is overlooked".[42] In Ban Gu's depiction, the official was dissatisfied with his low position and the limited political impact he had achieved; he felt that both were in conflict with his great talents and important ambitions. As if summarizing his own research the historian Ban Gu quotes Yang Xiong's appraisal of the "jester", that while far from being a model in deeds or words, Dongfang Shuo still enjoyed a great reputation.[43] The *Liexian zhuan* account is more ambiguous, claiming that his behaviour was sometimes well founded, sometimes superficial, sometimes frank and at other times clandestine, while in his speech he was at times loyal and at times joking, thus perplexing everyone.[44] The *Liexian zhuan* also adds different lives after the time he spent with Emperor Wu. Dongfang Shuo is said to have remained a court official until the reign of Emperor Xuan (73–49) when he left with the wind to sell herbs in the neighbourhood of Lake Tai until retiring as a star deity. This early account of Dongfang Shuo's immortality looks pale and, except for his abode in the planet Jupiter, insignificant when compared with more literary accounts, which depict the immortal as a figure of very high standing: in age he reaches back to early mythical figures, and through his influence over the emperor his personal power surpasses all challengers at the Han court.[45] The frustrated ambition, the imagined contradiction between talent and position, the intellectual maladjustment of the official, which dominate the *Hanshu* account, do not appear in Daoist texts. The *Lishi zhenxian tidao tongjian* quotes long passages from the *Hanshu* where it refers to the tricks played by its hero to gain entry into the Han court and ignores the later stages of his life when, according to Ban Gu, his lack of political impact became more pressing. This biography also contains quotes from the *Han Wudi neizhuan*,[46] which relate to the appearance of the Queen Mother of the West and a few passages whose source has not been identified.[47] In all, the biography creates the impression of a powerful figure whose spiritual powers were crowned by much worldly success. It contains the following sentences, supposedly from a letter written by Dongfang Shuo, which remain in the tradition of the studied melancholy that periodically struck any career official: "We must not let the dusty nets and reins of reputation shackle us. With a long guffaw I happily withdraw to the Ten Continents and Three

Islands. Let us meet each other there, pluck jasper grasses, swallow the rays of the sun and moon, and lightly ascend together."[48] The *Xuanpin lu*, more than other Daoist biographical collections concerned with official life, consists of quotes in praise of the hero; it also cites a certain Xiahou Zhan (possibly the Jin official of this name),[49] as well as Yang Xiong and a commemorative tablet designed by Yan Zhenqing, the Tang Dynasty grandson of Yan Shigu. While the *Hanshu* gives a reasonable account of how difficult it was to survive at the Han court while looking at the world from what later generations would call a Daoist point of view, intellectual conflict is put aside in the Daoist material, or at best transformed into the eternal pattern of the periodically ill-adjusted public servant, as in the *Xuanpin lu*.

Yu Ji

With Fan Li, Liu An and Dongfang Shuo we are on safe ground concerning their identity. From early on they were identified with certain political as well as religious activities. If these different traces originally stem from different traditions, their origins lie in the misty zone of legend-building which need not concern us here. We have every reason to believe that the three men were historical figures, and that Fan Li's career stretched from politics to business, while Liu An and Dongfang Shuo were important personages of Emperor Wu's reign. However, historicity is a serious problem with a figure named Yu Ji (or Gan Ji, if a different but similar character is accepted as the correct form of his family name) who has been linked to a scripture entitled the *Taiping jing*.

Yu Ji has two different faces: when healing diseases, or being healed, he was associated with other Daoist personalities and was, in the same context, also depicted as the recipient of a sacred text. In another context Yu Ji figured as a member of the entourage of Sun Ce, a follower of Cao Cao; in this position Yu Ji was popular enough to make Sun Ce jealous. Daoist and non-Daoist sources view the controversy between the two men from different angles. The Daoist biography contained in the Yuan dynasty *Lishi zhenxian tidao tongjian*[50] depicts Yu Ji as a figure whose popularity resulted accidentally from his success in healing Sun Ce's soldiers rather than from any careerist motives. The fault lay with Sun Ce: his envy and jealousy caused the conflict and he righteously fell ill and died of remorse after he had rashly ordered Yu Ji's execution. Here the *Lishi zhenxian tidao tongjian*[51] follows the *Dongxian zhuan*, a pre-Tang text which has been lost except for the excerpts preserved in the *Yunji qiqian*, where it states that only Sun Ce was to blame for the strains in the relationship between the two men.[52] The Daoist biography is mainly concerned with Sun Ce's retribution. Attention is focussed on his illness, his remorse and on his death, conveying the message that whoever opposes immortals is at fault and will suffer punishment. For

The Virtue of Conformity

the same reason the *Shenxian zhuan* mentions that the officials who in its view had caused the growing alienation between the emperor and Liu An were to die a violent death as a consequence. On the other hand non-Daoist sources depict Yu Ji as active in causing conflict. They describe how he paraded himself in formal dress in sight of the guests of a party given by Sun Ce, with the result that the guests felt obliged to leave the party in order to greet Yu Ji.[53] This episode has, as far as I am aware, not entered his Daoist biographies except for Chen Baoguang's *Sandong qunxian lu*[54] which quotes the *Jiangbiao zhuan*.

The Yu Ji of Daoist hagiography was an immortal who had no plans for a worldly career; all he did was heal diseases, control weather conditions and outlive his corpse. However, he concentrated on these skills at a time when Daoist religious activities were not remote from the struggle for political power, as can be seen from the many insurrections between the second and the seventh centuries which made use of Daoist slogans and concepts to strengthen their cause. This link between political opposition and social unrest on the one hand and certain Daoist religious circles on the other is well documented in historical writings. However, it is rarely addressed in the Daoist sources preserved in religious circles. For instance, we will look in vain for a Daoist biography of the rebel Sun En whose Daoist inclinations are well documented.[55] Anna Seidel, when dealing with the Daoist messiah Li Hong, had to base her work to a large extent on non-Daoist sources.[56] The fact that in the Daoist sources Yu Ji's image does not show any political traits is therefore in line with the religious tradition's general disregard for programmes of social reform.

Guo Pu

Guo Pu (276–324) was an expert on choosing the sites of graves and planning their construction and was also a fortune teller. The *Jinshu*[57] gives a sceptical account of his life resulting in the following evaluation: "By nature he was light-hearted, not concerned with severity and righteousness, he would drink and make love, and occasionally overstep the limits."[58] These sentences imply a negative critique of the hero and are quite typical of the distance between the official historiographer and his object. In Daoist biographies Guo Pu is given more weight. The *Lishi zhenxian tidao tongjian* version of his life,[59] while quoting extensively from the *Jinshu*, omits the text's final evaluation. The Daoist *Sandong qunxian lu*'s approach[60] differs from the *Jinshu*, even when it reports the doubtful episode of the hero using his considerable magical techniques for a minor purpose. Both texts record that Guo Pu, as guest of the Governor of Lujiang, took a liking to a female servant, and how he used magical tricks to frighten the governor into giving the servant away. He addressed his host: '"Your house should not keep this servant. She should be sold twenty miles to the north-east, and you should be careful not to fight over the price. Thereby this apparition will be dismissed." The host followed these instructions and Guo Pu instructed someone to purchase the servant. He then threw an amulet into the well and all of the several thousand men were bound to it and threw themselves one by one into the well.' Only the *Jinshu* continues: 'The host was pleased. Pu left, taking the servant with him . . .' The Daoist source tells the story as an example of Guo Pu's considerable expertise omitting the last sentence because the episode's happy and very personal end does nothing to make its hero look greater. The *Jinshu*, on the other hand, reminds the reader at the end of the episode of the purely personal scope of Guo Pu's use of magic.

As regards Guo Pu's political involvement, all sources agree that he died at the hand of the rebel Wang Dun because he had correctly prognosticated the failure of Wang's rebellion. The Daoist biography provides no further details. The dynastic history hints at the extent of Guo Pu's political involvement by giving the full story: 'When Wang Dun planned a rebellion, Wen Qiao (288–329) and Yu Liang (d. 340) asked Guo Pu for his prediction upon which he excused himself. The two asked again for a prediction of their own good luck or misfortune. Pu said: "Great luck". After they had left him, Wen Qiao and the others said: "Pu excused himself and did not dare speak. Perhaps Heaven will take hold of Wang Dun's soul. Since we all jointly serve the country in this great enterprise the fact that Pu said 'Great luck' must mean that an enterprise undertaken by us will necessarily succeed." They consequently advised the emperor to put Wang Dun to death.'[61]

According to this passage Guo Pu knowingly widened the rift between certain influential courtiers and the potential rebels by encouraging the courtiers to threaten their rivals, which consequently led to the armed uprising. The *Jinshu* allows us to conclude that Guo Pu was more involved in factional struggles and was a more active participant in the political power play than the Daoist biographer thought feasible to include in his account.

Xiao Ziyun

Xiao Ziyun's (492–553) official biographies do not contain any clue to his Daoist experiences. He was known as a scholar and ritual expert. Emperor Wu of the Liang commissioned him to write a new liturgy to accompany the new-style Buddhist-oriented official offerings which abolished the sacrifice of live animals.[62] We are also told that he was successful in his business ventures. He is said to have earned one million gold coins by producing thirty sheets of calligraphy in three days for a Korean emissary. He was also known, apparently, to use poor quality paper when producing

The Virtue of Conformity

calligraphy in return for a gift, and to present people with gifts for the sole purpose of receiving gifts in return. The *Lishi zhenxian tidao tongjian*[63] reduces all these specific elements of his life to information on his authorship of a *Jinshu* and his successful official career as well as to the odd remark that 'in spite of being a famous official he conversed in private with strangers' which is a benevolent account of his business transactions with the Korean emissary. The Daoist text adds to the account of Xiao's career a period spent as a wandering Buddhist monk, in the region of Mount Yusi in Jiangxi, in present-day Xiajiang. Later in the reign of Liang Wudi, he is found back at court. Historiographers portray him starving to death in a Buddhist monastery where he took refuge after having been driven from his official post by the rebellion of Hou Jing.[64] The Daoist biography reserves several sentences for praising the steadfastness of his resistance against the rebellion: 'When Hou Jing rebelled, he enlisted support among the court officials. However, Xiao Ziyun yearned only for righteousness, to an extraordinary degree. Although at that time beyond 60 years of age, he excelled in spiritual brilliance.'[65] This passage does not appear in the *Liangshu* and *Nanshi* biographies. The *Lishi zhenxian tidao tongjian* goes on to describe how the rebels finally forced Xiao Ziyun from his post despite his resistance and how he then retired into the region he had previously visited as a monk. A mountain in that region was named after his family where an altar and a cauldron were kept as his relics. The text also mentions the particular place where five years after his retirement from the world he changed into an immortal. On the one hand, the input from local cults is particularly strong in this biography in the form of a number of place-names and local details. On the other hand, the colourful and many-faceted personality of Xiao Ziyun created by the historiographers is transformed in the Daoist version into a simple paragon of virtue.

He Zhizhang

He Zhizhang's (659–744) Daoist biographies show little concern for the well documented personal complexity of this friend of Li Bai. From his political biography we know that as a poet and eccentric he managed to introduce a certain level of spontaneity to the high positions he held. The experience of strong contradictions in the social and cultural realms seems to have formed the background for his final step into a Daoist environment. This however was not the concern of the Daoist biographers. On the one hand their interest lay in his name which connoted high rank and great fame and on the other hand in the technical details of his conversion to their creed. While referring to his official career in only one short sentence they take great care to describe his conversion as if this event were divorced from He Zhizhang's previous existence. Two versions are presented of how his enlightenment took place; they cover the full breadth of Daoist activities. According to one version He turned Daoist when he obtained an elixir;[66] in the other when an old man proved the irrelevance of material goods to him.[67] The precious pearl he had received was quickly exchanged for cakes which were eaten just as quickly. Thereupon, He suddenly understood and retired from office. The Daoist biographers tell these anecdotes with the aim of giving a positive explanation for He Zhizhang's retirement which the official sources play down as nothing but the sign of an old man's mental weakness. The political and social clashes which arose from He's Daoist convictions, or which shaped these convictions, were beyond the interest of his Daoist biographers.

Yan Zhenqing

Yan Zhenqing (709–784)[68] was another official who died a violent death after a complex involvement with different factions of power. He came from an old family with Yan Shigu among his ancestors and was seen by his contemporaries as an eminent historian and intellectual who played a leading and often controversial role in shaping the discourse of the An Lushan period. Towards the end of his life he attempted to confront the imperial protege Lu Qi (d. 785) who, as a consequence, had Yan Zhenqing sent on the impossible mission of pacifying the rebellious Governor of Huaixi. After the governor's servants had strangled Yan Zhenqing[69] the emperor lamented the murder which he had done nothing to prevent. The *Lishi zhenxian tidao tongjian* mentions neither the controversy with Lu Qi nor the dubious position of the emperor. We are first told about Yan Zhenqing's academic credentials and the steps of his remarkable career.[70] The text then moves directly to his death, different elements of which stem from different traditions; he is said to have known in advance that he would die, it states that he turned into a ghost and sought revenge by frightening the family of the governor who had instigated the murder. He appeared in their midst 'as if he were alive, his whole body golden, claws growing from his hands, and the hair down his back several feet long.'[71] He is also said to have turned into an immortal: when his coffin was opened it was found empty. Adding still another element, this Daoist biography assures us that according to Ge Zhanggeng of the Song Dynasty (under his Daoist name of Baiyuchan) he turned into an Administrative Assistant of the Left residing in the pole star in charge of expelling evil influences.

If we trust the dynastic biographies Yan Zhenqing was known as a believer in Daoist and the Buddhist doctrines.[72] However, he was also a leading politician as well as a controversial one. His Daoist biography changes his position from that of an active political leader to that of an innocent victim of other people's political manoeuvres.

The Virtue of Conformity

The Realms of Religious Biography

Daoist biographies were characterized by a downgrading of the controversial aspects in a person's life, particularly in regard to his social and political involvement. This move to conformity parallels other essential elements in the formation and development of the religion, and it prevails in figures and sources from the beginnings of Daoism as well as in its more mature Tang dynasty state. The wish to conform with an accepted system of values had shaped the formation of Daoist ritual, textual tradition, and even longevity techniques from at least the fourth century. Daoist biography which played a vital part in popularizing the religious doctrine followed suit. Since political conformity was seen as an important religious virtue, the biographies of immortals tended to exclude material which implied non-conformity. At the same time they strongly recommended the superior and long lasting quality of spiritual achievement as opposed to doubtful worldly merit. However, the price for obtaining immortality was to refrain from social and political involvement and if involvement could not be avoided, at least from activities which could be branded as controversial or non-conformist.

This paper has been concerned to point out the constraints of Daoist biography. Of course, one could also turn the question around and ask what information the Daoists conveyed that was different from that of the official historiographers. They often added both a longer physical life to a person and more liveliness to that life, more situations in which the central figure was active in this world (the figures of Fan Li and Xiao Ziyun are good examples of this), and at least one life after death, or rather they replaced death with immortality. The doctrinal need to add an immortal existence to a person made his or her death or supposed death often the central element of a life story. For dramatic reasons, many of the figures depicted died a violent death. Gouyi furen the mother of Emperor Wu's successor Zhao was put to death to exclude her from the political scene. According to Zhu Shaosun's addition to Sima Qian's account of the "Empresses" she died a violent death;[73] in the *Hanshu* it is said that she died of grief while in prison.[74] The *Liexian zhuan*[75] chose the *Shiji* version, possibly for dramatic purposes, the violent death making her ensuing resurrection more impressive. Another specific element of religious biographies is their local flavour which became more prevalent as the religion spread and amalgamated local cults. In geographical terms, the life of the saintly figure stretches beyond his secular counterpart.

From a literary point of view the clash between the realm of worldly affairs on the one hand and the realm of personal longevity and spiritual excellence on the other can create contrast and tension in a piece of prose. Fantastic events interwoven into the fabric of an official career, or career steps built into a process of religious achievement add a specific narrative flavour to the religious biography of political figures.

Notes

1. *Shenxian zhuan*, Longwei mishu edition, 1.
2. Judith Boltz, "Taoist Literature Part II. Five Dynasties to the Ming," in W.H. Nienhauser, *The Indiana Companion to Traditional Chinese Literature* (Bloomington: Indiana University Press 1986), 156.
3. B. Penny, Early Daoist Biography: A Study of the *Shenxian zhuan*, unpublished PhD thesis, Australian National University, 1993, 3.
4. Penny, Early Daoist Biography, 124ff.
5. Stephen Durrant, "*Shen-hsien chuan*," in Nienhauser, *The Indiana Companion*, 677–78.
6. Boltz, "Taoist Literature Part II," 157.
7. A. Wright, "Values, Roles and Personalities," in A. Wright and D. Twitchett, *Confucian Persuasion* (Stanford: Stanford University Press, 1962).
8. W. LaFleur, "Biography," in M. Eliade, *The Encyclopedia of Religion*, vol. 2 (NewYork: Macmillan, 1987), 220–24.
9. K. Schipper, *L'Empereur Wou des Han dans la légende taoiste* (Paris: Publications de l'École Française D'Extrême-Orient, 1965).
10. *Liexian zhuan*, HY 294, 1: 6a–b, Volumes in the *Daozang* are identified by "HY" which precedes the number assigned to it in the index to Daoist literature in the Harvard-Yenching Institute Sinological Index Series; M. Kaltenmark, *Le Lie-sien tchouan* (Paris: Collège de France, Institut des Hautes Études Chinoises, 1987), 71–74.
11. *Shiji* (Beijing: Zhonghua shuju, 1959), 32: 1477ff.; É. Chavannes, *Les Mémoires Historiques de Se-Ma Ts'ien* (Paris: Adrien-Maisonneuve, 1967), 34ff.
12. See *Meixian guanji*: HY 600, 6a–b.
13. *Hanshu* (Beijing: Zhonghua shuju, 1975), 67: 2926.
14. A. Wright, "Values, Roles and Personalities"; D. Twitchett, "Problems in Chinese Biography," in A. Wright and D. Twitchett, *The Confucian Persuasion* (Stanford: Stanford University Press, 1960); P. Alheit and B. Dausien, "Biographie," in H.J. Sandkühler, ed., *Europäische Enzyklopädie zu Philosophie und Wissenschaften*, vol. 1 (Hamburg: Meiner, 1990), 405–18.
15. *Shiji*, 41: 1752ff.
16. *Guoyu* (Shanghai: Shanghai guji chubanshe, 1978), 21: 641ff.
17. *Wu Yue chunqiu*, Gujin yishi edition, chs 7–10.
18. *Yue jueshu* (Shanghai: Shangwu yinshuguan, 1956), ch. 7 and *passim.*
19. *Shiji*, 129: 3257f. and *Hanshu*, 91: 3683, cf. N. Swann, *Food and Money in Ancient China* (Princeton: Princeton University Press, 1950), 424ff.
20. Kaltenmark, *Le Lie-sien tchouan*, 3ff.
21. *Liexian zhuan*, 1: 20a; Kaltenmark, *Le Lie-sien tchouan*, 102.
22. *Shiji*, 41: 1752; Chavannes, *Les Mémoires Historiques*, 440.
23. See *Wu Yue chunqiu*, 6: 12b; W. Eichhorn, *Heldensagen aus dem unteren Yangtse-Tal* (Wiesbaden: F. Steiner, 1969), 146ff.
24. *Xuanpin lu*, HY 780, 1: 8b. The preface is dated 1335.
25. *Lishi zhenxian tidao tongjian*, DZ 296, 3: 8a.
26. *Shenxian zhuan*, 9: 2a and cited in the *Xianyuan bianzhu*, DZ 596, 2: 16a, which comes from the end of the Tang Dynasty and consists mainly of citations of earlier biographies.
27. B. Penny, Historicising Immortality, presented at the Australian Association for Asian Studies conference, Perth, 1994.

28 T.E. Smith, Ritual and the Shaping of Narrative: The Legend of the Han Emperor Wu, unpublished PhD dissertation, University of Michigan, 1992, 141ff.
29 A. Birrell, *Popular Songs and Ballads of Han China* (London, Sydney & Wellington: Unwin Hyman, 1988), 100ff.
30 *Shiji*, 118: 3082ff.; *Hanshu*, 44: 2146ff.
31 *Hanshu*, 44:2145.
32 *Shenxian zhuan*, 4: 1 a–5a; cf. B. Wallacker, "Liu An, Second King of Huai-nan (180?–122? B.C.)," *Journal of the American Oriental Society*, 92:1 (1972), 36–49.
33 *Shenxian zhuan*, 4: 4a.
34 *Hanshu*, 44: 2149.
35 B. Kandel, "Der Versuch einer politischen Restauration – Liu An, der König von Huai-nan," *Nachrichten der Gesellschaft für Natur- und Völkerkunde Ostasiens*, 113 (1973), 33–96.
36 Penny, Early Daoist Biography, 174.
37 *Hanshu*, 45: 2167ff.
38 Boltz, "Taoist Literature Part II," 157.
39 Smith, Ritual and the Shaping of Narrative, 147ff.
40 *Shiji*, 126: 3205.
41 *Hanshu*, 65: 2874; cf. Smith, Ritual and the Shaping of Narrative, 156f.
42 Translation by Smith, Ritual and the Shaping of Narrative, 156.
43 *Hanshu*, 65: 2873.
44 M. Kaltenmark, *Le Lie-sien Tchouan*, 137.
45 Smith, Ritual and the Shaping of Narrative, 439ff. and *passim*.
46 Schipper, *L'Empereur Wou des Han*, 122.
47 Smith, Ritual and the Shaping of Narrative, 664ff.
48 *Lishi zhenxian tidao tongjian*, 3: 20a; translation by Smith, Ritual and the Shaping of Narrative, 665.
49 Cf. *Jinshu* (Beijing: Zhonghua shuju, 1974), 55: 1491.
50 *Lishi zhenxian tidao tongjian*, 20: 1a.
51 *Lishi zhenxian tidao tongjian*, 20: 1aff.
52 *Yunji qiqian, Daozang jinghua* edition (Taipei: Ziyou chubanshe, 1973), 111: 1522.
53 *Jiangbiao zhuan*, preserved in the commentary to *Sanguo zhi* (Beijing: Zhonghua shuju, 1973), 46: 1110.
54 *Sandong qunxian lu*, HY 1238, preface 1154, 13:20a–b.
55 W. Eichhorn, "Description of the Rebellion of Sun En and Earlier Taoist Rebellions," *Mitteilungen des Instituts für Orientforschung*, 2 (1954), 325–52.
56 A. Seidel, "Image of the Perfect Ruler in Early Taoist Messianism," *History of Religions*, 9 (1969), 216–55.
57 *Jinshu*, 72: 1899ff.
58 *Jinshu*, 72: 1904.
59 *Lishi zhenxian tidao tongjian*, 28: 6b–10a.
60 *Sandong qunxian lu*, 14: 4a.
61 *Jinshu*, 72: 1909.
62 *Nanshi* (Beijing: Zhonghua shuju, 1973), 42: 1075.
63 *Lishi zhenxian tidao tongjian*, 31:12b–13a.
64 *Nanshi*, 42: 1076.
65 *Lishi zhenxian tidao tongjian*, 31:13a.
66 The Song Dynasty *Gaodao zhuan*, which is lost except for quotations: see *Sandong qunxian lu*, 40: 5f.; cf. J.R. Kirkland, Taoists of the High T'ang: An Inquiry into the Perceived Significance of Eminent Taoists in Medieval Chinese Society, unpublished PhD dissertation, University of Indiana, 1986, 116.

67 *Taiping guangji, Saoye shanfang yinhang* edition, 42: 3a; cf. Kirkland, Taoists of the High T'ang, 361.
68 Cf. David McMullen, "Historical and Literary Theory in the Mid-Eighth Century," in A.F. Wright and D. Twitchett, ed., *Perspectives on the T'ang* (New Haven: Yale University Press 1973), 307–44.
69 *Jiu Tangshu* (Beijing: Zhonghua shuju, 1972), 128: 3594.
70 *Lishi zhenxian tidao tongjian*, 32: 5b–7a.
71 *Lishi zhenxian tidao tongjian*, 32: 6b.
72 McMullen, "Historical and Literary Theory in the Mid-Eighth Century," 313.
73 *Shiji*, 49: 1986.
74 *Hanshu*, 97a: 3956.
75 Kaltenmark, *Le Lie-sien Tchouan*, 139.

3
Everyday Miracles

A.J. Prince

Das Wunder ist des Glaubens liebstes Kind[1]

Miracles[2] can be said to be a common and distinctive feature of religious biographies or hagiographies in most religious traditions. In such biographies, the occurrence of miracles testifies to the holiness of the saint whose life is being narrated, but explanation of the precise nature of such miracles, and interpretation of their significance, will differ from one religion to another.

In theistic traditions, miracles are supernatural phenomena produced by God (or by a god or goddess) to demonstrate some particular truth or lesson, for deities alone have the power to suspend the laws of nature. According to the *New Catholic Encyclopedia*, for example, "a miracle is an extraordinary event, perceptible to the senses, produced by God in a religious context as a sign of the supernatural."[3] The purpose of the miracle may be to express the deity's approval of the saint's virtues, to display the deity's power, to convey the divine will, and so on.

In nontheistic traditions such as Buddhism or Jainism (as well as to some extent in mixed traditions like Daoism and Hinduism), however, the power to perform miracles is generally held to lie within the mind of the saint himself or herself. In Buddhism, this power is understood to be intrinsic to the mind. It is normally obscured by delusive patterns of thought and feeling accumulated over innumerable lifetimes but becomes accessible when the mind is purified through the practice of meditation. To achieve this, it is necessary to withdraw one's attention and interest from the objects of the senses and to focus the mind on a single point. In a stock passage, the Pali Canon describes the process as follows:

> And again, monks, a monk, detached from the pleasures of the senses ... enters on and abides in the first level of meditation (*jhāna*) which is accompanied by initial and discursive thinking, is born of detachment

and is blissful and joyful... And again monks, a monk, after stilling initial and discursive thinking, with the mind made calm within and fixed on one point, enters on and abides in the second level of meditation which is free from initial and discursive thinking and is blissful and joyful.[4]

When the mind is thus focussed and settled, it becomes clear, and things become apparent that were not visible before. The metaphor of clear water is often used:

With the mind thus composed, purified and clarified, without blemish or defilement, supple and serviceable, firm and imperturbable, he applies his mind to the elimination of the Cankers (*āsava*). Monks, it is as if there were a mountain pool, clear, limpid and serene, and a man, with eyes to see, were standing on the bank: he would observe the various shells, the pebbles and gravel, and the shoals of fish moving and at rest... even so does a monk know as it really is (*yathābhūtaṃ*) "This is suffering."[5]

Just as the mind that is clarified in this way can be directed to a knowledge of ultimate reality (*yathābhūtaṃ*), so it can be directed to the acquisition of miraculous powers. The Pali Canon again has a stock passage:

With the mind thus composed, purified and clarified, without blemish or defilement, supple and serviceable, firm and imperturbable, he applies his mind to the production of a mind-made body... to the various miraculous powers (*iddhi* = S. *ṛddhi*)[6]... from being one he becomes many, and from being many becomes one again; he becomes visible or invisible; he passes unhindered through walls, ramparts and mountains as if through space; he plunges into and emerges from the earth as if it were water; he walks on water without disturbing the surface as if it were land; with legs crossed he travels through the air like a bird; even the sun and moon with all their miraculous power (*mahiddhike*) and majesty he touches and feels with his hand; in his own physical form (*kāyena*) he travels as far as the Realm of Brahma... with purified divine hearing, surpassing human ability, he hears the sounds of both worlds... with his own mind he knows the minds of other beings... he recalls his many previous existences (*nivāsa*, "abode, dwelling")... with purified divine vision, surpassing human ability, he beholds beings as they perish and are reborn.[7]

Four specific practices, called *iddhipāda* (S. *ṛddhipāda*, Ch. *ruyizu, shenzu*) or "bases of miraculous (or 'psychic') power" are often mentioned in the Buddhist scriptures, commonly as part of the Thirty-seven Aids to Enlightenment (S. *bodhipākṣika-dharma*, Ch. *zudaopin*). These four, which make the attainment of miraculous powers possible are all said to involve meditative concentration (*samādhi*) and to be "accompanied by active striving" (P. *padhāna-saṅkhāra-samannāgata*). They are described as concentration of will-power (*chanda*), of effort (S.*vīrya*, P. *viriya*), of mind (*citta*) and of examination or investigation (S. *mīmāṃsā*, P. *vīmaṃsā*).

The Buddhist texts that mention miraculous powers and events of this type do not go into much more detail than this about the precise nature and function of the processes involved. There are probably two reasons for this reticence. One is that such phenomena are regarded as being by definition beyond the comprehension (i.e. S. *acintya*, Ch. *bu (ke) siyi*) of the worldly, who lack understanding of the mind and of reality itself. The other and perhaps more important reason is that the Buddha himself is believed to have frowned on the display of such powers, regarding them as being, at best, distractions from the true task of seeking Liberation from suffering, and, at worst, an incitement to pride and egotism. A well known passage, as recorded for example in the *Kevaddha Sutta*[8] of the Pali Canon, has the Buddha speaking of three types of miracle (*pāṭihāriya*). The first is the power of *iddhi* – the ability to perform the various feats mentioned above – and the second (*ādesanā*) is, in effect, the power of telepathy – the ability to perceive other people's thoughts and feelings directly. In both these cases, the Buddha says, a skeptic will attempt to explain such things away by claiming that they are done with the aid of some magic charm or other. Clearly the Buddha feels that any accomplishment that can be so easily devalued is not worth the trouble of acquiring. More valuable, and more impressive, the Buddha suggests, is the third type of miracle, the miracle of education (*anusāsanī*), here referring to instruction in the Dharma. Therefore, for a monk or nun to lay false claim to such powers (the reality of which, be it noted, is never doubted) counts as one of the most serious offences against the Buddhist monastic code, the Vinaya.[9]

Nevertheless, in spite of this disapproving attitude, miracles do play a prominent and positive role in Buddhist biographies, including those of the Buddha himself. In some cases, in Mahayana Buddhism particularly, miraculous powers developed through meditation came to be regarded as a useful or even indispensible means of instructing the ignorant and helping to free them from their delusions. This is in accord with the Mahayanist doctrine of the "skilful means" (S. *upāya-kauśalya*, Ch. *fangbian*) that the bodhisattva must acquire for the endless task of liberating sentient beings. So Atīśa (Dīpaṃkara Śrījñāna, 982–1054) goes so far as to say that if one wants to accumulate the Two Resources (of merit and wisdom):

> And has the constant desire to work for others' good,
> But has not developed the Superknowledges,[10]
> Then he is acting like a blind man,
> And behaving as though insane.[11]

And he adds:

> My guru has spoken on this . . . "The Scriptures do not tell us that we can be helpful to others just from having studied the Teaching, and without first acquiring the superknowledges . . . A man who is incapable of maturing disciples because he lacks the superknowledges is sinking toward death himself."[12]

In the Buddhist hagiographies themselves, miracles can be seen to have various levels of meaning and to perform various functions. Dante, in his famous letter to Can Grande della Scala, distinguishes four levels at which Christian allegory can be interpreted, the literal (*ad literam*), the allegorical (*ad allegoriam*), the moral (*ad moralem sensum*) and the anagogical or mystical (*ad anagogium*)[13] In an analogous way, one might say that the miraculous events that occur in Buddhist biographies can be significant at four different levels: the inspirational, the political, the cosmological and the ontological.

At the personal level, the most obvious function of the miracle is to inspire the individual listener or reader to have faith in the one who performs it (although, as the Buddha pointed out, a determined cynic will always remain unimpressed). And in Buddhism at least, the purpose of inspiring faith is to encourage the devotee to practise. This is made clear, with naive explicitness, in the following passage from the biography of Marpa (1012–1096), the teacher of the great Tibetan yogi and poet Milarepa (1040–1123):

> Once when Jetsün Mila went before the guru, Marpa displayed various miracles – multiplying his own body, appearing as the four elements, disappearing, appearing as a rainbow, appearing as light, and so on. Then he asked Mila, "Did you see? Are you convinced by these?" Mila replied, "I saw them, sir, and I cannot help but be convinced. I also will meditate so that I can do this."[14]

At the social level, the function of miracles in biographical narratives could be said to be, in the broadest sense, political. This can be a matter of sectarian rivalry, as when stories of miracles serve as a means of demonstrating that "our" saints are holier than "yours", and that therefore Buddhism, for instance, is superior to its rivals, in India (Jainism and Brahmanism)[15] or China (Daoism and Confucianism). A simple example from China is the well-known – and fictitious – story of a dispute between two Buddhist missionaries, Kāśyapa Mātaṅga and Dharmaratna, and the Daoists that is supposed to have taken place in Luoyang during the reign of Emperor Ming (r. 58–76). In the course of the contest the Daoist scriptures were burnt in a trial by fire while the Buddhist texts remained unconsumed, and the triumphant Mātaṅga demonstrated his own powers by rising into the air and precipitating a rain of flowers.[16]

Everyday Miracles

But accounts of miracles can also have implications in a wider political sphere. They may indicate to the government or the ruling class that the religion in question produces saints with mysterious powers that are perhaps capable of directly affecting the country or the government itself. Such powers could, for example, be employed to protect the country from internal or external dangers, whether material (e.g. drought, foreign invasion) or spiritual (angry gods, demons, witchcraft etc.). The government may then draw the conclusion that the saints in question, and the religion they represent, are worth patronizing. And of course another possible conclusion might be that it would be unwise to antagonize these holy beings by slighting or persecuting their religion.

In the biography of Fa Zang, the so-called Third Patriarch of the Huayen School, by the Silla (Korean) scholar Ch'oe Ch'iwŏn (857–904?),[17] it is said that Fa Zang was several times called on to employ his powers on behalf of the state. Even though his character and reputation were those of a scholar rather than a miracle-worker, it was considered that his status as a holy and learned monk should be sufficient to give him access to powers beyond the normal.

> In the first year of Divine Merit (697 – reign of Empress Wu), the Khitan (Qidan) rebelled. An army was sent out to punish them, and Fa Zang was specially commissioned to curb the bandits' depredations by the means taught in the scriptures. He then submitted a memorial saying, "If I am to subdue malevolent enemies, I request permission to use the methods of the Left-hand Path [i.e. tantric methods]." This was granted, and the Dharma Master bathed, changed his clothing, and set up a shrine to the eleven-headed Guangyin,[18] installed an image of the deity and performed the rites. A few days later the barbarian rabble saw the approaching imperial army as a host of countless divine kings, with an image of Guanyin floating [above them] in the sky. Thereupon they retreated pell-mell like a pack of dogs or sheep.[19]
>
> In the second year of Radiant Dragon (708), the Emperor Zhongzong was distressed over the [lack of] rain in midsummer, so he commissioned Fa Zang to assemble a hundred Dharma Masters at the Source of Blessings Monastery and pray for rain according to the Buddhist practice. By the seventh morning [thereafter] a torrential downpour had begun that lasted for ten nights.[20]
>
> In the spring of 711 the seasonal rain was scanty, and in the winter there was no snow. All the people were crying out to Heaven, so the Emperor summoned Fa Zang to the palace and earnestly requested that he employ his arts to save the peasantry. Fa Zang replied, "I have searched through the scriptures and found the *Maheśvaradhāraṇī*.[21] If an altar were to be constructed and this *dhāraṇī* were to be copied out and cast into a dragon pond, we would certainly obtain a timely

response." The Emperor commanded that this request be complied with. Fa Zang then went to Awakening to the Truth Monastery on Indigo Field Mountain, where he performed the ceremony by the dragon pond, and within ten days there was a heavy fall of snow.[22]

Turning now to the significance of miracles in terms of the religious doctrine itself, one might distinguish two of the four aspects mentioned above: the cosmological and the ontological. In the former case, the miraculous powers exhibited by the saint are meant to indicate his or her status in the history of the world or in the cosmic scheme of things. Miracles of this type usually appear in connection with the founders of religions, such as Jesus Christ, for example, or with saints regarded as having equivalent or near-equivalent status. Thus Ibn al-'Arabī (1165–1240), referring to the Perfect Man (A. *al-insān al-kāmil*), the holiest type of sage, uses the term "the Pole" (A. *al-Quṭb* = axis, axle, pole, pivot), implying that such a person is the pivotal point around which the whole world revolves:

> The Pole is ... the mirror of God, the locus of disclosure for the holy descriptions and for the divine loci of self-manifestation. He is the Possessor of the Present Moment, the Eye of Time, and the Mystery of Destiny.[23]

In Buddhist literature, miracles with this kind of cosmic significance are associated above all with the Buddha, as will be seen below.

By miracles with ontological significance is meant those which involve an alteration in or breach of the very nature of reality as commonly perceived and understood. They demonstrate, in a Buddhist context, that such saints have reached the point at which they understand that this conventional view of reality is ultimately an illusion; hence they are no longer bound by ordinary physical laws. In Mahayana Buddhism in particular this aspect of the miraculous is closely connected with the Madhyamika doctrine of emptiness (S. *śūnyatā*) and with the Yogācāra teaching that world and self are only mental constructs (S. *citta-mātra*). Miracles of this type, or understood in this light, therefore, can be a means of conveying the profoundest teachings of Mahayana Buddhism.

For Buddhism, the archetypal saint is of course the Buddha himself, and miracles performed by him (of which many are recorded despite his apparent disapproval of such displays) may carry any of the four types of significance mentioned above, although the cosmological aspect is especially prominent in the traditional accounts of his life. There are passages in the Pali Canon that lack the miraculous element and so to modern eyes have a certain historical plausibility; for example, this account of his Renunciation, the simplicity of which contrasts strikingly with the elaborate and stereotyped accounts given in the traditional biographies:[24]

Everyday Miracles

And I too, monks, before my Enlightenment, when I was still an unenlightened bodhisattva, being subject to birth because of self, sought what was likewise subject to birth ... Then it occurred to me, monks: ... Suppose that I, though subject to birth because of self, having understood the danger in things subject to birth, should seek the Unborn, the ultimate peace transcending all bonds – Nirvana? ...

Then, monks, some time later, while I was still young, while my hair still retained its youthful black, in the flower of my youth, in the prime of my life – despite the tearful faces and the lamenting of my unhappy parents – I cut my hair and beard off, and left home for the homeless life, dressed in the robes of a mendicant.[25]

Elsewhere, however, miraculous occurrences serve to indicate clearly that it is the life of a person of exceptional holiness and cosmic significance that is being narrated:

And when the Lord was seated, he said to the Venerable Ānanda: "Fetch me some water Ānanda, for I am thirsty and would like to drink." When he had said this, the venerable Ānanda said to the Lord: "But just now, Master, some five hundred carts have gone past, and the water, choked off by the wheels, has dwindled and flows foul and turbid ..."

A second time ... A third time the Lord said to the Venerable Ānanda ... "Yes, Master!" said the venerable Ānanda ... and taking a bowl he approached the stream. Then he found that the stream which ... had been flowing foul and turbid, was now, as he approached it, flowing clear, pure and clean. Then Ānanda thought: "How wonderful, how marvellous is the Tathāgata's great might and miraculous power (*mahiddhikatā*)!"[26]

Not long after the Mallian Pukkusa had gone, the venerable Ānanda brought the two robes of cloth of gold, burnished and ready for wear, over to the Lord; but when they were brought near the body of the Lord, their brilliance faded ... "So it is, Ānanda. There are two occasions ... on which the colour of a Tathāgata's skin becomes extremely clear and bright."[27]

At that time the venerable Upavāṇa was standing in front of the Lord, fanning him, and the Lord rebuked Upavāṇa, saying: "Move aside, monk; do not stand in front of me!" ... And the venerable Ānanda said ... "... For what cause, for what reason, does the Lord rebuke Upavāṇa ... ?"

"Countless gods of the ten world-systems have gathered here to behold the Tathāgata, Ānanda. For twelve leagues (*yojanāni*) ... around ... the place is so thronged by powerful deities that there would be nowhere to insert so much as the tip of a hair."[28]

It is in the nature of things (*dhammatā esā*), monks, that when a Bodhisattva issues from his mother's womb, two streams of water should appear in the air, one cool and the other warm, so that the Bodhisattva and his mother may be suitably bathed. That, in such a case, is the nature of things.

It is in the nature of things, monks, that when a Bodhisattva is born, he should stand firmly on both feet and take seven strides towards the north, while a white canopy is held over him, and, looking around in every direction, should utter in a powerful voice like that of a bull: "I am supreme in the world, I am foremost in the world, I am unsurpassed in the world! This is the last birth! There will be no further becoming!" That, in such a case, is the nature of things.[29]

A particularly spectacular miracle attributed to the Buddha by relatively late Pali sources and often depicted in Indian Buddhist sculpture is the "Miracle of the Pairs" (S. *yamaka-prātihārya*; P. *yamaka-pāṭihāriya*):

For a long time the nature of this extraordinary performance was not understood, but now we possess canonical descriptions. *Paṭisambhidāmagga*, i.125; *M[ahā]vastu*, iii.115. Buddha rose in the air, flames of fire came from the upper part of his body and streams of water from the lower part. Then the process was reversed. Next fire came from the right side of his body and water from the left, and so on through twenty-two variations of pairs. He then created a jewelled promenade in the sky, and walking along it produced the illusion that he was standing or sitting or lying down, and varied the illusions in a similar way. The Jātaka says that he performed it on three other occasions, at his enlightenment to remove the doubt of the gods, at the meeting with Pāṭika, and at Gaṇḍa's mango-tree.[30]

Turning now to the Huayen School, we find that Fa Zang himself has collected a large number of biographies in his account of the lineage of the School, *The Transmission of the Avataṃsaka Sūtra* (*Huayanjing chuanji*), an unfinished work in five fascicles that he was apparently still working on in the last year of his life. Some of the miraculous events related in these biographies are simply testimonies to the special powers, and therefore the holiness, of the subject, as for example the following incident from the biography of Buddhabhadra (359–429):

On reaching Jiaozhi [in present-day North Vietnam, to the north-east of Hanoi] they boarded a ship and travelled along the coast. When they were passing a certain island, Buddhabhadra pointed to it and said: "We could anchor here." But the captain said: "One should not waste time on such a voyage, for it is not so easy to encounter favourable

Everyday Miracles

winds. We cannot afford to stop." After they had travelled another two hundred *li* or so [about seventy miles], they suddenly met with a contrary wind that blew them right back to the island. All the people on board then realized that he had supernatural powers . . .

Later a convenient wind sprang up and his companions wanted to leave. Buddhabhadra said: "We should stay here." The captain accordingly remained, while those who had already set out all perished together.

Later, in the middle of the night, he suddenly commanded that all the ships should set sail. Some were not willing to follow him, so Buddhabhadra cast off the hawser himself, and his boat alone moved out. Bandits then appeared, and all those who had remained behind were seized and killed.[31]

This seems to be a matter of telepathy and/or precognition. Another motif, as common in Buddhism as in other religious traditions, involves the emanation of light:

Once the Master went to the palace chapel, and in the middle of the night a brilliant light like an unfading rainbow streamed out from inside (the building). His Majesty saw this light and ordered his attendants to go and investigate. They went, and reported back, saying that it was light from the Master's eyes. His Majesty proceeded to where the Master was, and asked him what method of spiritual training he practised to obtain results such as this. The Master replied: "This monk's practice is nothing special." Thereupon a string of rosary beads on the low sutra-table rose spontaneously into the air and circled the Master three times, before coming to rest once more.[32]

On nights when the Elder was composing his *Commentary* . . . a bright light would shine from his mouth to illuminate the grotto, in place of a lamp or a candle.[33]

A particularly striking example of such spiritual luminescence was once related to Fa Zang by an eyewitness, a monk called Tan Xun. According to the latter's story, he and his guru, Tan Yi, were wandering through the mountains one day when they encountered a Buddhist nun who appeared to be living by herself in the wilderness. She directed them to a stone hut on the other side of the valley, "perhaps five or six *li* away", where they could spend the night. That evening the two monks heard the nun reciting the *Avataṃsaka Sūtra*, and when they looked they could "see light being emitted from the nun's mouth in the distance". As the recitation continued throughout the night, the amount of light steadily increased till "it lit the whole valley up as though it were broad daylight". After this it gradually contracted again, finally disappearing as the recitation ended. The next day the monks paid their devout respects to the nun, but when they subsequently returned with others (like the woodcutter attempting to return to the Peach Blossom Spring) they could find no trace of her.[34]

Another miracle testifying to the personal holiness of the saint concerned but with deeper, symbolic implications would presumably have been witnessed by Fa Zang himself, for it occurred at the funeral of Śikṣānanda, who had produced the 80-fascicle Chinese version of the *Avataṃsaka Sūtra* between 695 and 699, with the assistance of Fa Zang among others:

> An edict was issued giving permission for the funeral to be conducted according to foreign custom [i.e. cremation]. This was done on the 12th day of the 11th month [710], and the body was cremated on the Dīpaṅkara Platform outside the Kaiyuan Gate. When the fuel had been consumed and the fire had gone out, his tongue was found still intact. This was an auspicious sign of his [accomplishment in] spreading the Dharma.[35]

Here the symbolic significance of the miracle is pointed out by Fa Zang himself. In a similar miracle, related of Guṇabhadra (394–468), the implications are wider, for the story is meant to emphasize the power of the Sutra itself and the overtones are cosmological:

> Prince Qiao wanted him to expound the *Avataṃsaka Sūtra* but [Guṇa]bhadra considered that he had not yet sufficient skill in Chinese [for the purpose], and he felt sad and ashamed. So he practised the rite of repentance day and night and prayed to Avalokiteśvara for assistance. Then he dreamt that a person dressed in white, holding a sword and carrying a human head, came up to him and asked, "What is troubling you?" Guṇabhadra explained the whole situation. The other replied, "That's no great problem", and with his sword he struck Guṇabhadra's head off and replaced it with a new one. He bade him turn [his new head] round, saying, "It doesn't hurt, does it?" Guṇabhadra replied "Not at all", and all at once he experienced a great Enlightenment. His mind was flooded with joy, and after this he was perfectly fluent in Chinese . . . He subsequently lectured on the *Avataṃsaka Sūtra* dozens of times.[36]

One of the best known (and most historically dubious) stories of this type in the *Transmission* reads as follows:

> Formerly, in the first year of Great Harmony of the Northern Qi Dynasty (479–502),[37] the Emperor's third son prayed to the bodhisattva Mañjuśrī on Cool Clarity Mountain [i.e. Wutai Shan or Five Peak Mountain], where he burnt his body as an offering. This prince had a eunuch official

Everyday Miracles

[called] Liu Qianzhi who grieved over his mutilation, and when he saw the Prince's act of self-immolation, he asked the Emperor's permission to go into the mountains for spiritual cultivation. This was granted him. There he venerated the Sutra ardently day and night, performing rites of repentance, chanting the text, and praying with all his heart to Mañjuśrī, hoping for divine assistance. He continued thus, eating no grain and drinking only water, for twenty-one days, and although he had become feeble in body and vital energy, his ardour was undiminished. Then he suddenly felt hair growing on his head, and he once again bore all the marks of manhood. This miraculous phenomenon awoke in him a profound understanding of its hidden significance, and he went on to compose the above-mentioned commentary [the *Commentary on the Avataṃsaka* (*Huayan lun*) in 600 fascicles],[38] in which he gave a full account of the whole course of events. He also submitted a report to the First Emperor,[39] whose pious faith in the Source [of the miracle] was confirmed and deepened thereby. It was from this point on that the *Avataṃsaka Sūtra* started to become popular.[40]

Because the Huayen School regards the Sutra on which it is based, the *Huayan jing* or *Avataṃsaka Sūtra*, as ultimately coextensive with the reality of the universe (or, in Huayen terms, the "Dharma-realm" or *Dharmadhātu*, *fajie*), many of the miraculous events related in the biographies are primarily meant to demonstrate the cosmic significance of the Sutra itself, and the holiness of the saints in question is shown mainly by their ardent devotion to the Sutra.[41] In the story concerning Guṇabhadra related above, the deity appeared in a dream, although the effects became apparent in waking life; in another incident, from the life of Buddhabhadra, who produced the 60-fascicle translation of the Sutra between 418 and 422, the deities made a public appearance:

[Buddhabhadra] translated [the Sutra] at the Daochang Monastery ... where there is still an *Avataṃsaka* Hall ... When he began to translate the Sutra, two [spirits] dressed in green[42] would always emerge from the pond in front of the temple to offer incense and flowers. Everybody saw these beings. Other deities would [also] stand guard beside him.[43]

This must have been a popular story, for we find it again, slightly modified and elaborated, in the biography of Li Tongxuan (646–740), written perhaps a century or so after the latter's death:

After he had settled in these mountains, there suddenly appeared two maidens of unearthly beauty, both about fifteeen years old. They were dressed in homespun clothing and wore hoods of plain cloth over their heads. They would regularly draw water and burn incense for the Elder, and kept him supplied with paper and brushes. At daybreak they would prepare an assortment of vegetarian delicacies and place them before the Elder. After the meal they would collect the utensils and disappear, no one knew where. For five years they appeared regularly and without fail. Then, when the Commentary was nearly finished, they vanished without trace.[44]

The author of Li Tongxuan's biography, Ma Zhi,[45] himself comments on the similarity to the earlier story:

A careful examination of the old histories of the *Avataṃsaka* reveals that when Tripitaka Master Buddhabhadra of the Eastern Jin was translating the Sutra at Minister Xie's Monastery in Jiangdu, two boys dressed in green emerged suddenly from the pool in the courtyard to wait upon the Indian monk. Burning incense for him and keeping the vessels filled with water, they were in constant attendance on him. Every evening they would return to the pool. This went on day after day, becoming a regular routine. But when the copying of the translation was completed, they silently vanished without trace.[46]

Miraculous incidents of this type, suggesting a fundamental harmony between the saint and the universe itself, can in China blend easily with native Daoist ideas about the Sage who is at one with the Dao of Nature, as for example in the following passage, again from the biography of Li Tongxuan:

At the end of that period, he once more packed up his sutras and other texts and took to the road. He had proceeded some twenty *li* or more on his journey ... when he suddenly encountered a tiger. The tiger crouched down meekly on the road and appeared to be expecting something from him. The Elder spoke to it, saying, "I am about to compose a commentary on the *Avataṃsaka Sūtra*. You can help me choose a place to stay." When he had finished speaking, the tiger arose and the Elder stroked it gently. He then took up his satchel of books, hung it on the tiger's back, and entrusted to the beast the task of finding the place where they should stop. Thereupon, the tiger headed towards the Shenfu Plateau. They proceeded straight ahead in that direction for more than thirty *li* till they came to a grotto, whereupon the tiger sat down. The Elder took his satchel from the tiger's back and placed it inside the grotto. The tiger then lowered its tail and left, looking back repeatedly ...

On the night of the Elder's arrival, there arose a violent thunderstorm which uprooted an old pine that was over three hundred feet tall. The next day, where the pine's roots had been, there had magically appeared

Everyday Miracles

a pool many fathoms deep and over fifty paces in circumference. Its waters were sweeter than nectar and clearer than crystal ... Even today its waters are pure and sparkling, and have neither increased nor diminished.[47]

On the other hand, transcendence of the natural order as a process of inevitable decay is also part of the Daoist tradition, and one of the cases in Fa Zang's *Transmission*, purportedly a biographical note on a Sui Dynasty monk, Hui Wu, is clearly a Daoist fable of this type that has been edited to provide a Buddhist, and specifically Huayen, moral. According to this tale, Hui Wu was living in seclusion on Zhongnan Shan, where he devoted himself to recitation of the *Avataṃsaka Sūtra* and the *Mahāparinirvāṇa Sūtra*. One day he was approached by a mysterious individual who addressed him as "*Avataṃsaka* Master",[48] and who turned out to be the god of the mountain. The god conducted him to where a vegetarian feast had been set out. Over five hundred monks and nuns then arrived, flying through the air, and prostrated themselves before Hui Wu. The latter protested his unworthiness, but was told: "Since you have received and uphold the *Avataṃsaka Sūtra*, you are worthy of our veneration." After the banquet, one of the god's attendant medicine spirits flew into Hui Wu's mouth, enabling him to achieve immortality on the spot. He then flew back to his former residence, where he appeared

> sitting cross-legged in the air, and said to his companions from a distance: "Through the power of the *Avataṃsaka Sūtra* I have received the medicine that confers immortality. Humans and immortals do not share the same status, so we can no longer live together ... At some future date we will meet again in the presence of the Buddha." Thereupon he soared up into the sky and vanished in the distance, while the text [of the Sutra] that he used to recite from also followed after him.[49]

Nevertheless there remains a common Chinese cultural bias – among the literati, at least – in favour of accepting Nature and finding ultimate reality in immanence rather than transcendence, and perhaps for this reason miracles that explicitly disrupt the natural order of things are less frequent in Chinese than in Indian and Central Asian texts. Thus Indian Buddhist tradition speaks of Enlightenment in terms of "liberation" (*[vi]mokṣa*) and "extinction" (*nirvāṇa*), whereas Chinese texts seem to prefer metaphors like "going back to the Source" (*huanyuan*) or "returning to the Root" (*guiben*). So Li Tongxuan's discussion of the ontological significance of miracles, for example, is based on incidents described in the sutras themselves, as will be seen below.

For miracles of the transcendental type in a Buddhist biographical context, therefore, it may be better to look at traditional stories about the lives of the Indian siddhas or the yogis of Tibet. Two well-known stories from the life of Milarepa furnish particularly clear and explicit examples of this type of miracle. One concerns his encounter with a couple of scholars who were annoyed by the popularity of this ignorant yogi and engaged him in debate, with the idea of showing up his lack of learning and philosophical sophistication. At one point in the story Milarepa counter-attacks. He asks the scholars' spokesman whether space is obstructing or non-obstructing. The scholar replies that of course space is non-obstructing, but then finds that he is totally unable to move his body. Milarepa then indicates a large rock as being non-obstructing, and demonstrates his point by walking through it unhindered.[50]

The other story, which is very much in harmony with the Huayen teachings, and with the statements in the sutras on which they are based, has Milarepa out walking with his disciple Rechungpa. A violent hailstorm arises, and Mila takes shelter inside an old yak-horn that he had found lying on the ground. In language which echoes that of the sutras, and of the Chinese Huayen masters, the biography tells us that when Rechungpa looked into the horn, he "saw Milarepa seated comfortably within with ample room to spare; his body was no smaller and the horn no larger than before, just as the reflection of a large image may be seen in a small mirror."[51]

What is the significance of such stories? According to Li Tongxuan they are meant to indicate the true nature of reality, but he distinguishes between miracles which are performed for a particular purpose on a particular occasion and those which are not so restricted. The former involve an actual transformation, as indicated by Sanskrit and Chinese words for such displays (nirmāṇa, vikurvaṇa; hua, shentong bianhua etc.), but the miracles with true revelatory significance never change anything and are not limited to a particular time or place: instead they simply reveal the true nature of things, an intrinsically miraculous reality which is changeless, timeless and omnipresent. The former, he says, belong to the Provisional Teaching and the latter to the Complete or Perfect Teaching. Referring to events described in the Vimalakīrti-nirdeśa, he says:

> According to the Vimalakīrti-nirdeśa the miraculous powers of the bodhisattvas are such that they can fit Mt. Sumeru, in all its height and breadth, inside a mustard seed, or put the water of the four great oceans into a single pore. It is also said there that a single room can contain lion-seats[52] for 32,000 teachers, each seat being 84,000 leagues (yojana) tall, as well as 8,000 bodhisattvas, 500 Śrāvakas, and 10,000 devas. [Again,] Vimalakīrti takes the whole assembly up in the palm of his right hand and conveys them to the garden of the hermitage. Again, with his hand he brings the Buddha-realm Abhirati[53] to this world, shows it to the assembly, and then returns it to its original place.
>
> All these miraculous transformations are like those displayed by the Śrāvakas and the bodhisattvas of the Provisional Teachings or the Three

Vehicles. Why? Because their Enlightenment is not yet authentic and they have not yet ceased to [discriminate] between self and others. The miraculous powers displayed here are dependent on the faculties that perceive them, and all the [above] cases involve coming and going, discrimination and limitation. The Buddha's intention [in such cases] is, by means of a temporary display of miraculous transformations, to arouse [those with] lesser faculties and encourage them to make further progress. This is not the natural power of the Reality of things.

In the *Avataṃsaka Sūtra* it is possible, through the natural power of the Dharma, which is the very nature of Reality, to contain all the buddha-realms throughout the ten directions within a single atom, all the worlds of beings within an atom. And yet, the worlds do not shrink, nor does the atom increase in size. So it is with every atom in all the worlds throughout the ten directions. As the Sutra says, within the body of a single small creature there are bodhisattvas liberating beings everywhere, and yet the being [in question] remains unaware of all this.

One should know that the Buddha uses the Provisional Teachings to encourage those with lesser faculties, and it is for this reason that buddhas appear outside the body, displaying miraculous powers and coming and going. In the True Teaching, on the other hand, one realizes the intrinsic nature of one's own mind by means of one's own innate Enlightenment. The nature and attributes of one's body and mind are [here] no different from those of the Buddha, and there is no internal or external, no coming or going, nor any beliefs whatsoever.

Therefore Vairocana appears sitting on the Seat of Enlightenment everywhere, without moving from his original place. [Similarly,] the beings that come from all ten directions have never moved from their original places, and although they return [as though] by magical transformation, there is actually no coming or going at all, nor is anything effected by means of miraculous powers. Therefore the Sutra says: such is the nature of things.

Whenever the Sutra speaks of the Buddha's miraculous powers, or the power of the nature of things, this is to express reverence for the Buddha [in the first case] or for the inherent qualities of Reality itself [in the second case]. In neither case does any actual transformation take place.

Because all the various worlds and the bodies and minds [of those who dwell there] exist in dependence on this fundamental Reality, they are not under the sway of delusion, and so all objects of the senses, both great and small, are like light and shade: they interpenetrate and pervade all places, without coming or going and without division or limitation. So [it can be said that] every pore in the body of every single being pervades the whole of space.

This is quite different from the Provisional Teaching, where miraculous powers are employed, distinctions are made between coming and going, and things are brought to one place or taken to another. Such delusory concepts are far from the reality of the Dharmakāya, and obstruct the primordial wisdom of True Enlightenment. Therefore, the bodhisattva Vimalakīrti, after displaying his miraculous powers, proceeds to expound the True Teaching. The *Vimalakīrti-nirdeśa* says:

> "The true nature of the body should be contemplated as being the same as the Buddha. When I contemplate the tathāgatas I see that those of the future will not come, those of the past have not gone, and those of the present do not exist." This is explained at length in the "Akṣobhya" chapter.[54]

So the Provisional Teaching [is for those with] narrow views who delight in the strange and the marvellous. The bodhisattvas therefore adapt to the capacities [of their audience] and present [the Teachings] in a cruder form, in order to attract beings and encourage them to take delight in learning. Only then do they give them the True Teachings. One must not grasp at transformations as being [ultimately] real, for then the eye of Wisdom will be forever led astray.

One should know the provisional but follow the real, thereby entering the gate of the Dharma-realm. Contrived teachings are hard to perfect, but the Uncontrived Teaching that accords with conditions is easy to accomplish. The Contrived is laborious and achieves nothing, while the Uncontrived that accords with conditions accomplishes itself. Achievement that is not [consciously] achieved is never lost, while achievements that are achieved [through conscious effort] are always impermanent. [In the latter case,] aeons of practice will in the end come to nothing, but a single instant of the conditioned arising of the Unborn will transcend all the views of the Provisional Teachings of the Three Vehicles.[55]

This argument rests essentially on the idea of *śūnyatā*: everything is ultimately empty and all changes, including miraculous ones, are only the play of illusion. Li Tongxuan, says:

> According to the *Lotus Sutra* the Nāga Princess tranforms her body [into a male one], completes the practices of a bodhisattva, and attains Buddhahood [in a realm] to the south – all in the space of a single instant (*kṣaṇa*).[56] But the *Avataṃsaka Sūtra* is not like this: here one simply views things objectively, in the transcendent light of great wisdom, and everything will be seen as the essential Reality, without any sign of transformation. It is like the *Vimalakīrti-nirdeśa*, where Śāriputra asks the

Everyday Miracles

Goddess of the Ganges: "Why don't you transform your female body [into a male one]?", and she replies: "Śāriputra, for the past twelve years I have been seeking this quality of femaleness, but have been quite unable to find it. So what is there to change?" As she then explains: "[If you think that] you are male and I am female, you should know that all dharmas are Suchness (*tathatā*) by their very nature, so what is there that could be changed?"[57]

He also denies the reality of time, without which no change can occur:

Such is the nature of things: essentially time does not exist, and temporal divisions are created by the [subjective] beliefs, distorted by the Three Roots [of delusion], of those who follow the Provisional Teaching. In this way [beings] stray of their own accord from the real Truth, and turn to speaking of transformation, not realizing that all this lies within themselves.[58]

On this view, then, the highest function of the miraculous events related in the sutras and elsewhere is to demonstrate that ultimate reality (*li*, in Huayen terminology, as opposed to the apparent reality of *shi*, or observable events) is all-pervasive and unchanging while the transformations that phenomena undergo, whether natural or seemingly supernatural, are mere illusions. But this means that the difference between miraculous and everyday events must also be equally illusory. Li Tongxuan's idea, based on the teaching of the *Avataṃsaka Sūtra* itself, is that miracles occur because ultimately reality itself is miraculous, *māyā*, like the marvellous illusions conjured up by a skilful magician, that this is the very nature of things. In other words, miracles are an everyday occurrence, as indeed they are depicted throughout the *Gaṇḍavyūha Sūtra*, the last section of the *Avataṃsaka Sūtra* itself. So Li Tongxuan, echoing one of Sudhana's gurus,[59] says:

If one sees with the eye of Dharma, there is nothing worldly that is not ultimately true; and if one sees with the mundane physical eye, there is no ultimate truth that is not [merely] worldly.[60]

But the argument can also be inverted. If there is no real difference between miraculous and everyday phenomena, then instead of saying that miracles are an everyday matter, one could claim that everyday events, rightly understood, are sufficiently miraculous in themselves. Li Tongxuan himself does not hesitate to draw this conclusion:

The *Avataṃsaka Sūtra*'s teaching of the Conditioned Arising of the Dharma-realm makes it clear that worldling and saint are a single Reality. If one makes subjective distinctions, one is a worldling; if [such] subjectivity vanishes, one is a buddha. According to the [teaching of the] Arising of Ultimate Reality, looking up or down, going backwards or forwards, bending and stretching, bowing and yielding – all these are bodhisattva-activities. There is not a single thing that needs to be transformed.[61]

This is of course simply another aspect of the Huayen teaching that ultimate reality (*li*) and everyday phenomena (*shi*) in no way impede one another, that they interpenetrate and include one another, and are ultimately identical with one another. Certainly, miracles, as commonly understood, by violating the "normal" course of events point directly to the transcendent dimension of *li*, while at the same time, by occurring in a biography, in history, they also manifest as *shi*. Thus they are particularly striking evidence of the nonduality of the temporal and the eternal, illustrating as they do

> The point of intersection of the timeless
> With time . . .[62]

But the uncompromising nonduality taught by the Sutra and the Huayen School clearly asserts that *any* given phenomenon, no matter how "mundane", fully expresses the nature of ultimate reality[63] and embodies the totality of all other phenomena.[64] From this point of view the distinction between "ordinary" and "extraordinary" events is no longer relevant, for any event at all in anybody's biography displays the nature of ultimate reality for those who have eyes to see it, just as completely as the most spectacular miracle.

It was this approach that was to be taken up within the Chan School. In the Chan tradition, exemplary biographies or hagiographies play a more prominent role than in any other form of Chinese Buddhism, but miracles as conventionally understood are frequently either absent, disparaged, or treated humorously. One might see this, to some extent correctly, as a return to the point of view originally expressed by the Buddha. But at the same time it is also a concrete manifestation of the Huayen belief in the interpenetration of ultimate reality (*li, xing*) and ordinary phenomena, and of each phenomenon with every other phenomenon. Sometimes the Chan masters themselves point explicitly to the Huayen connection. In the following passage, for example, Dongshan Liang Jie (807–869) quotes from the *Avataṃsaka Sūtra*:

> A monk asked, "What is the mind of the ancient buddhas like?" The Master replied, "It is walls, tiles and gravel."[65] The monk said, "Aren't such things insentient?" The Master said, "Yes." So the monk said, "And yet they can still expound the Dharma?" The Master replied, "They do so constantly, fervently, incessantly." . . . The monk said, "On the basis of what canonical text do you claim that insentient things can

expound the Dharma?" The Master replied, "Haven't you seen where it says in the *Avatamsaka Sūtra* that 'the physical realm expounds it, living beings expound it, everything in the three periods of time expounds it?' "[66]

There are cases where the display of miraculous powers is even ridiculed:

> Once when the Master [Huangbo] was visiting Tiantai (Mountain), he met a monk on the way who smiled and chatted with him as though they were old friends. On looking more closely at him, [the Master noticed that] he had a piercing gaze and a rather unusual appearance. They travelled on together till they came to the rushing waters of a swollen stream. Then [Huangbo] stopped, planted his staff and took his hat off. The monk wanted to take the Master across, but the Master said, "Please go across." The other gathered up his robes and walked lightly across the waves as though he were treading on firm ground. He looked back at [Huangbo] and said, "Come on over." The Master abused him loudly, saying, "You egotistical scoundrel! If I'd known you were going to fabricate miracles, I would have broken your shins!" The monk sighed with admiration and said, "You are a true vessel of the Mahayana teaching!" As soon as he had said this he vanished.[67]

In other cases a disciple may be scolded and discouraged from displaying such powers:

> Yunju [769–835] later built a hut on Three Peaks and didn't come to the hall for ten days. The Master asked him, "Why haven't you been coming for meals lately?" Yunju said, "Heavenly spirits (*tianshen* S. *deva*) have been appearing and providing me with food every day." The Master said, "I took you for an exceptional person, and yet you still hold such views. Come and see me this evening." Yunju went that evening. The Master called to him: "Hut Master Ying!"[68] When he replied "Yes", the Master said, "Don't think of good or bad: what is it?" Yunju returned to his hut and sat tranquilly in meditation. From then on the heavenly spirits were quite unable to find him, and after three days they ceased to appear.[69]

These examples are taken from the Recorded Sayings (*yulu*) of the Chan masters, instructional texts set in a biographical context. But even in the more conventionally pious genre of the traditional biography or hagiography, the same irreverent attitude towards the miraculous can be seen. The following passage, for example, comes from an anonymous biographical preface to the *Recorded Sayings of Pang Yun*:

When the Layman was about to pass away, he said to his daughter Lingzhao, "Illusory transformations are without substance, and you should comply with circumstances. Go and check the position of the sun and let me know when it is midday." Lingzhao went to the door and reported. "It's noon already," she said, "but there's an eclipse of the sun. Why don't you take a look?" "Is that so?" said the Layman, and she replied "Yes," so he got up and went to the window. Lingzhao then sat down on his couch and promptly passed away. The Layman looked around and said with a smile, "My daughter has outsmarted me." Then he gathered some firewood and performed the last rites.

Seven days later, Mr. Yu [Yu Di, the current prefect of the area] came to see how he was. The Layman placed his hand on Mr. Yu's knee, gazed steadily at him for a while, and said, "Just try to see all existing things as empty, and be careful not to regard nonexistent things as real. Live at ease in the world, for it is all like shadows and echoes." When he had said this, a strange fragrance filled the room. He was sitting upright as if he were thinking, and Mr. Yu called to him several times, but he had already gone on the Long Journey . . .

When his wife heard about this, she said, "That stupid daughter of mine and my ignorant old husband have gone off without telling me. It's really too much!"

So she went to tell her son, and when she saw him digging in the fields, she said, "Mr. Pang and Lingzhao have gone." The son put his hoe down and said "Alas!" After a moment he also died, still standing there. His mother said, "What a stupid boy you are!" Then he was cremated too. Everyone marvelled at this.

Soon afterwards, Mrs. Pang visited everyone in the village and said goodbye to them. Then she went far away, no one knew where, to live in seclusion, and nothing was ever seen or heard of her again.[70]

In all these cases, as in the time of the Buddha, it is never the actual occurrence of the miracles that is in question: what is being challenged is the spiritual value of such displays. At this level of discourse the inspirational function of miracle-stories is no longer necessary, for it is taken for granted that the audience consists of those who have already set their minds on gaining Enlightenment. In that case, miraculous powers are a potentially dangerous distraction, and should be ignored or disparaged. For the same reason – namely, that the focus is on the individual's quest for Enlightenment – the political and cosmological implications of the miraculous are also irrelevant. And finally, at the ontological level, since the Huayen teaching of the perfect interpenetration of phenomena and ultimate reality has done away with the need to discriminate between the everyday and the miraculous, the normal and the supernormal, it has become possible to point to even the most commonplace activities as revealing the profoundest teachings of

Buddhism, and as soteriologically equivalent therefore to the most extraordinary miracles.[71]

The ninth-century Chan Master Linji Yi Xuan (d. 866) sums all this up very neatly in the following passage, in which he first restates the Buddha's objection to miraculous powers, contrasting them with the true nature of Enlightenment, then explains how the Mahayanist teaching of Emptiness (śūnyatā) exposes the futility of miracles that depend on an appeal to the senses, and finally, in language that echoes both Li Tongxuan and Zhuangzi, emphasizes that for the Enlightened, everyday activities are sufficiently miraculous in themselves:

> You say that the buddhas have six miraculous powers and that these are something inexpressibly wonderful. But all the gods, sages, asuras and powerful spirits have such powers. Are they to be considered buddhas? . . . All these powers are secondary phenomena dependent on karma. The miraculous powers of a buddha on the other hand are quite different. He enters the realm of form without being deluded by it, enters the realm of sound . . . smell . . . taste . . . touch . . . concepts without being deluded thereby. So he understands that the six types of sense-object are all characterized by emptiness and cannot bind him. Such an enlightened being is dependent on nothing, and although he is made up of the polluted five aggregates, he performs miracles just by walking on the ground.[72]

Notes

1 "Miracle is faith's favourite child." (Goethe, *Faust*, part 1, l.766).
2 By "miracles" here is meant occurrences, typically associated with deities or saints (or both), that attract attention because they appear to violate the natural course of events and to be inexplicable in terms of the laws of nature as commonly understood.
3 *New Catholic Encyclopedia*, vol. 9 (New York: McGraw-Hill Book Company, 1967), 890.
4 Robert Chalmers, ed., *The Majjhima-Nikāya*, vol. 3 (London: Luzac & Co. Ltd for the Pali Text Society, 1967), 92–93. Virtually identical descriptions can be found in *Majjhima-Nikāya*, vol. 1, 21–22, 40–41, 159, 181, 276; *Dīgha-Nikāya*, vol. 1, 73–74 etc.
5 V. Trenckner, ed., *The Majjhima-Nikāya*, vol. 1 (London: Luzac & Co. Ltd for the Pali Text Society, 1964), 279–80.
6 Terms given in their original language will be identified as follows: S. Sanskrit; P. Pali; A. Arabic; and Ch. Chinese.
7 See, for example, T.W. Rhys Davids & J. Estlin Carpenter, eds, *The Dīgha Nikāya*, vol. 1 (London: The Pali Text Society, 1975), 77–78, 212; *The Majjhima-Nikāya*, vol. 1, 34–35, 494.
8 This is *sutta* number 11 of the *Dīgha Nikāya*. For the Pali text, see *The Dīgha Nikāya*, vol. 1, 211–23; for an English translation, see T.W. Rhys Davids, trans., *Dialogues of the Buddha*, part 1 (London: Luzac & Co. Ltd, 1956), 276–84.

9 This is the last of the four *pārājika* offences entailing expulsion from the monastic order. For details, see Hermann Oldenberg, ed., *The Vinaya Piṭakaṃ*, vol. 3 (London: Routledge & Kegan Paul for the Pali Text Society, 1984), 90–92; English translation in I.B. Horner, trans., *The Book of the Discipline*, vol. 1 (London: Luzac & Co. Ltd for the Pali Text Society, 1949), 157–60. A translation of a Sanskrit version of the same rule can be found in Charles Prebish, *Buddhist Monastic Discipline* (Philadelphia: Pennsylvania State University Press 1975), 53.
10 That is, the *abhijñā*, Ch. *shentong.*
11 Richard Sherburne, S.J., trans., *A Lamp for the Path and Commentary*, London: Allen & Unwin, 1983), 115.
12 Sherburne, *A Lamp for the Path and Commentary*, 117–18.
13 Paget Toynbee, ed., *Dantis Aligherii Epistolae: The Letters of Dante* (Clarendon: Oxford University Press 1966), 173–74, 199.
14 *The Life of Marpa the Translator*, Nalanda Translation Committee (Boulder: Prajna Press, 1982), 196.
15 As, for example, in the tale of the Buddha's conversion of the five hundred ascetics led by Kāśyapa (P. Kassapa) through a display of his miraculous powers. See Oldenberg, ed., *The Vinaya Piṭakaṃ*, vol. 1, 28–34; translated by I.B. Horner in *The Book of the Discipline*, vol. 4 (London: Luzac & Co. Ltd, 1951), 37–44.
16 This story, described by Zürcher as a "fantastic tale" and a "rather clumsy fake", appears to date from the Northern Wei Dynasty (5th century). See E. Zürcher, *The Buddhist Conquest of China*, vol. 1 (Leiden: E.J. Brill, 1972), 22(g). See also the discussion in Ren Jiyu, ed., *Zhongguo fojiao shi*, vol. 1 (Beijing: Zhongguo shehui kexue chubanshe, 1981), 103–04.
17 Ch'oe went to China when he was twelve years old, passed the *jinshi* examination in 874 at the age of seventeen, and served for ten years as a Chinese official before returning again to his native Silla. See Kamata Shigeo, *Chūgoku Bukkyō shi jiten* (Tokyo: Tōkyōdō shuppan 1981), 121–22.
18 "Guang[shi]yin" is a variant translation of the name "Avalokiteśvara", usually "Guan[shi]yin" or "Guanzizai".
19 Ch'oe Ch'iwŏn, *Tang Dajianfusi gusizhu fanjing dade Fa Zang heshang zhuan*, *Taishō Tripiṭaka* (hereafter: *TT*), no. 2054, 283c, ll.16–21.
20 Ch'oe, *Fa Zang heshang zhuan*, 284a, l.28–284b, l.3.
21 There is a "Maheśvaradevarājamantra" Ch. *Da zizai tianwang zhou*, in the *Miscellaneous Dhāraṇīs* Ch. *Tuolouni zaji*, *TT*, no. 1336, 589b–c.
22 Ch'oe, *Fa Zang heshang zhuan*, 284b, ll.16–21.
23 William Chittick, trans., *The Sufi Path of Knowledge* (New York: State University of New York Press, 1989), 412, note 13.
24 The traditional biographies are based on scriptural texts that regard the career of a buddha as an unvarying archetype and a pattern of miraculous events. See for example the Mahāpadāna Suttanta of the Pali Canon (*Dīgha Nikāya*, no. 14).
25 "Ariyapariyesanāsutta", Trenckner, *The Majjhima-Nikāya*, vol. 1, 163.
26 "Mahāparinibbānasuttanta", Davids & Carpenter, *The Dīgha Nikāya*, vol. 2, 128–29.
27 Davids & Carpenter, *The Dīgha Nikāya*, vol. 2, 133–34.
28 Davids & Carpenter, *The Dīgha Nikāya*, vol. 2, 138–39.
29 "Mahāpadānasuttanta", Davids & Carpenter, *The Dīgha Nikāya*, vol. 2, 15. For other versions of this famous tableau, see Étienne Lamotte, *Le Traité de la Grande Vertu de Sagesse*, tome 1 (Louvain: Institut Orientaliste, 1966), 6–10.
30 E.J. Thomas, *The Life of Buddha as Legend and History* (London: Routledge & Kegan Paul, 1960), 98–99, note 2.
31 *Huayan jing chuanji*, *TT*, no. 2073, 154a–154b.

Everyday Miracles

32 This is an incident from the biography of the Korean Hwaŏm (Hua Yen) monk Kyunyŏ (923–973). See Adrian Buzo and Tony Prince, trans., *Kyunyŏ-jŏn* (Sydney: Wild Peony, 1993), 41.
33 This convenient desk-light is mentioned in the biography of Li Tongxuan (646–740), a younger contemporary of Fa Zang and an important commentator on the *Avataṃsaka Sūtra* and its teachings. He is described as a hermit, and his biography, which may have been written some time around 800 A.D., appears as a preface to the *Avataṃsaka Sūtra with Commentary*, which inserts Li's commentary into the text of the 80-fascicle version of the Sutra. This work, which was compiled by the Tang Dynasty monk Zhi Ning has been published in the *Xuzang jing*, and Li Tongxuan's biography can be found on pages 654–55 of vol. 5 of the edition published by Xinwenfeng publishing company in Taipei. It also appears on pages 7–8 of the two-volume edition of Zhi Ning's compilation from the same publisher (Taipei, 1977). For further information on Li Tongxuan and an English translation of his biography, see Robert Gimello, "Li T'ung-hsüan and the Practical Dimensions of Hua-yen", in Robert M. Gimello & Peter N. Gregory, eds, *Studies in Ch'an and Hua-yen* (Honolulu: University of Hawaii Press, 1983), 321–89.
34 *Huayan jing chuanji*, 166a–b.
35 *Huayan jing chuanji*, 155b, ll.5–6.
36 *Huayan jing chuanji*, 158b–158c.
37 There is no such reign period; presumably the reign period Grand Harmony (477–500) of the Northern Wei is intended.
38 *Sic*! This would make the commentary ten times longer than the huge Sutra itself.
39 No such title is listed for either the Qi or the Wei.
40 *Huayan jing chuanji*, 156c, ll.18–27.
41 For the cosmic significance of the *Avataṃsaka Sūtra*, see chapter 37 of the Sutra itself, "The Manifestation of the Tathāgata", which contains the famous metaphor of the sutra in every atom, a metaphor brilliantly elaborated by Fa Zang in his *Huayan jing yihai baiwen* (*TT* no. 1875). For the Sutra passage containing the metaphor, see *TT*, no.279, 272c, ll.7–22; English translation in Cheng Chien Bhikshu, trans., *Manifestation of the Tathāgata* (Boston: Wisdom Publications, 1993), 105–06. In the 60-fascicle version, this chapter is number 32, and has the title "The Arising of the Nature of the Tathāgata, the Precious King". See also, Fa Zang: "Every word and meaning, every chapter and assembly [of the Sutra] pervades all the ten directions of space throughout the Dharmarealm, and all the worlds that exist in every single atom or hairtip therein." (*Huayan jing chuanji*, 153a, ll.8–10).

For the cult of the sacred book in Mahayana Buddhism, see the remarks of Raoul Birnbaum in his *The Healing Buddha* (Boulder: Shambhala Publications, 1979), 85, 108–09, note 12. For the cosmic role of the scriptures in Daoism, a possible source of influence on the Huayen School in this regard, see the discussion in Isabelle Robinet, *Taoist Meditation* (New York: State University of New York Press, 1993), 19–28.
42 This translation assumes that the colour word *qing* means "green", associating the spirits in question with spring, the east and the forces of natural growth. Alternatively, but perhaps less likely, *qing* could mean "black", in which case the spirits would be assuming the role of servants or Buddhist novices.
43 *Huayan jing chuanji*, 154c, ll.3–8.
44 *Shi dafang guangfo huayan jing lunzhu Li changzhe shiji*. See note 31 above.
45 Otherwise unknown.
46 *Li changzhe shiji*.

47 *Li changzhe shiji.*
48 Fa Zang himself in later life came to be known as "the Huayen Monk" and "Master Huayen" See Fang Litian, *Fa Zang* (Taipei: Dongda tushu gongsi, 1991), 18.
49 *Huayan jing chuanji,* 165c–66a.
50 See C.C. Chang, trans., *The Hundred Thousand Songs of Milarepa,* vol. 2 (Boulder: Shambhala Publications, 1977), 384–87.
51 Chang, *The Hundred Thousand Songs of Milarepa,* 428–29.
52 The lion, as the king of beasts, is often used to symbolize the Buddha, as supreme among human beings. Similarly the lion's roar (S. *siṃhanāda*), on hearing which all other beasts become afraid and fall silent, represents the preaching of the Buddha-Dharma, which overcomes all other teachings: and the lion-seat (S. *siṃhāsana*) is the throne from which the Buddha preaches, represented in art as supported by or decorated with lions. (See, for example, Nakamura Hajime, *Bukkyōgo daijiten* (Tokyo: Shoseki, 1981), 543–44.)
53 The realm of the Buddha Akṣobhya.
54 Chapter 11 of the *Vimalakīrtinirdeśa.*
55 *Xin Huayan jing lun, TT,* no. 1739, 723c–724a.
56 See the *Lotus Sutra* (*Saddharmapuṇḍarīka Sūtra*), chapter 11, "Manifestation of a Stūpa", (in the Sanskrit text) or chapter 12, "Devadatta", (in the Chinese translation).
57 *Xin Huayan jing lun,* 726a–b. For the *Vimalakīrti-nirdeśa* passage, see Étienne Lamotte's superb translation and study of the sutra, *L'Ensignement de Vimalakīrti* (Louvain: Institut Orientaliste, 1962), 280–82. (See also the English version of Lamotte's book by Sara Boin, *The Teaching of Vimalakīrti* (London: Pali Text Society, 1976), 169–70.)
58 *Xin Huayan jing lun,* 726b, ll.17–18.
59 Namely, the king Mahāprabha, who tells Sudhana: "You may see this town as small and cramped or as a vast city; the ground as made of earth and sand or as adorned with many jewels... If the minds of beings are pure... they will see this town as pure and adorned with jewels – the rest will see only rubbish." (*Shi dafang guang fo huayan jing , TT,* no.279, 357b, ll.3–13.)
60 *Xin Huayan jing lun,* 726b, ll.7–8.
61 *Xin Huayan jing lun,* 726, ll.21–24.
62 T.S. Eliot, *Four Quartets,* "The Dry Salvages", v. 18–19.
63 This is the teaching of "no impediment between [ultimate] reality and phenomenon", and of "the arising of the nature [of ultimate reality in every phenomenon]".
64 This is the teaching of "no impediment between phenomenon and phenomenon". In the Sutra itself it finds expression in the frequent assertion that there are countless buddhas preaching within every atom, and in the "mirror-maze" imagery, as in the metaphor of Indra's Net, or when bodhisattvas are granted visions of themselves appearing simultaneously in many different worlds and periods of time. See A.J. Prince, "The Hua Yen Vision of Enlightenment", *The Journal of the Oriental Society of Australia* 15–16 (1983–84), 145–48.
65 See *Zhuangzi,* "The Master of the Eastern Suburb asked Zhuangzi, 'Where is this so-called Dao to be found?'... He said, 'It is in tiles and bricks.'" (See *A Concordance to Chuang Tzu* (Cambridge, Ma.: Harvard-Yenching Institute, Harvard University Press, 1956), 59, ll.435.)
66 *Dongshan lu.* Text in *Xuzang jing;* translation from *Chan yulu,* 2 vols, Feng Zuomin and Song Xiuling, eds (Taipei: Xingguang chubanshe, 1982), 341.
67 *Biyan lu,* case 11; see *Foguo Yuanwu chanshi biyan lu, TT,* no. 2003, 151b, ll.14–20.

Everyday Miracles

68 In accordance with a common Chan usage, Yunju is normally referred to by the place chiefly associated with him, in this case Yunju Mountain in what is now Jiangxi Province; but here his master addresses him by his monastic name, [Dao] Ying.
69 *Dongshan lu*; translation from *Chan yulu*, 397.
70 Pang Yun (courtesy name, Daoxuan) (d. 808) is perhaps the most famous lay teacher in the Chan tradition. For the Chinese text, see *Pang jushi yulu* in *Xuzang jing*: translation here from Iriya Yoshitaka, *Hō Koji Goroku* (Tokyo: Chikuma Shobō, 1973), 3–4.
71 This was also referred to by the so-called Second Patriarch of the Huayen School, Zhi Yan (602–668), as "Revealing the Dharma and Producing Understanding by Means of Phenomena", and is the last of his "Ten Profound Teachings Concerning the Conditioned Arising of the Unimpeded".
72 *Linji lu* (XVIII); see *Zhenzhou linji Hui Zhao chanshi yulu*, TT, no. 1985, 500a, ll.2–12. With Linji's final assertion here, compare the well-known statement in *Zhuangzi* that "to hide one's tracks is easy, but to walk without touching the ground is hard" (See *A Concordance to Chuang Tzu*, 9, 1.30).

4

Representing Wŏnch'ŭk (613–696)

Meditations on Medieval East Asian Buddhist Biographies

John Jorgensen

The Importance and Misrepresentation of Wŏnch'ŭk

Evidence gleaned from prefaces to translations of scriptures, the content of commentaries and the breadth of his influence, suggests that Wŏnch'ŭk was one of the most meticulous, erudite, historically-minded and linguistically capable of all East Asian monks. An assistant to and critic of the famous Chinese pilgrim to India, Xuanzang (600–664), Wŏnch'ŭk's life has been overshadowed by that of the great pilgrim and translator. A reason for this relative lack of appreciation of his life is the negative representation of Wŏnch'ŭk in the standard collection of hagiographies of Tang dynasty monks, the *Song Gaoseng zhuan – The Lives of Eminent Monks (compiled in the) Song Dynasty* – by Zanning. Another cause of this neglect was Wŏnch'ŭk's criticism of the theories of Dharmapāla (530–561) whose system of Buddhist thought was championed as normative by Xuanzang and his heir Dasheng Ji (632–682), who founded the Faxiang or Ci'en School which was generally accepted as the orthodox form of Vijñānavāda because of the authority of Xuanzang.

Yet many, both past and present, have been impressed by Wŏnch'ŭk's careful scholarship, in which he cited his sources,[1] and adopted what one scholar has labelled a "scientific scholarly spirit" that was superior to the work of Dasheng Ji in that he was more aware of the problems of translation and conflicting opinions.[2] He was an invaluable assistant in major translation projects, and understood from all his studies how Vijñānavāda, the system of thought these monks adhered to, had evolved.[3] Moreover, he defended some of the earlier scholarship against the new Dharmapāla version, for which reason he was misrepresented. Thus, aware of the misrepresentation of his ideas, the Japanese monk of the Hossō (Ch. Faxiang) School, Zenju (724–797) concluded the reason for this was that,

Representing Wŏnch'ŭk

> Ximing(Wŏnch'ŭk) and Ci'en (Ji) are both our unique teachers.
> How can we decide right or wrong and incline to attack Ximing?
> That Ci'en became the select pupil and mixed in the *lun* text,
> And Ximing was the one who did not, is why we now attack him.[4]

In other words, it was only because Dasheng Ji participated in the compilation of the *Cheng weishi lun*, the core text of Faxiang/Hossō studies, and Wŏnch'ŭk did not, that Wŏnch'ŭk's ideas were rejected. Yet that surely is a misrepresentation of the intentions of Wŏnch'ŭk, who wanted to have all the information made available on the ten Indian theorists of Vijñānavāda. Xuanzang had intended to translate this material in full, but Dasheng Ji who had a narrow and exclusive perspective wanted only the opinions of Dharmapāla made public. Dasheng Ji successfully persuaded Xuanzang to translate only the theories of Dharmapāla and place them in the *Cheng weishi lun*, and not include most of the contrary opinions of the other nine scholastics.[5] This misrepresentation of Wŏnch'ŭk's position, made from a partisan sectarianism, and perpetuated by Zanning, has dominated studies of Wŏnch'ŭk's life, for the contrary opinions of the other hagiographers of Wŏnch'ŭk, Song Fu and Ch'oe Ch'iwŏn, have long been left in obscurity, or ignored because of the stain on his character made by Zanning and the overpowering reputation of Xuanzang whose orthodox lineage supposedly passed through Dasheng Ji. Thus even the Chinese Buddhists and others who revived Faxiang early this century still saw Dasheng Ji as orthodox, and so the misrepresentation continued.[6] Thus it is ironic that a scholar of a theory sometimes called "Representation Only", which states that the mind distorts information received until it is enlightened, should be so represented.

Hagiographies were generally written to glorify the saint and the religion, but not to slander them. Although the Chinese authors of the various *Gaoseng zhuan* or "Lives of Eminent Monks" used some negative examples as a caution, it is rare to find strongly-worded attacks on a cleric or Buddhist group when other materials to the contrary suggest a positive evaluation. Yet the case of Wŏnch'ŭk is one of the few exceptions to this observation. Zanning (919–1002), the author of the *Song Gaoseng zhuan*, which was presented to the Song court in 988, writes most disparagingly of Wŏnch'ŭk, while Song Fu writing in 1115 and Ch'oe Ch'iwŏn (857–908+), probably writing in the late 890s in Korea, gave glowing accounts of this monk. The vilification found in the *Song Gaoseng zhuan* seems to have been initially created out of sectarian rivalry, with the slander reported uncritically, possibly because its object was foreign. An ethnic divide and sectarianism is to an extent still reflected in the modern literature, with the Korean scholar O Hyŏnggŭn characterising one side of the dispute, Dasheng Ji (632–682) and his Ci'en School (or Faxiang) as the Chinese lineage, and the other, that of Wŏnch'ŭk or the Ximing School as the Korean lineage,[7] even though the latter survived among Chinese at Dunhuang as late as the 780s and perhaps beyond that time. Hatani Ryōtai, who helped revive interest in this issue, described the school of Wŏnch'ŭk as a Korean Vijñānavāda ("Consciousness/ Representation Only") because virtually all the pupils of Wŏnch'ŭk, even those resident in China, were from Silla Korea,[8] and Kamata Shigeo calls Wŏnch'ŭk a "heretic of the Faxiang School".[9]

The polarisation in the sources may be due to the differences in their genres; with that of Zanning a *liezhuan* or "connected biography" in which Wŏnch'ŭk's hagiography is placed in the context of the hagiographies of other clerics, in particular, of the associates of Xuanzang; that of Song Fu a public inscription dedicated to the monk, and that of Ch'oe Ch'iwŏn a vow undertaken by an assembly on the anniversary of Wŏnch'ŭk's death. Moreover, all of the accounts were written at least three hundred years after the death of their subject, which possibly allowed greater distortion or misinformation to be included.

Therefore, despite considerable studies devoted to Wŏnch'ŭk's thought, these difficulties in the sources have detracted from a detailed examination of his biography. Of course, some of the materials for Wŏnch'ŭk's thought are readily available, leading to studies of his differences over theory with his rival Dasheng Ji, and of his theories of mind, classification of the teachings or periodisation of Buddhism, the One Vehicle, the bodhisattva career, and whether or not all beings possess the potential to become buddha.[10] Wŏnch'ŭk's commentary on the *Saṃdhinirmocana sūtra*, which was translated into Tibetan by Chödrub (a.k.a. Facheng) and used by the great reformer of Tibetan Buddhism and founder of the Gelugpa Order, Tsongkhapa, has attracted the attention of Tibetologists. Inaba Shōju has thus laboriously reconstructed from the Tibetan translation those sections missing from the extant Chinese text.[11] A similar back translation was made by the Chinese monk Guankong and was published in 1981 by the Chinese Buddhist Federation.[12]

Wŏnch'ŭk's pupils went on to found the Yuga School (Yogācāra) of Vijñānavāda in Silla Korea. His ideas were perpetuated for several generations in his home monastery of Ximingsi in Chang'an, the capital of Tang China. They survived the massive turmoil of the An Lushan Rebellion (755–757), which ruined most of the scholastic schools of Buddhism that required imperial patronage, by being taught in the remote north-west of China at Dunhuang. From there they were spread into Tibet, where they came to influence Tsongkhapa (1357–1419), the founder of the Gelugpa (popularly known as the Yellow Hat) Order of Buddhism that eventually dominated Tibet under the leadership of the Dalai and Panchen Lamas. Wŏnch'ŭk's theories were also transmitted to Japan, where they were cited by the Hossō School from the 8th century to the present day.

Wŏnch'ŭk is then important in the history of Vijñānavāda, for not only was his thought known in China, Korea, Tibet and Japan, but he also provided a critical insight on the development of this tradition and philosophy.[13]

Therefore, Wŏnch'ŭk is a crucial figure for our understanding of the development of Vijñānavāda and related or rival systems of Buddhist thought, such as Huayan, in East Asia.

He became famous, among other things, for his commentary on the *Saṃdhinirmocana sūtra*, the first of the sutras for the Vijñānavādins. This sutra was translated into Chinese between 443 and 453 by Guṇabhadra, giving Chinese Buddhists their first impressions of Vijñānavāda. Subsequently, Vijñānavāda came in three waves to China. Bodhiruci and Ratnamati introduced the first phase of Vijñānavāda to Northern Wei China in 508, which resulted in the formation of the Dilun School based on the *Daśabhūmika śāstra* (Ch. *Dilun*). The second wave arrived with the great eclectic of the tradition, Paramārtha, who was both criticised and yet respected by Wŏnch'ŭk. Paramārtha reached Canton in 546. His combination of Vijñānavāda with Tathāgatagarbhin themes (the *tathāgatagarbha* or "womb/matrix of the Tathāgata" is a posited substratum to sentient existence or mind), which thought is probably best termed *cittamātra* ("mind only", *weixin*), led to the foundation of the Shelun School, based on the *Mahāyāna samparigraha śāstra* (Ch. *Shelun*), by his followers in South China. The synthesis of Dilun and Shelun theories formed the "Neo-Shelun" School, which influenced the theories of the originators of the Huayan and Chan schools in the Sui and early Tang period.

The third phase of Vijñānavāda was brought to the Tang capital, Chang'an, in 645 by Xuanzang after fifteen years of study in India.[14] Xuanzang's new teachings were based primarily on the ideas of Dharmapāla (530–561), which Xuanzang championed over the earlier theories transmitted to China and those of nine other Indian Vijñānavāda theorists. Therefore, Xuanzang and his pupil Dasheng Ji considered all other Indian Vijñānavāda theories and Chinese syntheses to be faulty, and only that of Dharmapāla to be orthodox. Wŏnch'ŭk, who was already deeply learned in the Vijñānavāda theories and literature available in China, challenged some of Xuanzang's teachings, maintaining a critical attitude not only towards the concepts of Dharmapāla, but also in respect of all other Indian and Chinese Vijñānavāda. For this daring though, he was dealt with harshly by Chinese Buddhist historians such as Zanning, who had accepted the propaganda of Dasheng Ji and his pupils that their lineage, the Ci'en or Faxiang School, was orthodox, and that the ideas of Wŏnch'ŭk were aberrations. Zanning's account, which was adopted by the Faxiang revivalists in China from early this century, has seemingly precluded any critical study of Wŏnch'ŭk's life.[15]

This article will try to remedy the deficiency, while indicating some of the problems and benefits of representing a past life. One fundamental obstacle to such a representation of the life of this key figure is the dearth of information concerning his personality and many of his activities. This deficiency is common to virtually all of the medieval East Asian Buddhist monks, and for this reason the detailed psychological portraits and assessments or ideological analyses such as those made of Martin Luther by Erik Erikson in *The Young Luther* or of Wŏnch'ŭk's near contemporary, Mohammed by Maxime Rodinson in his *Mohammed,* cannot be attempted. However, to examine only the works written by the monk is to disembody and decontextualise him. Wŏnch'ŭk's commentaries seem dull and scholastic to the modern reader, despite their erudition and insight, but even the barest of outlines of his career indicate that his was a sometimes tumultuous and varied life. Thus his life deserves some attention to rescue it from the superstructure of ideas and theories.

The *Saṃdhinirmocana sūtra* and Vijñānavāda

The *Saṃdhinirmocana sūtra* of ca. 300 was the product of a tradition of Buddhist meditation in India that was concerned with analysing the relationship of mind and existence, and how and why meditation could lead to enlightenment. In a discussion of the images perceived in meditation and discursive thought, the Buddha in this sutra is asked why there is no apparent difference between the perceiving mind and the images that arise during certain types of meditation (*vipaśyana* and *samādhi*). In this meditation, as in dreams, there are supposedly no sense-data to create the percepts or images in the mind, which is why the questioner asked whence they came. The answer is from consciousness, which includes memory and imagination, that has the powers to project entire worlds.[16] The Buddha replied to the question as follows: "It is because those images are merely consciousness/representation (*shi*) . . . that I therefore say that what the consciousness conditions are merely what the consciousness has manifested". Wŏnch'ŭk in his commentary to this quoted a commentary by Agotra, one of the nine theorists, which explained that:

> The external percept (*jing*, object of perception, the image, not a physical object) conditioned by the consciousness is merely the projection and manifestation of the internal consciousness. . . . the percept conditioned by the consciousness is merely the image that is projected out of the consciousness; it has no other substance.

He further relied on Agotra to clarify the point. Agotra shows that the external percepts conditioned or caused by consciousness are "merely the appearances of the inner consciousness. That is, the conditioned percepts are taken by consciousness to be objects of themselves", which they are not. This answer raised the question that if the images and the mind are identical, how can one see the mind? This question was crucial, for examination of the mind is the basis of Buddhist meditation. The answer is that although images are projected as soon as thought (mind) appears, the substance of the mind that reflects the images is different from the images projected therein.[17]

Representing Wŏnch'ŭk

The concentration on the practice of meditation gave this movement the name Yogācāra [the practice of yoga] and the analysis of consciousness (*vijñāna*) gave their doctrines the title of Vijñānavāda [the way of consciousness]. Because they attempted to explain how the world is falsely constructed out of habitual ways of perception that distort the primary sense-data, which process they called representation or making known (*vijñāpti*), their teaching was also named Vijñāptimātra [representation only].[18] This also led them to examine the mind and how it creates the illusion of a self or ego. The ambiguity in the Chinese translation of *shi* for both Sanskrit terms *vijñāna* and *vijñāpti* can be explained by the idea that "knowing" or "consciousness" was divided into a subjective, perceiving aspect (*jianfen*) and an objective aspect of the characteristics or marks (*xiangfen*) of the *dharmas* (*fa*, elements of existence). This latter dimension is the origin of the name Faxiang for the school created by Xuanzang and his pupil Dasheng Ji.

Although modern theorists are much given to discussions of representation, usually in terms of power and the purpose of the author, or of representation as the necessary basis of culture and texts,[19] Vijñānavādins and other Mahayana Buddhists were aware of some of the implications of representation in textual interpretation and soteriology. They understood that all humans, except the enlightened, project their desires and predilections on to the received raw data of sensations, re-presenting those percepts in accordance with their cravings and preconceptions that derive from memory or the infused karma of past perceptions and deeds. These constructions or fabrications are then treated *as if* they are real, for such fictions are expedients that are instrumental for humans living in a profane world. People need to believe or operate as if they are individual, conscious entities living in an objective environment. Therefore the *Madhyānta-vibhāṅga* states;

> The vijñānas produce transformations resembling the objects
> Of sentient being, ego and cognition.
> These percepts in reality do not exist,
> And being non-existent the vijñānas also do not exist.

Wŏnch'ŭk in his elucidation of the *Saṃdhinirmocana sūtra*, quotes a prose commentary on the above verse;

> "Transformations resembling objects" means that there are appearances of the percepts themselves such as the semblances of matter etc. "Transformations resembling sentient beings" means the appearance of the body of five sense organs itself as if there are self and other. "Transformations resembling the ego" means because the tainted *manas* [vijñāna of consciousness, 'will'] and the delusion of ego are constantly associated . . .[20]

The mind, according to those Mahayana Buddhists of the "idealist" tendency, does not maintain its pristine state of non-discrimination and detachment, being tempted out of that innocence. The mind changes from being a mirror into a projector of images; images created and thus transformed from the reflections in the mind-mirror.[21] This projector mind itself "is evolved dependent upon a variety of conditions, just as a painting depends upon the wall (on which it is painted)".[22] The *Cheng weishi lun* describes this process as being

> Like a person who is suffering a nightmare, because of the power of the dream, mentally manifests the semblances of external objects. Conditioned by this, that person grasps them as being really existing external objects.

This Wŏnch'ŭk states is like "grasping as one's parents that which is not one's parents".[23]

This does not imply that the person or the sensations do not exist, as the Dharmapāla/Xuanzang line has it, but simply that the representations of them are fictional. Emptiness in Vijñānavāda philosophy, the claim that the world is "representation only", does not mean everything is non-existent or void. As Hamilton states,

> There still remains the final nature of things which is the true representation immediately apprehended in the perfect intuition of ... Buddhas. ... What the 'realization of the insubstantiality of elements' actually denies is any and every form of element falsely conceived by the common, unenlightened consciousness ... [which are] seemingly outer objects as well as sensory capacities [that] are nothing but representation in consciousness itself.[24]

All representations are a re-presentation of the reality of the past, conditioning and altering the earlier primal sense-data in accord with desires and biases formed previously. This occurs because the *manovijñāna* or "volitional brush" can only act or paint after it has received the raw sense-data, which due to the delay between the sensations received by sense organs (also called *vijñānas*) and those processed by the *manovijñāna*, are dated information. As the famous formulator of Vijñānavāda doctrine, Vasubandhu wrote in the *Viṃśatikā*, "to use a later memory to prove the existence of a previously seen external object cannot in principle be maintained".[25] Discrimination and memory are the mental prerequisites for representation.[26] In other words, representation is a re-presenting of the past as if it is in the present, and then the past representations or memories themselves become objects of further representation by the mind.

Representing Wŏnch'ŭk

Such a misapprehension of these projected mental constructs as being reality, is a delusory and continuous representation of the past. These representations are frequently verbal, and so language functions as memory or a meta-representation. Thus the ultimate or reality-as-it-is (Thusness, *bhūtatathatā*) is ineffable, for language is a form of representation and memory which is karmic and misleading. Only an awareness of the functions of language and a detachment from it makes language soteriologically useful or "live" in Chan terms.

These theories provoked considerable polemic within Indian Buddhism. Thus the Mādhyamika philosopher Candrakīrti averred that the "mind only" doctrine of the *Laṅkāvatāra sūtra*, a text long associated with early Yogācāra, was preached by the Buddha merely as an expedient to instruct those who could not grasp the higher level of truth.[27] But that posed the dilemma; how could one now know the Buddha's intention? The *Saṃdhinirmocana sūtra* implied even in its title, that it could explain that intention through reading the mind of the historical Buddha who is no longer physically present. By assaying to recapture that past moment of Buddha's thought, this scripture is engaged in a representation of the Buddha's supposed verbalised representation of a putative truth. Logically, this should lead to an infinite regression of representations, or supplements conditioning the preceding representations, for as "the presence sought by the interpreter can never be reclaimed, these supplements are multiplied one upon the other, thereby creating 'the mirage of the thing itself, of immediate presence'".[28] Although one should lay aside all such supplements and representations,[29] the author of the *Saṃdhinirmocana sūtra*, who attempted to give the definitive, final interpretation by representing the Buddha's purported intention and imposing a "meaning" on the text, engaged in and invited further supplementation.[30]

Wŏnch'ŭk, despite his cognisance of the history of this doctrine, does not seem to have realised this contradiction, for he still claimed that the *Saṃdhinirmocana* was the definitive teaching or the Final Turning (preaching) of the Dharma. However, unlike other commentators, he allowed that the *prajñāpāramitā sūtras* of the Second Turning, on which he spent much energy as a translator and commentator, could also be definitive and not provisional.[31]

Representation and Chinese Buddhist Biography

The implications of these Vijñānavāda theories of representation did not impinge on the Buddhist writing of biographies. This was despite the fact that the *Saṃdhinirmocana sūtra* attempted to represent the Buddha's mind in its ultimate intentions, which should have made the biographers aware of the problematic nature of biographical representation. The hermeneutics of the intentions of the scriptures naturally centred on the Buddha, the author. Yet the Buddha could only be a presence and present his life. The interpreters and hagiographers represented their subjects, including the Buddha, through the biased lenses of their own culture and their readers' expectations. The intent or meaning of an action of the biographical subject was represented by another idea or image, usually in the post-mortem assessment by the biographer to which there was no reply by that subject. The author was the mediating authority for an other to the readers. Others perforce have to be represented, and those representations are imaginations (but often collective images) of what the other ought to have been.[32]

Thus there was a disjunction between the representation theories of Buddhism and the practices of the hagiographers and historians. The reason, at least in East Asia, seems to have been due to the influence of Confucian notions that histories or biographies transmitted a truth or reality. Thus a form of mimesis, a portrayal of reality, was attempted, and that was "transmission". Of course, the hagiographers felt that they could reconstruct or fabricate the thought and speech of some of their subjects, and they also consciously fitted them into stereotypical categories, making them perform a set function.[33] However, in practice the individual personality can be glimpsed on occasion,[34] just as it can be in the secular Chinese biographies.

Of the three biographers of Wŏnch'ŭk, Zanning and Ch'oe Ch'iwŏn were aware of the themes of categories of exemplars and of transmission. Zanning's preface and memorial to the Song throne in the *Song Gaoseng zhuan* mentions the biographers of the past, transmission, categories of Buddhist monks, and the types of evidence gathered. There is no evident problematisation of "representation".[35]

This lack of problematisation of representation occurred despite the fact that Zanning was a member of the Vinaya School. In India, the *Vinaya* texts contained the biographies and histories of Buddhism.[36] The major concern of the Indian Vinayists was to legitimate the monastic rules and regulations by placing them in the framework of the Buddha's life and by providing evidence of their transmission through an unbroken line of teachers.[37] In China, the Vinaya School (Lüzong) was founded by Daoxuan (596–667), the author of the *Xu Gaoseng zhuan – Continuation of the Lives of the Eminent Monks* – abbot of Wŏnch'ŭk's monastery of Ximingsi, and assistant in Xuanzang's translation project as a composer and verifier in the period from 645 until at least 659.[38] There he joined Xuanze, who as we shall see, was probably the same person as Wŏnch'ŭk. Daoxuan in fact included a lengthy biography of Xuanzang in his *Xu Gaoseng zhuan*.[39] Daoxuan's Vinaya School used the Faxiang doctrines taught by Xuanzang as its theoretical base,[40] meaning that the Vinaya School biographers had to be aware of the theories of representation. Zanning was the tenth patriarch of the Nanshan Vinaya School founded by Daoxuan.[41] Zanning's "summation" (*lun*) on the exegetes demonstrates that he must have known of some of the theories of representation taught by the Vijñānavādins:

> In the Yogācāra treatises the substance of the sutras (are claimed) to be of two kinds; the text and the meaning. The text is what is depended on; the meaning is the depender. Thus these two kinds are general names for all the sense-data that can be known. . . . The key to the two themes of the Hinayana and the Mahayana was something that previous (Chinese) savants could not decide upon, which caused the saints a shared doubt. They simply thought that the deficiency formed an obstacle to knowledge. And then Master Xuanzang returned from the West and brought Sanskrit texts to the east, and enriched the treasure grove of Yogācāra and opened up the erudite treasury of Vijñānavāda.[42]

However, Zanning followed the form of Buddhist *liezhuan* (connected biographies/traditions) initiated by his predecessors Huijiao and Daoxuan. Moreover, as the *Song Gaoseng zhuan* was commissioned by the Song emperor and Zanning had a Confucian education (although it was used to overcome Confucianism),[43] these problems were not addressed or did not impinge sufficiently on his awareness when he was writing the biographies.

Likewise, in 904 when Ch'oe was writing his biography of Fazang (643–712), the Huayan champion of mind-only theory, this theory was not translated into the writing of the hagiography. Ch'oe realised that the biography he was composing was not structurally identical with those *liezhuan* or collective biographies written by the great historian Sima Qian who wrote biographies of the Confucian sages. To distinguish his subject, Fazang, from other saints, Ch'oe adopted the perfect number ten that appeared in Fazang's *Huayan sanmei guan* on the meanings of the honest mind, as a metaphor for the stages in Fazang's life.[44] Despite this, Ch'oe's hagiography of Fazang was fundamentally Confucian in outlook, in that Ch'oe adhered to the standard biographical techniques of Sima Qian and referred to the Confucian classics such as the *Chunqiu – Spring and Autumn Annals* – for *topoi*.[45]

Ch'oe further states that his brother Hyŏnjun encouraged him to write Fazang's biography because we "adopt the words of the ancient sages but discard their bodies/persons, for the mind is a thief. Now in studying we follow their instructions but ignore their actions." This leads, he averred, to people staining the character of the ancient thinkers with petty harping or overblown theories. So although there are biographies of Fazang and other great clerics, the monks are too lazy to read them and are all too ready to make false statements about their subjects. "It even reaches the extent of people (monks) ridiculing the study of history as a doctrine of the devil and rejecting the genealogical records of monks as useless."[46]

Therefore, even though Ch'oe studied, probably with the guidance of his monk brother, some of Fazang's theories, those theories did not sway Ch'oe from the broadly empirical and mimetic "transmission of the facts" restraints of Confucian historiography. Consequently, for all the biographers of Wŏnch'ŭk, there were no "crises of representation".

Nor was there a crisis of authority. Zanning wrote his account with the emperor as his patron, and consequently favoured an anti-sectarian Buddhist position in which Buddhists were all in harmony. From the political heights as the emperor's historian of Buddhism, Zanning in the *Song Gaoseng zhuan* imperiously surveyed the history of Buddhism and the lives of eminent monks,[47] evidently judging Wŏnch'ŭk to be a cause of disharmony and thus not a truly insightful member of the Buddhist fraternity.[48] Zanning's authority was unquestioned, for he could arbitrarily classify monks into the ten categories he had adapted from earlier Buddhist historians. He was also a consummate Buddhist politician, constrained only by the needs of the Order as a whole within the state.

Ch'oe Ch'iwŏn seems to have been situated a little less firmly, for although he was a high official with considerable bureaucratic credentials obtained from China, he was not a member of the true aristocratic ruling elite of Silla, a state that was showing signs of decline. Ch'oe was sure of his role as a biographer in the Confucian tradition, but his hagiography of Fazang was probably commissioned by his more Buddhologically learned elder brother, and his biography of Wŏnch'ŭk was written on behalf of the comrades in the religious society to which he belonged. His authority was restrained to the degree that any criticism of Wŏnch'ŭk would have been unacceptable as an undermining of the spiritual authority of the object of worship, and by the fact that the hagiography had to conform to the needs of the religious group.

Song Fu had the least authority, for he was a mere candidate for a higher examination, young and without prestige. Moreover, as his work was probably commissioned by the monk Guangyue, he was also writing under strict instructions and may have been constrained by monetary considerations. Thus his biography was the least known, for he was an insignificant figure who has left no other record. He was not a well-known writer whose reputation would have enhanced the value of the inscription.[49]

One feature, however, links all three biographies; they are representations of Wŏnch'ŭk for soteriological ends. All soteriology, by its nature, is future-oriented, with a purpose. Although Zanning has a political aim in the preservation of the Buddhist Order, his biographies were exemplars, models to be imitated and occasionally avoided. The imitation of the supreme exemplars was a means of attaining salvation. Ch'oe's hagiography is a self-confessed representation of Wŏnch'ŭk as a model for direct salvation. The religious society devoted to Wŏnch'ŭk vowed to follow his example, and by commemorating his death, wished to be inspired through his "compassionate

Representing Wŏnch'ŭk

protection". Song Fu's inscription was meant to inculcate salvation through devotion and proximity to the relics of Wŏnch'ŭk and the two other saints enshrined in Xingjiao Monastery. Faith in the powers of the relics and the pilgrimage to the sacred site was an indirect path to salvation.

These representations for soteriological ends illustrate one of the main uses of history: authors in the present representing the past as a way of influencing the future. The transmission of "the facts" was for the sake of educating those in the future by the provision of mirrors for conduct. Therefore the representation could be embellished to enhance the didactic purpose.[50] As Ch'oe noted, even though some monks evidently considered biography and history useless and even pernicious, clearly preferring to represent Buddhism as a supra-historical teaching, most Buddhists in East Asia adopted the Confucian didactic and moral approach to historiography.

Biography and Representation

History, of which biography is a subgenre, is a form of representation. Modern historians are now beset by "crises of representation" because of the onset of doubts in authors who think that they are through their writing "conveying some independent truth about the world, that [they] are relaying an authentic representation".[51] It has been realised that inevitably the past is partially lost. The biography, and historiography in general, is thus a form of mourning and "its writing is based on an absence and produces nothing but simulacra, however scientific. It offers representation in the place of bereavement". The historian's role, it is claimed, is to maintain a dialogue with the past and so " 'calms' the dead and struggles against violence [of change] by producing a reason for things (an 'explanation') that overcomes their disorder and assures permanence . . ."[52] This outlook leads some writers to abandon biographies, in particular those of premodern religious figures, as sources of historical value, and interpret them instead only as literary pieces that provide general paradigms and no individuality. The biographical reconstruction, with its attempts to find a chronological continuity, is dismissed as an "illusion" that "flourishes precisely owing to the scarcity of historical materials".[53] Yet coherence is of the nature of historiography, and of biography in particular,[54] for authors and readers alike see the apparent continuity in their own lives and project those on to others. This is why, despite all their doubts, modern historians and authors have continued to pen biographies and hagiographies, just as their predecessors, some of whom were aware of the problems of representation, did.

The Mahayana Buddhists realised from early in their history that beings had to share elements in common which made them resemble each other, such that humans recognised other humans and monkeys other monkeys etc. For the Vijñānavādins, this common aspect of beings (*zhong tong fen* or *nikāya sabhāga*) made the bodies and minds of human beings resemble each other.⁵⁵ By extrapolation, this also meant that the "container world" of external percepts is also shared, for

> Although the consciousness of each sentient being manifests itself in its own distinct manner, yet the result of this manifestation is "common"; that is to say, it is the same for all. In other words, the phenomena of the manifested world are each like the other so that there is no differentiation of the external localities. [Note: This signifies that such objects as mountains and rivers etc., are evolved out of common or universal Bijas (seeds) which belong to all Ālayavijñānas in common. Thus, they are not simply the product of any single consciousness.]⁵⁶

In other words, there is a basis for shared or collective representations, which are products of our shared humanity, whether physical or mental, conscious or unconscious. Representations do not have to compel one into solipsism, in which every representation is particular to an individual and cannot be shared. As representations are evidently shared, coherence in life eventuates. This means that the biographies of individuals can be written and communicated in an intelligible fashion.

A related question is what sort of biography or hagiography should one write. Where the literary or religious *topoi* or structural approach is adopted, the attempt is usually to write a collective biography or a "biography" of sainthood or of some such similar type, which is simply another form of representation. This attempt does not distinguish, however, between the historicity or fictitiousness of the account of the life, for the concern is with the perception and representations that are being examined, the "collective mental representation" of someone or some legend as a type. On the other hand, an engaged historian, attempting to elucidate individual lives as exemplars, focuses on the reconstruction of the life of an individual "historical" person.⁵⁷ The engaged historians attempt to learn the lessons of history themselves and to transmit those lessons to their readers.⁵⁸

Historians with a pretense to scientific accuracy and veracity do not adopt the engaged historian's approach. Yet despite all of the doubts raised about the value of reconstructing lives from (premodern) hagiographies and biographies, which are seen to be akin in their "substantialist" attitude,⁵⁹ and thus unreliable because they were representations, they do attempt to salvage value from the "lives" because the popular hagiographies may inform more about the practised "thought" of a person than their dry scholastic writings or "historical" biographies.⁶⁰ Thus it may be concluded, just as Ch'oe did, that the thoughts of individuals or "historical actors" can be revealed by their actions and choices of action, although there is no necessary correlation of the thought and the action. Perhaps this attempt to go beyond historicist representation by examining the deeds performed and the choices the actors

Representing Wŏnch'ŭk

faced "should expedite our attempt to 'present' the *present* they experienced rather than a *past* which we reconstruct; for they lived through dilemmas that we can do nothing but represent – since we cannot relive them". This is an attempt to "make the past more like the present".[61] This then is writing history to make events and lives intelligible, and is not simply another form of representation.[62] If the biography is to be more than just fiction, the representation must be dependent on sources, which should be acknowledged, and where possible, be allowed to speak for themselves.[63] Yet, because of the tyranny of different times, places, cultures and languages, even these informant texts cannot have their own voice and have to be translated,[64] which is another layer of representation. In other words, the past or the other have to be represented, leaving historians and biographers mired in an endless series of representations. All the historian has as the remotest hope of salvation is the awareness that the process of writing is one of representation. The historian then should write **as if** the coherence created is a "live" representation, one that assists others. As Vaihinger asserted, "It is not the correspondence with an assumed 'objective reality' that can never be directly accessible to us, it is not the theoretical representation of an outer world in the mirror of consciousness ... which ... guarantees that thought has fulfilled its purpose", but rather the practical test in which "the elaboration and adjustment of the material of sensation" leads to "the attainment of a richer and fuller sensational life of experience".[65]

History and biography, like religion and literature, are representations that attempt to enrich experience. Here I wish to represent Wŏnch'ŭk, in full knowledge that this account will be supplemented, with the hope that future readers will be inspired by the heroic efforts of Wŏnch'ŭk in translation and scholarship, in other words, as much by his actions as by his writings themselves, which are still studied by Buddhists from Japan to Tibet and beyond. The mind, being a thief, as Ch'oe Ch'iwŏn so bluntly wrote, tends to adopt only the ideas of eminent intellectuals like Wŏnch'ŭk, leaving them as disembodied traces, which is ultimately not satisfactory, producing a sense of loss, for the ideas emanate from a human actor whose deeds may be equally important as models.

Biography and Hagiography, East and West

Although biography and hagiography share some fundamental features, there are distinctions that need to be drawn. Firstly, hagiographies, whether of the European or the Indian Buddhist traditions, differ from biographies. The Indian Buddhist "lives", for example, are filled with the supernatural and mundane chronology and life phases are practically ignored,[66] a feature also of the lives (*vitae*) of the Christian martyrs,[67] which tended to pay little attention to time and place.[68] However, although hagiographies were written for religious ends by engaged writers to propagandise and to demonstrate their own faith, and thus use fixed *topoi* as exemplars of religiosity,[69] the place and period of the authoring is crucial.

Some attempts have been made to distinguish the "legendary" type of *vitae* that are dominated by the *topoi* of the stereotype in which the "hagiographer's purpose could be served equally well by facts or fictions" and the "'historical' type of *vita*" and *acta* which had greater evidence of individuality. This latter arose in Western Europe in the thirteenth century[70] when the evidence needed for canonisation created a greater sophistication and level of reliability in the accounts, and the better hagiographers named their sources, and explained their intention, which was to teach by example.[71] Likewise, in Indian Buddhist hagiography, *avadāna*, *carita* and Vinaya accounts of the origins of the rules and precepts became more sophisticated and self-aware over time. However, they also tended to become more literary and legendary.[72]

Therefore there are grounds on which to rescue hagiography from being considered mere literary fictions or simply idealisations of types and that "the representations of a function assumed by a person who represents this type is far more important to the authors than the cut of his biography".[73] Many of the authors did use the particulars of individuals' lives and personalities to illustrate the ideal,[74] and did place the saint into an historical context, and so have historical value.[75] Thus these premodern lives may approximate the modern idea of a biography that individualises rather than the supposed medieval hagiography that generalised.[76] This was particularly the case in China where the influence of Chinese secular historiography lessened the hagiographical elements in the writing of the lives of Buddhist clergy.[77]

While all premodern biographies and hagiographies tended to use stereotypes and not strictly distinguish between fiction and history, and permitted or rather actively believed in the intervention of the supernatural into lives,[78] the differences in the models for the hagiography or biography had major consequences for the reliability of the "life". Some medieval Christian *vitae* were probably based on the "lives" of the legendary Greek heroes who were idealised,[79] which led to an "ideal pattern" and legendary or literary *topoi*. However, other *vitae* were more individualised because the "lives" were needed as evidence for canonisation.[80] Indian Buddhist historiography began with the biography of a human being, the Buddha, who taught and transmitted a doctrine that was a human creation, unlike the Vedic, Brahmanical and Christian doctrines which were supposedly revelations. Therefore, Indian Buddhist historiography was concerned with the human realm,[81] and when the supernatural intervened, it was merely secondary or a confirmation of the sanctity of the human person involved. When Buddhism arrived in China, this historiography was further humanised by the secular tendencies of Chinese historiography, which emphasised time, place and the phases of life.[82] Thus to Zanning (921–1002), the Indians appeared to lack any clerical histories, despite the fact he must have been cognisant of Chinese translations of biographies/hagiographies of the Buddha and important monks and the histories of the councils and doctrinal disputes.[83] Yet the Chinese Buddhist hagiogaphers/biographers did retain the Indian Buddhist theme that their subjects were agents of karma and under its influence.[84] Karma made all actions related and of significance, and forced the life into a moral "patterning".[85]

Moreover, the native Chinese historiographical tradition of "biography" was similar to the medieval Western European hagiography in that the life had to follow "conventionalized *topoi*" and was an "exploration not of a life but of the performance by its subject of some function or role".[86] In this, the individual personality is muffled, but not totally absent, which was partly due to the different Chinese attitude to the individual, who was supposed to model their life on an exemplar and perform a set or group-determined role.[87] As a result, it was rare for a biography to be read on its own, except when it was a funerary inscription or "account of conduct" written for the group members. The standard form of biography was the *liezhuan* or "connected traditions" which were meant to be read collectively, not singly, for a "cumulative didactic effect".[88] And yet, Buddhism seems to have encouraged a revival of "separate biographies" (*biezhuan*) which dealt rather with the individual such as Xuanzang,[89] although some, such as that of Huineng, the so-called Sixth Patriarch of Chan, are clearly fiction. The *liezhuan*, whether those written by the Confucian state historian or the Buddhist Vinaya "hagiographer" such as Zanning, were based primarily on funerary inscriptions or *xingzhuang* ("accounts of conduct") which had commemorative purposes and were compiled for the family or group by private individuals who knew the subject or who were commissioned to write an account based on the testimonies of members of the group. These materials were far more detailed and vivid than the *liezhuan*, portraying their subjects more as individuals. Yet these too were didactic and embellished, being eulogistic encomia.[90]

However, the Chinese historiographical tradition had strengths and weaknesses. For example, although it had a victor's view of history in most circumstances,[91] it did approve of the careful listing of sources and the discarding of unreliable materials. The better historiographers also classified their materials, placing those with origins in popular rumour or miracle tale into special, separate categories of "lives".[92] The Chinese Buddhist collective biographers, who were from the Vinaya School, adopted the principles of the secular historians.[93] They similarly classified and ranked the veracity and functions of their sources. Thus "stele inscriptions" and "accounts of conduct" took pride of place in most categories of clerical hagiographies. These were probably followed in evaluation by eye-witness accounts, prefaces and scriptural material, and finally by popular stories and mirabilia which found their way mostly into the "Thaumaturges" and "Promoters of Good Works" sections.[94] Material that most closely conformed to the classical model of the standard history *liezhuan* and their prime sources, the "accounts of conduct" and funerary inscriptions were considered the most reliable. Moreover, because many of the accounts of conduct and funerary inscriptions for monks were written by lay literati, secular criteria were introduced into these Buddhist compilations, making them less like hagiographies and more like biographies.[95] However, the classificatory schemes and the discrimination of the value of the evidence meant that the collective biographers were selective, adopting the principles of "concealing and revealing" and making moral judgements on the life of a person or category of persons.[96] This does not mean that all the fictional elements were selected out of the Buddhist biographies, even of the biographies that were based on funerary inscriptions and accounts of conduct, for they were meant to glorify the subject and enhance the standing of the religion.[97] Therefore difficulties will be encountered in any attempt to reconstruct an "historical biography" of an individual as distinct from the "biographical image" with its collective approach,[98] but knowledge of the period, the author and the types of source materials can assist the biographer represent the life of the chosen subject.

Thus, for the reconstruction of Wŏnch'ŭk's biography, it is clear that the later accounts by Song Fu and Ch'oe Ch'iwŏn are more reliable. Although this reverses the historiographical expectation that the earliest sources are the most accurate,[99] there are numerous instances where the later biographies are more objective because they were free of the social and political constraints placed on the contemporary or near-contemporary biographer.[100] Song Fu's account, and probably that of Ch'oe Ch'iwŏn were clearly based on a stupa funerary inscription and possibly an "account of conduct", and thus were much longer and more detailed than any *liezhuan*, which tended to be "brief, dry and impersonal".[101] But Zanning's account is clearly not based on a funerary inscription or account of conduct, for he did not know Wŏnch'ŭk's surname or personal name (*zi*), his birth or death dates, and he did not reveal his foreign origins. In fact, Zanning's account may have been based on an account of conduct for Wŏnch'ŭk's rival, Dasheng Ji, for it is strikingly partisan. It violated the principle of the various *Gaoseng zhuan* as enunciated by Huijiao: "If men of real achievement conceal their brilliance, then they are eminent but not famous; when men of slight virtue happen to be in accord with their times, then they are famous but not eminent."[102] It is almost as if Zanning was accusing Wŏnch'ŭk of being famous, but cannot back that with the data associated with the famous. Zanning only gave grudging praise to Wŏnch'ŭk for his intelligence and literary skills.[103] Indeed, in general Zanning downgraded exegetes, as did society as a whole by the time Zanning wrote his *Song Gaoseng zhuan*.[104] But his entry on Wŏnch'ŭk goes against the overwhelming tendency for the biographers of exegetes to base their accounts on the "stupa inscriptions",[105] although it is remarkable that most of the pupils of Xuanzang given in chapter four (on exegetes) have their origins listed as "unknown".[106] The length of the accounts show that Dasheng Ji had pride of place,[107] with Wŏnch'ŭk having the shortest

Representing Wŏnch'ŭk

entry.[108] Even the Silla monk Sun'gyŏng has a longer account.[109] Two other Silla monks, Ŭisang and Wŏnhyo, the latter of whom never even came to China, have lengthy entries in the same chapter on the exegetes.[110] This suggests that Zanning was biased against, and perhaps ignorant of, Wŏnch'ŭk, and that that prejudice was less ethnic than doctrinal and source-based. Even so, Zanning's account, like that of Song Fu, was less literary and more "historical" in its form of representation. Ch'oe's account, although highly literary on its surface, seems to have been built upon an historical, biographical skeleton. Therefore it is possible to reconstruct a "biographical" representation of Wŏnch'ŭk, which is of a different order to that of literary representation.

The Biographies

Zanning's Account

Zanning's account, being the most influential, will be treated first to show the unsavoury elements that may have dissuaded researchers from further investigation. The hagiography reads as follows:

Biography of Wŏnch'ŭk of Ximing Monastery in the Tang capital

There is no information on the clan surname of the monk Wŏnch'ŭk. From his youth he was intelligent and sagacious, and he understood everything. When the Tripitaka Teacher (Xuan)zang was lecturing on his new translation of the *Vijñaptimātratāsiddhi śāstra*[111] for Master Ci'en Ji[112], Wŏnch'ŭk bribed the gate-keeper and listened in secret. After he returned (to his own monastery) he compiled an essay on its meaning.[113] When (Xuanzang)'s lectures were about to finish, Wŏnch'ŭk rang the bell of Ximing Monastery to summon the assembly, announcing his own lectures on the Vijñānavāda (*wei-shi*). Ji resented (Wŏnch'ŭk) for having stolen the ideas of others, but he resigned himself to Wŏnch'ŭk giving the lectures. Then when Xuanzang lectured on the *Yogā(cārabhūmi śāstra)*, (Wŏnch'ŭk) again stole a hearing as before and received (the teaching), and so again he was ahead of Ji.

During the last years of Gaozong's reign and the first years of Empress Wu's reign,[114] he was selected for the sutra translation institute due to his understanding of the meaning (of the texts). The assembly there all promoted him (as the leader), and they translated the *Dasheng xianshi (jing)*[115] and other sutras. Wŏnch'ŭk fully authenticated the meaning together with Bozhen, Lingbian and Jiashang who accompanied him. He wrote the *Weishi shuchao*[116] and his detailed explanations of the sutras and shastras were distributed throughout the Empire.[117]

These incidents are confirmed and the prejudices buttressed, in the hagiography of Dasheng/Kuiji,[118] which admits that Wŏnch'ŭk was brilliant, but bribed the gate-keeper so he could steathily listen to the lectures on the *Cheng weishi lun* and compile his own commentary. This he allegedly did only after a number of lectures had been delivered. He then gave his own lectures. Ji, humiliated at having been pipped at the post yet again, could not get over his disappointment, and so Xuanzang encouraged him by saying, "Although Wŏnch'ŭk has written the commentary, he does not yet comprehend (Buddhist) logic. So I will lecture on Dignāga's treatise (on logic) for you." As Ji was accomplished in the three elements of logic he was able to elucidate this difficult text by the chief logician of the Vijñānavāda, Dignāga, in an unprecedented fashion.[119] Zanning concludes:

> It is also said that Ji requested that (Xuan)zang lecture on the *Yogā(cārabhūmi)śāstra* for him alone, but just as previously, Wŏnch'ŭk stole a hearing and lectured on it first. Xuanzang said, "Only you are conversant with the Dharma of the thesis of the five natures,[120] and he is not."[121]

Dasheng Ji displayed a great possessiveness and jealousy regarding the teachings Xuanzang brought. He persuaded Xuanzang to not translate all ten of the Indian commentaries in his interpretation of the *Triṃśīkā* ("Treatise in Thirty Stanzas"),[122] but to concentrate on translating the theories of Dharmapāla. He thus succeeded in removing three of Xuanzang's other translation assistants from the project, probably in order to exclude Wŏnch'ŭk.[123] As a result, the nine other interpretations were not fully available to Wŏnch'ŭk or any other East Asian Buddhists, and this was meant to stop Wŏnch'ŭk gaining ammunition for his criticisms of the Dharmapāla version of Vijñānavāda. And yet, as Dasheng Ji's pupil, Huizhao (650–714) in his *Cheng weishi lun liaoyi deng* attacked Wŏnch'ŭk's text and interpretation, it is clear that Wŏnch'ŭk used a different text of the *Cheng weishi lun* to that edited by Ji.[124] Therefore, it is conceivable that Wŏnch'ŭk had gained access to some of Xuanzang's materials earlier, materials that Ji had attempted to jealously guard.

The temporary dominance of the Ci'en School may have been gained through the political connections of Dasheng Ji, who was of an eminent family. The authors of Ji's stupa inscriptions, Li Hongjing, a son by a second wife of the heir apparent and Commissioner with Extraordinary Powers for Jinzhou,[125] and Li Yi (– ca. 713), the Grand Master of Court Audiences and Acting Vice Minister of Personnel,[126] were imperial relatives or high court officials. The high status of the supporters of Ji's chief disciple, Huizhao (640–714), as shown by the author of his stele, the famous Li Yong (680–746), and his patrons, Wu Pingyi (active 705+ – ca. 741), Lü Zangyong (ca. 650–ca. 713), Lu Jing and Cui Shi (671–713),[127] may have overshadowed the school of Wŏnch'ŭk, before both lineages were dealt a severe blow by the An Lushan Rebellion, which deprived them of the material support they needed from the court and central bureaucracy. Wŏnch'ŭk's ideas survived in China for a generation or two, and then retreated to Silla and to the north-west frontier of China.

Song Fu's Account

But a local revival of Wŏnch'ŭk's reputation did occur, for in 1115, his stupa was erected alongside those of Xuanzang and Dasheng Ji at Xingjiao Monastery, and there an inscription for the stupa was written by Song Fu.[128] Wang Chang (1724–1806), writing around 1805 in the *Jinshi cuibian*, a collection of epigraphy, notes that Song Fu was only a candidate for the third degree and so is otherwise unknown. Wang quoted the local gazetteer, the *Shanxi tongzhi*, which states:

> The monastery is sixty *li* to the south of the city (Chang'an). It was built in 669. There are three stupas inside (the monastery), the highest and largest of which is the one in which the body of the Tripitaka Dharma Teacher Xuanzang is interred. It has an inscription by Liu Ke, the Minister and Director of the State Farm Bureau. To the left is the stupa of Ci'en Ji, with an inscription by Li Hongdu,[129] the son by the Secondary Wife of the Heir Apparent. To the right is the stupa of the Dharma Teacher Wŏnch'ŭk of the Great Zhou (dynasty). The writer of the inscription was the third-degree candidate Song Fu.[130]

The monastery was founded on the orders of Emperor Gaozong to be the site for the reburied remains of Xuanzang, which were placed in the stupa. His body was moved there because the mourners at his previous tomb in the suburbs of Chang'an could not be contained in the cemetery grounds and the devotees there often injured themselves. The name Xingjiao Monastery was granted in the reign of Emperor Suzong.[131]

This stupa has survived. Cho Myŏnggi reports that Yuki Reimon surveyed the site and the reliquary stupas, which as a result of centuries of weathering, had to be repaired in 1916. During the repairs, a wooden image of Wŏnch'ŭk was discovered enshrined in the stupa, so it was probably the model for the statue in front of the stupa mentioned by Song Fu. These days the place seems to have been made into a modern tourist attraction.[132]

Song Fu's encomium, the *Inscription on the Buddha-śarīra Stupa for the late Bhadanta, the Dharma Teacher Wŏnch'ŭk of Ximing Monastery of the Great Zhou*,[133] reads as follows:

The Dharma Teacher's taboo name was Mun'a, his personal name Wŏnch'ŭk. He was a descendant of the kings of Silla. When he was three he departed the laity, and at fifteen he requested the Work (of Buddhism). First he listened to the shastras from the two Dharma Teachers (Fa)chang and (Seng)bian.[134] Being innately intelligent, his attention was exceptional, so although (the shastras) were tens of millions of words, he did not forget them.

In the Zhenguan era (627–650), the Cultured Emperor Taizong had him (legally) ordained[135] as a monk and reside at Yuanfa Monastery in the capital.[136] There he read the *Abhidharma, Satyasiddhi, (Abhidharma)-kośa, Vibhāṣa* and other shastras. He was versed in all of the essays and commentaries of the past and present, and his reputation soared.

When the Tripitaka Dharma Teacher (Xuan)zang was about to return from India, Wŏnch'ŭk had a premonitory dream in which a brahmin offered him a fruit which fulfilled all his yearnings. What he had witnessed was a response to the excellent causation of a meeting in a past [life with Xuanzang]. As soon as he saw (Xuan)zang he was in total agreement with him.[137] So he devoted his life to the *Yogā(cārabhūmi)*, *Cheng weishi* and other shastras, and to the Mahayana and Hinayana sutras and shastras which they translated together. They were as clear to him as if he had been born with knowledge of them.

Later he was summoned to be bhadanta[138] of Ximing Monastery,[139] where he wrote a *Cheng weishi lunshu* in ten juan,[140] the *Jie shenmi jingshu* in ten juan,[141] the *Renwang jingshu* in three juan,[142] the *Jingang boruo*,[143] the *Guan suoyuan lun*[144] and commentaries on the *Boruo xin jing* and *Wuliangyi jing*,[145] which were the eyes and the ears for the people of the time to assist (in understanding) the abstruse texts. Therefore people praised him as the assistant to (Xuan)zang in bringing the Buddha-Dharma to the East and in greatly promoting the inexhaustible teaching.

By temperament Wŏnch'ŭk delighted in the mountains and rivers,[146] and so he went to stay in Yunji Monastery on Mt. Zhongnan. He went a further thirty-odd *li* from the monastery to rest in a place where he calmed his will for eight years. His monk followers of Ximing Monastery requested he give in to their demands and return to the monastery and lecture on the *Cheng weishi lun*.

At that time the Central Indian Tripitaka (master) Divākara[147] had arrived in the capital and had been imperially commanded to select and summons five bhadantas to help him translate the *(Dasheng) miyan jing* and other sutras. Wŏnch'ŭk was placed at their head.

Later he was again summoned to the eastern capital (Luoyang) to lecture on and translate the new *Huayan jing*.[148] Before he had finished a juan scroll he passed away in Foshouji Monastery on the 22nd day of the 7th month of the first year of the Wansui tongtian era (25th August 696) at the age of eighty-four.

Representing Wŏnch'ŭk

On the 25th day of that month he was cremated in the valley to the north of Xiangshan Monastery at Longmen[149] and there a white stupa was erected. His students in the capital, the abbot of Ximing Monastery, Dharma Teacher Cishan, and the bhadanta of Dajianfu Monastery, Sŭngjang,[150] and others at that time were grieved that they were making offerings without an object.[151] Subsequently, at the burial site in Xiangshan (Monastery) they separated out his skeletal remains (from the ashes) into one section, and placed them into a jewelled casket in a stone coffin, which were separately buried on the range to the east of Fengde Monastery on Mt. Zhongnan,[152] a place where Wŏnch'ŭk had roamed. They raised a stupa over the tomb and placed forty-nine śarīra pellets in the foundations of the stupa.

Now that road is almost impassable. Cliffs and precipices cut it off, and the forests are so dense they close it off. It was dangerous, isolated and disease-ridden, so people rarely venture there. This buried his brilliance and covered over his virtue, and time just passed, so who knew about or paid respect to him?

Because of this, Dharma Teacher Guangyue of Renwang Cloister in the Longxing Monastery of the same prefecture diligently made an earnest vow, and so on the 8th day of the 4th month of the Zhenghe reign of Great Song (3rd May 1115) he went to the Fengde (Monastery) portion (of the relics) to worship. He also reburied all of the buddha's (Wŏnch'ŭk) śarīra in Xingjiao Monastery to the left of Xuanzang's stupa, erecting a totally new stupa modelled on that of (Dasheng) Ji's stupa. There was not the slightest difference between the two. Moreover, Ji's stupa was old and so they renewed it. The gold wheels and precious bells (of the stupa) were erected in tiers, both of them soaring loftily as if created by magic. Each was circled by a broad corridor at the base. Their death images[153] were exalted and deep, and were on the left and right in order to attend upon Xuanzang. It caused those who came to view them with admiration, and induced faith such that (the viewers) were not even aware of the time passing. And then in front of the stupas they built an offertory hall formed with six pillars.

On the day of dedication there was no time to seek an accomplished scholar, so they begged me to directly preface that work. They linked it to the inscription, which reads:

Since the patra leaves (Buddhist scriptures) came from the West
    their merit has been great;
Since the teaching flowed into the Central Region (China) it has
    been forever relied upon.
The Dharma Master was a prop who truly brought the sides (India,
    China) together.

Xiangshan (Monastery) is distant and hidden in the depths of the palace (capital);
Fengde (Monastery) is precipitous and concealed his numinous traces.
Later people will take refuge in him, so how can one go there in vain?
There was a (Guang)yue who created the conditions with the help of the spirit (of Wŏnch'ŭk).
The pair of stupas stand imposingly with Ji's (stupa) as the model.
In worshipping Xuanzang can one reach a limit?
The Zhongnan (Mountains) are so lofty they lean on heaven.
The entombed bhadanta was so majestic an inscription was engraved on stone,
So that those who came to gaze with reverence will do so for 100 million years.

This preface, commissioned by an otherwise obscure monk and written by an unknown and lowly examination candidate, was probably based on local monastic traditions and some sutra catalogues and prefaces. It owes very little if anything to the *Song Gaoseng zhuan*, and although no earlier stele is mentioned, surely one existed at the graves. Certainly, this inscription means that Wŏnch'ŭk's light had not been completely extinguished by his rivals who accused him of heterodoxy.

There may have been a revival of interest in Wŏnch'ŭk because of the activities of the Koryŏ monk Ŭich'ŏn whose 1090 catalogue of extra-Tripitaka scriptures listed Wŏnch'ŭk's works, and who studied Vijñānavāda doctrines and wrote on them extensively, even though he is famed for his Tiantai and Huayan (Hwaŏm) studies. Ŭich'ŏn visited China in 1085 in search of missing texts.[154] Around this time, in 1119, the Faxiang lineage monk of Longxing Monastery in Zhending, Shouqian (1064–1143), edited the Silla monk Toyun's *Yuga saji nonjip* (Ch. *Yujia shidi lun ji*).[155] Toyun, a monk of Hŭngnyŭn Monastery in Kyŏngju, wrote eighteen works, of which only the above commentary on the *Yogācārabhūmi śāstra* has survived.[156] However, as Toyun's work detailed the various differing theories of the commentators on this text, over half of whom were Silla monks, including Wŏnch'ŭk and Wŏnhyo, and frequently quoted Dasheng Ji, he was probably neutral in the sectarian dispute. The re-publication of Toyun's commentary suggests that there was a resurrection of the theories of Wŏnch'ŭk and Dasheng Ji. As Toyun did not quote Huizhao (650–714), he probably wrote this work before 714,[157] and so would have provided insight for Song scholars into the early differences between the Ximing and Ci'en schools. Guangyue then may have promoted a restoration of Wŏnch'ŭk's position as an equal of Dasheng Ji because of a revival in interest in the re-evaluation of the Vijñānavāda philosophy.

Representing Wŏnch'ŭk

However, the reburial of Wŏnch'ŭk's relics and the reconstruction of the stupa of Dasheng Ji, together with the building of an offertory hall, suggests that a purpose of this activity was to revive the fortunes of Xingjiao Monastery by using the reputation of Xuanzang and his pupils. Thus Song Fu does not mention the rivalry or allegations of Dasheng Ji against Wŏnch'ŭk, for such a hint of jealousy and dispute would have undermined the reputation of this trio and the income to be gained from worshippers because it violated Buddhist ethics. Indeed, much of the inscription stresses Wŏnch'ŭk's relations with Xuanzang, such as their connections in a previous life, which would raise Wŏnch'ŭk in the estimation of the readers.

Despite these limitations, Song Fu must have had access to records other than that by Zanning, for he supplies information on Wŏnch'ŭk's background, names his early teachers, gives specific dates for his death and age, and records the burial sites. These were probably available locally, possibly at his tomb in Yunji Monastery. Funerary inscriptions as a genre were eulogies, and so eschewed any stains on the character of their subject. These were Song Fu's sources and genre, but he surprisingly did not use the third extant source for Wŏnch'ŭk's life, the *Text of the Death Anniversary of the Late Verifier of the Meaning of the Translated Sutras, the Bhadanta and Upādhyāya Wŏnch'ŭk*, written by Ch'oe Ch'iwŏn, which is of a similar genre.

Perhaps Song Fu did not have access to this text, for although the hagiography of the Huayan School founder, Fazang (643–712) written by Ch'oe Ch'iwŏn in 904 was likely known in China before 1115, being listed in Ŭich'ŏn's catalogue of 1090 and printed in Koryŏ in 1092, and included in the Song Tripitaka in 1145 and published separately in 1149,[158] there is no evidence that Ch'oe's work on Wŏnch'ŭk was available outside of Korea. But if Ch'oe had written such an account of Wŏnch'ŭk, it may likewise have been known in Song China, for Ch'oe's hagiography of Ŭisang (625–702), an associate and correspondent with Fazang, was possibly known to Zanning, as there are indications in the *Song Gaoseng zhuan* biography of Ŭisang that Zanning had knowledge of some Korean records.[159]

Ch'oe Ch'iwŏn's Vow Text

This anniversary text was written with a Silla audience in mind, for it was written in Silla as the vow of a monastery-centred society in Silla, a society which venerated Wŏnch'ŭk. Therefore it uses special terms adopted by Silla patriots, such as "the realm of humaneness" for the country, and mentions that Wŏnch'ŭk died "on foreign soil". It even uses the phrase, "the West is enlightened from the East", an expression of Silla pride in the country, its priority in Buddhism, and pride in Wŏnch'ŭk's achievements, lamenting that he did not return to Korea. The text reads:

Observe the dawning sun that rises out of Yuyi,[160] the light of which illuminates[161] the myriad images. The spring breeze which is born of the *chen* position[162] has a breath that moistens the eight compass points. Thus they can shatter the darkness of the world[163] and form a fruit on earth. Only after that does the crow (sun) fly as a fleeting shadow,[164] returning on its orbit into the depths of the valley of darkness. A tiger roared and heroes were in awe, and he halted at the gates of the distant suburbs of Shang.[165] This is to know that righteousness issues forth due to humaneness, just as the West is illuminated from the East.[166] Since that has been a metaphor for human talent, why should the nature of (physical) things differ?

And so it is with the bequeathed teachings of the Sugata (Buddha). In India[167] he manifested his form, and to the Chinese courts he transmitted his voice. Therefore, while many monks arrived from the region of India and became patriarchs of Tang, few people from the ocean country (Korea) left to be teachers of the Han (Chinese). But in having the rising sun that opens the mind, and the purifying breeze that harmonises strength,[168] the Black Mountains[169] are lit up first and the cold lands are all warmed, and so the reception of the wonderful is spearheaded by the outer countries.[170]

The person who hung up the clear mirror (of wisdom) in China was only our Master Mun'a. It is remembered that the bhadanta was of the P'ung village clan and a descendant of the kings of Yan. He had planted good shoots and acted to grasp the superior fruit,[171] and so became a dragon-child of the sea of Korea[172] and a phoenix-fledgling of Cock Forest.[173]

Therefore he left his (lay) home [entered the Order] when in swaddling clothes and departed from the troubles of the senses (the lay world) early in life. He boarded a ship to see the world[174] and beached himself far off at the imperial court. His learning was limited only by the seven continents (of the Buddhist world) and he came to understand the languages of six countries. Ultimately he was fluent in the Indian tongue[175] and he could reproduce it in the Chinese sound (translate). The oceanic assembly (of saints) was impressed upon his mind,[176] and so he superbly sought out[177] the sense of the Sanskrit. He was just like the talented people of Qin taking refuge in Jin,[178] or the jade of Zhao entering Qin.[179] Consequently he could conduct himself in the heights of the tenth stage.[180]

His fame reached to the supreme of the ninth heaven (the emperor) and so the Cultured Emperor[181] recognised him as a treasure and straightaway had him ordained as a monk. Empress Wu respected him as a saint and truly venerated him like a buddha. Each time an Indian missionary of the West was received, (the court) summoned the remarkable man of the East Ocean (Korea) and made him take part in the debate.

Representing Wŏnch'ŭk

Because he was gifted with eloquence, when there was discussion (translation) of the sutra he was certain to be made its leader. When he wrote commentaries he was independent of mind, and when he went into seclusion the numinous was moved most frequently.[182] When he rose to the pulpit his voice of the Dharma (sermon) corresponded (to the occasion). Great was he! He was unceasing in his illumination and his pathways overflowed (with benefits).[183] Ever since the marvellous (Dharma) flowed east[184] its meaning has been inexhaustible and yet many have adhered to delusions concerning the Western learning.[185]

In the Chuigong era (685–687) our Lord (King Sinmun of Silla) who loved the Dharma repeatedly memorialised (the Chinese ruler) requesting (Wŏnch'ŭk's) return. The Holy Emperor (of China) took pity and kindly (sent) an edict (to the Korean king) to show opposition (to the request). Therefore his arrival (birth) was as a sagely heir to those who had fled from Qin[186] and his departure (death) was as a compassionate saint to assist the Han (Chinese). It was due to this that this monk of our country was admired as if an eminent mountain.[187] His cultivation of the Work (of Buddhism) was like the four rivers returning to the sea[188] and his pronouncements were like the myriad panpipes (of Nature) piping in the wind.[189]

The virtuous (senior monks in Korea) deliberated on this, saying, "The late Master Mun'a's merit was transcendent and suddenly his spirit transmigrated on foreign soil. His bones were interred on an empty mountain, but just think of the roc riding on a typhoon[190] and do not look at the crane soul returning to the (grave) monument."[191]

His pupils divided up his skeleton and raised up a stupa. We comrades were silenced and had forgotten our schemes, and even though we contemplated his theme of non-duality, we are concerned at our deficiency in respect of the three obligations.[192] How much more, given that the *zhi* fungus and the epidendrum have been made metaphors for their enduring fragrance, and the trees and plums have formed (the subjects of) poems and so have always been regarded as good,[193] should we perform rites in honour of the patriarch as we have received the instruction of the strict teacher. Therefore, we planned a day of commemoration. We respectfully seek his compassionate protection and we humbly beseech him to travel aloft to the Buddha-land and from afar protect the realm of humaneness,[194] transmit the great voice of the Indian ranges, bring forth the best books from the dragon's palace,[195] and make the production of dharmas and the cessation of dharmas jointly shed light on causation, and being without ego or self, eternally expand merit and virtue. Even though he has gone to a parched grave, his sea of vows will eternally flow.[196]

Respectfully stated.

This paean to Wŏnch'ŭk was written as a preamble to a vow which was made by Ch'oe Ch'iwŏn and the assembly for whom he wrote. Thus, given the patriotic sentiments expressed, Ch'oe was most unlikely to refer to any defects in Wŏnch'ŭk or to any conflict he had with other Buddhist scholars. Commemorative encomia such as this contain little factual detail and tend to be overwhelmingly poetical outpourings of pride and piety written in ornate, laudatory styles. This can be confirmed by comparison with the similar vow text commemorating Ŭisang's date of death. Such occasions demanded praise, not concrete detail.

However, Ch'oe had to have drawn upon earlier sources, for some of the information here cannot be gleaned from the *Song Gaoseng zhuan*. The sources are unnamed and no longer extant. Song Fu did not use Zanning's account either, ignoring its slander and poverty of useful information, and he probably did not have access to Ch'oe's text, which was meant for worship in a society or assembly attached to a monastery, and so was not a public inscription engraved on stone from which rubbings or other forms of reproduction could be taken and the text disseminated. It may then have long been kept for the private use of that society and the monastery. These societies were made up of lay persons like Ch'oe and monks who vowed to commemorate the death of a patriarch by rites and deeds, or to chant a sutra. Such groups were often associated with Hwaŏm, both in China and Korea, and they attempted to spread that form of Buddhism among the people, being active especially when the state-supported or aristocratic Order was in decline, as was the case in late Silla. That the commemoration day for Wŏnch'ŭk seems to have been held by such a society of "we comrades" is suggested by the fact that such a society commemorated Ŭisang to repay his kindness in teaching.[197] The texts of those societies then were most likely to have been retained for the exclusive use of the society for some time before they became freely available to the general public.

Given that the sources for all three texts on Wŏnch'ŭk translated above were not identified and are no longer extant, the only means of reconstructing the life of the saint is through these three late, imperfect and slanted materials, supplemented by mentions of him in prefaces and Tripitaka catalogues. However, together they supply considerable data once the contexts of and constraints on these materials are known.

Reconstruction of Biography

Ancestry and Name

Wŏnch'ŭk's ancestry and family name pose the first conundrum. Ch'oe claims he was of the P'ung village clan and a descendant of the kings of Yan, while Song Fu states he was a descendant of the kings of Silla. No kings of

Representing Wŏnch'ŭk

Silla were named P'ung, or came from a village of that name, and so Ch'oe's reference must be to the Feng (K. P'ung), a clan which ruled the minor state of Northern Yan (408–437) in Liaodong and who were supposedly remote descendants of Bi Wan of the Spring and Autumn period.[198] Defeated by the Tuoba Northern Wei, the rulers of Northern Yan either ended up in Tuoba hands or shifted to Koguryŏ, the northernmost "Korean" state,[199] for the Feng had a close connection with Koguryŏ.[200] Although Ch'oe wrote a history of Korea, the *Chewang nyŏndae yŏk*[201] and knew of the existence of Bi Wan,[202] there is no other mention in Korean historical records of the Feng living in Silla, and indeed, the Koguryŏ king eventually had the entire Feng clan and their offspring slaughtered in 438 for arrogance and plotting.[203]

As Ch'oe also refers to Wŏnch'ŭk's arrival or birth as that of "a sagely heir to those who had fled from Qin", perhaps the allusion is to Wei Man (K. Wi Man), a man from the state of Yan who made himself king of Chaoxian (Chosŏn) when Qin conquered Yan, by leading refugees from Yan and Qi into Northern Korea.[204] The Ch'in Han "federation" that was one of the main components of early Silla and provided its mythical founder, claimed Ch'in Han was established by refugees fleeing the Chinese Qin oppression, using the *Hou Hanshu* and other sources as their evidence.[205] Ch'oe Ch'iwŏn is quoted as having written:

> The Ch'in Han were originally people who fled from Yan. Because they adopted the name of the T'ak River, they took (this word) into the names of their villages, calling them Sat'ak and Chŏmt'ak [note the Silla dialect reads the sound of *t'ak* as *to*, and so they sometimes write Sa(r)yang, with *yang* also read as *to*].[206]

Such a Ch'in Han connection can be detected in the story of a Wŏnch'ŭk in the *Samguk yusa*. According to Iryŏn, Wŏnch'ŭk was prevented from entering a monastery or carrying out priestly functions because of an incident that supposedly occurred in the reign of King Hyoso (r. 692–702). However, as Wŏnch'ŭk died in China in 693, this dating would make that incident too late to refer to the same person.[207] But it has been argued that the Iryŏn's dating is incorrect, and suggested that the incident happened in the reign of King Chinp'yŏng (r. 579–632), the story being that of an elderly *hwarang*, a member of a select, moral army corps, recounting the events of his youth to someone in the time of Hyoso.[208] Because the chieftain of Mo(r)yang district, one Ik-sŏn, tried to assert his customary rights over one of his people, a hwarang who also owed direct allegiance to the king, the king intervened to counteract this diminution of royal authority, which was being strengthened through the hwarang corps. Mo(r)yang district (*ri*) was on a strategic route out of Kyŏngju, the Silla capital, to the rival Paekche domain, and so the king could not permit any challenge to his power from traditional clan chieftains who held such castles and areas. The king therefore punished the ruling clan of Mo(r)yang by preventing them from obtaining any administrative or monastic posts.[209] As Wǒnch'ǔk was a member of this clan, he was barred from monastic office.

Mo(r)yang was one of the six villages that provided the founders of the Ch'in Han. It was controlled by the Son clan,[210] a clan which provided queens for a number of Silla kings, including the second consort of King Chinp'yǒng.[211] Although other clans such as the Kim and the Pak came from this district,[212] the Son were the controlling clan. Therefore, as a distaff relative of royalty through the Son clan, Wǒnch'ǔk could possibly have been counted as a descendant (son) of the Silla kings as Song Fu stated. Maybe Song and Ch'oe misunderstood the clan name Son for descendant (son).

If Wǒnch'ǔk was a descendant of a clan that provided consorts to the royal family of Silla, a clan later called the Son,[213] they may have had some specious claim to descent from the Feng clan of Northern Yan. This Feng clan had provided a consort to the Northern Wei ruler, Gaozong (r. 453–465). She later obtained real power as empress dowager, and at least in China, this clan was led by women.[214] If the Son had such a claim, precedents like that of the Feng in Northern Wei may have worried the Silla king about the strength of his distaff relatives, the Son, leading to the exclusion of Wǒnch'ǔk from office along with his clan members.

However, for early Silla society, which only introduced Chinese-style surnames for the aristocracy in the sixth century because of the needs of diplomatic exchanges with China, surnames were not firmly fixed as in China, and so "a descent group was hard pressed to identify itself with one single surname", which is why the *Samguk yusa* gives three surnames for Ich'adon (506–527).[215] Therefore, an apparent conflict over surnames is simply a product of viewing Silla society through Chinese eyes. Wǒnch'ǔk may well have been a descendant of a P'ung clan and of the Silla royal family, or of the Son, for Silla aristocratics may have claimed descent from both the maternal and paternal lines.[216]

Birth and Youth

According to Song Fu, Wǒnch'ǔk must have been born around 613 and was put into the care of the Buddhist Order at a very tender age, three years old in Song's account, and still in "swaddling clothes" according to Ch'oe. This must have occurred around 615 or 616. If he was of a prominent clan, as his taboo name Mun'a (Literary Elegance) suggests, the dedication of such a young child to Buddhism must have been motivated by a significant event. Perhaps the momentous event was the death of the queen of King Chinhǔng in 615. A native of Mo(r)yang, she died a nun.[217] The old empress dowager's death may have induced the second consort of Chinp'yǒng, who was of the Son clan of Mo(r)yang, to give one of her children to the Order in order to obtain merit for the departed woman.

Representing Wŏnch'ŭk

By 627, when Wŏnch'ŭk was around fifteen, he went to China by sea, most likely as a novice student. Monks were regularly sent from Silla as students to study in Chang'an, although this may have been difficult in 627, for monks arriving later in 634 were still suspected of being spies and were temporarily detained.[218] However, an official delegation from the Silla court arrived in the Tang capital sometime in late 626 or early 627. It was probably sent to congratulate Li Shimin, known formally as Emperor Taizong, on his accession to the throne in September 626.[219] As this delegation included sons of the Silla ruling class sent for an education in Chang'an, the teenage Wŏnch'ŭk, a novice with connections to the Silla royal house, was probably a member of the party, which explains why he was not detained.

At this stage in its history, Silla was attempting to build a centralised state with an educated bureaucracy. As part of this state-building, Silla took every chance to send young members of the elite, both lay and monk, to learn the requisite knowledge in Tang China. Monks were the earliest regular students from the Korean Peninsula to study in China. Between 613 and 614, the preceding Chinese Sui dynasty appointed prominent monks to teach these foreign students, most of whom came from southern Korea, the tenets of Buddhism.[220] The sons of the royal houses of states on the peripheries of China such as Silla, Paekche, Koguryŏ and Tibet only formally sent these students to the National College in 632.[221] As full diplomatic relations between Silla and Tang only commenced in 640,[222] Wŏnch'ŭk's probable inclusion in the delegation and his acceptance by the Tang officials must have been exceptional, attesting to his royal connections and his outstanding abilities. No doubt it was expected of him that he return to Silla to teach what he had learnt during his sojourn in China, otherwise he would not have been sent.

Chang'an, the Tang capital, was the cosmopolitan centre of East Asia, "the greatest city in the world", and was the model for all of the states developing in the region. It attracted merchants, students, missionary monks, political leaders and entertainers from all over Asia, as distant as Arabia in the west, India to the south and Japan to the east.[223] For a young Buddhist novice from the still relatively backward state of Silla which was located in an isolated corner of the Korean Peninsula, the massive, vibrant city of Chang'an would have been exciting. It was the location of rapidly evolving systems of Buddhist doctrine of extraordinary complexity and profundity, which must have fascinated and intrigued the youthful student. Indeed, through his connections, he soon became a pupil of two of the leading Buddhist scholars of the day.

Education

The young novice received instruction in the scholastic forms of Buddhism from Fachang (567–645) and Sengbian (568–642), with whom the young Xuanzang had also studied for some time before 629.[224] Both the elder monks were experts on the *Shelun* and other shastra literature[225] and attracted foreign students, with the Silla prince who became the monk Chajang (608–686) visiting Fachang sometime between 635 and 640.[226] Both teachers were appointed verifiers of meanings for the translation projects of Prabhākaramitra.[227] Sengbian was ordered by the emperor to reside in Hongfu Monastery, which was commissioned in 632 by Tang Taizong to commemorate his late mother, and it was this monastery where Xuanzang was first persuaded to live and begin his translations.[228] Fachang was the precepts teacher to the Empress Dowager in 635, and he used his position to resist Taizong's attempts to place new controls over the Buddhist Order, a move which seems to have hastened Fachang's death on July 24, 645.[229] Fachang was a most popular cleric, for his funeral attracted tens of thousands of mourners, including eminent statesmen, and miracles were attributed to him.[230]

Therefore, through the aegis of these two scholars, Wŏnch'ŭk would have received a thorough grounding in the Vijñānavāda theories of the Shelun and Dilun schools, and perhaps some insight or practice in the verification of the meaning of translations. To be a verifier of the meaning of a translation required a thorough understanding of the theories of Buddhism first, for in the translation process, the chief translator in the central hall rendered the scripture into an oral Chinese translation, and then the participants debated the sense of the passage. The results of these lectures and debates were transcribed and sent to the composers of the literary text in the east hall. Then the draft translation in literary Chinese was forwarded to the verifiers of the meaning, who had participated in the debates, in the west hall, to verify that the meaning corresponded to Buddhist principles and did not violate the content of the oral explanations and the outcomes of the debates. Therefore, the verifiers had to be skilled debaters, perceptive readers and thoroughly versed in Buddhist doctrine. They interrogated the text and the translators to be certain that the original Sanskrit or Indian sense was preserved in the translation.[231] As Wŏnch'ŭk later became one of the eleven verifiers for some of Xuanzang's translations, he must have been among the top twenty or thirty Buddhist scholars in China, for they were selected from all over the country.[232]

Ordination

Wŏnch'ŭk was probably not yet fully ordained as a monk, for that ceremony usually occurred around the age of twenty, for Wŏnch'ŭk around 633. It was possibly in order to be ordained in his native country of Silla that he may have returned around 632–633, the end of the reign of King Chinp'yŏng. In this he may have been fulfilling his duty to transmit what he had learnt in Chang'an over the previous four or five years. If we are to give credence to the *Samguk yusa*, he was there refused a monastic position, and perhaps ordination.

Representing Wŏnch'ŭk

Disappointed and frustrated at the lack of opportunity for a Buddhist monastic career in his homeland, he may have returned to Chang'an soon afterwards. About this time, probably in 635, he was legally licensed as an ordained monk and ordered to live in Yuanfa Monastery, Chang'an. He was probably ordained with the monk name Wenye (K. Mun'a), which was thereafter his usual name. Song Fu writes that Wenye was his taboo name, and that his personal name was Wŏnch'ŭk.

At the time of ordination, monks took a name, which was often called a *hui* or mourning name, probably because a monk was supposed to have died to the lay life once they entered the Śākya clan or Buddhist Order. Most monks who were near contemporaries of Wŏnch'ŭk were generally known by their *hui*. Thus Xuanzang was a *hui*.[233] The Tiantai School leader, Zhiyi, had as his *hui* Zhiyi, while his *zi* was De'an.[234] Falin was the *hui* of that monk who defended Buddhism against the Taoists in 639.[235] Similarly, the Huayan master Fazang who was sponsored by Empress Wu had a *zi* of Xianshou, but he was usually known by his *hui*, Fazang.[236] But there was some confusion over these names, for Mingxiang states that Xuanzang's *hui* was Yi and his *zi* Xuanzang,[237] and a lay report wrote, "the monk with the *zi* Xuanzang".[238] Here the *hui* probably refers to Xuanzang's lay personal name.

Wenye may also have been a taboo name (*hui*) because it was not used by Wŏnch'ŭk's contemporaries or by Wŏnch'ŭk in his own writings. The reason for this may have been the need to avoid the posthumous mourning name of Emperor Taizong who died in 649. His posthumous title was Wen Huangdi, the "Cultured August Emperor". To avoid the character *wen*, Wŏnch'ŭk and others probably stopped using Wenye.[239] The names of emperors that had to be avoided were their personal *hui*, such as Shimin for Taizong and Zhi (Li Zhi) for Gaozong, and their shrine or mourning *hui*. However, in 679, Gaozong permitted Buddhist translators to use these characters prohibited because they were in late emperors' names, which were called "state *hui*".[240] Therefore Wŏnch'ŭk seems to have adopted the name Xuanze (K. Hyŏnch'ŭk), possibly around the year 650.

The Translation Project under Xuanzang

He may have come back to study with his previous masters until sometime before Xuanzang returned from India in 645, an event which Wŏnch'ŭk anticipated in a dream. He certainly had gained great competence in translation and the technical literature of Buddhist scholasticism. Xuanzang arrived in Chang'an on February 8, 645 to a major reception. He proceeded to Luoyang, the secondary capital, to meet Emperor Taizong a month later.

However, Wŏnch'ŭk may have previously left Chang'an to reside in Luoyang under the name Xuanze, for in 730 Zhisheng stated that when Taizong ordered Xuanzang to start translating at Hongfu Monastery, a Xuanze of Tiangong Monastery, Luoyang, was summoned as one of the drafters of the translation.[241] This might imply that he had changed his name before 645 when he began to work with Xuanzang. Perhaps he had to avoid the posthumous name of the pro-Buddhist empress, Wende, who died in 636.[242] This probably explains why Ch'oe Ch'iwŏn consistently used Mun'a in the body of his vow text for Wŏnch'ŭk, for the prohibition did not apply under another dynasty in a different country. Thus, in contrast, the cataloguers mention that Xuanze was the amanuensis for translations of the *Shiyi mian shenchou xin jing* made at Daci'en Monastery in 656 and the *Abidamo fazhilun* made between 657 and 660 at Yuhua Monastery.[243] The prefaces to the vast translation of the *Mahāprajñāpāramitā sūtra* in 600 juan were all written by a Xuanze, now of Ximing Monastery, and as Ennin (in China from 840) says Dasheng Ji avoided Xuanze by going to Mt. Wutai, this Xuanze was probably Wŏnch'ŭk.[244]

Summoned from Luoyang to Chang'an, Wŏnch'ŭk found a fellow spirit in Xuanzang, immediately taking an interest in the new ideas and texts the pilgrim brought from India. He was clearly valued for his expertise in the Prajñāpāramitā literature, which explains why he was asked to write prefaces for translations of the most extensive text in this class. From around 656 or 658 he was a resident of Ximing Monastery, and he began work on the translation of the *Mahāprajñāpāramitā sūtra* in 659 and finished it in 663. Xuanzang had shifted his residence to a monastery on the outskirts of Chang'an in 659,[245] so either the translation was carried out at a distance with the verifiers in a separate monastery, or Wŏnch'ŭk commuted. He may, of course, have taken up residence at this other monastery, the Yuhuasi, which was located to the north of the city.

Because Wŏnch'ŭk had serious misgivings about the Dharmapala/Xuanzang version of Vijñānavāda, it is possible there were attempts to exclude him from the translation work on the *Vijñāptimātratāsiddhi śāstra/Cheng weishi lun* and the *Yogācārabhūmi śāstra* as Zanning related. The lectures mentioned by Zanning were in effect the debates and lectures that took place at the initial stages of translation. As too much disputation would have slowed the projects, gate-keepers were used to keep out the fractious or the simply curious, who apparently were a nuisance.[246] Dasheng Ji may have wished to exclude his rival from the debates, for those privileged to participate in them had the first chance to lecture on the new works before they were even published. Yet it is clear Wŏnch'ŭk gained access to this material, for he was apparently able to give lectures on it before Dasheng Ji, which caused a rift between the two. Perhaps Xuanzang separated them deliberately.

In any case, Wŏnch'ŭk may have learnt some Sanskrit and perhaps Khotanese through the translation process. It is alleged, and possibly his variants on the text of the *Cheng weishi lun* mentioned by Huizhao indicate this, that Wŏnch'ŭk directly consulted a commentary by Vasubandhu's pupil

Gopa, which was not translated into Chinese. He also supposedly amended Xuanzang's "translation" of the *Heart Sutra* adding one word to expand the object of a verb. He also seems to have known that the word *jie* is not a contraction of the Sanskrit *gāthā*, but of a Khotanese word.[247] At the very least he had some knowledge of languages other than Korean and Chinese, but his Sanskrit comprehension was probably only very elementary.[248]

Wǒnch'ŭk continued to reside at Ximing Monastery after being ordered to live there by Gaozong in 658. He pursued his translation work with Xuanzang's team until the master translator died in 664, after which the translation project was halted on imperial orders and all the monks involved sent back to their monasteries of registration.[249]

During the latter part of this period, he came into contact with eminent, pro-Buddhist officials who were probably attracted by Xuanzang and his project. Wǒnch'ŭk wrote two prefaces to a collection on Buddhism in two parts, the *Chanlin miaozhi* ["Marvellous Records of the Meditation Grove"], which had ten chapters and was in twenty fascicles. This work was based on an exhaustive search of Buddhist literature. The author was a high official who held the ranks of Grand Scribe of the Orchid Pavilion (Director of the Palace Library) and Policy Advisor of the Left (an attendant on the emperor whose role was to criticise the emperor's misdeeds). The author's name is not given by Xuanze, but as there was only one Policy Advisor of the Left in this period, the author was undoubtedly Lu Dunxin, who gained this post in the period between 661 and 663. Lu Dunxin was the son of the renowned Confucian scholar Lu Deming. As Policy Advisor of the Left, he was close to the emperor, and was ordered by the emperor to compile this work. He commenced it on July 27, 663 and completed it on June 3, 664. This is probably why Xuanze in his second preface directly addressed the emperor, Gaozong.[250] Xuanze's preface to the first half of the collection outlines the myth and life of the Buddha, and a brief history of Buddhism via Emperor Asoka to China; the second describes the work and its origins. It was included by the historian, Daoxuan, who was abbot of Xuanze's monastery of registration, the Ximingsi, into the *Guang hongming ji*, which Daoxuan compiled in 664, the very same year in which the prefaces were written.[251]

Retreat

Xuanze's activities retreat into obscurity until he was ordered to assist Divākara with translation of Buddhist scriptures in 680. In the interim he probably wrote more of his extensive commentaries at Ximing Monastery, and he may have changed his name from Xuanze to Yuance (Wǒnch'ŭk), for the catalogues now use this name for him in all cases after the death of Xuanzang.[252] He may have been showing his respect for the great master by avoiding his *hui*.

A number of factors may have combined to make Wŏnch'ŭk go into a form of voluntary retirement. Firstly, Xuanzang died in 664, and the imperial patronage of Buddhist scholarship came to an end in 665 as Gaozong turned increasingly to Daoism and Empress Wu manipulated Buddhism for her own aggrandisement.[253] Furthermore, the abbot of Ximing Monastery, where Wŏnch'ŭk was registered, died in 666. Internationally, Silla, which had been a staunch ally of Tang China since 640 – jointly attacking Koguryŏ and Paekche in concert with Tang forces – in the 670s turned against its erstwhile ally and gradually forced the Chinese to withdraw from the Korean Peninsula. Gaozong even considered an attack on Silla in 678, but did not do so, leaving Silla to occupy nearly all of the peninsula.[254] In 674 and 675, there were battles between the Tang and Silla forces, for which Silla supposedly apologised after being "defeated".[255] Relations with Silla must have remained icy for some time, for according to the *Jiu Tangshu*, the next Silla delegation to the Tang court did not arrive until 728, and the *Zizhi tongjian* only mentions missions going from Tang to establish or confirm the son of the late king as new king in 681 and again in 693.[256] Therefore, Wŏnch'ŭk, as a native of Silla, may have wished to keep a low profile, and retreated into the cloisters to write commentaries, and into the mountains to meditate. Certainly, none of the texts from the period that refer to him mention that he was from Silla.

Another reason for Wŏnch'ŭk's retirement may have been the jealousy of Dasheng Ji, whom Xuanzang had favoured. So tense did the relation become after Xuanzang's death in 664 that Dasheng Ji apparently left for Mt Wutai, probably in part to avoid Wŏnch'ŭk who was based in Chang'an.[257] The recriminations between the two leading clerics and their supporters were intense. Allegations were made that Ji was not merely a scholar, but also a libertine who took three carts with him on his travels, the first carrying his Buddhist books, the centre cart carrying himself, and the last transporting family retainers, sing-song girls, servants and food. The tale has Ji meet an old man, an incarnation of Mañjuśrī, the bodhisattva of Mt Wutai, who told him that to be accompanied by family retainers was not in accord with Buddhist regulations, causing Ji to repent suddenly and travel on alone. Zanning commented that this was most likely to have been an insult.[258] Zanning did not give Wŏnch'ŭk a similar benefit of the doubt concerning the allegations made against him, once again demonstrating his favouritism. Although the story of the three carts may have been derived from the metaphor of the three carts or three vehicles of Buddhism in the *Lotus sūtra*,[259] the fact that Ji went to Mt Wutai and Wŏnch'ŭk into the fastnesses of the Zhongnan Mountains for eight years,[260] probably in the period ca. 670+ to ca. 680, suggests a deliberate distancing between the two men, which in turn may have provoked slanderous allegations from the two camps in their absence.

Thus, sometime during this interval, Wŏnch'ŭk retreated into the seclusion of the Zhongnan Mountains to the south of Chang'an, presumably to meditate after his taxing translation tasks or to escape the controversies of which he was a part, or even to avoid the increasingly anti-Buddhist actions of Gaozong from 666, or anti-Silla sentiment. Again, it was probably no accident that he went to Yunji Monastery and beyond, for Chajang (608–686), who had already studied with Fachang, Wŏnch'ŭk's earlier teacher, had some time after 638 spent three years to the east of that monastery in a hermitage.[261]

Resumption of Translation Activities

Not long before 680, his pupils pleaded he return to Ximing Monastery to teach. Soon after, he and several of his former collaborators were again ordered to form a translation team of five people to assist Divākara, a missionary from Central India, who, possibly on Wŏnch'ŭk's urging, in 679 requested Empress Wu that a project be set up on the model of that headed by Xuanzang.[262] According to a preface written by Wŏnch'ŭk, now using the name by which he has usually been known to posterity, to what was presumably the first scripture translated, the ruler's request for the translation to be carried out in Hongfu Monastery, was made on December 11, 680. This work was completed in 681, on January 3.[263] The team did not include Dasheng Ji, who died in 682, and so may already have been too ill. The work continued until Divākara's death in 687.[264] There is a gap in our information on Wŏnch'ŭk's activities until 693, when he became a verifier for Bodhiruci's translations at Fo shouji Monastery in Luoyang.[265] In 695 he was also ordered by Empress Wu to aid the Khotanese Śikṣānanda (652–710) make a revised translation of the *Avataṃsaka sūtra* (Ch. *Huayan jing*) from a new Sanskrit text. This was evidently an extension of the Divākara and Bodhiruci team. However, almost as soon as the work on this massive eighty-juan work began, Wŏnch'ŭk died on August 25, 696, aged eighty-four.

His ashes were buried at Xiangshan Monastery, Longmen, near Luoyang, but his mourning pupils from Chang'an, both Chinese and Korean, desiring a *memento mori*, brought his bone fragments and śarīra back to the Chang'an area, burying them under a stupa to the south of the city in the mountain ranges he so loved.

Legacy

Wŏnch'ŭk's reputation remained high in some quarters for a considerable time. He was appreciated by everyone for his abilities in verifying translations, which probably justifies Ch'oe Ch'iwŏn's comment that "every time an Indian missionary was received, (the court) summoned him". His fame reached not just the Chinese rulers such as Taizong, Gaozong and Empress Wu, but even to his native Silla, with King Sinmun requesting Empress Wu that he be permitted to return sometime between 685 and 687. So valuable was he to the translation projects that the empress refused.

From the reactions of some of his Ci'en School rivals, it is clear that Wŏnch'ŭk's commentaries and criticisms of the Dharmapāla/Xuanzang version of Vijñānavāda had aroused sympathy and support. His broad perspectives on Vijñānavāda and Buddhist scholasticism in general gained him respect, for his writings were known from Dunhuang to Japan.

Wŏnch'ŭk had several pupils, including Cishan, who is only known from Song Fu's inscription, and Sŭngjang who continued in his master's footsteps, writing commentaries and working as a verifier in the translation projects of Yijing from 703 until 710 and in that of Bodhiruci from 706 to 713. Sŭngjang may have studied under Xuanzang just before 664, and only after became a pupil of Wŏnch'ŭk, for his writings reveal the influence of both camps of Vijñānavāda.[266] Wŏnch'ŭk's other Silla pupil, Tojŭng, was a fierce champion of his teacher's theories, thereby attracting a strong counter-attack from the Ci'en School. His works are mainly known from the quotations used by his rivals. It is possible that this polemic was conducted over a distance, for Tojŭng returned to Silla in 692.[267]

Taehyŏn, who is known to have attended the Silla court in 753 and was ordered by the king to live in Pulguk Monastery in 774, and who is sometimes alleged to have been a pupil of Tojŭng, has been called the founder of Korean Yogācāra. Given his dates, he was more likely to have been in the second generation from Tojŭng. Taehyŏn wrote over fifty commentaries and used the works of Wŏnch'ŭk, Tojŭng, Dasheng Ji and Xuanzang, evaluating their theories fairly. His books impressed the Chinese and were mentioned by the Japanese. He had a number of pupils, whose line continued into the Koryŏ period.[268]

Wŏnch'ŭk thus was not forgotten in Korea, for Ch'oe Ch'iwŏn wrote the vow text for Wŏnch'ŭk's commemoration, and the monks of Pulguk Monastery at some time claimed to possess a lecture hall or study dedicated to three saints, of whom Wŏnch'ŭk was one.[269]

In China, the Ci'en School seems to have gone into a rapid decline in the third or fourth generation from Dasheng Ji under the shocks from the An Lushan Rebellion (755+), and even Dasheng Ji's commentary on the *Cheng weishi lun* was lost by the Huichang Persecution (842+).[270] Moreover, Huayan critics also undermined the influence of Vijñānavāda.

In the meantime, the Ximing School of Wŏnch'ŭk maintained a precarious foothold in the north-west away from the rebellion. The monk Tankuang (ca. 700+ – ca. 782+),[271] who studied at Ximing Monastery after having studied Vijñānavāda elsewhere, seems to have subscribed to many of Wŏnch'ŭk's views, possibly learning them from Daoyin (d. 740),[272] who he describes as of a "different place but the same learning" as Zhizhou (668–723), a pupil of Huizhao.[273] As Daoyin was a master of the Vijñānavāda and taught for a while at Ximing Monastery,[274] the link between the two monks

Representing Wŏnch'ŭk

is almost certain. With the chaos brought by the An Lushan Rebellion, Tankuang left for the north-west, finally resting in Dunhuang,[275] where around 782 he wrote a text answering twenty-two questions on Mahayana Buddhism posed by the Tibetan king, Trisong Detsen.[276] Tankuang's eminence in Dunhuang and Tibet led in turn to Wŏnch'ŭk's commentary on the *Saṃdhinirmocana sūtra* being translated by Chödrub (ca. 755–ca. 849) into Tibetan circa 820.[277] This is how this commentary came to influence Tsongkhapa (1357–1419), who cited the translated commentary in his *Lekshé nyingpo* and elsewhere.[278]

Wŏnch'ŭk was remembered in Japan through the works of the Hossō School, which followed Huizhao's criticisms of Wŏnch'ŭk in books such as the *Jō yuishiki ryōgitō zōmyōki* by Zenju (724–797), or much later in the *Jō yuishiki kundokki* by Kōhan (1655–1723).[279] Wŏnch'ŭk's *Cheng weishi lun shu* was copied in Japan in 748, but is no longer extant.[280]

Conclusion

The supplementary representation of Wŏnch'ŭk presented above demonstrates how an influential individual may be misrepresented directly and by omission. The selective focus on Xuanzang and Dasheng Ji has left Wŏnch'ŭk, his ideas and scholarship, in an obscurity of the marginalised, which has resulted in more than the usual difficulties in creating coherence from the extant accounts and in making his life intelligible to modern readers. However, some context can be given to the ideas and writings of Wŏnch'ŭk despite the limitations of the sources. His commentaries are proof of his intelligence as well as linguistic and literary skills. Moreover, the life presented above demonstrates the obstacles Wŏnch'ŭk had to overcome in his pursuit of Buddhist knowledge and salvation. Furthermore, it dispels the pall cast over him by the slanderous Zanning account and places him in a far more human context. There is evidence of the respect he gave to and received from Xuanzang, and that emperors and kings requested his services, which meant that he was not an inconsequential figure. Certainly, there are enough hints about his diligence, intellect and refusal to be swayed by popular scholastic trends, even those taught by his master, and reverence from his pupils and contemporaries, to refute the suggestion that he has to be represented only as a collective or literary image and not as an historical individual. Although his personality cannot be known in detail or a psychological portrait of him be drawn to the requirements of modern taste, his thought should no longer exist in a disembodied, ahistorical limbo. While his life cannot be known at the absolute level of perfect truth which is available, according to Buddhists, only to the enlightened, it can be known at the conventional or relative level of worldly truth through analysis which removes delusory imagination, just as a viewer sees the illusion created by a magician but knows it to be false even though the means of the trickery is not immediately known.²⁸¹ Although such a biographical representation cannot convey perfect knowledge, neither does it fall prey to imagination which is attachment to representation. Rather, such a biography is written on the understanding it is dealing with representation and not an immediately perceived absolute truth.

Appendix: The Attribution of the Vow Text to Ch'oe Ch'iwŏn

There have been doubts raised about the correctness of the attribution of the *Text of the Death Anniversary of Wŏnch'ŭk* (hereafter DW) to Ch'oe Ch'iwŏn. Firstly, the DW has only been found in the *Hwaŏm Sa sajŏk* ("The historical gazetteer of Hwaŏm Monastery", hereafter HSS) of 1636, which was first printed in 1697. Ch'oe had no demonstrable connection with Hwaŏm Monastery on Mt. Chiri. Moreover, the compiler of the HSS, trading on the similarity of the name of his monastery, Hwaŏm Sa, with that of Hwaŏm Pulguk Sa, included, sometimes with distortions or omissions of the word Pulguk from the titles, a number of texts attributed to Ch'oe Ch'iwŏn that were originally associated with Pulguk Monastery, which was situated on the outskirts of distant Kyŏngju.²⁸² The HSS includes eight texts attributed to Ch'oe Ch'iwŏn, five of which can also be found in the Pulguk Monastery records; three in the *Pulguk Sa sajŏk* and five in the *Pulguk Sa kogŭm ch'anggi* (hereafter PSC).²⁸³ The *Pulguk Sa sajŏk* is claimed to have been written in 1046 by Iryŏn, the author of the *Samguk yusa*, a major Buddhist "history" of early Korea, which is impossible, for Iryŏn lived from 1206-1289. The text rather dates from after the death of Iryŏn, possibly as late as 1368, and it was re-edited in 1708.²⁸⁴ The PSC was written in 1740 based on earlier sources, but it contains many errors in dates and deliberate distortions, in an attempt to create the impression that Wŏnch'ŭk was one of three saints to whom a lecture hall was dedicated.²⁸⁵ Comparison of the "Hwaŏmgyŏng sahoe wŏnmun" (Vow of the *Avataṃsaka sūtra* Society) that is recorded in the *Wŏnjong mullyu* of Ŭich'ŏn (1055-1101) with that in the PSC and the HSS reveals that the PSC has an incorrect date, has inserted an entry on Wŏnch'ŭk and changed a character in the name of a monk Hyŏnjun so that it coincided with the name of Ch'oe Ch'iwŏn's elder brother, Hyŏnjun, who was an eminent monk in Haein Monastery.²⁸⁶ As all the additions or embellishments seem to concern Wŏnch'ŭk, Kim Poksun thinks that texts, possibly by Ch'oe Ch'iwŏn, from the Hwaŏm School headquarters of Haein Monastery where Hyŏnjun was resident, were appropriated or invented by the compilers of the PSC or its sources to strengthen Pulguk Monastery's claim to being a Hwaŏm Monastery, even though it was originally a Yogācāra School monastery. Thus texts were falsely attributed to Ch'oe Ch'iwŏn to raise the profile of Wŏnch'ŭk as a monk connected to the monastery. As a consequence, the DW has been suspected of being a forgery.²⁸⁷

Representing Wŏnch'ŭk

Kim Sanghyŏn has countered that Pulguk Monastery was not truly a Yogācāra School monastery, for the title *Yuga* is really the name of a monk from the monastery, and not the name of the school the monastery belonged to. However, Kim Sanghyŏn is quoting from a text that Kim Poksun thinks is corrupted. That monk, Yuga, is quoted by Kyunyŏ (923–973) in respect of Hwaŏm thought, and Kim Sanghyŏn writes that the name P'yŏhun in the list of the three saints to whom the hall was dedicated refers to a well-known Hwaŏm School monk. Therefore, Wŏnch'ŭk is listed among the three because he was involved, albeit for a short time, in the translation of the *Huayan jing*.[288] Moreover, the HSS text has inserted a reference here to Hwaŏm Monastery on Mt. Chiri, which is definitely out of place.[289] Hence, there are question marks over both sets of monastic records, but they are insufficient to dismiss the DW as a forgery or false ascription.

Firstly, there are many overlaps between the texts, confusions and competing claims; but the HSS contains two "death anniversary (vow) texts" attributed to Ch'oe Ch'iwŏn, one for Ŭisang and the other for Wŏnch'ŭk. The eulogy for Ŭisang is also found in the WM by Ŭich'ŏn with a slightly different title but identical content.[290] In other words, the "anniversary text for Ŭisang" existed in the times of Ŭich'ŏn (1055–1101), and as the WM was a collection of texts concerned only with Huayan/Hwaŏm (Wŏnjong is a synonym for Hwaŏm), and only three out of the twenty-two chapters of it are extant,[291] the DW was probably not included and so cannot be found therein.

Secondly, the style of the two "death anniversary texts" is very similar, and much of the distinctive vocabulary of the DW is shared with other works known to be by Ch'oe Ch'iwŏn. This suggests that the "death anniversary texts" were by a common author, almost certainly Ch'oe Ch'iwŏn. Even Kim Poksun considers the text dedicated to Ŭisang a genuine Ch'oe Ch'iwŏn piece that was written in 885 at the request of a Hwaŏm society of Haein Monastery.[292] Therefore, the text for Wŏnch'ŭk may have been written around the same time in Kyŏngju, for Ch'oe wrote a "Hwaŏm Society Vow" for the monks, including Kyŏl'ŏn, of Hwangbok Monastery, in the capital,[293] the monastery where Ŭisang had lived and been first tonsured.[294] In addition, as the Pŏpsang (Faxiang) lineage or Yogācāra was influential in Kyŏngju (through the activities of Wŏnch'ŭk's pupil Tojŭng, and Taehyŏn, the so-called founder of Korean Yogācāra, who was active in Kyŏngju and at Pulguk Monastery in the 750s to 770s), stronger possibly than the Hwaŏm School,[295] Ch'oe may well have written this eulogy between 885 and 890.[296]

So even though the text of the DW did not reach China or Song Fu, the vow text for Wŏnch'ŭk should also be considered genuine because of the similarity in style and language with other texts by Ch'oe. It only came to be recorded in the HSS because confusion between the names of Hwaŏm Pulguk Sa and Hwaŏm Sa led the compiler to include virtually everything written by Ch'oe about Buddhism as relevant to his monastery.

Notes

1 Shōju Inaba, "On Chos-grub's Translation of the *Chieh-shen-mi-ching-shu*," in Leslie S. Kawamura and Keith Scott, eds, *Buddhist Thought and Asian Civilization* (Emeryville: Dharma Publishing, 1977), 109.
2 Kim Tongju, *Yuance zhi weishixue guan* (Taibei: Huiwen tang, 1987), 19–25, although most of Kim's comments are related to the *Heart Sutra*, which was not a translation according to Jan Nattier, "The *Heart Sutra*: A Chinese Apocryphal Text," *Journal of the International Association of Buddhist Studies* 15:2 (1992), 153–223.
3 O Hyŏnggŭn, "Wŏnch'ŭk Pŏpsa ŭi sinsiksŏl e taehayŏ," *Pulgyo hakbo* 13 (1976), 7–8, especially the quote by Taehyŏn of Wŏnch'ŭk to the effect that Buddha knew there were many levels of representation or consciousness, but preached only one, mind. Then, 900 years later Asanga and Vasubandhu claimed that there were the perceived and perceiving aspects to consciousness. Then Dignāga and others added the self-conscious or self-witnessing aspect, and finally, 1,100 years after Buddha's death, Dharmapāla added a fourth aspect, the "consciousness of being self-conscious".
4 O Hyŏnggŭn, "Wŏnch'ŭk Pŏpsa ŭi sinsiksŏl e taehayŏ," 136, citing Zenju's *Jō yuishiki ryōgitō zōmyōki*. Terms given in their original language will be identified as follows: S. Sanskrit; K. Korean; and Ch. Chinese.
5 See the lament of Shōtarō Iida, "The Three Stupas of Ch'ang An," *Papers of the 1st International Conference on Korean Studies* (Seoul: The Academy of Korean Studies, 1980), 486–87, and "Who Best Can *Return* the Dharma-cakra?," *Indogaku bukkyōgaku kenkyū* 34:2 (1986), 942, note 9.
6 Holmes Welch, *The Buddhist Revival in China* (Cambridge, Ma.: Harvard University Press, 1969), 195–96. See also a doctoral thesis by Edward F. Connelly on Xiong Shili, Australian National University, 1978. However, Wŏnch'ŭk's *Jie shenmi jing shu* ["Commentary on the Saṃdhinirmocana sutra"] was published as a separate volume in 1922 by the Jinling Sutra Printery, one of the centres of the Faxiang revival. See Kim Yŏngt'ae, *Han'guk Pulgyo kojŏn myŏngcho ŭi se'gye* (Seoul: Minjoksa, 1994), 81.
7 O Hyŏnggŭn, "Wŏnch'ŭk Pŏpsa ŭi sinsiksŏl e taehayŏ," 136. Note the term school is used here for a line of theory and not so much as a separate organisation, although there were affiliations with certain teachers. It should be noted however, that Dasheng Ji's ancestry could be traced back to a Khotanese tribe (*Song Gaoseng zhuan*, T50.725b), which lessens the probability of differences between the two on ethnic grounds. Foreign monks or those with non-Chinese ancestry had an enormous influence on the formation of what are often held to have been distinctively Chinese Buddhist doctrines, for which see Ishii Kōsei, *Kegon shisō no kenkyū* (Tokyo: Shunjūsha, 1996), 10–11, 336–38.
8 Hatani Ryōtai, "Yuishikishū no iha – Chōsenkei no Yuishikishū," in *Hatani hakushi bukkyō ronsetsu senshū*, (1916; Tokyo: Daitōshuppansha, 1971), 856–857.
9 Kamata Shigeo, *Chōsen bukkyō no tera to rekishi* (Tokyo: Daihōrinkaku, 1980), 161. Faxiang or Dharmalakṣaṇa is another name used for Vijñānavāda, or more strictly, for the Ci'en School.
10 A sample would include Ko Ikjin, "Sŏmyŏng yusik ŭi kibon ipjang," *Tongguk sasang* 10:11 (1978), 33–45; O Hyŏnggŭn, "Wŏnch'ŭk Pŏpsa wa Ilsŭng sasang," *Han'guk pulgyohak* 2 (1976), 85–101; Sin Hyŏnsuk, "Tang Kyugi wa Silla Wŏnch'ŭk ŭi sangwisŏl yon'gu I," *Han'guk pulgyohak* 4 (1979), 77–94; Hwang Sŏnggi, "Wŏnch'ŭk ŭi yusikhakgwan e kwanhan yŏn'gu," *Pulgyo hakbo* 9 (1972), 15–66; Wŏn Ŭibŏm,

"Wŏnch'ŭk ŭi yusik sasang," in Sungsan Pak Kiljin paksa hwagap ki'nyŏm saŏphoe, ed., *Han'guk pulgyo sasangsa*, (Iri: Wŏn pulgyo sasang yŏn'guwŏn, 1975), 277–285; O Hyŏnggŭn, "Silla Wŏnch'ŭk Pŏpsa ŭi yusik sasang yŏn'gu," *Pulgyo hakbo* 25 (1988), 65–105. Also refer to other articles mentioned below.

11 *Enjiki Gejinmikkyōsho sanitsububun no kenkyū: kambun'yaku*, Kyoto: Hōzōkan, 1972.

12 Kim Yŏngt'ae, "Pulguksa ŭi Hwaŏm Pŏpsa Wŏnch'ŭk e taehayŏ," *Han'guk Pulgyohak* 19 (1994), 81. The text is reprinted in Tongguk Taehakkyo Han'guk Pulgyo ch'ŏnsŏ p'yŏnch'an wiwŏnhoe, comps, *Han'guk Pulgyo ch'ŏnsŏ*, 12 vols (Seoul: Tongguk Taehakkyo, 1992), 11:1–11:42 (hereafter, *HPC*). The compilers noted some slight differences between the two back-translations. Inaba's reconstruction is reprinted in the same series, 1.443ff.

13 O Hyŏnggŭn, "Wŏnch'ŭk Pŏpsa ŭi sinsiksŏl e taehayŏ," 7–8.

14 These three phases are outlined in Fukaura Seibun, *Yuishikigaku kenkyū*, 2 vols (Tokyo: Nagata bunshōdō, 1954), 1:199ff.

15 Shōtarō Iida, "A MuKung-hwa in Changan: A Study of the Life and Works of Wŏnch'ŭk (613–696), with special interest in the Korean contributions to the development of Chinese and Tibetan Buddhism," *Proceedings of the International Symposium Commemorating the 30th Anniversary of Korean Liberation* (Seoul: National Academy of Sciences, 1975), has not been available. However, I suspect that Shōtarō Iida, "Wŏnch'ŭk (613–696) ŭi saeng'ae wa chŏsŏ yŏn'gu: t'ŭk'i Han'guk'inŭrosŏ Chungguk Pulgyo wa T'ibet'an Pulgyo ŭi paljŏn e ibajihan ŏpjŏk ul chungsim hayŏ," *Kwangbok 30 chu'nyon chonghap haksul hoeŭi nonmunjip* (Seoul: Haksulwon, 1975), 161–79, is the same work in translation. See also Inaba Shōju, "Chōsen shusshin-sō Enjiki hosshi ni tsuite," *Chōsen gakuhō* 2 (1952), 41–51. Inaba, pages 48–49, gives four possible reasons for the criticisms of Wŏnch'ŭk: a reaction to his sharp intellect; Chinese chauvinism directed towards a foreigner; that he was not considered a true pupil of Xuanzang because he was much older than Dasheng Ji and so was not shown the same favour; and that the Ci'en School was made orthodox.

16 For dreams, see David J. Kalupahana, *Buddhist Philosophy: A Historical Analysis* (Honolulu: University Press of Hawaii, 1976), 144–45; Junjirō Takakusu, *The Essentials of Buddhist Philosophy*, Wing Tsit Chan and Charles A. Moore, eds, 3rd ed. (Honolulu: Office Appliance Co., 1956), 86–87.

17 Tongguk Taehakkyo Han'guk Pulgyo ch'ŏnsŏ p'yŏnch'an wiwŏnhoe, comps, *HPC*, 1:304c–1:306b.

18 Yokoyama Kōitsu, *Yuishiki no tetsugaku* (Kyoto: Heirakuji shoten, 1979), 5–6, 14–15. For some of the questions investigated in this school, see Richard H. Robinson, *The Buddhist Religion: A Historical Introduction* (Belmont: Dickenson Publishing, 1970), 70.

19 For example, Edward W. Said, *Orientalism: Western Concepts of the Orient*, (1978; Harmondsworth: Penguin, 1991), 20–22, 272–73; James Duncan and David Ley, "Introduction: Representing the Place of Culture," in James Duncan and David Ley, eds, *Place/Culture/Representation* (London: Routledge, 1993), 2–4, 8.

20 *Jie shenmi jingshu*, *HPC*, 1:218a12–18. See the analysis by Kim Tongju, *Yuance zhi weishixue guan*, 70 and 90–91, note 60. Cognition is here a translation of *liaobie* or *vijñāpti*, and pages 54 and 59 where it also equals *shi*.

21 Cf. H. Vaihinger, *The philosophy of 'As If'*, C.K. Ogden, trans., 2nd ed. (London: Routledge & Kegan Paul, 1935), 2, who writes, "consciousness is not to be compared to a mere passive mirror, which reflects rays . . ." It moulds all external stimuli "according to its own nature" and "independently changes what has been appropriated . . .".

22 D.T. Suzuki, *Laṅkāvatāra Sūtra* (London: Routledge & Kegan Paul, 1932), 234.
23 Yi Man, "Silla'in ch'ansul ŭi *Sŏng Yusiknon* so san'ibon pug'wŏn," *Pulgyo hakbo* 30 (1993), 394. This article contains all the quotes of lost commentaries on the *Cheng weishi lun* by Silla monks. For a free translation into English of the *Cheng weishi lun*, see Wei Tat, *Ch'eng Wei-shih Lun: Doctrine of Mere-Consciousness* (Hong Kong: Ch'eng Wei-Shih Lun Publication Committee, 1973), 13. This is adapted from the French translation of Louis de La Vallée Poussin, *Vijñāptimātratāsiddhi: La Siddhi de Hiuan-Tsang*, 2 vols (Paris: Paul Guenther, 1928–29).
24 Clarence H. Hamilton, trans., *Wei Er Shih Lun*, American Oriental Series, vol. 13 (New Haven: American Oriental Society, 1938), 10.
25 Hamilton, *Wei Er Shih Lun*, 13.
26 Cf. *Long Scroll* XLII, Yanagida Seizan, *Zen no goroku I: Daruma no goroku* (Tokyo: Chikuma shobō, 1969), 174: "If one sees appearances and remembers and discriminates [them], one will experience . . . [hell]."
27 Donald S. Lopez, Jr, "On the Interpretation of the Mahāyāna sūtras," in Donald S. Lopez, Jr, ed., *Buddhist Hermeneutics* (Honolulu: University of Hawaii Press, 1988), 54–55.
28 Lopez, "On the Interpretation of the Mahāyāna sūtras," 60, quoting Derrida. For this infinite regress in modern theory, see the "Epilogue" by David Ley and James Duncan in *Place/Culture/Representation*, 330.
29 Buddhists, both Indian and Chinese, generally condemned infinite regression (*anavastha* or *wuqiong*) as an error, Ishii, *Kegon shisō no kenkyū*, 299–300. Cf. Vaihinger, *The Philosophy of 'As If'*, 68 on the Greek sceptics. In Chinese, the classic expression of this was that words are to be discarded once the meaning is apprehended, just as the trap is put aside once the fish is caught. For Buddhists, all expedients are ultimately meant to be self-destructive, as the teachings are expedients to be treated just like a raft is left behind once the river is crossed. Cf. Michael Pye, *Skilful Means: A Concept in Mahayana Buddhism* (London: Duckworth, 1978), 136, 160. Buddhism itself will disappear as an expedient when all beings are enlightened, a utilitarianism close to that of Vaihinger.
30 Lopez, "On the Interpretation of the Mahāyāna sūtras," 60–61, 65.
31 Iida, "The Three Stupas of Ch'ang An," 944–46. Note that this idea inspired Tsongkhapa's work, the *Lekshé nyingpo* (*legs bshad snying po*), which deals with the distinction between provisional and definitive meaning or teaching, or what Lopez, in his excerpt from this book, translates as interpretable and definitive meaning, "On the Interpretation of the Mahāyāna sūtras," 66.
32 Cf. Said, *Orientalism*, 67; Donna Haraway, "The Promises of Monsters: A Regenerative Politics for Inappropriate/d Others," in Lawrence Grossberg, Cary Nelson and Paula A. Treichler, eds, *Cultural Studies* (New York: Routledge, 1992), 313.
33 Arthur F. Wright, "Biography and Hagiography: Hui-chiao's 'Lives of Eminent Monks'," *Silver Jubilee Volume of the Zinbun Kagaku Kenkyūsyō* (Kyoto: Kyoto University, 1954), 386, 391, 407; and Denis Twitchett, "Chinese Biographical Writing," in E.G. Pulleyblank and W.G. Beasley, eds, *Historians of China and Japan* (New York: Oxford University Press, 1961), 108, 112.
34 See, discussion of Régis Boyer's paper, "An Attempt to Define the Typology of Medieval Hagiography," in Hans Bekker-Nielsen, Peter Foote, Jørgen Højgaard Jørgensen, and Tore Nyberg, eds, *Hagiography and Medieval Literature: A Symposium* (Odense: Odense University Press, 1981), 161, distinguishing "legendary" and "historical" types of *vitae* in medieval Christian hagiographies. See also the discussion of Thai Buddhist hagiographers for similar themes

in Stanley Jeyaraja Tambiah, *The Buddhist Saints of the Forest and the Cult of Amulets: A Study in Charisma, Hagiography, Sectarianism and Millennial Buddhism* (Cambridge: Cambridge University Press, 1984), 124–27.
35 See T50.709a–710a.
36 Tambiah, *The Buddhist Saints of the Forest and the Cult of Amulets*, 116–17.
37 Erik Frauwallner, *The Earliest Buddhist Vinaya and the Beginnings of Buddhist Literature*, Serie Orientale Roma VIII (Rome, 1956), 62–65; A.K. Warder, *An Introduction to Indian Historiography* (Bombay: Popular Prakashan, 1972), 27–28.
38 Cao Shibang, "Zhongguo Fojiao shizhuan yu mulu yuanchu lüxue shamen zhi tantao: zhong," *Xinya xuebao* 7:1 (1965), 336; Huili, *DaTang Daci'ensi Sanzang Fashi zhuan*, T50.253c28, 254a3.
39 T50.446c–458c.
40 Mizuno Kōgen, ed., *Shin Butten kaidai jiten* (Tokyo: Shunjusha, 1966), 30–31.
41 Entry by Shioiri Hōdō in Mizuno, *Shin Butten kaidai jiten*, 227.
42 T50.753b6–8, 753b27–c2.
43 Cao Shibang, "Zhongguo Fojiao shizhuan yu mulu yuanchu lüxue shamen zhi tantao: xia," *Xinya xuebao* 7:2 (1966), 123–25.
44 *Tang Dajianfusi gusizhu fanjing dade Fazang heshang zhuan*, T50.280c28–281a5.
45 Kim Poksun, *Silla Hwaŏmjong yŏn'gu* (Seoul: Minjoksa, 1990), 211.
46 T50.285c2–17; cf. Kim Poksun, *Silla Hwaŏmjong yŏn'gu*, 198–201.
47 Cf. Albert A. Dalia, "The 'Political Career' of the Buddhist Historian Tsan-ning," in David W. Chappell, ed., *Buddhist and Taoist Practice in Medieval Chinese Society: Buddhist and Taoist Studies II* (Honolulu: University of Hawaii Press, 1987), 147, 153, 168. For stories of Zanning's flattery of the emperor, see the story, not accepted by Buddhists, by Ouyang Xiu of Zanning and the Song emperor going to burn incense at Xiangguo Monastery. When the emperor asked whether he should bow or not, Zanning replied, "Do not bow . . . because the present buddha [emperor] does not bow to a past buddha." See Guo Peng, *Song Yuan Fojiao* (Fuzhou: Fuzhou renmin chubanshe, 1981), 154–55.
48 Dalia, "The 'Political Career' of the Buddhist Historian Tsan-ning," 153, for those not thought to be harmonious.
49 Cf. Koichi Shinohara, "Two sources of Chinese Buddhist Biographies: Stupa Inscriptions and Miracle Stories," in Phyllis Granoff and Koichi Shinohara, eds, *Monks and Magicians: Religious Biographies in Asia* (Oakville, Ontario: Mosaic Press, 1988), 125.
50 Denis Twitchett, "Problems of Chinese Biography," in Arthur F. Wright and Denis Twitchett, eds, *Confucian Personalities* (Stanford: Stanford University Press, 1962), 29.
51 Denis Cosgrove and Moria Domosh, "Author and Authority: Writing the New Cultural Geography," in James Duncan and David Ley, eds, *Place/Culture/Representation*, 36.
52 Michel de Certeau, *The Mystic Fable, volume 1: The Sixteenth and Seventeenth Centuries*, Michael B. Smith, trans. (Chicago: University of Chicago Press, 1992), 10–11.
53 Bernard Faure, "Bodhidharma as Textual and Religious Paradigm," *History of Religions* 25:3 (1986), 188–90.
54 See de Certeau *The Mystic Fable*, 9, on the correlation and coherence in historiography.
55 *Weishi ershi lun*, T31.74aff. Mochizuki Shinkō, *Bukkyō Daijiten*, 10 vols (Tokyo: Sekai seiten kankō kyōkai, 1933–1936). Reprint, (Taibei: Diping xian chuban she, 1979), 2500b–2501a.

56 Wei, *Ch'eng Wei-shih Lun*, 145. A literal translation reads, "Although that which is evolved (out of the consciousness) of each separate being is distinct, their (what is evolved) characteristics resemble each other, and so the locality lacks differentiation ... [Dasheng Ji's *shuji* comments: 'It is like the karmic (results) such as mountains and rivers etc., which to masses of people are shared in their resemblances, and in their minds function together without barrier.']", see Takakusu, 86–87. Ālayavijñāna is a store-consciousness, rather like the unconscious, which contains "seeds".

57 Donald Weinstein and Rudolph M. Bell, *Saints and Society: The Two Worlds of Western Christendom, 1000–1700* (Chicago: University of Chicago Press, 1982), 1–2, 9. These two approaches are called here the realists and the nominalists. Cf. Albert Welter, "The Contextual Study of Chinese Buddhist Biographies: The Example of Yung-ming Yen-shou (904–975)," in Phyllis Granoff and Koichi Shinohara, eds, *Monks and Magicians*, 247–48, 261 on this practice of collective representation in respect of Buddhist biographies.

58 See Dale S. Wright, "Historical Understanding: The Ch'an Buddhist Transmission Narratives and Modern Historiography," *History and Theory* 31:1 (1992), 43–45. An example of this engagement is clear in the dedication by the authors to Korean Buddhist Research Institute, *Buddhist Thought in Korea* (Seoul: Dongguk University Press, 1994), which reads, "We dedicate this book to all the Masters of the past, present and future, who by their own realization and teachings, have inspired us on the path to enlightenment".

59 Faure, "Bodhidharma as Textual and Religious Paradigm," 188.

60 Bernard Faure, "Random Thoughts: Wonhyo's 'Life' as Thought," *Bulgyo Yongu* 11/12 (1995), 198–99, 222–23.

61 George M. Wilson, *Patriots and Redeemers in Japan: Motives in the Meiji Restoration* (Chicago: University of Chicago Press, 1992), xii, 74. Of course, the problem of the agent is clouded in Buddhism by the doctrine of no-ego. The actor then is an expedient and the ego is a misrepresentation created by karma and memory, and so even the notion of the agent in history should be a fiction. Soteriologically the notion of the agent is a barrier to enlightenment, but historiographically it is a necessary fiction.

62 Cf. Robert Young, *White Mythologies: Writing History and the West* (London: Routledge, 1990), 78.

63 Young, *White Mythologies*, 130, states that representation of necessity needs to have some connection with its putative object (in criticism of some elements of Said's *Orientalism*). Duncan and Ley, *Place/Culture/Representation*, 9, show that there are limitations on permitting informants their own voice.

64 George Steiner, *After Babel: Aspects of Language and Translation* (Oxford: Oxford University Press, 1975), 132, 134–37.

65 Vaihinger, *The Philosophy of 'As If'*, 3, 6.

66 Wright, "Biography and Hagiography", 385–86.

67 Peter Brown, *The Cult of the Saints: Its Rise and Function in Latin Christianity* (Chicago: University of Chicago Press, 1981), 80.

68 Régis Boyer, "An Attempt to Define the Typology of Medieval Hagiography," in Hans Bekker-Nielsen et al., eds, *Hagiography and Medieval Literature*, 28–29.

69 For Buddhist "biographies," Tambiah, *The Buddhist Saints of the Forest and the Cult of Amulets*, p. 116; Boyer, "An Attempt to Define the Typology of Medieval Hagiography," 28–38, on the typology of the hero.

70 Cf. Discussion of Boyer's paper in Bekker-Nielsen et al., *Hagiography and Medieval Literature*, 161–62. See also Tambiah, *The Buddhist Saints of the Forest and the Cult of Amulets*, 124–27.

71 Michael Goodrich, *Vita Perfecta: The Ideal of Sainthood in the Thirteenth Century*, Monographien zur Geschichte des Mittelalters, vol. 25 (Stuttgart: Anton Hiersemann, 1982), 28–30, 62–64.
72 Tambiah, *The Buddhist Saints of the Forest and the Cult of Amulets*, 113–16.
73 Boyer, "An Attempt to Define the Typology of Medieval Hagiography," 31.
74 Discussion of Boyer's paper, 162.
75 Goodrich, *Vita Perfecta*, 4–5.
76 Tambiah, *The Buddhist Saints of the Forest and the Cult of Amulets*, 125, quoting Donald A. Stauffer, *English Biography before 1700* (New York: Russell and Russell, 1964), 5.
77 Wright, "Biography and Hagiography", 385–86.
78 Cf. Wright, "Biography and Hagiography", 388–89; Boyer, "An Attempt to Define the Typology of Medieval Hagiography," 30, 33, 35; Tambiah, *The Buddhist Saints of the Forest and the Cult of Amulets*, 124.
79 Boyer, "An Attempt to Define the Typology of Medieval Hagiography," 31, and discussion of Boyer's paper, 162. Cf. Twitchett, "Problems of Chinese Biography," 34, on the absence of the "hero epic" in China, which possibly meant a lessening of the semi-divine image of humans.
80 Discussion of Boyer's paper, 162.
81 Tambiah, *The Buddhist Saints of the Forest and the Cult of Amulets*, 118–19.
82 Wright, "Biography and Hagiography", 386.
83 Cao Shibang, "Zhongguo Fojiao shizhuan yu mulu yuanchu lüxue shamen zhi tantao: shang," *Xinya xuebao* 6:1 (1964), 419.
84 Peter H. Lee, *Lives of Eminent Korean Monks: The Haedong Kosŭng chŏn* (Cambridge, Ma.: Harvard University Press, 1969), 10, 13.
85 Warder, *An Introduction to Indian Historiography*, 30.
86 Twitchett, "Problems of Chinese Biography," 34–35; Twitchett, "Chinese Biographical Writing," 112.
87 Twitchett, "Problems of Chinese Biography," 35.
88 Twitchett, "Problems of Chinese Biography," 32–33.
89 Twitchett, "Problems of Chinese Biography," 36–37.
90 Twitchett, "Problems of Chinese Biography," 25, 27–29; cf. Shinohara, "Two sources of Chinese Buddhist Biographies," 124.
91 Twitchett, "Problems of Chinese Biography," 31.
92 Cao, "Zhongguo Fojiao shizhuan yu mulu yuanchu lüxue shamen zhi tantao: zhong," 150; Lien-sheng Yang, "The Organization of Chinese Official Historiography," in E.G. Pulleyblank and W.G. Beasley, eds, *Historians of China and Japan*, 48; Wright, "Biography and Hagiography," 387–88; Shinohara, "Two sources of Chinese Buddhist Biographies," 213–14, who shows that stupa miracle stories were "used in two different ways by Tao-hsüan, one as an equivalent of miracle stories and the other as biographies. Tao-hsüan seems to have known how to distinguish between the 'biographies' that were no more than miracle stories written in the form of biographies . . . and the more authentic biographies, which also happened to contain stories of miracles".
93 Cao, "Zhongguo Fojiao shizhuan yu mulu yuanchu lüxue shamen zhi tantao: xia," 126, 150; Cao, "Zhongguo Fojiao shizhuan yu mulu yuanchu lüxue shamen zhi tantao: zhong," 432–34; Wright, "Biography and Hagiography," 384–85.
94 Shinohara, "Two Sources of Chinese Buddhist Biographies," 120–22, 194, note 3; I have modified the priorities.
95 Cf. Shinohara, "Two Sources of Chinese Buddhist Biographies," 126.
96 Wright, "Biography and Hagiography," 384, 388, calls this "inclusion and exclusion"; Yang, "The Organization of Chinese Official Historiography," 51,

calls it "concealment"; Twitchett, "Chinese Biographical Writing," 101–02; Wright, "Biography and Hagiography," 391–92, 407, on the "summation" and "appreciation"; Twitchett, "Problems of Chinese Biography," 30, on selection.
97 Welter, "The Contextual Study of Chinese Buddhist Biographies", 247–48; Jan Yün-hua, "Portrait and Self-portrait: A Case Study of Biographical and Autobiographical Records of Tsung-mi," in Phyllis Granoff and Koichi Shinohara, eds, *Monks and Magicians*, 242.
98 Welter, "The Contextual Study of Chinese Buddhist Biographies", 247–48, note 4, 264, 261–62. Cf. discussion of Boyer's paper, 165, for problems with *vitae*. Here the narrower historical approach which evaluates the actual behaviour versus the author's embellishments is distinguished from the broader literary approach. "But distinctions between the narrower and the broader kinds are essential."
99 Faure, "Bodhidharma as Textual and Religious Paradigm," 189.
100 Jan, "Portrait and Self-portrait," 231.
101 Jan, "Portrait and Self-portrait," 229.
102 Wright, "Biography and Hagiography," 393.
103 T50.725c24, biography of Dasheng Ji and T50.753c8–9 where Wŏnch'ŭk is ranked with three others in the summation (*lun*).
104 Shinohara, "Two sources of Chinese Buddhist Biographies," 126.
105 Shinohara, "Two sources of Chinese Buddhist Biographies," 128.
106 The pupils are Kuiji (Dasheng Ji), origins known; Daoshi, known but date of death unknown; Puguang, origins unknown, death date known; Fabao, unknown; Wŏnch'ŭk, unknown; Yuankang, unknown; Jingmao, known, death date unknown; Sun'gyŏng, known, death date unknown; Jiashang, unknown; Huizhao, unknown; Yancong, unknown; T50.725b–729a.
107 T50.725b17–726c5.
108 T50.727b4–14 or ten lines; the next shortest is that of Huizhao, T50.728a1–14 or 14 lines; most are longer, a number being two to three times as long.
109 T50.728a4–728b10, including the evaluation.
110 Ŭisang, T50.729a3–c3; Wŏnhyo, T50.730a6–b28, although much of the latter is on the legendary origins of the *Kŭmgangsammei gyŏng*, a sutra allegedly forged in Silla.
111 *Cheng weishi lun*.
112 i.e. Dasheng Ji; Ci'en was the name of his monastery.
113 Possibly his *Cheng weishi lun biezhang* (not extant).
114 Zhongzong took the throne in 683 from Gaozong, and in 690 Empress Wu established the Zhou dynasty.
115 T15, no. 347.
116 Either the *Cheng weishi lun yingchao* or *Cheng weishi lun guangchao*. See Sin Hyŏnsuk, "Shiragi yuishikigaku no tenseki shōsō," in Kim Chigyŏn and Ch'ae Inhwan, eds, *Shiragi bukkyō kenkyū* (Tokyo: Sankibo busshorin, 1973), 164–65.
117 *Song Gaoseng zhuan*, T50.727b4–14.
118 For the name of this monk, see Stanley Weinstein, "A Biographical Study of Tz'u-ên," *Monumenta Nipponica* 15 (1959–60), 130–34.
119 For Dignāga's treatise, see Theodore Stcherbatsky, *Buddhist Logic*, 2 vols (New York: Dover reprint, 1962 (original, 1930)). Dasheng Ji's commentary is the *Yinming ruzhengli lunshu*.
120 The five natures or potentials to become buddha asserted by Dharmapāla are: 1) the fixed nature of the bodhisattva, 2) the fixed nature of the pratyekabuddha, 3) the fixed nature of the śrāvaka, 4) the unfixed nature which may

share in some of the previous three natures, but is not guaranteed to be able to become buddha, and 5) those beings who lack any nature or potential to become buddha. Wŏnch'ŭk, like many Chinese, thought that all beings, no matter how evil, had the potential.

121 T50.726a1–4 for the translated section. The preceding summary is from T50.725c.
122 Taisho no. 1585, completed in 659. See Hamilton, *Wei Er Shih Lun*, 3.
123 T50.725c17–22; Iida, "Three Stupas," 487; Fukaura, *Yuishikigaku kenkyū*, 247; Weinstein, *Monumenta Nipponica* 15, 145–46 writes that Ji claimed he became the only assistant and "it was to himself alone that the full meaning of the doctrines of the *Vij[ñāptimātratāsiddhi śāstra]* was revealed". Weinstein considers that there is no indication that the two monks ever debated each other, and Inaba, "Chōsen shusshin-sō Enjiki hosshi ni tsuite," 50, thinks the disputes never occurred in their lifetimes, but were the products of later rivalries.
124 Kitsukawa Tomoaki, "Enjiki Yuishikigaku ni okeru *Jō yuishikiron* no shiryoteki mondai," *Indogaku bukkyōgaku kenkyū* 42:2 (1994), 608–11.
125 Ouyang Xiu and Song Ji, comps, *Xin Tangshu*, 20 vols (Shanghai: Zhonghua shuju, 1975), 8: 2562; and stele for Ji in *Xuanzang sanzang shizi zhuan congshu*, in vol. 150 of the *Xu zang ching* (Z). Weinstein, *Monumenta Nipponica* 15, 124, states that he wrote the inscription in 830 during repairs to the stupa. For Dasheng Ji's family, see 134–35.
126 *Jiu Tangshu*, 16 vols (Shanghai: Zhonghua shuju, 1975), 10: 3135; and Weinstein, *Monumenta Nipponica* 15, 124.
127 For Li Yong, see *Jiu Tangshu*, 15: 15039–43. He was thought corrupt and was killed, but was an excellent writer of stelae. For Wu Pingyi, see *Xin Tangshu* 14: 4293. A son of the Prince of Yingchuan, he was pro-Buddhist but averse to Empress Wu. He was later pressed into service by his relatives. Demoted by Xuanzong. For Lü Zangyong, see *Jiu Tangshu* 9: 3000 and *Xin Tangshu* 14: 4374. He was known as a good writer and was made Vice President in the Board of Personnel and the Board of Works. He assisted Yijing in translation of Buddhist texts, T50.710c29. For Cui Shi, see Denis Twitchett, "Hsüan-tsung (reign 712–756)," in D. Twitchett, ed., *The Cambridge History of China*, vol. 3, *Sui and T'ang China, 589–906*, part 1 (Cambridge: Cambridge University Press, 1979), 342–45. He was a good writer who was involved in plots and was a favourite of the female relatives of the imperial clan, for which he was forced to commit suicide. The information is derived from the stelae collected in the *Xuanzang sanzang shizi zhuan congshu*, Z150.175–181; and from *Song Gaoseng zhuan* T50.728c9–10.
128 Iida, "Three Stupas," 484.
129 Error for Li Hongqing.
130 *Jinshi cuibian* 146: 9b–10a.
131 Maejima Shinji, *Genjō Sanzō* (Tokyo: Iwanami shinsho, 1952), 186–187; Huili, T50.278b12–13; Daoxuan, *Xu Gaoseng zhuan*, T50.458b7–11.
132 Cho Myonggi, *Silla Pulgyo ui i'nyom kwa yoksa* (Seoul: Sin t'aeyang chulbansa, 1962), 162. Yuki's report was published by the Tōhō Gakuin, 179, note 4. Photographs of the stupa can be found in Hibino Takeo, *Kareinaru Zui-Tō teikoku: Zusetsu Chūgoku no rekishi 4*, (Tokyo: Kodansha, 1977), 92 (plate 118) and 145 (colour plate 48), and map, 193, which shows it approx. 20km south of Xi'an.
133 *Jinshi cuibian* 146, and in *Xuanzang sanzang fashi shizi zhuan congshu*, Z 150.181b–182b and Kim Yŏngt'ae, "Haeoe munhŏn chung ŭi Han'guk pulgyo saryo," *Pulgyo hakbo* 13 (1976), 230–32.
134 Biographies in *Xu Gaoseng zhuan*, T50.540a–541b. Fachang (567–645) and Sengbian (568–642) lived in Chang'an.

135 In 627 Taizong ordered the death penalty for illegally ordained monks, and as Wŏnch'ŭk was twenty in 633, the proper age for ordination, his ordination may have been as one of the three thousand people ordained by Taizong's order in 635 to commemorate his late father. See Stanley Weinstein, *Buddhism under the T'ang* (Cambridge: Cambridge University Press, 1987), 14–15.

136 This monastery was established in 586 in the mansion of Zhang Ying, the President of the Ministry of Rites during the Sui. It faced the eastern market in Chang'an. See no. 29 on the frontispiece map in Tsukamoto Zenryū, *Tō chūki no Jōdokyō* (Kyoto: Hōzōkan, 1975).

137 *Jinshi cuibian* has a reading probably related to a phrase meaning a very close friendship. This may be a literary flourish, but it is evident from Huili's account that dreams were very important to Xuanzang and his colleagues and admirers, cf. T50.222c13ff, 223b4ff, 276c10ff.

138 Literally "Great Virtue", one of excellent conduct. At this time the title was especially given to monks involved in translation.

139 Established by Gaozong in 656, it had over 4,000 rooms. Xuanzang was made take up residence there when it was completed in 658, but he did not stay long. The historian and Vinaya master Daoxuan was abbot there in 662. See Weinstein, *Buddhism under the T'ang*, 28, 30, 32.

140 Probably the *Cheng weishi lunshu*, also known in twenty juan, which was copied in Japan in 748, but is now lost. See Tongguk Taehakkyo Pulgyo munhwa yŏn'guso, comp., *Han'guk Pulgyo ch'ansul munhŏn ch'ongnok* (Seoul: Tongguk Taehakkyo, 1976), 12 (hereafter *Catalogue*), and Sin Hyŏnsuk, "Shiragi yuishikigaku no tenseki shōsō," 161–63.

141 Juan one to seven are extant in *Xu zang jing* Z 34, juan nine in Z 35, along with the first part of eight. Tongguk Taehakkyo Han'guk Pulgyo ch'ŏnsŏ p'yŏnch'an wiwŏnhoe, *HPC*, 1:123b–1:479c. Juan ten went missing in early times, but the missing sections have been back-translated from Tibetan by Inaba Shōju in 1949 as *Enjiki-sen Gejinmikkyōsho sanitsububun no kambun'yaku* (Kyoto: Hōzōkan), and reissued in print form in 1972 with corrections. Tongguk Taehakkyo Pulgyo munhwa yŏn'guso, *Catalogue*, 11. The Tibetan text was a translation by Chödrub titled, *'phags pa dgongs pa zab mo nges par 'grel pa'i mdo'i rgya cher 'grel pa*, Sin, "Shiragi yuishikigaku no tenseki shōsō," 141–44.

142 The *Renwang boruo jingshu*, in Taisho vol. 33 and Z 40, and Tongguk Taehakkyo Han'guk Pulgyo ch'ŏnsŏ p'yŏnch'an wiwŏnhoe, *HPC* 1:15–1:123a; Tongguk Taehakkyo Pulgyo munhwa yŏn'guso, *Catalogue*, 10.

143 *Diamond Sutra*, commentary unknown.

144 Also called *Guan suoyuan yuan lunshu*, Tongguk Taehakkyo Pulgyo munhwa yŏn'guso, *Catalogue*, 13; Sin, "Shiragi yuishikigaku no tenseki shōsō," 204–05.

145 Tongguk Taehakkyo Pulgyo munhwa yŏn'guso, *Catalogue*, 9–10 lists *Boruo xin jingshu* ("Commentary on the Heart Sutra") and *Boruo boluomiduo xin jingcan*, the latter extant in Taisho vol. 33 and *HPC* 1:1–1:15a. It also lists a *Wuliangyi jingshu* in two juan and another in three juan.

146 *Lunyu* VI:21 which has Confucius say that sages and the wise delight in mountains and rivers.

147 Weinstein, *Buddhism under the T'ang*, 44, states that Divākara arrived several years prior to 680 when he was ordered by Empress Wu to translate sutras together with ten assistants.

148 This was the project to translate the eighty-juan *Avataṃsaka sūtra* led by Śikṣānanda who was invited from Khotan by Empress Wu at the request of Fazang. Empress Wu assisted the work which took place at Fo shouji Monastery. See Weinstein, *Buddhism under the T'ang*, 44–45.

Representing Wŏnch'ŭk

149 Erected by Xue Huaiyi in 691 near Luoyang to commemorate Empress Wu's ascension to the throne. See Weinstein, *Buddhism under the T'ang*, 44.
150 This monastery was close to the entry to the imperial city in Chang'an, Tsukamoto, frontispiece map, no. 2. Sŭngjang was a Silla monk. He is known from the testimony of Huizhao. He assisted in the many translations of Yijing and Bodhiruci as a verifier of meaning in the period 703–713. See Tongguk Taehakkyo Pulgyo munhwa yŏn'guso, *Catalogue*, 54–57; Hatani, "Yuishikishū no iha – Chōsenkei no Yuishikishū," 828–33.
151 *Wuyi*, literally "without reliance". Although this could mean that Wŏnch'ŭk had entered final nirvana, that "without residue," it probably means that the corpse was in Luoyang, while they, his pupils, were in Chang'an, without any object to venerate.
152 Mochizuki Shinkō, *Bukkyō Daijiten*, 10 vols (Tokyo: Sekai seiten kankō kyōkai, 1933–36; reprinted Taibei: Diping xian chuban she, 1979), 2319c, states it was founded in 571 by Zhizang.
153 Statues of the deceased, the model(?) for Wŏnch'ŭk's statue being found in 1916.
154 Tongguk Taehakkyo Pulgyo munhwa yŏn'guso, *Catalogue*, 101–02; O Hyŏnggŭn, "Silla yusik sasang ŭi t'ŭksŏng kwa kŭ yŏksajŏk chŏn'gae," in Han'guk ch'ŏlhak hoe, ed., *Han'guk ch'ŏlhak yŏn'gu*, 3 vols (Seoul: Tongmyŏngsa, 1977), 1:265–66.
155 Lü Cheng, *Zhongguo foxue yuanliu luejiang* (Taibei: Liren shuju, 1985), 418.
156 Tongguk Taehakkyo Pulgyo munhwa yŏn'guso, *Catalogue*, 67–69.
157 Eda Toshio, "Shiragi no Tonrin to 'rinki' so'in no Tōdai shoka," in *Chōsen bukkyōshi no kenkyū* (Tokyo: Kokusho kankōkai, 1977), 187, 190, 198, 202 for Toyun. See also Fukaura, *Yuishikigaku kenkyū*, 264–65.
158 Kim Poksun, *Silla Hwaŏmjong yŏn'gu*, 188–89.
159 T50.729c2–3 where Zanning mentions a stupa in Korea for Ŭisang, and that he was called the first patriarch of Korean Hwaŏm. This should be compared with the *Samguk yusa* account, which is heavily indebted to Ch'oe's hagiography of Ŭisang. Cf. Yi Pyŏngdo, comp. and trans., *Samguk yusa* (Seoul: Kwangjo ch'ulpansa, 1980), 143–44.
160 The text reads *yuni*, but *ni* is an alternative for *yi*. See Morohashi Tetsuji, *Dai Kan-Wa jiten*, 13 vols (Tokyo: Daishukan shoten, 1966), reduced reprint, no. 7635.4 (hereafter M plus no. of the character). Cf. Yi Nŭnghwa, *Chosŏn Pulgyo t'ongsa*, 3 vols in two, (1974 reprint, Tokyo: Kokusho kankōkai; originally Keijō: Sinmunguan 1918), 3:167. The word is an old name for Korea or the Dongyi, M.8281.1. A similar word, *yuyi*, appears in Ch'oe's stele for Tohŏn, a Sŏn monk, for which see Ch'oe Yŏngsŏng, trans. and annotator, *Chuhae sasan pimyŏng* (Seoul: Asea munhwa sa, 1987), 166 (hereafter *SP*), and in his inscription for a monastery, 161. The term is found in *Shiji* as a place, "the valley of sunshine," and in the *Shangshu*, Yaodian, for which see Ch'oe, *SP*, 136, note 91.
161 The same wording also appears in Ch'oe's stele for Hyeso, another Sŏn monk, *SP*, 101.
162 *Chen* is one of the eight trigrams of the *Book of Changes* and indicates the east and spring. A similar use of "position" and "direction of movement" can be seen in Ch'oe's stele for Tohŏn, *SP*, 164–65.
163 The idea that light "shines on the gloomy dark of the world" is found in Ch'oe's "anniversary text" for Ŭisang in *Wŏnjong mullyu*, *HPC*, 4:645a1.
164 Possibly a conflation of two allusions, one in which the sage emperor Shun saw birds fly off, which caused him to think of his (late?) parents, and an allusion to the speed of the passing of the sun and moon, M.18998.299–300.

165 That is, he went to Chang'an, see M.3803.17, the "land of Yin".
166 Ch'oe Chun'ok, comp., *Kug'yŏk Koun Sŏnsaeng munjip*, 2 vols (Seoul: Poryŏnkak, 1982), 2:327, note 4 (this section translated by Yang Sangch'ŏl) in the correlations of directions, virtues and seasons used in the Sinitic realm, humaneness equals Spring and the East, and righteousness equals Summer and the West.
167 *Zhuqian*. India (*Zhu*) and Gandhāra (*Qian*)? See in another Ch'oe stele, *SP*, 284, note 10.
168 In Ch'oe's stele for Muyŏm, another Sŏn monk, *SP*, 41, 46, note 66, citing *Shijing* (Book of Songs), which means "south wind and morning sun".
169 Ch'oe, *Kug'yŏk Koun Sŏnsaeng munjip*, 2:327 says this equals Korea.
170 In Ch'oe's stele for a monastery, *SP*, 161; "The compassionate king of Kapilavastu (Buddha) is the Great Sun of Yuyi that shines on the Western Lands, and comes out of the East." The image comes from the *Huayan jing*, M.45313.383, meaning that the highest mountains or spiritual beings are enlightened by the sun Buddha first.
171 That is, he aimed to achieve buddhahood.
172 Literally, "the flat-fish sea." M.46322.2; a flatfish or plaice is particular to the sea off Korea. Ch'oe used a similar expression in the stele for a monastery, *SP*, 137, note 100, in a stele for Tohŏn, *SP*, 170, 182, note 119, and in a vow text dedicated to Zhiyan, the teacher of Fazang, *Wŏnjong mullyu*, 4.645b14. "Dragon-child" is used in his stele for Muyŏm, *SP*, 85, 88, note 60.
173 Kyerim, another name for Kyŏngju, the Silla capital.
174 M.34993.80, from *Daode jing*, 54.
175 *Tianyan* could also mean the "divine speech".
176 Probably a contraction of "the oceanic assembly of the saints" and "the samadhi of the ocean seal" wherein all phenomena are reflected or imprinted on the calm ocean of the mind without distortion. This is an image from the *Huayan jing*. "Oceanic assembly" means a vast assembly, just as all the waters flow into and meet up in the ocean.
177 The text here is corrected according to Yi Nŭnghwa's edition.
178 *Zuozhuan*, Rang 26 meaning the talents of one country benefit another.
179 M.21269.56: from an incident recorded in the *Shiji*, "to return something to its original owner," but again here, meaning something valuable from one country going to another.
180 The tenth stage is the highest and final stage of the career of the bodhisattva.
181 Li Shimin, reigned 627–650 as Taizong; had the posthumous title Wen Huangdi; Liu et al., *Jiu Tangshu* 3:62.
182 A similar expression is found in Ch'oe's stele for Hyeso, *SP*, 112.
183 M.34091.13, from the *Huainanzi*: "wine barrels set up all along the roads so everyone can drink at will," a metaphor for people obtaining their desires. Also used in Ch'oe's stele for Hyeso, *SP*, 122, note 51. Ch'oe Chun'ok, *Kug'yŏk Koun Sŏnsaeng munjip*, 2: 329, note 12, "The mirror on his stand constantly shone, and the path of learning was always open."
184 Used in Ch'oe's stele for Muyŏm, *SP*, 58, note 42; in vow dedicated to Zhiyan, *Wŏnjong mullyu*, 4.645a1.
185 Probably refers to Buddhism. However, Ch'oe Yongsong glosses it as study in China by Koreans, *SP*, 41, note 1, stele for Muyŏm; and vow for Chih-yen, *Wŏnjong mullyu*, 4.645a1 where it is paired with the flow east of Buddhism.
186 The Koreans of Silla believed in the light of Chinese records that their region received refugees from the horrors of the Qin empire, who then helped found the state.

Representing Wŏnch'ŭk

187 M.45313.377, from *Shijing*. James Legge, *Shijing* vol. 4 of *The Chinese Classics* (reprint; Taibei: Wenshizhe chuban she, 1972), 393, translates as "the high hill is looked up to". The same phrase is found in the vow dedicated to Ŭisang, *Wŏnjong mullyu*, 4.646a4.

188 Ch'oe Chun'ok, *Kug'yŏk Koun Sŏnsaeng munjip*, 2:331, note 4, the four rivers (Ganges, Indus, Brahmaputra, Sutlej?) coming out of the sacred lake of Buddhism, Anavatapta, which is supposedly located north of the Himalayas.

189 From *Zhuangzi*; see Burton Watson, trans., *The Complete Works of Chuang Tzu* (New York: Columbia University Press, 1968), 36-37. A similar expression is found in Ch'oe's stele for Tohŏn, *SP*, 164.

190 *Zhuangzi*, "Free and easy wandering" chapter, Watson, *The Complete Works of Chuang Tzu*, 29-31. Ch'oe Chun'ok, *Kug'yok Koun Sonsaeng munjip*, 2:331, note 5, a metaphor for his nirvana.

191 M.31241.392, states that the *Soushen houji* has a story of Ding Lingwei of Liaodong. After he died he turned into a crane and one thousand years later returned to his home village, stopping at the gate in front of the graveyard, but he was fired on by a youth and so flew away. "The roc manifests itself and the crane returns" is found in Ch'oe's stele for Muyŏm, *SP*, 43, note 22, meaning the "roc" is strong and lively, the crane is quiet and unobtrusive. The request is to think of Wŏnch'ŭk's actions in life, and not to think of his death or hope that his remains will be brought back to Silla. There could be a double meaning here, for *Huabiao* could mean China, in contrast to the "east side" (*tongbiao*) in the stele for Tohŏn, *SP*, 171, note 1 or "ocean side" (*haibiao*) for Silla, 117, note 49. Normally *huabiao* means a stone monument or a guide post at the city gate.

192 Meaning unclear. A similar expression appears in Ch'oe's stele for Muyŏm, which Ch'oe Yŏngsŏng, *SP*, 38, note 55, glosses as "no concern for the three relations with lord, father and teacher". But the three could also refer to the three levels of truth in Vijñānavāda, the three jewels of Buddhism, or perhaps in this context, the three stupas of Xingjiao Monastery. Probably means, "although we have studied his teachings on non-duality, we are concerned that we are still wanting in proper respect for him as a teacher".

193 The *zhi* and *lan* are metaphors for friendship, M.30699.73; "they are fragrant not because people are present," just as sages cultivate the Way. In other words, even if a sage had no followers, the sage's influence will still be exerted. The latter line seems corrupt, so "trees and plums" could instead be "peaches and plums," a metaphor for excellent scholars. The first line is echoed in Ch'oe's stele for Hyeso, "the perfume (of Buddhism) was planted on the ocean shore (Korea), and for a long time it has been full of fragrance". So the sense of this line is something like, "Moreover, he was a good friend (Buddhist term for the spiritual guide) whose influence remained, and that influence was continued through the excellent writings of his pupils."

194 *Renfang*, means Korea. Cf. Ch'oe's stele for Muyŏm, *SP*, 96 note 23, equals the East, *Renyu*, meaning the "realm of humaneness," and in his stele for a monastery, *SP*, 150.

195 Reference to the bringing of the *Avataṃsaka* and other Mahayana sutras from the Nāga king or dragon king's palace in a "rediscovery" of Buddhist scriptures.

196 Like a bodhisattva who vows not to enter nirvana until all beings have been saved. This is a plea for his assistance.

197 Kamata Shigeo, *Chūgoku Kegonshisōshi no kenkyū* (Tokyo: Tokyo Daigaku shuppankai, 1965), 244-45, 248.

198 Jennifer Holmgren, "Social Mobility in the Northern Dynasties: A Case Study of the Feng of Northern Yen," *Monumenta Serica* 35 (1981-1983), 21.

199 Holmgren, "Social Mobility in the Northern Dynasties," 27. The ruler of Northern Yan, Feng Hong, when attacked by Northern Wei in 436, requested the Koguryŏ king, Changsu, for assistance, and so the Northern Yan ruler and peasants were shifted to Pingguo in Liaodong under Koguryŏ protection. See Yi Man'yŏl, "Samguk ŭi hangjaeng," in Kuksa p'yŏnch'an wiwŏnhoe, comp., *Han'guk sa*, 24 vols (Seoul: Taehan min'guk mungyobu Kuksa p'yŏnch'an wiwŏnhoe, 1981), 2:472, note 14.

200 The Feng had put a descendant of a Koguryŏ family on the throne of Northern Yan, but when he proved incompetent, had him murdered, and ruled in his stead. See Chi Paesŏn, "Puk-Yŏn e taehayŏ I," *Tongbang Hakji* 54.55.56 (1987), 870–71.

201 *SP*, 3, testimony of the *Samguk sagi*.

202 *SP*, 171, cf. 185, note 152, in the stele for Tohŏn.

203 Yi Man'yŏl, "Samguk ŭi hangjaeng," 472, note 14. Kim Pusik, *Samguk sagi*, (Seoul: Kyong'in munhwa sa, 1982), 189–90; Wei Shou, *Wei shu*, 8 vols (Beijing: Zhonghua shuju, 1974), 97: 2128–29.

204 According to the *Shiji*. See Inoue Hideo, *Kodai Chōsen* (Tokyo: NHK Bukkusu, 1972), 30–31 for a translation and explanation. K.H.J. Gardiner, *The Early History of Korea*, Oriental Monograph Series 8 (Canberra: Australian National University Press 1969), 9–13, analyses these accounts, showing that Wei Man extended his authority into southern Korea. Note references on page 13 to a Liqixiang or "Minister Yŏkkye" who fled to Ch'in Han, the core area of Silla. Perhaps then a "Minister P'ung" also fled south in similar circumstances and claimed descent from the kings of Yan, mistaking those of Northern Yan with the earlier state of Yan ruled by Lü Guan. Also noted in Yi Pyŏngdo, *Samguk yusa*, 28, with possible confusion making the "minister" into a village, for *xiangshi*, "village gentleman," can mean an officer in charge of policing in a number of villages, while the very similar *xiangtu* means a village land or district.

205 Qin and Ch'in represent the Chinese and Korean pronunciations of the same character.

206 Yi Pyŏngdo, *Samguk yusa*, 34. Mishina Akihide et al., *Sankoku iji kōshō*, vol. 1 (Tokyo: Hanawa shobō, 1975), 64–65, notes 101, 101a. The text within brackets is a note in the original.

207 Pak Chonghong, "Han'guk ch'ŏlhaksa – kodae p'yŏn," in Han'guk sasang yŏn'gu hoe, comp., *Han'guk sasangsa – kodae p'yŏn* (Seoul: Pŏmmunsa, 1966), 40, 58, note 1, thinks this date has been given due to confusion of the master with Wŏnch'ŭk's pupil Tojŭng who returned to Silla in the first year of King Hyoso's reign. Cho Myŏnggi, *Silla Pulgyo ŭi i'nyŏm kwa yŏksa*, 164–65 thinks that this rejection explains Wŏnch'ŭk's retreat into the Zhongnan Mountains. See Yi Pyŏngdo, *Samguk yusa*, 59.

208 Mishina Akihide, *Shiragi Karo no kenkyū*, republished in *Mishina Akihide rombunshū*, vol. 6 (1943; Tokyo: Heibonsha, 1974), 64–65. Referred to in Kim Ch'ŏljun, *Han'guk kodae sahoe yŏn'gu* (Seoul: Chisik san'ŏpsa, 1976), 227. Mishina Akihide et al., *Sankoku iji kōshō*, vol. 2 (Tokyo: Hanawa shobō, 1979), 62, thinks that the Chukji-rang of the story became a hwarang in the time of King Chinp'yŏng. Inoue, *Kodai Chōsen*, 205, lists this man as a high-ranking army officer during war in 661 and 668. Although the *Samguk yusa* states that "at that time the Dharma Teacher Wŏnch'ŭk was an eminent cleric, because he was a person of Mo(r)yang . . . ," which would support Cho Myŏnggi's theory that Wŏnch'ŭk returned to Silla after the death of Xuanzang in 664, this was a period of intense warfare on the peninsula, with Japan's navy being defeated by Tang forces on Paekche territory and the savage fighting continuing into 664

(Inoue, 202–03). I suspect the rank given Wŏnch'ŭk is another example of an anachronism, but the possibility that he returned to Korea after 664 cannot be ruled out.
209 Kim Ch'ŏljun's interpretation, *Han'guk kodae sahoe yŏn'gu*, 227–31.
210 Yi Pyŏngdo, *Samguk yusa*, 35; Mishina et al., *Sankoku iji kōshō*, vol. 1, 424. Mishina thinks that the names of the clans only came into use from late Silla times in imitation of famous Tang dynasty clan names, 432.
211 Mishina et al., *Sankoku iji kōshō*, 424, but with some doubts, and 193. The mother of King Chinhŭng (r. 540–576), the empress dowager and regent for Chinp'yŏng, was a member of a clan from this district, 180–81, and possibly his queen also.
212 Kim Ch'ŏljun, *Han'guk kodae sahoe yŏn'gu*, 176.
213 Shōtarō Iida, "Wŏnch'ŭk (613–696) ŭi saeng'ae," 163, writes, "Wŏnch'ŭk was born into a *p'yo* (?) family of royal descent of Silla's Mo(r)yang-bu".
214 Holmgren, "Social Mobility in the Northern Dynasties," 21, 30.
215 Martina Deuchler, *The Confucian Transformation of Korea: A Study of Society and Ideology* (Cambridge Ma.: Harvard University Press, 1992), 84–85.
216 For the example of Ŭisang, see Kim Tujin, *Ŭisang: kŭ ŭi saeng'ae wa Hwa'ŏm sasang* (Seoul: Min'ŭmsa, 1995), 74.
217 *Samguk sagi*, Silla Annals, 36th year of Chinp'yŏng, 47. See also *Samguk yusa*, 96, which reports the event, but with emendations.
218 Yan Gengwang, "Xinle xueTang xuesheng yu sengtu," in his *Tangshi yanjiu zengkao* (Hong Kong: Xinya yanjiusuo, 1969), 443–44.
219 In the 8th lunar month, *Jiu Tangshu* 1: 2: 32; Sima Guang, *Zizhi tongjian*, annotated by Hu Sansheng, 11 vols (Taibei: Hongshi chuban she, 1974), 192:6030, implies that the delegations from the states of the Korean Peninsula brought letters of apology for their "misdemeanours" of attacking each other. These delegations also included the sons of the elites sent to China to receive an education from the university. Their professor was named as Zhu Zishe (d. 641). Zhu, a Confucian scholar, had been given the task of making the three Korean states apologise for the attacks made by Koguryo and Paekche on Silla. Silla had sent a mission to the Tang court to report on the crisis. Because of his dignity, Zhu impressed the kings of those states, who apologised by letter. Zhu was also supposed to teach Confucianism, but he soon returned to China. See *Jiu Tangshu* 15: 189A: 4948; *Samguk sagi* 48th year, autumn, 7th lunar month of King Chinp'yŏng's reign. Silla Annals, page 48, mentions the mission and Zhu's arrival on the orders from Gaozu to make peace.
220 Yan, "Xinle xueTang xuesheng yu sengtu," 443; Yamazaki Hiroshi, *Zui-Tō Bukkyōshi no kenkyū* (Kyoto: Hōzōkan, 1967), 147–49; the title of "Teachers of Foreign Monks" was changed to "Teachers of the Three Han Monks". As Three Han was a term for the area in southern Korea, this probably meant that the bulk of the students were from Silla and Paekche.
221 Yan, "Xinle xueTang xuesheng yu sengtu," 426.
222 Sin Hyŏngsik, "Sug'wi haksaeng ko: Namal Yŏch'o ŭi chisikin ŭi tonghyang e taehan ilgu," in Yŏksahakhoe, comp., *Han'guk sa nonmun sŏnjip (Kodae p'yŏn) II* (Seoul: Ilchogak, 1976), 325–26.
223 Denis Twitchett and Arthur F. Wright, "Introduction" in Twitchett and Wright, eds, *Perspectives on the T'ang* (New Haven: Yale University Press, 1973), 1.
224 Huili, *DaTang Daci'ensi Sanzang fashi zhuan*, T50.222b23ff. These monks inspired the pilgrimage. See also Zhisheng (730), *Kaiyuan shijiao lu*, T55.557c22ff.
225 For these two monks' studies of the *Shelun*, see *Xu Gaoseng zhuan*, T50.540b12; 540c12; 540c17, 23; 541b6, 20.

John Jorgensen

226 *Xu Gaoseng zhuan*, T50.540b22–23; 541a12–15.
227 *Xu Gaoseng zhuan*, T50.540b19–20; 541a6. For Prabhākaramitra, see *Xu Gaoseng zhuan*, T50.439c–440a; *Kaiyuan shijiao lu*, T55.553b–554a.
228 *Kaiyuan shijiao lu*, T55.559a and Weinstein, *Buddhism under the T'ang*, 22, 24, 156, note 22.
229 *Xu Gaoseng zhuan*, T50.541a9–10 as precepts teacher, and for his dispute with the imperial rulings on Buddhism, T50.541a18ff and Weinstein, *Buddhism under the T'ang*, 16–17. For an account of Taizong's attitudes towards and actions against Buddhism, see Wright, "T'ang T'ai-tsung and Buddhism," in Twitchett and Wright, *Perspectives on the T'ang*, 259–62.
230 *Xu Gaoseng zhuan*, T50.541b.
231 Summarised from Cao Shibang (Tso Sze-bong), "Guanyu Fojiaodi 'yizhang'" *Hsien-tai tsa-chih*, offprint (n.d.), 1–9. Offprint courtesy of the author. See also J.W. de Jong, "Buddha's word in China," 28th George Ernest Morrison Lecture, 1967 (Canberra: Australian National University, 1968), 13, for a summary based on an earlier 1963 article by Tso Sze-bong.
232 Cao, "Guanyu Fojiaodi 'yizhang'", 4. Xuanzang had twenty-three regular assistants.
233 Huili, *DaTang Daci'ensi Sanzang fashi zhuan*, T50.221b21.
234 Evidence provided by his pupil Guanding, *Sui Tiantai Zhizhe Dashi biezhuan*, T50.191a24.
235 Yancong, *Tang hufa shamen Falin biezhuan*, T50.198b18.
236 Yan Chaoyin, *DaTang Daxianfusi gu Dade Kang zang Fashi*, T50.280b10.
237 Mingxiang, *DaTang gu Sanzang Xuanzang Fashi xingzhuang*, T50.214a5.
238 Huili, T50.223a22–23.
239 Suggestion made by Kim Yŏngt'ae, "Pulguksa ŭi Hwaŏm Pŏpsa Wŏnch'ŭk e taehayŏ," *Han'guk Pulgyohak*, 23; cf. *Jiu Tangshu* 3: 62 for the emperor's names. His *hui* was Shimin, for which see *Jiu Tangshu* 2: 21.
240 Weinstein, *Buddhism under the T'ang*, 39–40; Zhisheng (730), *Xu gujin yijing tuji*, T55.368c25–28.
241 *Kaiyuan shijiao lu*, T55.559b8, and *Daci'ensi Sanzang Fashi zhuan*, T50.254a2–3.
242 *Jiu Tangshu* 3: 46; Wright, "T'ang T'ai-tsung," 248.
243 *Kaiyuan shijiao lu*, T55.556a, 557a. Also, a preface to the *Abidamo biposha lun*, states that Xuanze was a text composer for this translation in 656 along with Huili, T27.5a3.
244 For the prefaces written by Xuanze of Ximing Monastery, see T5 (no. 220).1a. T7.1a, 427a, 763a, 865a, 921a. These were written as each "assembly" (*hui*) was finished, the last being completed in 663 and the first started in 659.
245 Weinstein, *Buddhism under the T'ang*, 30.
246 Cao Shibang "Guanyu Fojiaodi 'yizhang'", 4–5. Note that Wŏnch'ŭk is not listed among the verifiers etc. for the translation of the *Yogācārabhūmi śāstra*, T30.283–284, a work which commenced in 647.
247 Iida, "Wŏnch'ŭk ŭi saeng'ae," 164; Hatani, "Yuishikishū no iha – Chōsenkei no Yuishikishū," 793. *Jie shenmi jingshu*, *HPC*, 1.177b.
248 See the cautions of Robert H. van Gulik, *Siddham: An Essay on the History of Sanskrit Studies in China and Japan* (Nagpur: Chandra, 1956), 13, 18, 45, who claims only those who studied in India really knew Sanskrit; the others, even Dasheng Ji who was credited with knowledge of Sanskrit, probably could only pronounce the script without understanding the meaning or grammar. However, Weinstein, *Monumenta Nipponica* 15, 143–44 suggests Ji may have consulted a Sanskrit text, but his emendations may rather have been a result of the discussions he took part in during the translation process.

Representing Wŏnch'ŭk

249 Weinstein, *Buddhism under the T'ang*, 31.
250 Daoxuan, *Guang hongming ji*, T52.245c24–26, 246a2–b2. For Lu Dunxin, see *Jiu Tangshu* 189A: 4945; for the post, see notes to *Zizhi tongjian*, 200: 6326–27; for titles, see Charles O. Tucker, *A Dictionary of Official Titles in Imperial China* (Stanford: Stanford University Press, 1985).
251 T52.97a; the text is in T52.245a–246b; the first preface is found in the early Ming dynasty collection, the *Zimen jingxun*, T48.1092b–1093b; Dong Gao et al., *Quan Tang wenji shiyi*, 5 vols, punctuated, with index, Dahua shuju, 908: 4253c–4254c, where the name of the preface writer is given as Yuanze, which is another case of avoidance of taboo characters, for Xuan was a character in the personal name of the Manchu Kangxi emperor.
252 See *Kaiyuan shijiao lu*, T55.564a20 as a verifier with Divākara, and 570a20 as verifier for Bodhiruci in 693.
253 Denis Twitchett and Howard J. Wechsler, "Kao-tsung (reign 649–83) and the Empress Wu: the inheritor and the usurper," in Twitchett and Fairbanks, *The Cambridge History of China, Sui and T'ang China*, 263–65.
254 Twitchett and Fairbanks, *The Cambridge History of China, Sui and T'ang China*, 282–85. *Zizhi tongjian* 202: 6385.
255 *Jiu Tangshu* 5: 98, 100; *Zizhi tongjian* 202: 6375.
256 *Jiu Tangshu* 8: 192; *Zizhi tongjian* 202: 6405, 205: 6490.
257 T50.726a4. Iida, "The Three Stupas of Ch'ang An," 485, note 8, quotes the Japanese pilgrim Ennin as stating that Ji came to the monastery of Tongzi to "avoid the Silla monk Hyŏnch'ŭk, coming from Chang'an here to first lecture on the *Wei-shih*." Hyŏnch'ŭk (Xuanze) was commonly used earlier in Wŏnch'ŭk's life rather than Yuanze (Wŏnch'ŭk). *Hyŏn* or *xuan* was often substituted for *yuan* ("original"), a homophone of the *yuan* ("perfect," "circle") used in Wŏnch'ŭk. Tongzi Monastery is named after the incident reported in the *Song Gaoseng zhuan* biography of Dasheng Ji, T50.726a4–19.
258 T50.726a19–23, cf. T50.725c4–7, translated in Iida, "The Three Stupas of Ch'ang An," 487 for another story on the origin of the three carts of desire that led Ji to be called the "Three Cart Monk" in the capital region. See also Weinstein, *Monumenta Nipponica* 15, 140–41, who thinks the stories a much later fabrication, 122, 141.
259 Fukaura, *Yuishikigaku kenkyū*, 247; Weinstein, *Monumenta Nipponica* 15, 142–43 who thinks that Dasheng Ji's unusual interpretation of the Three Vehicles gave rise to this slander.
260 Cf. Iida, "The Three Stupas of Ch'ang An," 487–88. The calculation of the years of retreat is based on the account of Song Fu.
261 *Xu Gaoseng zhuan*, T50.639b18ff.
262 *Song Gaoseng zhuan*, T50.719a20–29.
263 *Zuota gongde jingxu*, in *HPC* 12. 1a.
264 *Kaiyuan shijiao lu*, T55.564a20; Weinstein, *Buddhism under the T'ang*, 44.
265 *Kaiyuan shijiao lu*, T55.570a20; Weinstein, *Buddhism under the T'ang*, 44.
266 Tongguk Taehakkyo Pulgyo munhwa yŏn'guso, *Catalogue*, 54–57; Hatani, 828–32; *Kaiyuan shijiao lu*, T55.568c5; 569a4; 570c4.
267 *Samguk sagi*, Silla Annals 8 (Hyoso 1st year), 92; Tongguk Taehakkyo Pulgyo munhwa yŏn'guso, *Catalogue*, 52–54; Hatani, "Yuishikishū no iha – Chōsenkei no Yuishikishū," 833–46, who assesses his theories.
268 Tongguk Taehakkyo Pulgyo munhwa yŏn'guso, *Catalogue*, 72–82; Hatani, "Yuishikishū no iha – Chōsenkei no Yuishikishū," 847–55; Ch'ae T'aeksu (Inhwan), "Shiragi Daiken to *kosekki* ni tsuite," in Kim Chigyŏn and Ch'ae Inhwan, eds, *Shiragi bukkyō kenkyū* (Tokyo: Sankibo busshorin, 1973),

50–52, notes that Shōen, writing in 1333, stated that Taehyŏn was a pupil of Wŏnch'ŭk, but others claimed he was a pupil of Tojŭng. Hatani notes he was influenced by Hwaŏm and took a conciliatory approach. The *Samguk yusa* called him the founder of Korean Yogācāra.

269 Kim Yŏngt'ae, "Pulguksa ui Hwaŏm Pŏpsa Wŏnch'ŭk e taehayŏ," disputes this, suggesting that there was a much later monk called Wŏnch'ŭk who lived and lectured at Pulguk Monastery just before the time of Ch'oe Ch'iwŏn.

270 Weinstein, *Buddhism under the T'ang*, 62; Fukaura, *Yuishikigaku kenkyū*, 270.

271 W. Pachow, "A study of the Twenty-Two Dialogues on Mahāyāna Buddhism," *The Chinese Culture* 20:1 (1979), 45. Cf. the table in Ueyama Daishun, "Tonkō to Tonkō no bukkyōgaku," *Tōhō gakuhō* 35 (1964), 109.

272 Pachow, "A study of the Twenty-Two Dialogues on Mahāyāna Buddhism," 25ff.; Ueyama, 151.

273 Ueyama, "Tonkō to Tonkō no bukkyōgaku," 149.

274 *Song Gaoseng zhuan*, T50.734c13–14; 734a10.

275 Ueyama, "Tonkō to Tonkō no bukkyōgaku," 148; Pachow, "A study of the Twenty-Two Dialogues on Mahāyāna Buddhism," 27–28. Paul Demiéville, "Récents travaux sur Touen-Houang." T'oung Pao, LVI (1970), 29–30, apparently believed Tankuang stayed in Chang'an until 774.

276 Ueyama, "Tonkō to Tonkō no bukkyōgaku," 152–53; Pachow, "A study of the Twenty-Two Dialogues on Mahāyāna Buddhism," 32–33.

277 Wu Jiyu, "Daibankoku Daitoku Sanzōshi Hōsei denkō," in Makita Tairyō and Fukui Fumimasa, comps, *Tonkō to Chūgoku Bukkyō*, Kōza Tonkō, 7 (Tokyo: Daitō shuppansha, 1984), 402. Chödrub is usually identified as a Tibetan (Wu, 386–90; Ueyama, 144, 204). Pachow, "A study of the Twenty-Two Dialogues on Mahāyāna Buddhism," 62, also says he was Tibetan by birth. However, Iida, "Wŏnch'ŭk ŭi saeng'ae," 174, citing Mark Tatz, claims Facheng was the son of a Chinese soldier-settler leader, Wu Zhuzhi, and was born in Dunhuang ca. 755, becoming a "director of Buddhism and professor" during the Tibetan occupation, dying ca. 849 after the Chinese had reoccupied Dunhuang.

278 Shōju Inaba, "On Chos-grub's Translation of the *Chieh-shen-mi-ching-shu*," in Leslie S. Kawamura and Keith Scott, eds, *Buddhist Thought and Asian Civilization* (Emeryville: Dharma Publishing, 1977), 111.

279 Hatani, "Yuishikishū no iha – Chōsenkei no Yuishikishū," 787.

280 Fukaura, *Yuishikigaku kenkyū*, 261; but Tongguk Taehakkyo Pulgyo munhwa yŏn'guso, *Catalogue*, 12 gives 736.

281 Cf. Robinson, *The Buddhist Religion*, 72; Gadjin M. Nagao, *Mādhyamika and Yogācāra: A Study of Mahāyāna Philosophy*, Leslie S. Kawamura, trans. (Albany: State University of New York Press, 1991), chapter 6, esp. 67–72. Wŏnch'ŭk addresses these questions of levels of truth through the metaphor of the magician in his *Jie shenmi jingshu*, HPC 1.173b–174c, 1.232a–243b.

282 See Imanishi Ryū, "Chōsen Chi'isan Kegonji jiseki ki ni tsuite," in Hwang Suyong, *Pulguk Sa Hwaŏm Sa sajŏk*, Kogo misul charyŏ 7 (Seoul: Kogo misul tong'in hoe, 1975?), Appendix, 35–36, 40–41. Imanishi's article was originally published in *Bukkyō shigaku* 2, Dec. 1912.

283 Hwang, *Pulguk Sa Hwaŏm Sa sajŏk*, 8–18 for the PSC and 60–64 for the *Pulguk Sa sajŏk*; and in the Asea munhwa sa reproduction, Han'guk hak munhŏn yŏn'guso, comp., *Pulguk Sa ji (oe)*, Han'guk saji ch'ongsŏ 11 (Seoul: Asea munhwa sa, 1983), 51–64 for the PSC and 25–34 for the *Pulguk Sa sajŏk*. For the HSS, see Hwang, 110–30; the five equivalent texts are on 110–22.

284 Kim Sanghyŏn, *Silla Hwaŏm sasangsa yŏn'gu* (Seoul: Minjoksa, 1991), 188–89.

285 Kim Sanghyŏn, *Silla Hwaŏm sasangsa yŏn'gu*, 189–90, 200.

286 Kim Poksun, *Silla Hwaŏmjong yŏn'gu*, 171–72. The characters changed were not only homophones but also homonyms, which weakens the argument. Moreover, the monk Kyŏl'ŏn who appears with a monk of this name, Hyŏnjun, was famed as a Hwaŏm monk of Hwangbok Monastery, and so the identification or interchange of characters may have been legitimate. For the *Wŏnjong mullyu*, see the text in *HPC*, 4:646b–647b.
287 Kim Poksun, *Silla Hwaŏmjong yŏn'gu*, 174–76.
288 Kim Sanghyŏn, *Silla Hwaŏm sasangsa yŏn'gu*, 200.
289 Hwang, *Pulguk Sa Hwaŏm Sa sajŏk*, 121–22.
290 *Wŏnjong mullyu*, 4.645b–646b; Hwang, HSS, 125–28.
291 Tongguk Taehakkyo Pulgyo munhwa yŏn'guso, *Catalogue*, 103.
292 Kim Poksun, *Silla Hwaŏmjong yŏn'gu*, 173–77.
293 *Wŏnjong mullyu*, 4.646b7.
294 Yi Pyŏngdo, *Samguk yusa*, 144; and Han'guk Pulgyo yŏn'guwŏn, *Silla ŭi p'yesa I*, Han'guk ŭi sach'al series 3 (Seoul: Iljisa, 1974), 61.
295 Kim Sanghyŏn, *Silla Hwaŏm sasangsa yŏn'gu*, 291–92.
296 For a chronology of Ch'oe Ch'iwŏn's life, see Ch'oe Yŏngsŏng, trans. and annotator, *Chuhae sasan pimyŏng* (Seoul: Asea munhwa sa, 1987), 298–99.

5

The Mirror of Life

The Structure of a 16th Century Tibetan Hagiography

David Templeman

The Tibetan Tradition of Hagiography

An ongoing concern of Tibetan scholars from at least the 12th–13th centuries has been the writing of biographies of spiritual masters, either as individual works or as collections of texts dealing with successive reincarnations. It has often been a preoccupation of Tibetans to trace spiritual lineage back to an Indian antecedent, and due to the extremely close relationship between the two countries in the formative stages of Buddhism in Tibet between the 11th and the 13th centuries, this has mostly been a relatively easy and felicitous task. The purpose of tracing this relationship between the current holder of the incarnatory lineage and his Indian antecedents is not for the aggrandisement of either the incumbent or the lineage, although there are obvious examples where this patently did occur. It is rather to firmly establish the genuine nature of the teachings which the master's lineage is in possession of and which is in itself regarded as a guarantee of the impeccability of the teachings, to be able to maintain that they have an unimpeachable antecedent and to demonstrate that they have manifestly been passed from master to student in an unbroken chain to the present time.

This essay considers two such biographies, both of the same person, the great Indian Mahāsiddha Kṛṣṇācārya. In the first biography under discussion the establishment of lineal integrity is a major concern. Its author Kün-ga Dröchog had inherited the mantle of a reincarnating lineage from some quite renowned Tibetan masters after the lineage left its illustrious origins in India and passed into Tibet in the 12th or 13th century. It was important that he write clearly about his spiritual inheritance, as he came from a fairly insignificant part of the Tibetan cultural area, quite distant from the deep sources of the great lineages already set up centuries before, and by his time themselves seats of great power, both spiritual and temporal. His magnum opus is a vast hagiography of his lineage, tracing the string of rebirths from Kṛṣṇācārya right up to his own life. His autobiography occupies the final part of the work.[1]

The Mirror of Life

After the death of Kün-ga Dröchog in 1566, the lineage inexplicably reverted to India, adopting the form of a Prince of the small state of Tripurā.[2] Unfortunately he lived only for eight brief years and his rebirth was found back in Tibet in the form of Tāranātha, who would later become one of Tibet's most renowned scholars and liturgists.

Due to the proximity in time of the writing of Kün-ga Dröchog's massive work and the later version by Tāranātha, in 1632, there was probably no need for the latter to rewrite any of the biographies of the masters intervening between the Indian primogenitor and himself because his predecessor-but-one had already done so. However, what Tāranātha did see as imperative was to refute some of the "errors" which had been allowed to find their way into the hagiographies of the Mahāsiddha Kṛṣṇācārya in several previous accounts of his Life and which were almost sanctioned by their appearance in the version of Kün-ga Dröchog.[3] This point will be discussed in more detail later in this paper.

Several crucial questions dealing with the nature and status of what one writes in an autobiography have been referred to previously by Janet Gyatso in the context of the Life of the 13th century discoverer of hidden texts, Guru Chöwang, in her penetrating paper on the Tibetan autobiographical tradition.[4] I wish to narrow their purview and make them more applicable to the present context of a "semi-autobiographical" genre in which a master writes about his own lineal predecessor. One of the major questions raised by Gyatso may be rephrased as, "Why do those within a lineage appear to have such hazy and evanescent recall of their predecessors?" Other questions which owe much to her work and which must be considered in any serious treatment of the genre, concern the status of the hagiographies of lineal predecessors in relation to those of the current lineage holder, the question of the automatic legitimation of retrospective visionary experience (that is, when one dreams one is some figure from the past, was one in fact that person and how may such an experience be verified and enacted *in re*?), what constitutes legitimate knowledge concerning one's lineage and under which circumstances does such acquired, relative knowledge become absolute knowledge?

The Hagiography

This small account of the life of Kṛṣṇācārya has been drawn from a variety of sources, particularly those by Kün-ga Dröchog and Tāranātha.

Kṛṣṇācārya was born in the 10th or 11th century in Orissa, India. He trained under various tantric masters and at first learned the teachings and meditational instructions of the Hevajra Tantra. At the bidding of his master, the Mahāsiddha Jālandharipa, himself a most important figure in the transmission of both the Hevajra and Cakrasaṃvara Tantras, he visited the ḍākinī site of Urgyen in the north west of India where he was empowered in a mystic ceremony into the rites of the tantric deity Cakrasamvara.[5]

David Templeman

He travelled to Siṅgaladvīpa where he found the person who was to become his consort in the tantric practices. Thereafter he wandered around India with his entourage, performing many miracles of subjugation and spectacular conversions of Hindus and Jainas to Buddhism.[6]

His various biographies show clearly his direct and forthright attitude and his rather confrontational manner in both his spiritual and his day-to-day life. He even had the temerity to disobey his Guru, the mighty Mahāsiddha Jālandharipa, and towards the end of his life, as a direct result of breaking the master's injunction about never going to Devīkoṭṭa in Assam, he was inadvertently slain by a rampant demoness on the spot where he had planned to build a Buddhist temple to demonstrate the subjugation of that locale to Buddhism, and its abandonment of the old cultic ways.

The main literary inheritance we have from him is a series of texts dealing with systematization of various tantric cycles, including those of Cakrasamvara, Hevajra and Vasantatilaka as well as a series of spiritual songs of great profundity and beauty known as dohā and caryā songs. These latter songs, the so-called Caryāgīti, will be an important part of the later discussion.

Early Biographies

The earliest existing hagiography of the Mahāsiddha Kṛṣṇācārya was written by Abhayadatta in India in the late 11th century, as part of a book which contained brief lives of the masters consisting of a few pages each written in an epithetical manner.[7] As I have demonstrated elsewhere,[8] although the writing of a string of biographies of tantric masters was not beyond the abilities of Abhayadatta, the sympathetic recording of any one particular life was something he did not do well, and there is no better example of this failure to do justice to a Mahāsiddha's life than the case of Kṛṣṇācārya. To make his hagiographical collection a teaching tool (albeit a fairly basic one) Abhayadatta insisted on ending many of the vignettes (for they were merely fragments rather than full biographies) with didactic lines to demonstrate to the reader the correct frame of mind to adopt if one were to emulate these masters in any way. Unfortunately this has the effect of reducing the lives simply to mere moral lessons with "throwaway" endings such as, "One should know that pride and jealousy are hindrances" in the case of Kṛṣṇācārya.

Even so, this text found great popularity in Tibet, and it formed the Procrustean bed on which many subsequent biographies of the Mahāsiddha were based.[9] Although the Tibetan hagiographers were somewhat more circumspect about the stories themselves, they nevertheless borrowed a certain number of incidents directly from Abhayadatta and from other Indian sources, unfortunately unknown to us now except in name. Perhaps the earliest Tibetan scholar to write a hagiography of Kṛṣṇācārya was the 12th century Sakyapa cleric Kün-ga Nyingpo and he appears to have provided a model for one of the most notable of Tibetan writers, the great Butön Rimpoché who, in 1354, incorporated a short biography of Kṛṣṇācārya into his major synoptical history.[10] So great was Butön's position as the doyen of Tibetan polymaths that it earned him the sobriquet "kün khyen" or "Omniscient One". Nevertheless, even he appears to have transmitted several stories about the life of the Mahāsiddha Kṛṣṇācārya which Tāranātha took exception to. The appendix to this paper lists a selection of eleven aspects of Kṛṣṇācārya's life out of which Tāranātha felt six did not truly reflect the life of the Mahāsiddha. Tāranātha appears to have been the first in the lineage stemming from Kṛṣṇācārya to publicly denounce those stories. Although he condemned those who transmitted what he felt were spurious stories as the truth, he did not ever mention Kün-ga Nyingpo or Butön by name, reserving his open ire for others of much lesser status. Many of the accounts which Butön employed were in their turn adopted by one of the subjects of the present paper, the 16th century lineal descendent of Kṛṣṇācārya himself, Kün-ga Dröchog, who wrote his extensive biography between the years 1525 and 1560. It was with Kün-ga Dröchog's lineal successor-but-one, the great scholar Tāranātha, that many of these erroneous stories were "corrected" so they might more fully tally with the dignity and the puissance of their mutual lineal founder, as well as to align them more perfectly with the predictions made about his life in several tantric texts, most notably the Nātha Abhyudaya Tantra and the Kālacakra Tantra.[11]

The Hagiographies by Kün-ga Dröchog and Tāranātha

The work of Kün-ga Dröchog appears to concentrate almost exclusively on the mystical aspects of Kṛṣṇācārya's life, in particular the initiatory process and the many miracles he performed during his peregrinations around India. It is a work whose defining mark appears to be outright amazement at the siddha's astoundingly unconventional life, and which, via certain hermeneutic devices, attempts to explain the miraculous events without detracting from their mystery and majesty.

By contrast, Tāranātha's hagiography (written in 1632) is a much more self-conscious work, a putting together of what he regards as the justifiably correct accounts concerning the Mahāsiddha's life. One of its other major aims is to display the magnificence of the fuller lineage of Indian teachers attached to the cult of the tantric deity Cakrasaṃvara.

There are many major variations between the two accounts, even in the recounting of some episodes which should have displayed at the very least a common awareness of the facts of the Mahāsiddha's life. I have outlined these variations elsewhere[12] and suggested that Tāranātha takes a swipe not only at Kün-ga Nyingpo and the omniscient Butön Rimpoché, but also at his own lineal predecessor Kün-ga Dröchog, perhaps for their uncritical belief in many of the unfounded, but commonly believed, stories concerning Kṛṣṇācārya, but more importantly for diminishing his grandeur by transmitting such apparently incorrect data. Indeed Tāranātha points out to the reader that out of some dozen incidents in the biography at least four are taken quite uncritically from the lives of other siddhas altogether, although they too come from the lineages of Cakrasaṃvara practitioners.

In contrast to this rather normative vision of Tāranātha, Kün-ga Dröchog sees exemplars of something he himself had hinted at early in his own work in several of these same incidents. Quite early in his biography he said, apparently as a disclaimer, that the episodes themselves were in fact meant to be quite inexplicable because, "... for the sake of convenient appearances, this mighty siddha himself adopted the stratagem that he would not gain siddhahood in this very body".[13] Thus his strange and inexplicable actions, apparently not those of a Fully Enlightened Being, were able to be explicated by this most adroit of hermeneutic devices. Over and above this clear statement, Kün-ga Dröchog also adopts a rather poetic device for his explanation of these episodes. He says for example, to justify one particular incident in which Kṛṣṇācārya appears, at least outwardly, to be quite lacking in compassion,

> On a fearful, narrow path, under the sway of doubts,
> Even people who know each other, treat each other with suspicion.
> How can the secret denouement of the pretence of "knowing" and "not knowing" which he manifested,
> Even be evaluated (by people like us)?[14]

This is not so much a hermeneutical device to explain the mystery of the events themselves as a confession by Kün-ga Dröchog that Kṛṣṇācārya was working on a quite different plane even to himself, the inheritor of Kṛṣṇācārya's reincarnatory mantle. He appears to be saying that this plane operates at a level which we mere mortals cannot even aspire to understand. However, both this and several other poetic disclaimers which appear throughout the hagiography appear to be quite unnecessary, firstly because they serve to undercut Kün-ga Dröchog's overall view of his own predecessor's life and secondly inasmuch as they merely repeat one of the common criteria of hagiographies of mahāsiddhas, that is that they frequently work on two levels of truth. One level, the outer narrative level, is relatively easy to understand even by non-initiates, but the inner level of hagiographical meaning is written in a dense, often symbolic language, quite impossible to fathom for the non-initiate. Nevertheless on both levels of understanding the hagiographies themselves deal with ostensibly the same narrative events. For example, the Mahāsiddha Virūpa, while in Orissa, refused to pay his bar tab until the sun's shadow passed a certain point. He then held the sun in its position until time went haywire and the King paid his bill for him.[15]

The Mirror of Life

We may well glean some outer data about such things as locations and conditions of society from this story but the inner meaning has much more to do with the place and the circumstances which the siddha found conducive to perform his yoga praxis, for which holding the sun's progress with one's finger, and the meaninglessness of time are simply ciphers for the technique and its result.

The Structure of Kün-ga Dröchog's Biography

The Caryā Songs

As mentioned above, Kṛṣṇācārya is renowned for his remarkable collection of Songs of Practice, the so-called Caryāgīti, which occur as part of a larger collection of fifty similar songs known as the Caryāgītikoṣa[16] sung by other Mahāsiddhas. These songs were commented on in the 13th century by the Indian Munidatta and in their extensive version, elaborated as they are to this day, especially in Nepal, by initiation, oral explanation and accompanying ritual dance and song, are said to form a sort of "initiation through hearing". Among Tibetan yogins and savants even now, the songs are guarded extremely carefully and are not intended for the ears of any except the most advanced students on the tantric path. As to the songs themselves, it seems to be generally understood that they are to be kept in the order set in the original text (dating from perhaps the 11th or 12th century) as they are said to form a hierarchy of understanding within themselves, leading the student ever higher in the practices as they proceed along the text.

However, Kün-ga Dröchog quite consciously uses the whole collection of Kṛṣṇācārya's Caryā songs in a purely narrative format throughout the biography, employing in many cases their outer (that is relative, limited level of understanding) meanings as paradigms or as amplifiers for the actual events of the text itself. This leads of course to the very interesting question of how Kün-ga Dröchog was able to justify a re-ordering of the generally accepted sequence of the songs, thereby shifting them from a purely spiritual realm into a purely narrative realm.[17]

Out of the fifty extant Caryā songs, thirteen of them were sung by Kṛṣṇācārya and it was those which Kün-ga Dröchog employed as part of the process of internal sequencing and reconciling of the songs with the series of narrative events which made up the Mahāsiddha's life.[18]

The spiritual songs have certain imageries which make an interesting comparison with the narrative events with which Kün-ga Dröchog chose to link them. It will be noted that there is a remarkable concordance between the imagery of the songs and the narrative context they have been joined to, which might suggest that the songs were originally part of some narrative hagiography, now long forgotten even in the Tibetan tradition.

David Templeman

I here summarise the nine songs out of the thirteen which Kṛṣṇācārya sang which have a strong and definite link with the narrative events of his life.

Caryā No.	Caryā Imagery	Narrative Context
7	Blocked psychic veins. Homelessness of the siddha.	Equalising psychic channels. Ongoing peregrination through the twenty four tantric lands.
24	Guru as a seed growing. Sun dispelling gloom.	Joy at the Guru's permission to practise the yogic path.
40	Qualities of a false Guru.	Asked to teach when spiritually unready and immature.
12	Chess, the Royal game.	Royal Princes of Bengal are converted to Buddhism.
13	Boating imagery.	Sea journey to Siṅgala.
10	Consort and Kṛṣṇācārya appear as outcastes.	Kṛṣṇācārya dejected when spurned by his outcaste consort, a non-Buddhist.
18	Kṛṣṇācārya rejoices in the "outcasteness" of his consort.	Consort offers herself to Kṛṣṇācārya.
19	Kṛṣṇācārya exults at winning the love of his drunken consort.	Consort makes offerings at a Buddhist ceremony.
42	Death is an illusion. "How can Kāṇha[19] not exist?" "The world is full of people who neither come nor go . . ."	Kṛṣṇācārya dies at the hands of a rampant demoness in Assam, but manifests many times in the after-death period.

The level of similarity between the imagery of the songs and the narrative events in itself is worthy of note. However, there is another such set of similarities in the hagiography which is perhaps even more noteworthy as it throws the structure of the work into relief even more clearly.

The Ḍākinī Songs

A similar parallelism exists within the structure of a lengthy initiatory song sung to the Mahāsiddha Kṛṣṇācārya by the ḍākinīs in the mythic land of Urgyen in the west of India.[20] The song clearly differentiates between some thirteen aspects of the Guhyasamāja and Cakrasaṃvara Tantras, especially the differentiation between Mother and Father Tantras. Each verse contains an important point which delineates some aspect or other of the tantras.[21]

When the verses of the ḍākinī song are broken down into their basic component ideas, we can see that according to Kün-ga Dröchog, Kṛṣṇācārya exemplified some aspect of each one in the narrative events of his life, and moreover incorporated several of the attitudes and iconographic aspects of the deity Cakrasaṃvara in his own bodily form.

To summarize the above;

Verse of the Ḍākinī Song	*Corresponding Narrative Events*
1 Great passion of means (vajra) and wisdom (lotus), exemplified in union of Cakrasaṃvara and his consort.	Kṛṣṇācārya finds and weds his consort in Siṅgala. His caryā songs rejoice in her passionate nature.
2 Cakrasaṃvara wears only bone ornaments representing lack of selfhood.	Kṛṣṇācārya journeys to Urgyen to seek the ḍākinī's blessings on to the bone ornaments.
3 Cakrasaṃvara appears to be out of control with compassion.[22]	Kṛṣṇācārya's tempestuous nature matches that of Cakrasaṃvara.
4 Cakrasaṃvara holds no symbolic attributes except for weapons or drums.	Seven small drums sound spontaneously around Kṛṣṇācārya at all times as he proceeds around India.
5 After visiting the eight Great Cemeteries, places of cult worship must be avoided.	Kṛṣṇācārya persists in visiting the "cult" site of Devīkoṭṭa, the forbidden twenty fourth place, where he is slain.
6 Outer pilgrimage is transformed into inner maṇḍala. Buddhahood is gained in that very life.	Kṛṣṇācārya visits all the places in the maṇḍala, but fails to attain Buddhahood until the after-death period.[23]
7 Cakrasaṃvara enjoins the worshipper to fuse psychic channels, seed and the psychic winds.	Kṛṣṇācārya fully masters this technique of yoga praxis.

8	The vajra master employs the "inner essence" as a protecting agent.	Kṛṣṇācārya partakes of the "sixteen red heart-essences of the demon yak" at the ceremony with the ḍākinīs in Urgyen.
9	Sacred sealing of secret practices with vajra (immutable) knots.	Kṛṣṇācārya breaks those sealing knots on the bone ornaments, without the permission of his Guru or the ḍākinīs.
10	Psychic channels are to be blessed by mantra sounds.	(no evident narrative concordance)
11	Symbolic items which reflect the heroic ascetic practices.	Kṛṣṇācārya wears all the symbolic items and performs all the designated practices from the tantra.
12	Mastering the twenty four pilgrimage places is the utpattikrama (arising) stage of Cakrasaṃvara practice.	Kṛṣṇācārya visits all twenty four places, despite being warned about the twenty fourth place by his Guru.
13	Kissing the Vasantatilaka is the sampannakrama (perfection) practice of Cakrasaṃvara.	(no evident narrative concordance)

Conclusion

It may be noted from the above table that there is a high degree of reflection between the secret song of the ḍākinīs, the narrative events of the hagiography and the persona of Kṛṣṇācārya. This is precisely the point I wish to make by the title of this paper. The effect of this multiple-level concordance is indeed rather like a mirror. The life is seen not only in a series of "life incidents" but those same events are mirrored in every aspect of the text, particularly in the most crucial aspects, those which contain the quintessential secret tantric teachings in song form.

With Kün-ga Dröchog's biography of Kṛṣṇācārya we appear to have something quite rare in the Tibetan hagiographical tradition. While it is relatively common to find hagiographies modelled on other eminent lives such as that

The Mirror of Life

of the Buddha himself or purely eulogistic accounts, mystical narratives and even august and rather pompous "Great Lives", I suggest that this particular work under consideration delineates yet another type, hitherto unremarked upon. The Life of Kṛṣṇācārya by Kün-ga Dröchog is a literary exemplar of the *most secret teachings themselves becoming manifestly real in the form of the subject of the hagiography*. In this process almost every aspect of the subject is reflected in the structure of the text, the deployment of the tantric songs and most importantly in the secret tantric teachings themselves.

It appears to me that what has been suggested by the structure of Kün-ga Dröchog's text in this case is that it is extremely hard, if not impossible, to separate the ostensibly ordinary events of a life from the deeper spiritual ones. There is no doubt at all within the tradition that the life of Kṛṣṇācārya was a perfect one, that is one which reached the tantric goal of enlightenment within this lifetime, even though his attainment of it was slightly delayed until the after-death period. However, precisely which incidents went to make up this description of perfection and how they were to be interpreted within the confines of a hagiography remained in some doubt. There is no doubt that Tibetan Buddhists used the lives of the Mahāsiddha as models for their own spiritual pursuits. Here indeed were real *vitae*, ones which profoundly influenced countless anchorites and hermits in the Land of Snows. And yet there were some nagging doubts as to how these lives would be understood. Tāranātha said in his work on Kṛṣṇācārya that it was unfortunate that there was a considerable number of people in his own time who wished to, "compare today's Lamas and their blockheaded, ordinary disciples, who have hardly embarked on the path, to the Siddhas" and acknowledged that, "even though the sphere of activity of the siddhas is other-worldly, and even though it appears to be without order and system, you must have no doubts or reversion in your views."[24] Nevertheless, despite his rather wide claims in favour of accepting the apparent lack of order and system in the lives of the siddhas he went on, as the appendix demonstrates, to assiduously correct several stories he found unacceptable. Perhaps ideally, hagiographies written by direct lineal descendants would all be more or less identical, reflecting a commonly shared series of memories. However it seems that, at least in the case of Kün-ga Dröchog and Tāranātha, their own agendas and predilections coloured the possibility of a more uniform version, despite the brilliance of each work when taken by itself.

It has become a commonplace observation to note that the genre of Tibetan hagiographical literature may become more than merely a record of past spiritual triumphs and that they may also be regarded as lives of inspiration. I would add that they also have the possibility of adopting a new dimension, that of actually becoming the teachings themselves through the structure of their narrative and their incorporation of specific doctrinal truths. Kṛṣṇācārya's life as recorded for example by Kün-ga Dröchog, appears as one in which the highly secret teachings and the narrative events have been totally unified,

David Templeman

a life which necessitates that even its written account be as perfect as the subject's existence itself. Indeed it may even be said that such a life is not only an exemplar of the teachings, but has become the teaching itself.

Notes

1 Kün-ga Dröchog's work on Kṛṣṇācārya is entitled "Nag po spyod pa'i rtogs pa brjod pa'i yal 'dab," in *The Autobiographies of Jo-nan Kun dga' grol- mchog and His Previous Embodiments*, 2 vols (New Delhi: Tibet House, 1982), vol. 1, 49–127. I have recently translated the section dealing with Kṛṣṇācārya, which is now being prepared for publication in the Library of Tibetan Works and Archives, Dharamsala, India.
2 The hagiography of this young Prince is entitled "rGyal bu dga' byed sa skyon gi rtogs brjod", in *The Collected Works of Jo-Nan rJe btsun Tāranātha*, vol. 12 (Leh, Ladakh: Smanrtsis Shesrig Dpemzod Series, 1985), 685–96. For the English translation see, David Templeman, "The Account of the Prince Rāmagopāla," *The Tibet Journal* XVII:4 (Winter, 1992), 33–56.
3 Tāranātha's own work on Kṛṣṇācārya is entitled "Slob dpon chen po spyod 'chang dbang po'i rnam par thar pa ngo tshar snyan pa'i sgra dbyangs," in *The Collected Works of Jo-nan rJe btsun Tāranātha*, vol. 12, and Tseten Dorje, ed., *Five Historical Works of Tāranātha* (Arunachal Pradesh: Tibetan Nyingma Monastery, 1975). An English translation has been published as David Templeman, *Tāranātha's Life of Kṛṣṇācārya/Kāṇha* (Dharamsala: Library of Tibetan Works and Archives, 1989).
4 Janet Gyatso, "Autobiography in Tibetan Religious Literature: Reflections on its Modes of Self-Presentation," in S. Ihara and Z. Yamaguchi, eds, *Tibetan Studies: Proceedings of the 5th Seminar of the International Association for Tibetan Studies, Narita, 1989*, (Narita: Naritasan Shinshōji, 1992), 465–78.
5 This ceremony itself has been the subject of a small preliminary study: D. Templeman, "A Narrative Account of a Ganacakra and the fulfilment of Guhyasamāja through Cakrasaṃvara," *Studies in Central and East Asian Religions*, vols 5/6 (1992/1993), 64–77.
6 These miracles of subjugation and conversion are part of the commonly acceptable structure of the hagiographies of Buddhist mahāsiddhas. They demonstrate in symbolic form the superiority of the Buddhist path as exemplified in the lives of siddhas in the same way that Buddhist deities manifest their superiority over those who would compete with them. For the *loci classici* which deal with the process of subjugation of the Hindu deity Maheśvara by the Buddhist deity Cakrasaṃvara see R. M. Davidson, "Reflections on the Maheśvara Subjugation Myth: Indic Materials, Sa-skya-pa Apologetics, and the Birth of Heruka," *The Journal of the International Association of Buddhist Studies* 14:2 (1991), 197–235; R. A. Stein, "La Soumission de Rudra et Autres Contes Tantriques," *Journal Asiatique* 283:1 (1995), 121–60.
7 This work, the *Grub thob brgyad cu rtsa bzhi'i lo rgyus* has been translated by K. Dowman as *Masters of Mahāmudrā* (New York: State University of New York Press, 1985). Pages 385–88 of the above-mentioned work discuss the text itself and the sources of further information within the Tibetan bsTan 'gyur (Tenjur).
8 D. Templeman, "Reflexive Criticism – The Case Of Kun dga' grol mchog and Tāranātha," in P. Kvaerne, ed., *Tibetan Studies, Proceedings of the 6th Seminar of the International Association for Tibetan Studies, Fagernes, 1992* (Oslo: Institute for Comparative Research in Human Culture, 1994).

The Mirror of Life

9. Here I refer to hagiographies such as those by Butön Rimpoché (1354), Pawo Tsuglag (1564) and Sumpa Khenpo (1748), all of whose brief works are modelled on that of Abhayadatta, if not wholly in substance then certainly in their manner of presentation.
10. E. Obermiller, *History of Buddhism (Chos-hbyung) by Bu-ston*, part 1, *The Jewelry of Scripture* (Leipzig: Harrassowitz, 1931).
11. The appendix to this paper will show how many of Abhayadatta's stories were considered worth reproducing by Tibetan hagiographers and will also demonstrate the flexible nature of what may be considered "core" accounts within a hagiography. I am aware that Butön appears to have adopted several of his accounts of Kṛṣṇācārya's life from the 12th-century Sakyapa writer Kün-ga Nyingpo, but have not included a summary of this earlier account due to space limitations. There are many other Tibetan savants who have written hagiographies of Kṛṣṇācārya certainly as recently as the 18th century, as exemplified by Sumpa Khenpo, but these too have been ignored for the same reason.
12. D. Templeman, "Reflexive Criticism – The Case Of Kun dga' grol mchog and Tāranātha".
13. Kün-ga Dröchog, *The Autobiographies*, vol. 1, section A, folio 2B, line 5-folio 3A, line 1.
14. Kün-ga Dröchog, *The Autobiographies*, vol. 1, section A, folio 30 B, lines 3–4.
15. D. Templeman, *The Seven Instruction Lineages* (Dharamsala: Library of Tibetan Works and Archives, 1983), 15.
16. P. Kvaerne, *An Anthology of Buddhist Tantric Songs: A Study of the Caryagiti* (Oslo, Bergen & Tromso: Det Norske Videnskaps-Akademi, Universitetsforlaget, 1977).
17. I suspect that the answer to this question, if indeed there is one, depends on an extremely detailed search through all recensions of the Caryā songs as they might have been found in outlying parts of the Tibetan cultural area, that is in peripheral areas where we already know certain early versions of texts have appeared from time to time. As Kün-ga Dröchog came from the area of Loyul, also known as Mustang, on the Nepalese–Tibetan borderland it would seem appropriate to commence with a survey of which versions of the songs were commonly found there, in the area of Tsang in southern Tibet as well as in the Kathmandu valley in the 16th century.
18. The usual order for the songs is (following the numbering system of the whole collection of fifty songs): 7, 9, 10, 11, 12, 13, 18, 19, 24, 36, 40, 42, 45.
    Kün-ga Dröchog employed the songs in the following order to fit the narrative series of events in the hagiography: 7, 24, 40, 9, 12, 13, 10, 18, 19, 36, 45, 11, 42.
19. Kāṇha is the name by which Kṛṣṇācārya is known in the Caryā songs.
20. Urgyen, also known as Oḍḍiyāna, is the earthly place where the paradise of the ḍākinīs is said to be found. It is generally said to be located in the area of the present day Swat Valley in Pakistan. However, Buddhaguptanātha, the Indian Guru of Tāranātha, is said to have visited Urgyen and his biography recounts that it was in the area of Ghazni in present day eastern Afghanistan. Tāranātha, "Grub chen Buddha gupta'i rnam thar rje btsun nyid kyi zhal lung las gzhan du rang rtog gi dri mas sbags pa'i yi ge dag pa'o," in *The Collected Works of Jo-Nan rJe btsun Tāranātha*, vol. 17. The reference is to folio 5A, lines 3–6. For others, the process of initiation and instruction by the ḍākinīs occurs solely as a series of mental events and attempting to find such a location in an earthly site is considered futile.
21. The Guhyasamāja Tantra is seen by comparison to be somewhat more restrained and fastidious in nature. The wilder and more energetic aspects of the Mother Tantra

of Cakrasaṃvara are seen to "enhance" the more conservative Guhyasamāja Tantra and to add further levels of understanding to it. In "A Narrative Account of a Ganacakra and the fulfilment of Guhyasamāja through Cakrasaṃvara" I have demonstrated that what is apparently being said is that the Guhyasamāja is actually *incomplete* without the abovementioned extra dimensions which the Cakrasaṃvara Tantra bestows on it, and that there appears a *prima facie* case for suggesting that there is a gradation of Tantras within the category known as Anuttaratantra, or "Those than which no higher exists".

22 Passion is transmuted into compassion with no loss of intensity in tantric practice. In the same manner that Avalokiteśvara's head split into eleven pieces when he viewed with compassion the follies of earthly existence, so too compassion is the informing aspect of all tantric deities no matter what their outer form may be, wrathful, amorous, playful, malignant etc. Cakrasaṃvara, a wrathful deity, manifests many of the aspects of wrath – his snarling teeth grind the world of dualistic appearances, the warlike implements he holds are symbols of his victory over the ego-centricities of the world and his pose is that of a warrior to symbolise his heroic stance towards the world of apparent appearance. Nevertheless he merely assumes these wrathful activities so that suffering beings may learn from his compassionate example that the world is not only their snare but also their very means of liberation.

23 There is an implied criticism here. Indeed, Kṛṣṇācārya is the only one amongst the eighty-four siddhas whose hagiographies are referred to in note 7, who did not attain Buddhahood in his lifetime but who instead had to wait until the after-death period. Despite this, in terms of relative importance, Kṛṣṇācārya remains one of the most highly regarded of all the great siddhas despite this black mark against him.

24 D. Templeman, *Tāranātha's Life of Kṛṣṇācārya/Kāṇha*, 12.

Appendix

Abhayadatta	Butön	Kün-ga Drōchog	Pawo Tsug	Tāranātha
Date of text, c. 1050–1150 (Abbrev. *Abhaya*)	Date of text, 1354 (Abbrev. *Butön*)	Date of text c. 1525–1560 (Abbrev. *Kün-ga*)	Date of text 1564 (Abbrev, *Pawo*)	Date of text 1632 (Abbrev. *T.*)
Born Somapuri, Bengal.	Born Orissa.	Born Orissa.	Born Bengal.	Born Orissa.
Caste-scribe.	Caste-warrior.	(*Kün-ga adopts Butön's version of caste*) Caste-warrior.	Caste-warrior.	(*T corrects Kün-ga*) Caste Brahmin.
No mention of bone ornaments.	Wears bone ornaments to gain mundane siddhi powers.	Opens the ḍākinī-sealed knots which bind the bone ornaments and wears them in defiance of Guru.	Wears bone ornaments after seeing their power in action.	As for *Kün-ga*.
No specific mention of being permitted to practise the caryās.	Guru bestows permission to practise caryās as Kṛṣṇācārya has already told his disciples he would get them.	Guru bestows full permission to practise caryās.	Guru denies permission to practise the caryās but Kṛṣṇācārya goes ahead anyway.	Guru bestows full permission to practise the caryās.
No mention of being forbidden to visit Devīkoṭṭa by Guru.	Forbidden to visit Devīkoṭṭa by Guru.	Forbidden to visit Devīkoṭṭa by Guru.	No mention of being forbidden to visit Devīkoṭṭa by Guru.	Forbidden to visit Devīkoṭṭa by Guru.
On his journey to Lankā he equates his own siddhi powers with those of his Guru. Sinks into ocean as a result.	Meets leper woman on Ganges banks. Refuses to help her across due to fear of contagion. Walks across water. Becomes arrogant and sinks into river. Siddha disciple helps woman over.	(*Kün-ga adopts Butön's story*) Meets leper woman on Ganges banks. Refuses to help her across due to fear of contagion. Siddha disciple helps woman over.	As for *Kün-ga* but Kṛṣṇācārya's role is not so central.	(*T. corrects Kün-ga's story*) Tāranātha says that this story belongs to a disciple's hagiography. Soundly rejects any story of Kṛṣṇācārya being arrogant or sinking into water.
Kṛṣṇācārya meets siddha Tantipa the weaver and eats flesh of a corpse crudely. Is chided by Tantipa who amazes him with a feast made out of apparently little.	Story not mentioned.	(*Kün-ga adopts Abhaya's story*) Story substantially the same as Abhayadatta.	Kṛṣṇācārya eats a corpse with a knife and is chided by a manifestation of his Guru who transforms himself into a crow.	(*T. corrects Kün-ga's story*) Tāranātha denies this story is part of Kṛṣṇācārya's hagiography.

No mention of this story.	Kṛṣṇācārya meets with ploughman and is refused beer. Kills oxen and is unable to revive them. Ploughman revives them instead.	(Kün-ga adopts Butön's story) Story substantially the same as Butön.	Kṛṣṇācārya meets with ploughman and is refused water. Warned about tigers. Fails to protect oxen which are killed. Ploughman returns and manifests as his Guru.	(T. corrects Kün-ga's story) Tāranātha denies this is part of Kṛṣṇācārya's hagiography.
Kṛṣṇācārya meets an orchardess. Steals fruit. Engages in siddhi power competition with her. Severely wounds her. Drops own protection momentarily to help her and is killed by her ritual gaze.	As for Abhayadatta but Kṛṣṇācārya loses only the competition, not his life.	As for Butön.	No mention of this story.	As for Butön.
No mention of this story.	Kṛṣṇācārya meets a yogin reading. Questions his status as a yogin. Is unable to understand the text yogin was reading.	(Kün-ga adopts Butön's story) Story substantially the same as Butön.	No mention of this story.	(T. corrects Kün-ga's story) Tāranātha denies this is part of Kṛṣṇācārya's hagiography.
No mention of this story.	Kṛṣṇācārya visits graveyard for ceremony. Meets blue yogin who assumes leadership. Argues with yogin who reveals himself as Heruka and identifies the leper woman as Vajravārāhī and the ploughman, orchardess and yogin reader as Heruka.	(Kün-ga adopts Butön's story) As for Butön.	No mention of this story.	(T. corrects Kün-ga's story) Tāranātha attributes blue yogin story elsewhere.

6
Peng Shaosheng or Peng Jiqing?
Biographies of a Confucian Buddhist

Colin Jeffcott

How much can it tell us to say that a biography is the account of a life? What are the understandings by which writers or readers can recognize the terms for such a project?

It is not that narrating events within a life is any way an unfamiliar undertaking. Stories about ourselves and others, after all, are the everyday currency in which we deal with the world and each other. At home, at school, as employees, as managers, as parents, children, litigants, judges, criminals, jurors: in all kinds of different contexts, human beings form understandings of each other, and ways of dealing with each other and with themselves, by presenting and receiving narratives of the events of their lives. Much of each person's sense of identity must surely be built from such narratives. Someone with no sense of any series of particular actions and experiences as belonging to her life as distinct from that of some other person has no full way of knowing who she is. Certainly bare naming can convey nothing of this identity without being connected to the stories which belong to the individual who is named.

Philosophers, historians and literary and social thinkers have all become very conscious in the last half century or so of the need for publicly available criteria for these ubiquitous questions of narrative and identity. We need social, linguistic and cultural forms to give intelligible pattern to the selection and naming of even those experiences thought of as "private" or "internal". This insight is as crucial to the thought of the later Wittgenstein as to that of Foucault, however different their reactions to it were. The notion of "publicly available criteria", of course, need carry no implication that those criteria belong to a single system, or are dictated by a single objective reality. The suggestion that there is never such a reality, that the world is constituted for us solely by the signs we use to refer to it, seems to me to be simply self-defeating.[1] On the other hand, the emphasis on the variety of our systems of signs, of their specific, contingent social and cultural forms – as distinct from the supposed certainties of rationalism or phenomenology – has surely brought

Peng Shaosheng or Peng Jiqing?

a great advance in understanding. This is so not only for specifically social institutions and patterns – from kinship to ideals of the state – but also for notions of subjective experience and the ways in which they are used to provide the materials for the building of consistent "selves."

Now a good deal of our everyday dealing in narratives takes place within the contexts of particular practices. Within these contexts, re-evaluation, even re-selection and re-definition, of what is relevant, may always be in principle open. Without some degree of agreement about what sorts of stories are to count, though, it is hard to see how we could continue to understand and carry on our socially defined practices, use the theories and ways of talking which go with them, or even find terms to criticise and reform them.[2]

One way of conceiving of "biography" would be to see it as a genre which involves more general and self-conscious versions of these everyday narratives. Like them, it would thus involve a main focus on a broad area of practice (politics, art, warfare, literature, administration). It would often draw, of course, on more than one (adding in, say, to accounts of political activity a "background" of family life, friendship, marriage, sexual liaisons), thus achieving what reviewers might call a "rounded" account. Biography might thus be seen as essentially the summation of narratives about a person, for which there is surviving evidence, evidence which was produced in the course of the subject's activity in a number of social contexts. The terms of the narratives would, broadly, be drawn from the accepted understandings (ideally, those accepted in the time being written about) of the practices involved in these contexts. Skill in the biographer would be found in the richness of the different narratives and the imaginative grasp with which they were related to the historical conditions of their contexts, as well as the consistency of the overall story. The ways that a person's record in different social contexts is brought into some kind of consistent structure of evaluation will itself very often derive, of course, from ideas which give one or other of these contexts priority. What is seen as consistent, therefore, will itself be a historical matter, and what is more one that is contested by differing evaluations of what I have been calling practices.[3]

If I call the sort of narrative I have been describing the "life-and-times" pole of the notion of biography, I don't mean to imply that work structured according to such ideas has been produced only in sets of two volumes by industrious nineteenth-century European gentlemen. While the range is thinner and much of the understanding of social practice more stereotyped, Chinese biographies of statesmen and literary figures seem to me at least sometimes to be recognizable as belonging to this pattern. And the Roman notion of *res gestae* surely involves some of the same ideas.

Of course, writing such general accounts of lives must be seen as itself a social practice, or perhaps an important part of a wider one. As cultural products, biographies themselves are part of some practice of writing. Whatever the standards and ideals of that practice are (and they are of course very various across cultures and periods) those standards and ideals will connect with a far wider range of conceptions than simply those to do with the production of life-and-times accounts. In the culture of modern Europe and its offshoots, in particular, a crucial influence has been the idea that consistency will come from delineating an inward, individual self as a focus of understanding and of moral commitment, and as the source of all kinds of ways of expressing "what we are".[4] Quite explicitly, writers possessed of this notion disavow the conception that human beings are centrally constituted by their social spheres of activity. The message is as strong in Montaigne:

> There is no man (if he listen to himselfe) that doth not discover in himselfe a peculiar forme, a swaying forme, that wrestleth against the institution, and against the tempests of passion which are contrary unto him.[5]

As it is in Rousseau:

> I long for the time when, freed from the fetters of the body, I shall be myself, at one with myself, no longer torn in two, when I myself shall suffice for my own happiness[6]

Biographical writing informed by such ideas clearly will demand different kinds of insight, and different definitions of the persons whose lives are being narrated, from those I have described as belonging to the "life-and-times" pole of such writing. Whether they are understood as fiction or fact, accounts of lives – and parts of lives – written from such a standpoint will necessarily see the narratives of social participation as being in the main subordinate to the presentation of the nature, experience and development of the inner self. Rather than constituting a life, involvement in social practices will become its setting. Narrative practice – in biographical writing as well as the modern novel – will demand consistency, not just in the account of "actions in the world", but in the view which is presented of the emotional, intellectual, spiritual life of the subject, seen from the inside. If I call this pole of biographical writing the "confessional" style, I don't mean to imply that it is produced only in autobiography, though clearly autobiographical writing lends itself to the confessional perspective. And the particular modern sense of the self – that it is the real source of what is to be taken as the individuality of the person – is not to be found in all works called *Confessions*: certainly not, for example, in the *Confessions* of Saint Augustine.

Now I don't want to make large claims for the notions I have presented here as two polar conceptions of biographical writing. For one thing, the social understandings which underlie them are always likely to be contested, and this will be reflected in the concepts which guide the biographer and so in the forms of the narratives chosen. So there will be disagreement and debate, often quite radical, over the character and worth of the practices which define the "life-and-times" pole, and over the subject's participation in them. The "inner self" of the "confessional" pole is even more liable to conflicts of interpretation. Evidence to support choosing one story over another in this context is much harder to evaluate. In more practical terms, even leaving aside these questions of self-conscious theory, no real biography is ever likely to belong solely to one or other pole. My suggestion is simply that, nevertheless, modern western expectations of biographical writing include these two rather different approaches to the definition of a life, and the structure of meaning involved in the narration of it.

Specifically religious biography of course introduces some different perspectives into this general picture. In many cases, though, religious biographies do in fact fit fairly well with the understanding of the "life-and-times" pole which I have tried to outline. The deeds of the people involved in the growth, spread, development and maintenance of religious faiths and their institutions will of course be seen in a very special perspective by biographers from their own community of belief. Nevertheless, accounts of their activities naturally enough fall largely within the history of the practices which together give the religion its social identity. This is seen clearly enough by many religious biographers themselves. To take an illustrious example from the history of Chinese Buddhism, here are the words of Huijiao, the sixth-century compiler of the great biographical collection *Gaoseng zhuan – Lives of Eminent Monks*:

> I reflect that the Dharma depends on men for its dissemination, that principles depend on teaching for their manifestation. In propagating the Dharma and explaining the teachings, none excel the eminent monks. Therefore, from its inception, they have illumined the Dharma bequeathed by Buddha. Since their extraordinary merit and wonderful accomplishments have flourished throughout the ages, and provide an inspiration to posterity, it is reasonable and proper to write a comprehensive and connected account of them.[7]

Arthur Wright's study of Huijiao's biographies shows that in his practice as well as his intentions, Huijiao was concerned above all to give what I have called "life-and-times" accounts of the monks who were his subjects. Of course, his beliefs meant that these lives might well go beyond the normal world and involve supernatural deeds, or intervention by supernatural beings. And often enough his accounts would be interpreted in such a way as to illustrate the workings of the laws of karma in the pattern of the life he was describing. Nevertheless, his biographies were accounts of the activities of men involved in the well-recognized task of "disseminating the Dharma". They were narratives of human lives in this socially involved context: as Wright points out, they were very different from the Indian hagiographies, in which "their subjects move through a sequence of supernatural events with the majesty of demi-gods", and in which "the biographical element – the chronological record of the commonplace events and actions of mundane existence – is lacking or subordinate."[8] Long before Huijiao's time, the Chinese historiographical tradition had established forms and conventions for biography. These narratives are perhaps not well described as "Confucian", but they were most certainly "socially oriented", as Confucianism prescribes. Huijiao's biographies were explicitly designed to give the world of Buddhist practice the same dignity in the record which was enjoyed by the spheres of social practice recounted by Sima Qian, Ban Gu, Fan Ye and their successors.

The nature of religious belief poses much more of a problem for what I have called the "confessional" pole of biographical writing. This is partly, of course, because of the specifically modern conceptions which go with its notion of "exploring the self". Saint Augustine's *Confessions* will be read by those whose expectations have been formed by the modern notion of "confessional biography" in a way which focuses on the author rather than his Creator. This despite his insistence that his message is a different one: that it is only God who can provide unity, coherence and intelligibility to man's sense of himself. It is Augustine's religious beliefs which provide meaning for his own emphasis on the inner life. Yet modern readers who do not share those beliefs at all, however much they may understand about them at an intellectual level, can read his work from the perspective of their own notions of inwardness, as a record of the development of a particular individual self.

If this is a distortion, it is perhaps an inevitable one. The modern sense of the inner self is drawn from developments in religious thought, but no longer belongs to the world in which the inner is read in terms of the divine or the cosmological. The radical imperfection of Man, his separateness from God and his dependence on God's grace for wholeness and salvation: these are ideas which now seem external to narratives of lives. Biographies might be used as texts for sermons on such themes. It is hard to read the narratives themselves as involving them directly. Autobiographies may claim to be the record of struggles which take their whole meaning from the realization of truths about God and His relation to Man. They are often read now as accounts of how it came about that such faith became crucial for the self-understanding of particular individuals, and as guides for our own understanding of the inner lives of those individuals.

This dichotomy is of course largely due to the loss of religious perspectives in the dominant culture of the modern world. Nevertheless, it seems to me that some such element of disjunction is never very far away from the enterprise of biography in a religious context, at least in a religious context which involves anything like the radical break between the religious and the secular world which is to be found in Augustine. Actions which are undertaken in the world of social institutions must be described in terms of the social practices which belong to them. This is so even when those institutions are built around religious belief, and however edifying are the religious interpretations the author may offer. Works like Huijiao's *Lives of Eminent Monks* aim to show the effects and tokens of faith, rather than to delineate the contents of that faith itself. In terms of inner experience, on the other hand, the right vision of the divine or the transcendent is never something which can be directly communicated in narrative words. In any case, it is the quest for that vision which is the story to be told. Expressing the vision itself through the narrative of an actual human life must be undertaken in the knowledge that the means are inherently unequal to the task. The telling of the quest, though, inevitably throws the focus back on the subject of the narrative. Allegory, as in Bunyan's *Pilgrim's Progress*, can delineate the stages of a version of the Christian life by naming its components, its episodes and even its actors as abstractions. Accounts of real lives cannot keep the world so much at bay.

This essay is about Peng Shaosheng (1740–1796) and his biographies. Peng was not a Christian, but a Buddhist, who retained for much of his life the hope of reconciling Buddhist belief with the philosophy and values of Confucianism. This might seem to make his religious world more compatible with the kind of secular systems of belief which I have been arguing inform what we now recognize as "biography". Buddhism, after all, does not insist as Christianity does on a radical break between the world of the divine will and the world of human competence. This is what makes Peng's attachment to the idea of reconciling his Buddhist and his Confucian commitments so readily understandable. The specifically religious view of human beings which is at the centre of Buddhist understanding, though, seems to me to be quite as antithetical to the one which goes with modern "confessional biography" as is that of Christianity. The goal of Buddhist enlightenment or awakening is a full and total acknowledgement of the emptiness and unreality, the lack of metaphysical substance, of human persons. To perceive, or rather to experience completely, that it is craving and nothing more which has provided what has seemed to be the unity of the self, is to be released from the illusion of that unity itself. It would be hard to find a more striking contrast to what I have been describing as the modern European sense of the self. Rousseau's moment of deliverance, after all, is to come when he can be himself without contradiction, and be able to rely solely on himself for his own happiness. Concern with the inner life as providing this kind of sense of the source of real unity of human experience, understood in terms of individuality, is surely radically at odds with the ultimate Buddhist vision. That vision is one of the dissolution, not the celebration, of the self.

If it is crucial to understand that our sense of real self belongs to the sphere of *saṃsāra*, it is also true that that sphere is not as radically different from the world of enlightenment as, in Christianity, the divine power is from the world it has created. There is, in fact, no separate world, no separate power. Buddhist enlightenment is in essence the full comprehension of the laws which actually operate in the world, the understanding of the nature of all things as seen from the standpoint of totality. Mahayana teachings, with their innumerable realms of buddhas and bodhisattvas and their varied modes of calling on them for salvation through faith, complicate this understanding. They do not change the essential perception of the Buddhist task: to come to a full comprehension of the real nature of the world of saṃsāra and thereby to transcend it. Given this relative or provisional acceptance of the world of change, the examination of a life lived in this world is something which could have its own place in the gaining of a higher understanding.

———•———

It is time to turn to Peng Shaosheng himself, or to give him his Buddhist name, Peng Jiqing. In his own short account of his life down to about 1774, which appears at the end of perhaps his best-known work, the *Jushi zhuan – Biographies of Buddhist Laymen*, Peng does not use either name. He calls himself instead the "Master who knows his true home (Zhiguizi)", the literary name which he uses throughout the book to introduce his own comments on the biographies. This is not because of any hesitation about his Buddhist identity. At the end of his preface to the book he includes a devotional poem, or *gāthā*, and identifies himself as its author by using the name Peng Jisheng, which he had in fact taken along with his full Bodhisattva vows as an *upāsaka* lay disciple only about a year before the completion of the book.

Peng saw no reason either to be apologetic about his Buddhist faith, or to think that that faith required him to shed his commitment to Confucianism. As I shall argue later, the form he chose for his autobiographical sketch, and the name he used for himself in it, both express this conviction that his Buddhist and Confucian identities were to be understood as a unity. Peng's commitment to Confucianism was very much bound up with his adherence to the School of the Mind (*xinxue*) within Confucian philosophy. This was not a position which was any longer held in the dominant schools of Confucian thinking in his time. I believe that Peng eventually found it very difficult to mount a defence of his views on the compatibility of Buddhism and Confucianism which could cope with the philosophical arguments of Confucians who were his contemporaries.[9] Of more particular interest, though, are the internally focused preoccupations of Peng's kind of Confucianism. There is undoubtedly a similarity here, at the most general level, with the "inward trend" in European thought which has had such a large influence on notions of personal and social identity.

The family into which Peng was born was part of a prominent and very successful example of the Jiangnan gentry lineage.[10] It had produced *jinshi* graduates since the last century of the Ming dynasty. Peng Shaosheng's great-grandfather, his father, and the second of two elder brothers had been placed in the palace examinations, and his eldest brother was a *juren* or provincial graduate. The father and the two elder brothers had official careers, the father becoming President of the Board of War and the second brother a Reader in the Hanlin Academy. As he grew up Peng was given the standard literary education which went with the status of the family, oriented toward the examinations and dominated by the orthodox Confucian texts and their selected commentaries by Zhu Xi. He was clearly well-suited to the tasks involved, passing the provincial examinations, and thus obtaining the status of *juren*, at the notably early age of seventeen[11]. Despite his success, it is hardly surprising, given the constricted and artificial nature of such an education, that he felt that his real commitment to learning began only after his first phase of examination training was well behind him.

An attempt at the *jinshi* examinations in Beijing the next year, 1757, was not successful, and Peng returned in the autumn of that year to his home in Suzhou prefecture. There his mother soon fell ill and died a year later, much to her son's distress. During the period of mourning for her, and afterwards, he recalls his development as going through three stages. First was one in which he re-read the older classics and histories, gaining from them an ideal of direct political involvement, and dreaming of emulating some of the heroic figures they presented. After a time, he took stock of himself, and decided that after all this was not for him. In the next stage he set himself a program of introspective self-discipline of his motives and conduct, trying to model his behaviour completely on the rules of propriety. But again after a time he took stock and came to an unhappy conclusion: "Without yet being clear about my own mind, what is there I can do?" At this point "someone told him about Daoist practices" and the third stage involved three years of attempting to realize Daoist religious goals such as "flying upward (*feisheng*)" and "release from the corpse (*shijie*)": to no avail, needless to add.[12]

It was at this time, he says, that he first really set his mind to learning.[13] This is clearly a loaded phrase. He had done a good deal of quite serious study, and reports himself as having done so, in the years after the death of his mother. What "setting his mind to learning" refers to is something more specific. It was at this time that he found a way of engaging with learning which he says truly answered the needs which his previous reading had failed to satisfy. The crucial question which he had begun to find a way of answering is the one he reports himself as having asked three years before: "What can I do to be clear about my own mind?"

In a number of accounts of this period of his life, Peng recalls his conviction that the programme of reading he had embarked on was evoking in him for the first time true insight and inward enlightenment. This sense of new understanding is recorded as coming from reading the works of the Song and Ming neo-Confucian writers. When he read the Song and Ming philosophers at the age of twenty-four, he writes, "For the first time I felt completely convinced about how the sages must be studied if we are to learn: sitting silent, I had such clarity of vision that it seemed as if things were there in front of my eyes."[14] From these works of neo-Confucian philosophy he was learning about their concepts of the mind and of human nature or essence (*xin* and *xing*).[15] Peng was reading these philosophers and understanding their concepts in a particular way. Despite his protestations that he did not pay attention to the differences of view among his masters, his account of his understanding of their works reveals a fundamental affinity with the views of the School of Mind associated with the names of Lu Xiangshan and Wang Yangming. For both of these philosophers, study of external texts or authorities is for the purpose of illuminating and giving order to what is already present in the mind, available to those who can heed it with the reverence and simplicity required. Peng is quite explicit that this was the conception which brought him at the age of twenty-four to the conviction that he had found the way to true learning:

> It was at the age of twenty-four that I first set my mind to learning. I formed the conviction that the scholar is seeking only what is already innate within him. From the works of the two schools, that of Lu Xiangshan and that of Zhu Xi, I took only those things which touched my own mind and heart, realizing their truth by silent introspection. When it came to matters over which they might be said to agree or disagree, I gave no time to spelling out the differences.[16]

Like others who had learned to think and read with this conviction, Peng found that the familiar texts of the Classics took on a fresh significance. When he returned and looked for the message to be found in the works of Confucius and his disciples, and of Mencius, "I felt that every word and every sentence was flowing straight from my own heart, and from the first there was nothing so lofty or so deep that I could not come close to grasping it."[17]

Peng's reading of the Song and Ming neo-Confucians, then, allowed him the liberating conviction that the answers to the questions of how he should live, and how he should conceive of his relation to the world at large, were available within his own mind. They did not need to be found in externally imposed authority of any kind. These are matters on which he is quite explicit. In one letter, for example, he writes:

> The only value in studying texts and doing philosophy is to liberate the mind, to learn from your own resources: it is not a question of looking for something to be applied from outside. You say that learning has always involved knowledge as a priority, and that is indeed true, but this knowledge surely cannot be sought from outside? The distinction between the knowledge we gain through the senses and the knowledge we have from the conscience which is our natural essence is a very fine one, and scholars often confound the two . . . If you are not sincerely true to your own inner being, you will not be able to keep yourself clear and free from confusion between them.[18]

Peng Shaosheng or Peng Jiqing?

Peng records his movement toward intellectual engagement with Buddhism as coming after his reading in neo-Confucian philosophy, and as having been at least partly a result of his close friendship with two men from the Suzhou area, Xue Qifeng and Wang Jin. Xue was influential in making the teachings of Buddhism seem worth serious consideration.[19] Wang, according to Peng's later memorial inscription to him after his death, was a close intellectual companion to Peng at every stage of his life, first in Confucian readings and later in Buddhist investigations.[20] In fact, of course, it was not only from these particular men that Peng came into contact with Buddhism. Buddhist practices and scriptures were a regular part of the general culture of literate families of the time, particularly but not exclusively among the women. Thus, to go no further, Peng Shaosheng's own father, Peng Qifeng, made a regular practice of reading from the Diamond Sutra, and had a pond built to continue a family tradition of keeping fish, as one sort of "releasing living things". It was probably more important, at least in the long run, that Peng's wife, whom he had married at the age of twenty, was herself a devout Buddhist.[21]

The form in which Buddhism presented itself to Peng in his early reading was very much influenced by syncretism. His early advisers encouraged him to read the works of an influential group of late Ming monks: Zhenke (1544–1605), Zhuhong (1535–1615), Deqing (1546–1623) and Zhixu (1599–1655). These men share a set of attitudes which make their religious commitment notably open and relaxed. They treat Buddhism as one way to understanding among others, they emphasize practice rather than doctrine, they particularly value the invocation of the Buddha to be found in the Pure Land tradition. In particular, they stress the importance of Buddhist commitment among lay people. Zhuhong, for example, writes of inward commitment rather than the division between lay and cleric as the crucial question: "As long as one can realize the nature of his own mind and obtain salvation it is unnecessary to ask whether that person has taken the tonsure or not." And this in turn means that the secular obligations of lay life must be included in the nature of Buddhist commitment. For Zhuhong, this is particularly true of filial piety (*xiao*). To fail in this duty is to fail in one's Buddhist vocation. Such ideas were particularly congenial to Peng, whose formation had been Confucian, but whose ideas about Confucianism itself laid so much stress on notions of inward understanding and sincerity. It is no surprise to find that he is drawn to Buddhist as well as to Confucian writers of the later Ming period.

Peng's intellectual development toward Buddhism was undertaken in close contact with a small number of friends, with whom he kept up a correspondence involving debate and critical comment as well as mutual encouragement. Peng himself was probably the most personally committed in the group, and sometimes seems to have found the effects of the questioning and debate rather hard going.[22] He took the first step toward formalizing a Buddhist notion of himself quite quickly. His later account of this action – taking the first in the series of five lay vows – is very interesting in its analysis of his own mentality. It is characteristic of him in its insistence that by taking his eventual decision to be strict in observing his vow he was not following any sort of externally prescribed programme, but being true to his own sense of himself:

> When I was twenty-five, I first took the vows against killing, and at that time I ate only meat which had been bought in the market. If I found a louse on my chest, I would straightaway let it go. I gave myself the sort of explanation Confucian scholars usually do, for I really did not want to give up eating meat altogether. But after four years, I suddenly examined my own motives, and said to myself, "Scholars are always saying: 'See all creatures as one body'". 'One body' means that at base there is no division. Doing violence to other creatures to fatten oneself is like cutting off one's four limbs to please one's mouth. The suffering inflicted is just the same. It is taking one body and treating it as two things. Acting in this way comes from paralysis of the mind. What is more, if I borrow someone else's hand to do the killing, then even though I get no reputation as a killer, and even though I don't need to do the slaughtering myself, I can sit at my ease and enjoy the results. This is what the law calls 'deliberately procuring the commission of a crime'. It is more disgraceful than putting the knife to a victim's throat oneself. From this time on I gave up eating meat altogether. This decision was not the result of fear of any Buddhist doctrine of future rebirth in animal form. It was just a matter of practising what would put my mind at ease, no more. And what can put my mind at ease is simply to know that life is to be treated well, simply to know that other creatures should be treated with love, no more.[23]

In 1769, the same year as his decision to abandon eating meat, Peng went once more to the capital to take the examination for the *jinshi* degree. This time he was successful. Offered a county magistracy, though, he refused it, and returned home. This was a turning point in his life. From then on until his acceptance of the last of the five vows of the dedicated *upāsaka* layman in 1773, he studied Buddhist doctrines, those of Pure Land in particular, and involved himself in a variety of charitable works. Most significantly for the development of his ideas, he began work in 1769 on the collection of biographies which was completed in 1774 as *Biographies of Buddhist Laymen*.[24] There can be no doubt that the motive for deciding to compile this collection was to provide patterns and justifications for a role which Peng had chosen for himself at the time he began to work on it. In the Preface which Peng asked his friend Wang Jin to write for the book, Wang speaks of Peng "explaining the Dharma in showing forth the nature of lay devotees", and goes on, "To see the self-discipline of the past as being close at hand; to show how the myriad dharmas converge on one end; to examine others through examining oneself and to examine oneself through examining others – the intentions behind this book deserve to be called apt."[25]

Peng sets out to give dignity to the role of the lay devotee by providing it with a collection of exemplars, written according to the standards of serious scholarship with which his education has made him familiar. In effect he is doing for laymen what Huijiao did so long ago for monks, in compiling the *Lives of Eminent Monks*. Reading Peng's own "Explanatory note",[26] in fact, it is very hard to believe that he is not quite explicitly trying to evoke Huijiao's work. There is the same listing of previous works, the same kinds of criticism of their shoddy scholarship, their lack of discrimination, their narrow focus or their failure to treat their subjects with proper seriousness. Like Huijiao's, Peng's work is written very much according to the canons of secular history. At the end of each of his biographies he lists his sources, which as he says include previous collections of lives of laymen, the standard dynastic histories, collected writings, prefaces and commentaries on the scriptures, and philosophical and miscellaneous writings.[27]

If Peng's work seems to owe something to the example of Huijiao's lives of monks, it is after all about men who stayed in the secular world, and in many cases were highly active in politics or scholarship. The lives they led did not involve the sort of break with secular ideals, particularly with Confucian ones, that the choice of the monastic role had involved for Huijiao's subjects. It was thus more easily possible for Peng to insist on the compatibility of Confucianism, and indeed Daoism, with Buddhist commitment, as part of his explanation of his intentions in writing his biographical collection:

> Of those who have written about the Three Doctrines, surely none is greater than Dazhu. When someone asked him about the differences and similarities among the Doctrines, he replied, "In their broad meaning and their function, they are the same: it is only if you cling to their details that they are different. They all take their origin from the one human nature, but as they work themselves out they diverge and are seen as three different things. Ignorance and enlightenment belong to human beings: they are not to be found in the differences among the Doctrines themselves." Among those who have attained to such a conception are surely Li Boji [Li Gang] of the Song and Zhao Dazhou [Zhao Zhenji] of the Ming. In the period of division between Northern and Southern courts, Buddhists and Daoists fought each other, and in Song and Ming times Confucians and Buddhists competed with each other. This was always because of their failure to realize that the truth of human nature is constant within us, that in fundamental tenets there are no differences to be found. They looked only at the branches, picked the leaves: how could they realize the whole?[28]

In Peng's conception, for Buddhist and Confucian alike, the key to understanding the fundamental unity of doctrines is to recognize that all have their point of origin in that human nature that is available within us all. He shared the conception of this nature which was common to all neo-Confucian teaching, that it was the source of the moral sense which is the essence of human persons. So it is not surprising to find him seeing the virtues and rules of conduct to be found in Buddhism and Confucianism as fundamentally the same:

> Advancing toward enlightenment and realizing the fruits of Buddhist discipline find their foundation in the Five Commandments, and the Five Commandments take their whole substance from the Five Virtues. Without practising the Five Virtues, how can you keep the Five Commandments?[29]

An equation between the Confucian Five Virtues of humanity, justice, propriety, wisdom and trust, and the Buddhist Five Commandments against killing, stealing, sexual misbehaviour, lying and alcohol, had of course been common in Chinese Buddhist writing for a long time. Beneath the coincidence of number is an argument that both religions share a commitment to the same fundamental moral principles.[30] In Peng's thinking, though, the idea takes its plausibility from his understanding that both the Confucian and the Buddhist injunctions derive from an inner human nature or essence. The Commandments are then to be seen simply as the practical working out of the innate principles expressed by the Virtues. To digress for a moment, this tendency to see sets of strongly held general moral principles or injunctions as being equivalent to each other seems to be quite a common one in ethical thought. In a quite different context, admittedly, Kant could assert the equivalence of his formulations of the Categorical Imperative with as much certainty, and almost as little justification, as Peng brought to his equation between Confucian and Buddhist ethics.

Peng himself was quite explicit about the didactic purpose he claimed his book was to serve. In selecting and condensing his sources into the fifty-five chapters on his subjects, he said:

> I have gone into detail about the reasons for which they came into the Buddhist faith, about the way they kept to it and their achievements in it. The aim is to bring each person who has the will to do so, to follow the Nature which is at his root, and whether he belongs to the Huayan tradition, to the Chan or to the Pure Land, to ponder and respond with a will to bliss, and to possess to the full the assistance of these teachers.

Despite this emphasis on the inward lessons to be taught, Peng's criteria for inclusion were quite strict. They had more to do with the honesty and integrity of the conduct and the surviving writing of his subjects than with any introspective message they might communicate to the readers. The writing of some historical figures was indeed perfect in its elegance, yet its art exceeded its substance: "what could it have to do with our Way?" And those writers from the Yuan and Ming periods who, like Peng himself, demonstrated sympathies with both Buddhism and Confucianism: only if their conduct matched their understanding were they chosen for inclusion. Otherwise, what they had written was no more than a game, unfit for consideration.

In fact, despite the great stress on the inner nature of men to be found in Peng's statements of his understanding of the faith and of his intentions in writing the work, the biographies in this book are very plainly of the "life and times" kind. In many of them, what Peng did was to supply for his subjects a supplement to the biographies they already had in other contexts. He gave narratives of the Buddhist practice which the evidence showed them to have been involved in, to add to the other social practices (literary, political), on which existing biographies concentrated. As Peng himself says,

> In some of the pieces I have given no detail of the actions of the men concerned ... what is not concerned with the Buddhist Dharma I have not recorded. Taking material which is included in a dynastic history and retelling it is not the plan of this book.

This results in a sense of quite marked disjointedness and incompleteness to the biographies, considered as accounts of the lives of specific people. Chinese biographies, from those of Sima Qian on, regularly concentrate on restricted, predetermined categories of activity for their structure, exhibiting the life as the working out of some of the possibilities in the category. This produces the impression that a good deal of the evidence on other elements of the life is being left out. The resulting short narratives sometimes seem to lack the connexions which might make intelligible the relationship of one episode with the next. Peng's concentration solely on what can be explicitly narrated as Buddhist certainly makes this impression a very strong one in many of his accounts. This is especially obvious in some of the biographies of Song lay Buddhists, of whom there are more in the work than those from any other period. Like other Chinese biographies, they might be seen as offering materials toward the judgement of a life, from the perspective of selected records to do with one or a few particular fields of social practice – in this case just those which can be identified with Buddhist faith – rather than attempting to make intelligible as full a range of connexions among the episodes of that life.

The selection of the subjects, in addition, brings the intention of the collection closer to hagiography. In his prefatory remarks to the 1783 collection of accounts of the lives of Pure Land figures, the *Jingtu sheng xian lu*, whose compilation he supervised, Peng makes it clear that this work is designed to celebrate the faith and the "good deaths" of the people whose lives it records. In this it is a contrast to the earlier *Biographies of Buddhist Laymen* in its principles of selection:

> In the *Biographies of Buddhist Laymen* and the *Biographies of Buddhist Laywomen*[31] the choice of the subjects of the records was always based on the purity of their conduct. If they had some faults, then the general rule was to leave them out. In this work, the standard for inclusion is only their faith at the end of their lives: no account is taken of the faults they might have committed previously.[32]

Another source of this sense of incompleteness in *Jushi zhuan* is that many of the pieces rely on the reader's knowledge of the lives or works of the subjects to make much sense at all. The one on Pang Yun of the mid-Tang period, whom Peng greatly admired, gives a brief narrative of his relations with major clerical figures, and some striking episodes to illustrate his unworldliness. The substance of all this is taken from the *Chuan deng lu*. In addition, the piece quotes a few of his *gāthā*. Yet in his comment in the role of historian, after the biography proper, Peng makes it clear that what has made the greatest impression on him is reading the poems left by Pang Yun. Nothing is said to give Pang's poetry any place at all in the biography itself, though on any reading it was closely connected with his Buddhist faith. Perhaps the biographies themselves are best read as contributing not to explicit setting-out of the pattern of lives but to conversation among the interested literate public about the worth and the significance of the lives of men about whom a good deal was actually already taken for granted. The comments after each biography, sometimes quite long, were written not only by Peng himself but also by his friend Wang Jin, and on occasion also by Luo Yougao. Quite often they expressed a degree of disagreement about the subjects. It is clear that these comments were an essential part of the work. In effect, they were the first contributions to the conversation which it was the point of the book to stimulate.

The last chapter of the *Biographies of Buddhist Laymen* is a very particular one. It consists solely of "Zhiguizi zhuan": "Biography of the Master who Knows his True Home". This is often called Peng's "Autobiography", but it is well to remember that it was written when he was only thirty-five, at the beginning of a career of Buddhist writing which was to last for nearly twenty more years. To my mind, it is as much the statement of a very particular stance as the record of a life. Since it is a short piece – and this itself is significant – I translate it here in full:

Biography of the Master Who Knows his True Home

The real name of Zhiguizi, the Master Who Knows his True Home, has not come down to us. In his life he was solitary, and happy with his own company, so that there was no-one who really knew him. He did at one time keep company with the Master who Recognizes Emptiness (Kongkongzi), who thought he was out of the ordinary. Zhiguizi's ancestors were Confucian scholars, and his father and elder brother were made officials of the state on the basis of their literary learning. Before Zhiguizi reached the age of twenty and was formally capped, he took an examination degree by using the words that Confucian scholars use. After that, he threw himself even more into the study of the ancient Classics and their Commentaries, as well as more worldly literature, working on them day and night without resting. At this stage, he was full of admiration for the conduct of upright scholars of the past who had the spirit of resistance, like Jia Yi of Luoyang under the Han. He dreamt of modelling himself on their example, so that he could write proposals which would bring peace and order to the world, and create a glorious reputation for himself in his own time. After a time, he reflected on himself and said, "This is not my calling." Then he gave himself up to quiet thought, turning inward to build up his inner virtue and doing no action which was not in accordance with the rules of propriety. After some little time, he again reflected on himself and said, "I have not yet understood my own mind: what is to be done?" He asked Kongkongzi about it, but Kongkongzi remained impassive and said nothing. Someone told him about Daoist practices, and he followed them for three years with nothing to show for it.

Later, he read the Buddhist books and his mind was opened: he came to the conviction that here was the destination to which the Way led. He heard that in the west there is the Buddha Amitābha, source of great radiance, who welcomes all the beings of this present world of imperfection to rebirth in the Pure Land, and he yearned for that with his whole heart. Every day he faced west and made obeisance. Kongkongzi said to him, "Can this be called anything else but knowing your true home?"

When he was thirty years old the government sent a letter appointing him to an official post at level seven of the service. He declined it, writing a *gāthā*:

Green grass in the garden,
A nice breeze in the woods,
Bring happiness to my state of peace
Without winter, without summer.

After a while, he gave up eating meat and involvement in sexual desires, writing two more *gāthā*:

Your body is my body,
Your flesh is my flesh:
Life is the greatest of virtues:
I will nurture it with you.

> It is from illusion there grows love,
> A myriad deaths, a myriad births:
> Cut it sharply away:
> The world is clear and serene.

After a little while more he went into hiding, leaving yet another *gāthā*:

> We come from no source;
> We leave for no destination:
> The utmost joy is not far;
> Call on it and there it is.

Kongkongzi says, "There have been reports that Zhiguizi is coming and going in the city and that people are running into him on occasion, but when I have looked for him he has been nowhere to be found."[33]

One of the things which seems to me to be striking about this piece is that, though it does give an account, however brief and unspecific, of the sorts of inward states which Peng went through before he found his commitment to Buddhism, the inner process which took him to that decision is left entirely without comment. From his other writings – and he was by no means unable to discuss his inner life in ways which would be relevant – it is quite plain that the sense of illumination he gained from the Confucian School of Mind was very important in this movement. This is passed over completely, though he was soon to embark on a work, *Yisheng jueyi lun*, which was an attempt to answer the criticisms of Buddhism made by Confucians of that school and to "bridge the gap" between them and Buddhist belief.

My own understanding of Peng's short account of himself here is that it needs to be read, not so much as an autobiography, as the account of a particular cultural stance. The tone is set at the beginning, with the assertion of the anonymity and lack of social identity of the hero, despite the fact that any reader of *Biographies of Buddhist Laymen* would have been aware that Zhiguizi was in fact the author of the book. The genre to which this kind of literary game belongs goes back to the self-portrait of Tao Qian (365–427), "Biography of the Master of Five Willows (*Wuliu xiansheng zhuan*)." This is not to suggest that Peng's piece is a detailed parallel to Tao Qian's. Tao's biography lacks the narrative structure of the one by Peng, and even the picture of the elusive figure at the end of "Zhiguizi zhuan" has no parallel in the Five Willows piece, though it was a very familiar literary device by Peng's time. But the fictitious obscurity of the supposedly unknown subject, expressed in very similar phrases, and most importantly the overall tone of ironic, take-it-or-leave-it simplicity, make it impossible to read Peng's autobiography as other than deliberately framed in the mode of self-description first adopted in the Five Willows piece. It was, as I've said, a well-established literary genre.[34] And it carried a clear self-conception. This was that of the literary recluse, with links to the ideal of the hermit. While this was not necessarily an ideal which was in its origins explicitly Confucian, it had become very much part of the armoury of the post-Song literary elite whose orientation was in fact very much Confucian.

Ouyang Xiu, whose credentials as a leader of the Song Confucian revival, and opponent of Buddhism, could hardly be questioned, had in fact written one of the best-known versions of the Five Willows style of self-explanation in 1070, under the title "An account of the scholar-in-retirement One-of-Six". There was a story, not based on any very strong evidence, that Ouyang had turned to Buddhism at the end of his life, and his little essay is sometimes read in this context. Nevertheless, the essay itself is quite devoid of anything which could be read as expressing religious commitment: the attitude is that of the contented and contemplative recluse.[35] Peng Shaosheng's conception of the *Jushi* in the title of his book may thus be seen as including the sense which Ouyang and other writers in the Confucian tradition give it, that of "scholar-in-retirement", "recluse", as well as its Buddhist sense of "lay devotee". His "autobiography", recounting his progress toward a committed Buddhist religious life, is cast in a form which presents itself also as a statement of the position of a recluse, on the pattern of such figures as Ouyang Xiu. In the end, the elusive hermit, in and out of the city but definitely not of it, is the same person as the one who composes the *gāthā* summing up the impermanence of the self and the immanence of paradise. This *zhuan*, I am convinced, is as little meant as a full account of a life, as much the expression of a cultural stance, as were Tao Qian's and Ouyang Xiu's. In Peng's case, the stance is the same as the one he set out explicitly in some detail in later work: namely that Confucianism and Buddhism are not incompatible, as so many Confucians have held. Rather, Buddhism is a way of understanding a position with which the literary world of Confucian culture is perfectly familiar. It is a way of realizing at least some of the aspirations of Confucians themselves.

Cursory though it is, Peng's little account of himself is certainly not what I have been calling a "life-and-times" biography. What is important in defining the changing position of its subject is his state of mind rather than his actions in any social sphere at all, including those of his religion. Once Peng has realized his Buddhist commitment, though, it seems that his interest in providing any personal explanation at all of his state of mind lapses, except for what can be found in the *gāthā*. (He wrote a very large number of these over the rest of his life, in all kinds of contexts.) It is worth remembering how far Peng moved during the seven years after he took his *jinshi* and turned down the offer of an official post, the years while he was writing the *Biographies*. He went from acceptance of the full importance of the vow against killing, to taking the full five vows of the *upāsaka* layman. His reading of these vows included an acceptance of celibate relations with his wife, with which she was in full concurrence. He read widely in Pure Land literature and began to publish works on Pure Land faith even before the *Biographies* was completed. Yet he feels no need to include any of this in his account of himself. Once Zhiguizi has realized the truth of Buddhism, Peng implies, it is time for him to withdraw his own self from the story: what matters now is the general and rather abstract attitudes and faith which are expressed in his *gāthā* and in the form of the *zhuan* itself.

Peng's intellectual and emotional life was certainly not uneventful after the completion of the *Biographies*. We have records of debates he involved himself in, especially detailed in the case of the famous one with Dai Zhen the next year (1777). He wrote a great deal, including works such as the *Yisheng jueyi lun – Resolving Doubts about the One Vehicle of Truth* – explicitly designed to reconcile Confucianism with Buddhism. He was involved in leading a number of community and charitable enterprises. And after his father's death in 1784, he went through a personal crisis, which ended in his leaving home and living as what has been called a "lay monk" until shortly before his death twelve years later. It is not hard to find places where he discusses his thoughts and feelings about many of these episodes in his books and letters, sometimes at some length. Yet nowhere in the Chinese record is there to be found any kind of biographical account which focuses on the movement of his inner thoughts and feelings in all this, not even in the brief and schematic terms of the "Zhiguizi zhuan". Perhaps there is no reason to expect Peng himself to have written such an account, though in fact both Confucians and Buddhists from the late Ming period, whose thought he so much admired, did write quite full spiritual autobiographies.[36] It is notable, though, that none of the biographical sketches written about him after his death show any more interest in drawing on the quite plentiful materials available on this aspect of his life.

The fullest of these biographical sketches from the Buddhist side is in the continuation of the *Jingtu shengxian lu*.[37] The compilation of the original work under this name, a collection of Pure Land biographies, had originally been a project carried out under Peng's instructions by his brother. Its continuation was undertaken by Hu Ting, and includes biographies of both the Peng brothers. The one of Peng Shaosheng is composed very largely of texts taken from his own writings: a number of *gāthā*, some other poems, and the oath he took at the time he completed his lay disciple's vows. The narrative which frames these quotations is very brief. In its earlier sections, it is in effect a summary of the account Peng gives in his own "Zhiguizi zhuan". It records, in addition, his admiration for particular figures of the past. It explains, for example, that one of the literary names he used, "Erlin" ("Two groves"), derived from the fact that the Buddhist Liu Yimin, a lay member of the Jin dynasty White Lotus Society of early Pure Land devotees around Huiyuan, was associated with the Eastern Grove Temple (Donglin si) on Lushan, while the Confucian Gao Panlong of the late Ming period was a leader of another institution named Eastern Grove, the famous Academy in Wuxi.[38] It mentions Peng's movement into a life of retirement, meditation and study and then into more than a decade spent as a lay associate of monasteries in Suzhou and Hangzhou. And it gives a full and pious account of his faith in the last few months of his life after he returned home. Aside from the material from Peng's own account of his early life, and the extensive quotations, perhaps the only direct comment offered in the text itself on Peng's motivations comes in the explanation offered for his writings which attempt to reconcile opposing philosophical or religious viewpoints:

> He was saddened that in this degenerate period of the Law, sentient beings do not have right understanding, and so enter into conflict among themselves. So he wrote *Resolving Doubts about the One Vehicle of Truth* to allow communication across the barrier between Buddhism and Confucianism, and *Huayan nianFo sanmei lun – On the Invocation of the Buddha as the Samādhi of the Law*[39] – to solve the disputes between the Chan and Pure Land schools of Buddhism.[40]

In this decidedly hagiographical text, the attitudes which seem to underlie the lack of interest in the inner self behind Peng's Buddhist persona are perhaps best explained in the brief critical comment which is given after the narrative proper:

> When I heard people say, "Belonging to one of the 'Groves' is better than belonging to two: if you go to Lushan you should leave Wuxi", I was very much in agreement. But when I came to read [Peng's work] on "The single course", I was full of admiration for his judgement about what should be left and what should be kept to. When I read his works *Resolving Doubts* and *On the Invocation of the Buddha*, I realized there was no first and no second, no ego and no other, and I was lost to myself.[41]

The view of the world and of humans which Peng was trying to present in the works of his Buddhist maturity was one in which distinctions were obliterated, where the sense of the unity of all things was more vividly present than the sense of distinctions between particular creatures, and where the meditative vision of this unity could achieve a kind of freedom from specified roles, both social and cultural. Neither in his own work, nor in those of the biographers who knew that work, was this vision easily compatible with any focus on a particular self as the carrier of individual identity and personal definition.

Biographies of Peng from a more orthodox, or Confucian, perspective see him mainly as a writer, or as a thinker in the "Song learning" tradition. *Qingshi liezhuan – Biographies for the Qing History* – puts its piece on him in the "literary figures" section, along with his friends Wang Jin and Luo Yougao.[42] Zhang Zhidong, toward the end of the Qing dynasty, categorized the men as neo-Confucian philosophers: "These three men were all neo-Confucians who were also versed in the Buddhist classics. This was a particular school of neo-Confucian thought in the [Qing] dynasty." The fullest biographical sketch of Peng from a Confucian perspective in fact comes from a study of Qing dynasty thinkers in the "Song learning" tradition of speculative metaphysics, as opposed to the "evidential scholarship" of "Han learning": this is the *Guochao Songxue yuanyuan ji* of Jiang Fan.[43] It is not a source which could be expected automatically to be favourable to Peng. In its biography of his friend, the *juren* Luo Yougao, considerable space is devoted to an undignified fracas in which Luo was involved when county runners tried to arrest him, suspecting that the size of the dealings he was transacting in silver must mean that he was a robber. Luo had been fond of martial arts in his youth. He resisted arrest, knocking down three of the runners before voluntarily going to the county office. There he was berated by the magistrate, and tied up when he refused to answer questions. Only the intervention of an acquaintance from a nearby monastery managed to have the situation sorted out. The biographer's ironic comment is

> There is no impiety worse than allowing the body given one by one's parents to be harmed. No-one with the slightest understanding would act like this. Do those who are students of the Buddha?[44]

Peng was not a person to provoke this kind of amusement. Jiang Fan praises the honesty of his character, and the earnestness with which he embodied his family's tradition in his early efforts to live up to Confucian ideals. There is a hint of regret that he was led astray into Buddhist studies by his association with Xue Qifeng and Wang Jin. Nevertheless, the strictness with which he kept his vows, and his record of charitable undertakings (by which "many people in the region were influenced for the good") are treated as entirely admirable. All the same, this account of Peng is almost entirely concerned with actions and words which make sense in the context of the intellectual and scholarly practices associated with Confucianism. Even relaxation in his leisure time came from collecting inscriptions, and from executing calligraphy in the Han style, both of which he characteristically defended by reference to Zhu Xi (who also collected inscriptions) and to Confucius ("I take my recreation in the arts"). He was an accomplished scholar, both of ancient works and writings of the recent past. He wrote accounts of the lives of officials and statesmen, as well as studies of Confucian writers, all of which are reliable, soundly based, and eminently suitable to be passed on to later generations. His writings on philosophical themes are subtle, closely argued, and expressed in model prose. Even his works which discuss Buddhist contemplation are elegantly phrased, and avoid the vulgar habits of the genre of Sayings (*Yulu*) associated with the Chan school. His reading of the *Daxue* is quoted at such length that it takes up over half the section: as might have been expected, it stresses the inward, natural, spontaneous sources of understanding and knowledge to a degree that takes it close to mysticism. Even here, however, Jiang Fan is tolerant: Peng

> bases himself on the the theories of Wang Yangming but pushes them further and wider. Phrases like "when in thought there is no thought [then thought has truly gone forward]" and "the mind fundamentally has no location" are close to Chan. But when he explains his programme for study, he shows that he understands what its basis must be.

And in general, his understanding of Peng's position within Confucianism points to a characteristic which almost all commentators on Peng notice, his desire to reconcile opposing positions and thus not to lose what is valuable in them: he

> was deeply involved with the school of Lu Xiangshan and Wang Yangming, so he was not able to keep himself from having some doubts about Zhu Xi. Yet he respected what he understood in each of the schools, and took his arguments no further.[45]

In all, this main biography of Peng from a Confucian viewpoint is something of a mirror image of the one written from the Buddhist perspective. While noticing Peng's commitments to the other teaching, and giving some recognition to his desire to bridge the gap between them, it concentrates on listing the ways in which he contributed to the practices involved in Confucian scholarship. The extent to which each side saw Peng in terms of its own enterprises is so striking as to be rather sad. Among his written works, his Buddhist biographer notes *Resolving Doubts about the One Vehicle of Truth* as the fruit of an effort to bridge the gap between Confucianism and Buddhism which Peng so much regretted. All the other writings which he mentions are firmly within the Buddhist tradition. Jiang Fan does not even go so far as to notice *Resolving Doubts*, but includes only works which deal with Confucian concerns: biographies, essays on neo-Confucians, commentaries. Neither the Buddhist nor the Confucian biographer sees it as his task to investigate the processes of thought or attitude which took Peng to the particular positions which he adopted, let alone to give attention to the whole range of them. Nor indeed was either interested in providing interpretations of the personal meanings which these positions had for Peng. Each is content to concentrate his attention on the practices which define the tradition to which he belongs, and simply to record Peng's contribution to them.

What the Confucian writers do notice, something which his Buddhist biographer neglects completely, is the crisis which Peng passed through after the death of his father. Jiang Fan ends his account of Peng's life:

> After the death of [his father] the Grand Marshal in 1784, he went deep into the mountains to engage in undisturbed reflection and thought, and to make progress toward Ultimate Truth. He himself said, "Truly I am in a sinking ship, a broken vessel, a war to the death. When I have swept away all my demons, I will return to the light of day." He wrote "Bitter words to show my nephews". After a long time he went back home to live, but died shortly thereafter.[46]

The inadequacy, not to say unintelligibility, of this passage as explanatory narrative seems to me to be symptomatic of the limited ambitions which informed Chinese biographies of this kind. By including this reference, Jiang Fan showed that he was certainly not indifferent to the inner life of his subject. Nevertheless, rather than giving his own explanation or interpretation of such a critical episode, he seems to have been content to offer a pointer for his readers who wished to do so, to allow them to explore the matter in the works left by Peng Shaosheng himself. Those who did so would have found that the passage Jiang quotes is one of the more dramatic parts of a long and very revealing document, "Bitter words". It is a kind of open letter to family members. In it Peng makes very plain his sense of the incompatibility of his search for inner harmony and peace, on the one hand, and the practical demands of the roles asked of him in his family, on the other. Far from being some kind of natural intellectual progression, his movement toward what amounted to a monastic life as a lay associate of Suzhou and Hangzhou temples was the result of a process of very considerable inner turmoil. This in turn was precipitated by the death of his father, which broke the link between his own inner sense of emotional commitment and the obligations which went with a Confucian identity.[47] Yet the brief lines I have quoted above are the most which any of the Chinese biographers offer, in order to make sense of this major shift in the pattern of Peng's life and commitments.

———•———

The conclusion which must be given after this examination of his biographers' treatment of Peng Shaosheng is that, whichever perspective they took on his life, their accounts were defined and structured by recounting his place in the sets of practices that they found important to their own traditions. Peng's own "autobiography" is better described as a way of communicating the cultural significance of the combination of social and intellectual positions he was choosing to adopt. Those who wrote about him after his death provided materials selected and structured to show him as involved in the patterns of activity appropriate to an identity as an intellectual figure in either Buddhism or Confucianism. All the biographies belong quite unequivocally to the "life and times" pole as I defined it at the beginning of this essay.

Why is this so? It is not as if the Chinese world of Peng's day lacked a conception of, or an interest in, notions to do with inner experience. Peng's own philosophical writings, indeed, stress this to an almost extreme degree. Yet the interest which he and many others took does seem to me to be different in kind to that which I have described as belonging to the culture of modern Europe. The truths which Buddhism and the Confucian School of the Mind hoped to find in inner experience were general truths. They were not conceived of as revealing the particular, individual self of each human being. Neither were they primarily seen as a way of differentiating the moral, emotional and intellectual worlds understood to belong to the perspectives of those individual selves. Now of course it is true that the development of a focus on the inner world of experience, in the history of Chinese conceptions of persons, did allow for a sense of individual differentiation. The philosophical and literary world of the late Ming, under the influence of extensions of Wang Yangming's thought, saw a good deal of emphasis on individual inner experience, emotional as well as intellectual. It is not surprising that this was the time in which Chinese biography – more particularly autobiography – of the confessional kind was perhaps most highly developed.[48]

The general intellectual climate of the eighteenth century, however, was very different. While there was an acceptance, even an emphasis, on the different makeup, needs and wants of particular, individual people – given philosophical expression by Dai Zhen – this went with a marked focus on the world of everyday empirical experience and social life. Stress on the world of inner experience did not usually go with this valuation of the everyday as it did in modern European thought, though there is of course the outstanding exception of the *Hong lou meng*.[49] It was precisely the notion that moral and social truths could be accessible to introspection – "as if they were things available to perception" – which Dai Zhen made the focus of his most intensive attack on the philosophy, not only of Wang Yangming but also of Zhu Xi. Dai's philosophy did not have a wide direct influence, admittedly. It does seem nevertheless to have given explicit conceptual form to general understandings which were widespread in the cultural world of the high Qing period.[50]

Peng Shaosheng, then, believed for much of his life in the worth of a philosophy which gave great importance to the inner life and believed that the most important moral and social truths belonged to it. The religious view which he came to adopt did not demand that he denied the force of these truths, but it made them relative. It confined them to the world of illusion which it was the aim of enlightenment to transcend. In Peng's own life the demands of his own nature, his need for peace and a sense of freedom from social and emotional entanglements, meant that he eventually cast off the required social roles of ordinary life as "fetters", in the search for "autonomy". Nevertheless, his sense of his spiritual goal was of course toward a stilling of the sense of a real and valued self rather than its assertion. The same was true of his Buddhist biographer. His presentation of Peng's life is in such abstract terms that it lacks even the briefest acknowledgement of the crisis which made him choose to leave behind the everyday life which he had been living in the context of his family. To the contrary, his Confucian biographer Jiang Fan notices this crisis, and refers to it. But because it is not part of the set of roles which are validated by Confucian commitments, he does not connect it explicitly with the rest of his account. Peng's philosophical discourse on the *Daxue* is noted and evaluated as a part of his more extreme version of the ideas of Wang Yangming, and as itself a kind of writing which was part of the accepted range of Confucian practices. Yet such ideas themselves were no longer the lens through which lives were understood, and they are not used by Jiang to explore the ways in which the other – quite abundant – material he had available on Peng's own understandings of his inner life might be structured in to his biographical treatment. His own biography of Peng thus stays almost entirely "on the surface" by amassing a series of accounts of conventionally Confucian activities.

There is nothing inevitable about the ways in which the culture of modern Europe and eighteenth-century China differed in the kinds of narrative and the place of inner accounts which went into unifying biographical writing. Many of the ingredients, so to speak, were similar enough to give rise to some strikingly similar attitudes and formulations. The particular religious, philosophical and social configurations of the two cultures, and the practices which belonged to them, gave rise to very different conventions of understanding and of writing about the patterns of lives, which it has been the purpose of this paper to explore. Yet the fact that neither Peng's Buddhist nor his Confucian biographer incorporated much of the history of his own inner life into their narratives has more to do with their understanding of what those narrative should look like, than with the kinds of discussion available in Peng's own more personal writings. Cao Xueqin, of course, gives his readers a great deal of analysis of the inner selves of his main characters, and to a lesser extent so did other writers of fiction. And writers who commented on the lives of real people, but were not trying to structure *biographies*, could sometimes make telling comments of a kind which could have served well to inform biographical writing of a "modern" kind, if anyone had been interested in doing that. I should like to end with what is in fact no more than a brief comment on Peng's life, and a fairly conventionally Confucian one at that. It seems to me, though, that its focus on motivation and psychological understanding demonstrates that the relative lack of interest in these subjects in the biographies is a matter of form and genre rather than of personal perception. It is taken from a collection of essays by Zhang Weiping (1780–1859).

Peng Shaosheng or Peng Jiqing?

The *jushi* Chimu[51] was descended from a family illustrious for its achievement. But he cared little for the state of the world and was taken up instead with the attractions of Buddhist meditation. One would think that this must have been something innate, resulting from a previous life. Yet in his writing collected in his *Erlin juji*, he searched out materials on the lives of ministers and scholars with high reputations, and upright officials, from recent times, putting together records which showed the particular qualities of his subjects. He was especially appreciative of men who had been scrupulous in their character and conduct, and of actions which brought help to people in need or benefit to other creatures, noting them and giving them praise. This was not done just because he put store by documents. He must have had a deep desire to make a contribution to the needs of the world and to support the educational endeavour [of Confucianism]. In my opinion, Mr Peng did not shrink from being a Confucian. But because of the nobility of his spiritual nature, he rejected the dust and vulgarity of the world, so that he found that, without his noticing it, he had come into agreement with the teachings of the Buddha. How sad it is to think of the number of people in the past who have called themselves Confucians and yet have been led astray by Buddhism![52]

Notes

1 For a very lucid and useful discussion of ideas on this subject in a broad philosophical context see Frank B. Farrell, *Subjectivity, Realism and Postmodernism: The Recovery of the World in Recent Philosophy* (Cambridge: Cambridge University Press, 1994).
2 Alisdair MacIntyre's rather idealized delineation of the idea of "practice" has given rise to a good deal of discussion which I have found useful in giving this notion substance: MacIntyre's most-quoted definition is in his *After Virtue: A Study in Moral Theory*, 2nd edition (London: Duckworth, 1985), 187. There are a number of useful critical essays in John Horton and Susan Mendus, eds, *After MacIntyre: Critical Perspectives on the Work of Alisdair MacIntyre* (Cambridge: Polity Press, 1994), see especially the treatment by Elizabeth Frazer and Nicola Lacey, 267–75.
3 MacIntyre's discussion of this theme in chapters 14 and 15 of *After Virtue* makes very clear the problems involved in providing consistent overall assessments in modern accounts of a life: it is far from clear, though, that his own suggestions about the nature and definition of the virtues go far toward solving them.
4 By "modern" here I mean simply to indicate the period from roughly the sixteenth century on. My treatment of the theme of the inward conception of the self is largely drawn from Charles Taylor, *Sources of the Self: The Making of the Modern Identity* (Cambridge, Ma: Harvard University Press, 1989). Farrell's work cited in note 1 above puts forward very interesting arguments on what he sees as the mediaeval theological background of the more extreme versions of this notion of the inward self and the powers attributed to it.
5 *Les Essais de Michel de Montaigne*, as quoted in Taylor, *Sources of the Self*, 182. The English is by Florio – his "swaying" would perhaps be translated "controlling"

or "mastering" today. The original reads, "Il n'est personne, s'il s'escoute, qui ne descouvre en soy une forme sienne, une forme maitresse, qui luicte contre l'institution, et contre la tempeste des passions qui lui est contraire."

6 *Émile*, as quoted in Taylor, *Sources of the Self*: 362. The English is by Barbara Foxley. The original reads, "J'aspire au moment où, délivré des entraves du corps, je serai moi sans contradiction, sans partages, et n'aurait besoin que de moi pour être heureux."

7 Translated in Arthur Wright, "Biography and Hagiography: Hui-chiao's Lives of Eminent Monks," reprinted in *Studies in Chinese Buddhism*, Robert M. Somers, ed. (New Haven: Yale University Press, 1990), 75.

8 Wright, "Biography and Hagiography," 76.

9 The key texts here are: firstly the exchange of letters Peng had with the scholar and philosopher Dai Zhen, shortly before the latter's death in 1777 (the text of Peng's letter can be found in Dai Zhen, He Wenguang, ed. *Mengzi ziyi shu zheng* (Beijing: Zhonghua shuju, 1961), 170–72 and a well-annotated text of Dai Zhen's reply is in An Zhenghui, *Dai Zhen zhexue zhuzuo xuanzhu* (Beijing: Zhonghua shuju, 1979), 223–51); and secondly Peng's attempt at rebuttal of Confucian arguments against Buddhism, *Yi sheng jue yi lun*, in *Zoku Zōkyō* (*Supplement to the Buddhist Canon*), 1, 2, 9, 1: 75–83 (in vol. 104 of the Hong Kong reprint). The latter work, completed in 1780, does not deal with any writer later than the end of the Ming dynasty.

10 For accounts of Peng's life and background, the most useful works are two excellent recent articles, which both give quite full references to earlier studies: Richard Shek, "Testimony to the Resilience of the Mind: The Life and Thought of Peng Shao-sheng (1740–1796)," in Richard J. Smith and D.W.Y. Kwok, eds, *Cosmology, Ontology, and Human Efficacy: Essays in Chinese Thought* (Honolulu: University of Hawaii Press, 1993); and Miura Shūichi, "Hō Shōshō no shisō," *Tōhō gakuhō* 60 (March 1988), 439–79.

11 There is some confusion in the literature about the dates of Peng's examination degrees. Shek claims that he obtained the *jinshi* before he was twenty: Miura gives the year as Qianlong 22 (1757) when Peng was eighteen *sui*. The biography in *Jingtu sheng xian lu, xubian* (*Zoku Zōkyō* 1, 2, yi, 8: in vol. 135 of the Hong Kong reprint), 1:1a says explicitly that he gained the *jinshi* in 1757. Makita Shigeo, in the much cited chapter on Peng in his *Chūgoku kinsei Bukkyōshi kenkyū* (Kyoto: Heirakuji shoten, 1957), adds to the muddle by giving the year of Peng's *jinshi* as Qianlong 34, but calculating that to be equivalent to 1759 (page 138). Shi Dongchu makes the same mistake in his *Zhongguo Fojiao jindai shi*, vol. 1, 39. Hayashi Tadayoshi, *Chūgoku Bukkyō shiseki yōsetsu* (Kyoto: Nagata bun shōdō, 1979), also gives the date as Qianlong 34, but gets his sums right and gives the correct equivalent, 1769 (p. 275). This is the date given by the biographies of Peng in *Qingshi liezhuan* (Beijing: Zhonghua shuju, 1987), 72:5924, and in *Guochao qixian leizheng chubian*, which at 437:19a gives the same date in cyclic form as Qianlong *sichou*. This last source identifies what is probably the source of the problem by commenting that "he was selected by the province at an early age". Shek is clearly taking his information from "Zhigui zi zhuan", translated in the text below, but while Peng does say there that he "gained a degree" before he was twenty, he does not specify the level of that degree. The source which is cited by Miura from Peng ("Xuwen", *Erlin juji*, 3:5b) certainly demonstrates that he took the examinations for the *jinshi* in 1757: the language he uses about what happened later ("after the results were published"), and his account of the family social connexions he was involved in at the time, imply that he did not succeed at this try. (I do not have access to *jinshi* lists to show this conclusively). To have

been accepted for the metropolitan examinations in 1757 would imply that he had passed the provincial examinations, and taken the degree of *juren*, the year before, at seventeen *sui*: certainly an early age. 1769 seems to be the most likely year for Peng's *jinshi*: the offer of an official post in that year fits this choice.

12 "Zhiguizi zhuan", *juan* 56 of *Jushi zhuan*, *Zoku Zōkyō* 1, 2, yi, 12, 5 (in vol. 149 of the Hong Kong reprint), 505b. The references to specific Daoist phrases are in "Wenjin luxu", Peng Shaosheng, *Yixing juji*, 3:16b.
13 "Wenjin luxu", *Yixing juji*, 3:16b.
14 "Xuwen", *Erlin juji*, 3:5b.
15 "Wenjin luxu", *Yixing juji*, 3:16b.
16 "Da Song Daoyuan", *Erlin juji*, 3:14a.
17 "Fu Zhuang Shengke shu", *Erlin juji*, 4:10a.
18 "Yu Han Gong fu", *Erlin juji*, 3:13b.
19 "Xue Jiasan shu", *Erlin juji*, 22:1a–b.
20 "Wangzi wenlu xu", *Erlin juji*, 6:6b.
21 Shek's and Miura's articles both give references to this family background. On the general subject of the influence of religious belief among the women of gentry families, see David Johnston, "Communication, Class and Consciousness", in David Johnson et al., eds, *Popular Culture in Late Imperial China* (Berkeley: University of California Press, 1985), 61–62.
22 The most accessible study, well-documented with full Chinese versions of the sources used, is in the middle sections of Miura's article cited above. But see also Araki Kengo, "Hō Shōshō o meguru futari no jinbutsu," in his *Yōmeigaku no kaiten to bukkyō* (Tokyo: Kenbun shuppan, 1984). Unfortunately I do not have access to the primary sources for this correspondence, aside from Peng's own contributions.
23 "Ti ren lu", *Erlin juji*, 6:1b.
24 *Jushi zhuan*, *Zoku Zōkyō*, 1, 2, yi, 12, 5 (in vol. 149 of the Hong Kong reprint). The *jushi* in the title presents insurmountable problems of translation, originally meaning "scholar in retirement", with hermetic overtones, in the Confucian tradition, and then being borrowed for "lay devotee" in the Buddhist.
25 *Jushi zhuan*, 1:396a.
26 This is to be found in *Jushi zhuan*, 1:396a–397b.
27 There is a convenient list of 39 works Peng cites three times or more in the biographies, in Hayashi, *Chūgoku Bukkyō shiseki yōsetsu*, 271–72. As Hayashi points out, many other works are cited just once or twice: his own count of the total number of identifiable works Peng used as source material is 192.
28 *Jushi zhuan*, 1:396d.
29 *Jushi zhuan*, 1:396c.
30 The Song monk Qi Song offers a good example of this argument that they were "different expressions with the same substance": "Yuan jiao" in *Tanjiao wenji* (*Taishō Dai Zōkyō*, no. 2115), 1:651b; and "Guang yuan jiao", *Tanjiao wenji*, 2:654b.
31 This refers to *Shannü zhuan*, completed in 1780.
32 *Jingtu sheng xian lu*, *xubian*, (*Zoku Zōkyō* 1, 2, yi, 8: in vol. 135 of the Hong Kong reprint), 1:1–9.
33 *Jushi zhuan*, 56, 505b–c.
34 For more detail on this genre, see Wu P'ei-yi, *The Confucian's Progress* (Princeton: Princeton University Press, 1990).
35 Ouyang's piece is not even as much of an autobiography as Tao Qian's is. Both of them are personal statements, and self-justifications for choosing life in retirement, rather than narrative accounts of their authors' lives. In Ouyang's case, the choice of retirement comes only at the end of a career of public service. The

argument of the piece, though, is unambiguously un-Buddhist: that "the affairs of the world" bring Ouyang "entanglement" in travail and worry, whereas to be "entangled" in his five pleasures (his library, his collection of old inscriptions, his *qin*, his chess-board and his regular jug of wine) is to have made himself at ease. A convenient annotated text of Ouyang's "Liuyi jushi zhuan" is in *Ouyang Xiu xuanji*, Chen Xin and Du Weimo, eds (Shanghai: Guji chuban she, 1986), 421–24. For the story about Ouyang's supposed move to Buddhism, see James T.C. Liu, *Ou-yang Hsiu: An Eleventh-Century Neo-Confucianist* (Stanford: Stanford University Press, 1967), 170, and for a modern example of acceptance of the story in a work from a Buddhist point of view, Nogami Shunjō et al., *Bukkyō shi gaisetsu – Chūgoku hen* (Kyoto: Heirakuji shoten, 1968), 137–38.

36 Gao Panlong (1562–1626), for example, a leader of the Donglin group, for whom Peng had great reverence. Wu P'ei-yi describes Gao's work as "the last Confucian spiritual autobiography", *The Confucian's Progress*, 141.

37 *Jingtu shengxian lu, xubian* (*Zoku Zōkyō* 1, 2, yi, 8: in vol. 135 of the Hong Kong reprint), 2:208a–09a.

38 Peng himself explains this in "ErLin jushuo", *Erlin juji*, 3:1b–2b.

39 Completed in 1783. On this work see Nakamura Kaoru, *Kegon no jōdo* (Kyoto: Hōzokan, 1991), 304–27.

40 *Jingtu shengxian lu, xubian*: 208d.

41 This last phrase is a reference to the historian's comment at the end of the *Shiji* biography of Jia Yi (in *juan* 84), which runs, "When I read the *fu* on 'The Owl', life and death were the same to me, I thought nothing of whether I came or went, and I was lost to myself." *Shiji* (Beijing: Zhonghua shuju, 1959), 8:2503. The quotation as a whole comes from *Jingtu shengxian lu, xubian*: 209a.

42 *Qingshi liezhuan* (Beijing, Zhonghua shuju, 1987), 72:5924–27. On page 5925 there is a quotation from Peng about the proper way to learn a good individual style of writing. His ideas about this are unmistakably in a Confucian tradition going back at least to Han Yu in the Tang dynasty. One must start by writing according to the style of some model author of the past, but the eventual goal is to develop a style of one's own which is no longer that of the model.

43 *Guochao qixian leizheng chubian* (1890, reprinted Taibei: Wenhai chuban she 1965) also includes its collection of biographical material on Peng in its section on literature, in *juan* 437:19a–21a, though in fact its fullest entry is extracted from *(Guochao) Songxue yuanyuan ji*. Since most of the section on Peng in the *Qingshi liezhuan*, and also that in *Guochao xianzheng shilue* (preface 1866, 1900 edition, 30:16a–b) is also clearly derived from this latter material, the biography originally given in *Songxue yuanyuan ji* (Guangzhou: Yueya tang, 1822: *fuji*: 10a–13b) is the most important Confucian-oriented one on Peng. Zhang Zhidong's categorization is from the appendix ("Qingdai zhushu zhu jia xing ming lüe") to Zhang's *Shumu dawen*, as quoted in Makita, *Chūgoku kinsei Bukkyōshi kenkyū*, 241.

44 *Songxue yuanyuan ji*, as quoted in *Guochao qixian leizheng chubian*, 438:24a.

45 *Guochao qixian leizheng chubian*, *juan* 438:21a. *Guochao xianzheng shilue* is less understanding: it says of Peng not only that he crossed over into Chan, but that he and his friends Luo Yougao and Wang Jin, all three, wanted to "go over the boundary between Confucianism and Buddhism and wander without cares in Great Unity." It implies that the letter which Dai Zhen sent to Peng was in order to reprimand him for this unfortunate and anti-social tendency (30:16b).

46 *Songxue yuanyuan ji*, as quoted in *Guochao qixian leizheng chubian*, 438:21a. The original of the passage quoted is in *Erlin juji*, 3:10b. It is worth noting that Jiang Fan not only takes it out of context but misquotes it in a way which makes its actual meaning extremely hard to understand without reference to the original.

47 I hope soon to publish a fuller study of the difficulty Peng found with reconciling his Confucian and Buddhist commitments in the practical circumstances of his time. "Bitter words" is a major element in this story.
48 Among other standard references on these themes, see Wm. T. De Bary, ed., *Self and Society in Ming Thought* (New York: Columbia University Press, 1970); Patrick Hanan, *The Chinese Vernacular Story*, Cambridge, Ma.: Harvard University Press, 1981), especially ch. 4; and Wu Pei-yi, *The Confucian's Progress*.
49 On this theme in the history of European thought, see Taylor, *Sources of the Self*, ch. 13; and especially pages 327–28 for an analysis of Enlightenment versions of the "ethic of everyday life" which provides material for an illuminating comparison with Dai Zhen's ideas.
50 The idea that Dai Zhen's philosophical ideas were neglected less because they were radical in their implications than because they simply offered intellectual arguments for what were in practice generally accepted values is put forward by Watanabe Hiroshi in his article in *Confucianisme et sociétés asiatiques*, Yuzo Mizoguchi and Léon Vandermeersch, eds (Paris: Harmattan, 1991).
51 Chimu was Peng Shaosheng's *hao*.
52 From Zhang Weiping, *Tingsong lu wenchao*, as quoted in *Guochao qixian leizheng chubian*, 438:21b.

7

The Epic and Nationalism in Tibet

Geoffrey Samuel

Introduction

The subject of this essay is the Tibetan Epic of King Gesar of Ling, considered as a form of discourse about the nation and the state in Tibetan societies. To begin with, I shall introduce the epic and give a brief sketch of the history of the state in the Tibetan region.

The Tibetan epic consists of a series of episodes linked by their central characters, a Tibetan king called Gesar and his entourage.[1] These Gesar stories are also found in Mongolia, and among several minor peoples in the Tibetan region, such as the Tu or Monguor of Qinghai, the Lepcha of Sikkim, and the Burushaski-speaking people of Hunza in northern Pakistan, but they are primarily associated with Tibet, and particularly with the Khampa people of Eastern Tibet (Kham). For the Khampa, who have a strong tradition of political autonomy and martial pride, the Gesar epic is an expression of central values of their society. Gesar, however, is not just a warrior. His victories result as much from his magical or spiritual power as from his fighting ability, and much of his behaviour in the epic calls to mind the archetypical figure of the trickster.[2]

The epic, usually performed by a solo singer without instrumental accompaniment, consists of a prose narrative interspersed with lengthy songs for the various characters.[3] It may be performed from memory, or through visionary inspiration, as with the small number of "inspired bards" or babdrung who are particularly valued and authoritative performers of the epic. Many episodes have been written down, however, and modern performances are usually based on one or another of these written texts, now available cheaply in printed versions. Often, two or more Khampa men will gather together to read and sing from the epic from one of these published texts. Women rarely sing the epic, although there are exceptions, and one of the most famous contemporary babdrung is a woman.

The Epic and Nationalism in Tibet

There may have been a historical Gesar, who perhaps lived in East Tibet in the 11th century, just as there may have been a historical King Arthur. As in the case of Arthur, however, the relationship between any such historical figure and the narrative of the epic is remote, at least from the point of view of Western historical scholarship. It is not necessarily remote for Tibetans, who have a strong indigenous historical tradition, but do not generally indulge in Western-style historical criticism.[4]

This does not imply that all Tibetans "believe in" Gesar as a historical figure. However, views on this topic have less to do with the historical plausibility of the events of Gesar's life than with the extent to which the speaker "believes in" Gesar as a significant spiritual entity. As I will explain later, Gesar has affiliations with the Tibetan mountain-deities, who are invoked for protection and good fortune. Tibetan lamas describe the mountain-deities as local, pre-Buddhist deities who were converted to Buddhism and bound to obedience to the Buddhist teachings by the great Indian teacher and Vajrayāna (Tantric Buddhist) magician Padmasambhava. They are nevertheless of considerable importance in the lives of Tibetans, particularly, but not only, lay people.

Gesar is also regarded by a significant number of Tibetans as a Vajrayāna Buddhist deity, and in this context he becomes, in effect, equivalent to the major deities of the Tibetan Buddhist pantheon.[5]

Whether Gesar is a significant figure in the spiritual life of a particular Tibetan can be fairly closely predicted from his or her regional origins, and his or her location in relation to the traditional Tibetan religious and political system. In regional terms, East Tibetans (Khampa) are much more likely to believe in Gesar's existence and importance than Central Tibetans, with the Amdowa of North-East Tibet somewhere in between. As far as religious affiliation is concerned, the closer the speaker's association with the Gelugpa tradition, the religious order which dominated Central Tibet, and particularly to its more conservative factions, such as that associated with the great monastery of Drepung, just outside Lhasa, the less likely he or she is to regard Gesar as a significant figure.

Two examples can illustrate the two extremes. The first is a monk of the Gelugpa order who teaches at the secondary school at the Tibetan settlement in Chandragiri, Orissa, which I visited in August 1990.[6] When I mentioned in an address to the local school that I was carrying out research on Gesar, this monk reacted with a diatribe in which he claimed that such research was a total waste of time, and that there had never been any such person as Gesar. He went on to imply, more or less, that the whole thing was a Chinese plot of some kind. (This accusation is not quite as bizarre as it might sound, as will be seen.) My second example is the reincarnate lama Drugu Chögyé Rimpoché, of the Drugpa Kagyupa, whom I visited at the refugee settlement of Tashi Jong in North India in July 1989. For this non-Gelugpa lama, the historical Gesar was merely an earthly projection of a transcendent power acting through history to achieve peace and harmony in the world.

The meaning of Gesar, in other words, is a matter of contest within Tibetan society, and any consideration of the epic as a form of discourse about the nation in Tibet needs to take into account the contested nature of Gesar. That the meaning of Gesar is under dispute is not really surprising. I have suggested elsewhere[7] that many aspects of Tibetan society are contested. Perhaps the primary line of cleavage concerns the role of state power.

The State in Tibet

In the late Ernest Gellner's entertaining survey of human history and its underlying social mechanisms, *Plough, Sword and Book*, he suggests

> as a provisional hypothesis that concentration of power will generally obtain, unless special countervailing factors operate.[8]

Two examples of countervailing circumstances which he instances are pastoral societies and peasant societies in difficult terrain.[9] In each case, economic exploitation and the development of centralized government tends to be limited. For the pastoralists, this is because their wealth is mobile, for peasants in inaccessible areas (such as the Moroccan Berbers Gellner himself wrote about in his *Saints of the Atlas*)[10] it is because it is not worth the effort for any state to extract what surplus they manage to produce. Now, these two cases cover between them a large part of the population of Tibet. A third set of circumstances which Gellner cites is also quite relevant to Tibet; that of a society where diversified trade is prevalent, and is carried on by large numbers of relatively independent and autonomous traders.[11]

Whatever the causes, Tibetan societies, as I have suggested elsewhere[12] were on the margins of viability for states, and centralized government in pre-modern times was established only to a limited and fluctuating degree. The early Tibetan state, which I refer to following Beckwith[13] as the Tibetan Empire, grew out of a lineage of local chieftains, the so-called Yarlung dynasty, who seem to have functioned as more or less Frazerian sacred kings.[14] They claimed semi-divine status and descent from one of the major mountain-gods of Central Tibet, Yarlha Shampo. I shall refer to this set of ideas below as the "Mountain God scenario".

In the early 7th century, the Yarlung state became an expansionist military entity which temporarily rivalled the Arab, Turkic and Chinese who were competing for control of the Central Asian trade routes. After barely two centuries, it collapsed into a multitude of local regimes and stateless areas, who were nevertheless now linked by a common written language and early forms of what was to become a common religious culture.[15]

The Epic and Nationalism in Tibet

Central Tibet was the one area where there was enough relatively accessible agricultural land to form the foundation of a stable state of any size. This regime was the nearest the Tibetans had in subsequent times to large-scale indigenous states. There were four of these between the collapse of Mongol rule in the mid-14th century and the imposition of direct Chinese rule in 1950-59. The first was established by Tai Situ Changchub Gyentsen, originally a subordinate ruler under the Mongol system, during the last years of Mongol overlordship. The last and most successful Tibetan state was that centred at Lhasa and headed by the Dalai Lamas, senior incarnate lamas of the Gelugpa order, and established in 1642 with the aid of the Mongol chieftain Güüshi Khan. While subject to intermittent Manchu interventions, especially during the 18th and early 19th century, this Lhasa regime was for most of its history an independent state, if a weak one.

The Lhasa state, like its predecessors, had some influence in the pastoral areas to the north and north-east of Central Tibet, and in the agricultural and pastoral communities of Kham to the east, but they established direct rule over these regions for only limited periods. By the end of the 19th century Kham was divided into numerous small states and stateless regions. Some of these were loosely incorporated into the Lhasa state, in a weak version of what Stanley Tambiah has called a "galactic polity",[16] others were even more loosely incorporated into the Chinese administrative system.[17] From the point of view of the Manchu rulers of China, all of Tibet was difficult and inaccessible territory along the margins of the civilized world. Small Chinese garrisons were stationed in a few places along the two main trading routes, Tibetan local rulers were awarded *tusi* titles which theoretically integrated them into the Manchu hierarchy, but in practice the Tibetans ran their own affairs.[18] This situation continued until 1950, when most of Kham was integrated into the Chinese province of Sichuan and a much more direct system of rule established.

The epic was, as I have mentioned, particularly associated with East Tibet (Kham). The social and political system of East Tibet in the pre-modern period, prior to 1950, was dominated in both the agricultural and pastoral regions (generally fairly close together in Kham) by a number of high-status lineages or families (rüpa).[19] Some of these were ruling families of petty states, or local aristocratic families within those states, generally enjoying considerable autonomy in their own regions. These families might supply officials at court on a similar model to that of the Lhasa government (as in the states of Dergé and Nangchen). Other rüpa were in effect local aristocratic lineages within stateless areas (Gonjo, Gyandé); this pattern was particularly common in primarily pastoral regions.

The head lamas of the major East Tibetan monasteries also mostly came from these same high-status families, usually being chosen through the process of recognizing rebirths, though occasionally through direct inheritance. High-status religious families, descended from famous non-monastic lamas, generally intermarried with these high status secular lineages.

The same families played a key role in large-scale trade, since they had both the financial resources necessary to organize large trading caravans, and the connections in the big trading towns of Eastern and Central Tibet such as Lhasa itself, Jyekundo, Kandzé or Dartsedo (Kangding) and outside Tibet in places such as Delhi, Kalimpong, Calcutta, Srinagar, Kathmandu or Xining. Khampa politics seems to have been based on these networks of linkages between relatively autonomous high-status lineages, with lower-status lineages attached through various kinds of patron-client relationships, including hereditary attachment to estates, particularly in the case of agricultural regions. The Khampa were, however, constantly threatened with encroachment by the more politically centralized regions surrounding them, including the Lhasa government itself, the Chinese state and the Mongols. Buddhism had come into Tibet as a state ideology, and though it survived in forms that were not directly linked to the state, it still had concepts that could sanction a much more centralized model of government such as obtained in Central Tibet.

Tibetan Discourse on the State

As might be expected given this background, Tibetan discourse on the state was and is complex and multivocal. The Tibetans imported, along with Buddhism, many of the Indian-derived conceptions that are familiar from the Hinduized states of South-East Asia, such as the *cakravartin*, or universal monarch, and the *dharmarāja*, or just king. The Lhasa state also developed a complex theory based on the so-called priest-patron (chö-yön) relationship between Dalai Lama and Manchu Emperor, which was itself held to be a renewal of the relationship between a previous series of lamas and the Mongol rulers.

In addition, the Lhasa regime followed the practice, introduced by the earlier regime of Changchub Gyentsen (reigned 1354–73) of emphasizing their links with the early Tibetan Empire. Several of the early Tibetan emperors had been discovered retrospectively to be emanations of Tantric deities, most notably of the bodhisattva Chenrezig (S. Avalokiteśvara), who became a kind of patron deity of the Tibetans and was also identified with the mythical ancestral monkey who fathered the ancestors of the six Tibetan tribes. The Dalai Lamas established their capital in Lhasa, rebuilding the palace of the old Tibetan emperors on the Potala, and they too came to be regarded as emanations of Chenrezig. We can call this the "Bodhisattva Emanation Scenario". We may note its similarities to the old "Mountain God scenario," but also that it has close links with the *cakravartin* and *dharmarāja* concepts and with the galactic polity model. The Manchu emperors were also regarded as Bodhisattva Emanations, in this case of the deity Jampeyang (S. Mañjuśrī). However, while the identity of the Dalai Lama with Chenrezig is well-known and often repeated, the Manchu emperor's bodhisattva status seems to have been more a doctrine given formal recognition by the Gelugpa in Tibet for reasons of state than an active belief.

Other Tibetan states used a variety of lines of legitimation. Monastic regimes, such as that in Bhutan, usually had some version of the Bodhisattva Emanation approach. The chief reincarnate lama lineage of the Karma Kagyupa order, like the Dalai Lamas, were regarded as Chenrezig emanations, the hereditary chief lamas of Sakya were also held to be emanations of various bodhisattvas, and the most senior Gelugpa incarnation after the Dalai Lama, the Panchen Rimpoché, were emanations of the Buddha Öpagmé (S. Amitābha). Lay regimes generally either claimed to derive from the old imperial lineage (as with the kings of Ladakh and of Powo), or else produced their own version of the Mountain God scenario used by the early kings, and perhaps common to most or all Tibetan aristocratic lineages in earlier times.

Generally speaking, the Bodhisattva Emanation story, especially when combined with elements of the *cakravartin* ideology, constitutes the ruler as the centre of the galactic polity on a model rather similar to that of the Indianized states of SE Asia. The Mountain God scenario is much less Indianized and constitutes the ruler in essentially indigenous terms. In fact, since each region has its own major mountain-god, and many aristocratic lineages claim descent from the mountain-gods, the Mountain God scenario defines the ruling lineage as one of a number of local ruling lineages, as *primus inter pares* rather than universal monarch. Perhaps for this reason, the early Tibetan emperors eventually came to be regarded as descended not from a mountain-god but from an Indian prince who came to Tibet.[20]

Elsewhere I have written of a polarity between "wild" and "tame" in Tibetan society,[21] the "wild" polarity corresponding to the decentralized and pastoral areas, the "tame" to the centralized and agricultural regions. The Bodhisattva Emanation theory and the Indic approach in general is associated with the "tame" end of the continuum. The function of a Bodhisattva emanation is precisely to "tame" his or her followers, where the term "tame" implies "civilize" and "convert to Buddhist practice".[22]

Gesar and the State

Having explored Tibetan conceptions of kingship, we return to the figure of Gesar. Gesar is himself a king or gyebo. Perhaps significantly, he is never called tsempo, the old term for the rulers of the Yarlung dynasty, equated with the Chinese emperor. His legend includes both Bodhisattva Emanation and Mountain-God Descent elements, with some tension noticeable between them. Thus Gesar is often described as an emanation of a bodhisattva, most usually of three of them conjointly (the so-called Rigsum Gönpo, corresponding to the S. Mañjuśrī, Vajrapāṇi and Avalokiteśvara). He is also the earthly representative of Guru Rimpoché or Padmasambhava, the deified Indian teacher who played a central role in the conversion of Tibet to Buddhism, and who is himself an emanation of Avalokiteśvara.

However, Gesar in the epic also has strong connections to the mountain-deities. Iconographically, he resembles them quite closely, being shown as they mostly are in the form of an armed and mounted warrior. Gesar in the epic is the rebirth of a heavenly deity, and as such has a heavenly father, usually Brahma in the Tibetan versions, but he is also the son or adopted son of the mountain-god Gendzo, and seems to have a special relationship to the principal mountain-god of Eastern Tibet, Machen Pomra. He is protected by the female sky-goddess Manéné. Machen Pomra and Manéné are both defenders of Buddhism but also powerful folk-religion deities with non-Buddhist associations.

The relationship between these two sets of elements, Indic and indigenous, is complex, and they reflect the complex history of the Gesar epic, which I have attempted to reconstruct elsewhere.[23] It seems that Gesar at an earlier stage was a figure with strong folk-religion overtones. He is still evoked as a god of good fortune, including success in warfare, in both Tibet and Mongolia.[24] He plays a pivotal role in relation to East Tibetan origin myths, in that most of the high-status lineages of East Tibet claim descent from one or another of Gesar's ministers or warriors. Possibly this situation developed during the dominance of the East Tibetan state of Lingtshang, whose rulers claimed descent from Gesar's half-brother. Gesar himself has no direct descendants in the epic; again the story seems to sanction a situation in which one local lineage is the most powerful of many local lineages, rather than a regime of centralized dominance by a ruling family endowed with some claim to absolute power.

In a recent paper, Samten Karmay has argued that the story of the epic, with its gradual incorporation of defeated neighbouring peoples into the Ling state, describes a transition between "a clan or tribal society" and "a kingdom with many vassals and with a chief now styled as a universal monarch".[25] There is undoubtedly truth in this, and the centralizing elements in the epic perhaps reflect its appropriation as state ideology by the Lingtshang kingdom. The epic as a whole, however, does not really describe Gesar as the ruler of a centralized state. He is a leader in times of war and crisis, but at other times he characteristically goes into religious retreat rather than being concerned with day-to-day administration. His wars, too, are not wars of conquest as such. They are essentially defensive in nature, and are almost always set off by aggressive action on the part of the king or leader of a neighbouring people, the Hor (Uighurs in Amdo), Jang (Naxi), Lhomon (?Bhutan), Khaché (Kashmir), Drugu (Turks), Sogpo (Mongols), Ladakh, etc. The king is often a demon, rather than a human being, and his removal by Gesar is an act of Buddhist compassion, since his own people are suffering under his oppressive and anti-Buddhist rule.

The Epic and Nationalism in Tibet

Significantly, the enemy king usually has a dzong or fortress, suggesting that he is a representative of intrusive state power threatening the people of Gesar's country. Once he has been defeated, Gesar and his generals replace him by a more worthy successor, who becomes an ally of Gesar. It does not seem that the conquered people are incorporated directly into Gesar's kingdom. They are allies, not vassals, and take part in future wars on that basis.

As a model for political relations, this picture bears a striking similarity to the realities of Eastern Tibetan politics in the pre-1950 period. The main difference is that in practice the intrusive state powers – primarily the Chinese governments and local warlords in Sichuan and Qinghai provinces, the various Mongol groups who intervened in Tibetan politics, especially from the 18th century onwards, and perhaps the Tibetan government at Lhasa itself – were not always dealt with as skilfully nor as successfully as by the epic hero.

Later, however, primarily in the 19th and 20th centuries, the Gesar stories acquired a rather different colouring. They were reworked under the influence of the East Tibetan Rimé lamas, in particular the great Nyingmapa scholar Ju Mipam (1846–1914), who was responsible for carving woodblocks for the printing of three central episodes of the epic and for creating (or rather "revealing") a large and influential body of Gesar rituals.[26] It was at this time that the idea of Gesar as a full-blown Vajrayāna deity presumably began to gain currency.

These various developments generated three ways of reading Gesar for contemporary Tibetans:

1. he can be seen positively as a folk-religion figure, associated with this worldly success and good fortune, with close relationship to the mountain-gods, and affinities to the old dominant lineages of Kham;
2. he can be seen positively as a Bodhisattva emanation, still associated with this-worldly success and good fortune, but also with the more transcendent aim of Enlightenment, and with connections to the galactic-polity model of the centralized state;
3. he can be seen negatively as a folk-religion figure, as associated with marginal and dubiously-Buddhist cults, and with the independent and "untamed" nature of the East Tibetans as contrasted with the more "civilized" people of Central Tibet.

To which we could add a fourth possibility: Gesar can be seen negatively as part of an alien and intrusive state system, that of China. A form of the Gesar cult was promoted in Tibet from the 18th century onwards by the Manchu dynasty. The Manchus were familiar with the Mongolian version of Gesar, whom they assimilated to the Chinese war-god Guandi or Guan Yü.[27] In Central Tibet, in particular, where the cult of the Tibetan Gesar was much less developed than in the East, the only temples of Gesar were actually temples of this syncretic Manchu-Mongolian cult. This is part of the background to the Gelugpa monk's comment that Gesar was all part of a Chinese plot.

More recently, Gesar has been heavily promoted (as folklore, certainly, rather than as religion) within the People's Republic of China. While the epic was suppressed during the Cultural Revolution, it made a remarkable comeback from around 1980 onwards. It is now officially described as a great *Chinese* epic (it is found, as I mentioned earlier, among several other minority nationalities besides the Tibetans, in particular among the Mongolians), especially since it is, by Chinese calculations, supposed to be the longest epic in the world.[28] A large-scale campaign to collect and preserve the epic has been organized throughout Tibetan regions and in Inner Mongolia. Around 100 episodes from the epic have been published in Tibetan in recent years, along with numerous Chinese translations. An 18-episode TV version of the epic has been broadcast. Several local conferences and three international conferences have been held on the Gesar Epic.

I attended the first two of these international conferences, in Chengdu in 1989 and Lhasa in 1991, and I have been studying scholarly work on Gesar in the People's Republic of China with some attention in recent years. I will conclude this rather condensed survey of the significance of the Tibetan epic as discourse about the state with some speculations on the meaning of Gesar today. Has Gesar simply been appropriated by the Chinese rulers of Tibet for their own purposes?

Conclusion: Gesar in the People's Republic of China

Superficially, the answer would seem to be yes, and the Gelugpa monk's diatribe against Gesar would seem to have some basis in reality. I have no doubt that the promotion of Gesar in the PRC is related to its being seen as a safe "folkloristic" topic, not directly involved with Buddhism,[29] and politically neutral or even positive, since Gesar can be seen as fighting for the welfare of the Tibetan masses as against the arbitrary and oppressive rule of the demon-kings. The epic as folklore is also quite consonant with the general Han Chinese stereotype of minority populations as simple, unsophisticated people, fond of singing, dancing, and other such cosy ethnic pursuits. I am sure all this has much to do with why the Gesar epic received such conspicuous official sanction, though many of the Chinese and Tibetan scholars who were actually working on the epic were doubtless aware, as the reader will be by now, that matters are more complex than the stereotype might suggest.

The validation of Gesar as a relatively "safe" topic has however created an arena within which some interesting things can happen. Reading and listening to some of the recent contributions on Gesar by scholars from the

PRC, one can sense that Gesar studies is a context within which, for example, the question of the autonomy of Tibetan culture can be asserted, and a dialogue with foreign scholars, including refugee Tibetan scholars, entered into. To validate Gesar is also, in a sense, to validate the Tibetan way of life, and as Gesar studies develop to greater levels of sophistication, they are bringing about a confrontation with aspects of Tibetan culture which in other contexts might simply be dismissed as archaic superstition. The question of the shamanic or inspired bards (babdrung), and the religious aspects of Gesar in general, are examples.

Consequently, I do not feel entirely negative about the Chinese appropriation of Gesar. Or, to put it in slightly different terms, Gesar, who always had a strong component of the trickster in his make-up, perhaps retains an ability to subvert the dominant Chinese modes of discourse about Tibet in a way not open to more straightforward political critiques. At least, I hope so.

Notes

1 For a survey of the epic and scholarly literature pertaining to it, see Geoffrey Samuel, "Gesar of Ling: The Origins and Meaning of the East Tibetan Epic," in S. Ihara and Z. Yamaguchi, eds, *Tibetan Studies: Proceedings of the 5th Seminar of the International Association for Tibetan Studies, Narita, 1989*, (Narita: Naritasan Shinshoji, 1992), 711–22. Karmay outlines the major episodes of the epic in its East Tibetan version, giving references to modern text-editions for the various episodes. See Samten Karmay, "The Theoretical Basis of the Tibetan Epic, with Reference to a 'Chronological Order' of the Various Episodes in the Gesar Epic," *Bulletin of the School of Oriental and African Studies* 56 (1993), 234–46.
2 Radin, *The Trickster: A Study in American Indian Mythology* (London: Routledge & Kegan Paul, 1955); Geoffrey Samuel, *Mind, Body and Culture: Anthropology and the Biological Interface* (London & New York: Cambridge University Press, 1990), 119.
3 Geoffrey Samuel, "Music and Shamanic Power in the Gesar Epic," in Jamie Kassler, ed., *Metaphor: A Musical Dimension* (Sydney: Currency Press, 1991).
4 Cf. Matthew Kapstein, "The Purificatory Gem and its Cleansing: A Late Tibetan Polemical Discussion of Apocryphal Texts," *History of Religions* 28:3 (1989), 217–44.
5 Cf. Geoffrey Samuel, "Some Tibetan Ritual Texts about King Gesar," paper for the 2nd International Conference on Gesar Epic Studies, Lhasa, Tibet, August 1991.
6 I would like to acknowledge the assistance in this research of Mr Tashi Tsering of Amnye Machin Institute, Dharamsala, himself a noted Gesar scholar.
7 Geoffrey Samuel, *Civilized Shamans: Buddhism in Tibetan Societies* (Washington DC: Smithsonian Institution Press, 1993).
8 Ernest Gellner, *Plough, Sword, and Book* (Harmondsworth: Penguin, 1988), 149.
9 Gellner, *Plough, Sword, and Book*, 149–50.
10 Ernest Gellner, *Saints of the Atlas* (London: Weidenfeld and Nicolson, 1969).
11 Gellner, *Plough, Sword, and Book*, 152–53.
12 Geoffrey Samuel, "Tibet as a Stateless Society and Some Islamic Parallels," *Journal of Asian Studies* 41:2 (1982), 215–29, and *Civilized Shamans*.

13 Christopher Beckwith, "Tibet and the Early Medieval *florissance* in Eurasia," *Central Asiatic Journal* 21:2 (1977), 89–104, and *The Tibetan Empire in Central Asia*. (New York: Princeton University Press, 1987).
14 Giuseppe Tucci, "The Secret Characters [=Sacral Character] of the Kings of Ancient Tibet," *East and West* 6:2 (1955), 197–205; Erik Haarh, *The Yar-luṅ Dynasty* (Copenhagen, 1969); Russell Kirkland, "The Spirit of the Mountain: Myth and State in Pre-Buddhist Tibet," *History of Religions* 21 (1982), 257–71.
15 Beckwith, *The Tibetan Empire in Central Asia*; Samuel, *Civilized Shamans*.
16 S.J. Tambiah, "The Galactic Polity in Southeast Asia," in S.J. Tambiah, *Culture, Thought and Social Action: An Anthropological Perspective* (Cambridge, Ma. & London: Harvard University Press, 1985).
17 Samuel, *Civilized Shamans*, 64–86.
18 Takeshi Hamashita, "The Tribute Trade System and Modern Asia," *Memoirs of the Tōyō Bunko* 46 (1988), 7–25; Samuel, *Civilized Shamans*.
19 For the term rü, rüpa elsewhere in the Tibetan cultural world, see Nancy E. Levine, "The Theory of *rü* Kinship, Descent and Status in a Tibetan Society," in C. von Fürer-Haimendorf, ed., *Asian Highland Societies in Anthropological Perspective* (New Delhi: Sterling, 1981), 52–78; Samuel, *Civilized Shamans:*, 128–30. As far as I know, no serious research has yet been done on Khampa kinship (cf. Samuel, *Civilized Shamans*, 593, n9).
20 Haarh, *The Yar-luṅ Dynasty*.
21 Samuel, *Civilized Shamans*, 217–22.
22 Samuel, *Civilized Shamans*, 219–20.
23 Samuel, "Gesar of Ling".
24 Walther Heissig, *The Religions of Mongolia* (London: Routledge & Kegan Paul, 1980); Samuel, "Some Tibetan Ritual Texts about King Gesar".
25 Karmay, "The Social Organization of Ling and the Term *Phu-nu* in the Gesar Epic," 313.
26 Samuel, "Some Tibetan Ritual Texts about King Gesar" and *Civilized Shamans*, 537, 540.
27 Heissig, *The Religions of Mongolia*, 99–100.
28 Wang Yinuan "Incomplete Statistics of Sections and Lines in the Tibetan *King Gesar*" [in Chinese] *Gesar Yanjiu* 1 (1985), 184–211.
29 See two articles by the part-Tibetan Gesar scholar Jiangbian Jiacuo, of the Institute of Nationalities Literature of the Chinese Academy of Social Sciences in Beijing, in both of which a somewhat unconvincing attempt is made to present the epic as intrinsically non-Buddhist. Jiangbian Jiacuo, "Gesar and the Tibetan Culture," paper for the 5th Seminar of the International Association for Tibetan Studies, Narita, Japan, 1989, and [= Vjam-dpal rgya-mtsho] "Gesar and Religion," *Tibet Studies: Journal of the Tibetan Academy of Social Sciences* 1 (1989), 202–17.

8

Biography by Instalment

The Tibetan Periodicals *Sheja* and *Trunggö Böjong* on the Lives of Reincarnate Lamas

Kevin Garratt

Contemporary Tibetan society and culture, at least outside the boundaries of the People's Republic of China, remain inextricably linked with religious belief and practice, handed down from generation to generation for at least a millenium. Within the PRC, the seemingly moribund state of Tibetan Buddhism[1] may well have caused erosion of much of traditional Tibet's distinctive religious and cultural heritage. Yet the panoply of religion, in its myriad forms, continues to exert an influence across the Tibet plateau and to permeate the very fabric of Tibetan life elsewhere. The last decade does not appear to have witnessed any significant diminution in the strength of their religious traditions – be it those of the Buddhist majority or of a somewhat resurgent Bön animism or the pockets of Islam in the Tibetan Muslim communities of Kashmir.

The paper's focus is on how two current, secular periodicals, appearing in the Tibetan language and representing very different interests, present and contribute to the long tradition of textual religious biography found within the Buddhism of Tibet. All four schools of Tibetan Buddhism have long maintained a strong tradition of religious biography, which may be broadly categorised under the following headings:

textual: principally by way of a longstanding woodblock-printed hagiography – a tradition still extant both in and outside the PRC, though now, of course, competing with the wealth of material produced using modern technologies;

iconographic: painted scrolls, murals and frescoes adorning the interiors of temples, shrines and caves; also stupas, rock paintings and other adaptation of the natural landscape. Fine examples of these approaches can still be seen in and around the Potala and the Summer Palaces of the Thirteenth and the

Fourteenth (the present) Dalai Lamas in Lhasa; many have been added to those already in south Asia, mostly as a result of the post-1959 Tibetan exodus southwards across the Himalayas;

oral: religious and political material, ranging from the devotional songs of the yogi Milarepa from almost a millennium ago; the tales of professional itinerant storytellers; the irreverent social comment of Tibetan street songs earlier this century and popular songs referring to the Dalai Lama still heard in Lhasa today.

While those traditions remain intact to varying degrees within the Tibetan diaspora and in the PRC too, they have had to weather tremendous upheavals since 1949, adapting to environments almost unheard of in the traditional – some may say feudal – Tibet of a mere 50 years ago. Thus both periodicals – *Sheja* and *Trunggö Böjong* – operate in political, social, cultural and technological milieux vastly different from those confronting the traditional hagiography of pre-1949 Tibet.

Sheja

Sheja (Knowledge) is a monthly newspaper, published for thirty years from Dharamsala, the seat of the Dalai Lama in the Himalayan foothills of north-west India. Initially established in 1969 under private imprimateur, *Sheja* became a government publication in 1971. It has a wide circulation among the approximately 120,000 Tibetans living outside their homeland, mainly in south Asia. Its overall reportage may be characterised as a reflection of the Tibetan government-in-exile's policy of the day; besides that inevitable political function, it continues to serve as a channel of information on Tibetan religious affairs generally.

Rarely of less than twenty-eight closely printed pages, it is easily recognisable by a striking five-coloured masthead – otherwise it remains a black and white product throughout. Until recently the quality of paper, printing and artwork (including photographs) fluctuated considerably – in the one issue, columns of crisp print can suddenly give way to an indecipherable jumble of Tibetan vowels and consonants. Nearly all articles are anonymous and publication data amounts to just an Indian registration number. In contrast to *Trunggö Böjong*, neither a business address nor the editor's identity appears; there is no immediate English language counterpart for *Sheja* though translations of some articles – word for word or in summary and usually bolstering Dharamsala's position – feature in the bimonthly *Tibetan Bulletin: the Official Journal of the Tibetan Administration of His Holiness the Dalai Lama*. While unswerving editorial allegiance to the official line in *Sheja* may not parallel that of, say, the PRC's *Renmin Ribao*, the paper does

Biography by Instalment

sometimes offer a degree of muted criticism of the Dharamsala body politic – be it the Kashag (the Cabinet), the Assembly (the Parliament) or the Central Tibetan Administration.

The pivotal role of Buddhism in Tibetan society leads *Sheja* to place considerable emphasis on the religious affairs of Tibetans, from in and outside the PRC, through news reports and in a discrete 'religion' (*chos*) section. For Tibetan communities in India and, to a lesser extent, those in Nepal and Bhutan, the paper serves as both noticeboard and diary in terms of the public life of prominent lamas as well as for related matters like the publication, sale or reprinting of lamas' collected works or religious texts in general.

Trunggö Böjong

This quarterly magazine published from Beijing since 1990 may be better known to a Western readership in either its English language or Chinese incarnations (*China's Tibet* or *Zhongguo Xizang*). Indeed, the Tibetan sibling only removed those Chinese characters (as a subtitle) from its glossy cover in 1994, perhaps to anticipate, or ward off, criticism of making a more than geographical statement. In sharp contrast to *Sheja*, its standard forty-eight page format appears on high-quality paper and routinely includes colour photo covers, endpapers and a four-page centrespread. One or more black and white photographs accompany most articles. Although neither handsome nor lavish, it is by international standards a quality product; that in itself suggests ample government funding to underwrite what must surely be considerable production costs, since it seems unlikely that the modest subscription alone could possibly defray the cost of such a specialist work.

Articles range across Tibetan life within the PRC, with most portraying 'progress' – from a Chinese Communist Party standpoint – in areas of the PRC that are ethnically Tibetan. Indeed, economic, social and cultural aspects of life are recurrent, almost exclusive, themes, tending to become laboured through repetitive interviews with prominent PRC Tibetans. Thus senior government officials of the Tibetan Autonomous Region provide a wealth of statistics to support the latest official initiative for improving the people's welfare; religious leaders routinely applaud the benign hand of the Party, for guiding life along an ideologically correct line. The unsuspecting reader may well gain an impression of unreconstructed Stalinism and a command economy still at work. Content and style range from the informative to the vacuous but articles carefully shun controversy; the rare reference to a sensitive political issue is clothed in casual language or oblique allusion. Items concerning religious events and personalities are, for the most part, conspicuous by their absence.[2] Of the 1993–94 issues under review (Table 1), only five articles are relevant at all.

Table 1 *Trunggö Böjong 1993–94*

Number of articles; original Tibetan text; articles with religious biography content (1993 figures in brackets; * = unavailable, edition not received from Beijing)

Issue	No. of articles	Tibetan original	Religious biography content
1	12 (11)	4 (1)	1 (1)
2	13 (12)	3 (6)	1 (1)
3	9 (12)	2 (6)	0 (1)
4	10 (*)	3 (*)	0 (*)

Sheja 1984–94

The ten year period under review (December 1984 – December 1994) reveals twenty-two *Sheja* articles on religious figures (Table 2), ranging from detailed formal obituaries, resembling those found in Tibetan religious texts over centuries, through to the briefest reports in a couple of paragraphs covering the subject's decease, containing very limited biographical material.

The *namtar*, the traditional religious biography

The inevitable compression of information in order to meet space constraints in a newspaper with limited financial resources has led to a considerable stylistic reappraisal of the form of the standard religious biography or *namtar* (*rnam mthar*) to suit a contemporary journalistic medium. The many *namtar* found in Tibetan religious texts have tended to present their material in a standard basic format of a narrative account of the life and death of the deceased, usually couched in elaborate, formal language and structured into clearly demarcated sections. Usually that sequence commences with a homage to objects of worship, usually Buddhas, a tutelary deity or lineage of spiritual masters. That is followed by verses of praise and a general introduction to the deceased, which includes an outline of the text's component parts. They would normally cover sections on the deceased's birth, upbringing, studies, teachings received and given, travels, spiritual attainments and other religious or temporal accomplishments. Details surrounding the circumstances of death would come towards the end of the text, which concludes with auspicious verses and a colophon. A *namtar* would restrict itself to a single life of the reincarnate in question; the next 'instalment' dealing with the deceased's subsequent incarnation would not appear until after the passing of the successor. By contrast of course, modern newspaper reportage allows more or less contemporaneous coverage of events so the interested reader can follow a lama's career as it occurs, rather than life by life.

Biography by Instalment

Obviously, the exigencies of space alone would prevent a modern newspaper format from even attempting to maintain that traditional presentational approach and the material discussed below will demonstrate the inevitable degree of divergence that has occurred from the *namtar* form. Still, the abbreviated formal biographies appearing in *Sheja* clearly derive their inspiration from the structure and language of the *namtar* genre of classical Tibetan. Comparing *Sheja's* obituaries with a modern example of that genre, like Geleg Rimpoché's seventy-four page 1977 biography of the Drepung Gomang lama, Jamyang Zhépa (d.1721),[3] reveals an apparent editorial policy of drawing freely on, and in a few cases retaining, the traditional framework of the *namtar*. Adaptation to modern influences and journalistic constraints occurs through the replacement of often florid verbosity with a simple factual presentation that is more appropriate in a current affairs newspaper setting.

Coverage

Sheja has consistently emphasised the religious activities of leading Tibetan Buddhist luminaries: not just the Dalai and Panchen Lamas but other eminent and respected figures in the complex religious hierarchy which, from 1959 on, has been successfully transplanted across the Himalayas to south Asia and beyond. News items and features include reports on major Buddhist teachings and initiations given by high lamas both outside and within the PRC. Discussion also covers constraints on such figures' activities in the PRC, the progress of monastic building and education (mostly in India) and information on significant events in various lamas' lives, all of which remain of great importance to Tibetan believers. As with many cultures, obituary notices cover the passing of major religious as well as secular figures and in the case of celebrated religious teachers may feature a lengthy review of the subject's life. Matters do not rest there, of course, for Buddhist tenets on the cycle of lives enable reportage to proceed on into the lama's subsequent life. Thus the discovery of a reincarnation is followed by reports on a sequence of significant events, such as a new incumbent's enthronement and commencement of religious training. In this way, the newspaper has become over time an important repository of biographical records and historical biographies – in many cases recording events which occurred early this century. Ready access under the one roof to such records in Tibetan of events from around the world is otherwise very hard to find.

The dates of birth given in Table 2 are necessarily approximate as that information is often omitted in *Sheja*, in favour of just giving an age at death. That imprecision is compounded by the fact that Tibetans count the first twelve months of life as year '1', not as '0' as in Western computation, for instance, Zepug Rimpoché's dates do not tally with his age, given as seventy-three. Cited birth dates may also be questionable – Gyalsay Tulku's 1941 is

Table 2 *Sheja 1984–94*

Obituary notices and/or condensed biographies of Tibetan religious figures

Issue	Name/dates	Background
84.12	Zong Rimpoché (1905?–84)	Ganden Shartsé ex-abbot
85.5	Tenpai Gyentsen (1914?–85)	Tantric adept
85.10	Pema Gyentsen (1919–85)	Drepung Loseling ex-abbot
86.8	Lozang Samten (1932–86)	Dalai Lama's brother
87.1	21st Ling Rimpoché (1903–83)	Dalai Lama's senior tutor
87.1	Yeshé Gyentsen (1896?–1986)	Tantric adept
87.9	Thubten Ngödrub (1957–)	Nechung Oracle medium
87.11	3rd Wöntrül Rimpoché (1925–87)	Teacher of present Tai Situ; (died in Belgium)
89.2	10th Panchen Lama (1938–89)	Head of Tashilhunpo
90.4	Ngawang Nyima (1907–90)	Drepung Gomang ex-abbot
90.10	Nangchen Achen Rimpoché (?–1990)	Son of 98th king of Achen (Kham, Eastern Tibet)
91.1	Sanggyé Tenzin Rimpoché (1904?–90)	Gum Sakya abbot
91.7	Tara Rimpoché (1926–91)	Sharpa Chöjé
91.10	Dilgo Khyentsé Rimpoché (1910–91)	Head of Nyingma tradition
91.10	9th Jetsun Dampa (1932–)	Senior Mongolian lama
92.5	3rd Kongtrül Rimpoché (1954–92)	Karma Kagyu regent
92.9–10	9th Ratö Rimpoché (1915?–92)	Senior Gelugpa lama
92.12	Gonpo Tseten (1920?–92)	Panchen Rimpoché's father
93.9	3rd Zepug Rimpoché (1921–93)	Sera Mé lama
93.10	Pangnang Rimpoché (1935?–93)	Drepung Loseling lama
93.12	Lingtsang Gyalsay Tulku (1941?–93)	Died in Australia
94.9–10	8th Taglüng Rimpoché (1915–94)	Taglüng Kagyu head

far from the 1952 deduced from two English language sources.[4] Dating and chronology are constant problems as the obituaries are mostly very selective in the use of information – except for the most exalted lamas – economy of detail remains essential to meet the dictates of space in *Sheja*. For example, a half column devoted to Achen Rimpoché[5] gives only the date of his death in Tibet (9 June 1990); material casting China in an unfavourable light is preferred over mundane biographical detail such as a date of birth or his age. As with the *namtar*, the modern idiom appears not to be overly-concerned with a need for precise dating, which perhaps reflects a Tibetan preference for other-worldly, spiritual issues rather than simple mundane details. Certainly, the strength of traditional concerns is consistently reflected in the way the articles concentrate on the aspect of spirtual attainment and para-normal phenomena. There again a healthy circulation figure is no doubt important to the paper's survival.

As might be expected, these obituary notices tend to follow a standard pattern with content and length dependent on the perceived stature of the

Biography by Instalment

subject – ranging from a half column brief for Tenpai Gyentsen to a three-page article for the twenty-first Ling Rimpoché, published some three years after his death. The latter included a condensed biography and details of the near completion of the processes relating to the embalming of the body (the only occurrence during the decade), complete with a sculpted visage based on his death mask. The longest aggregate entry is perhaps the most elusive from a biographical perspective: while the tenth Panchen Lama's passing filled some ten pages of a twenty-eight page issue, the emphasis throughout is far more on the somewhat unexplained circumstances surrounding his sudden demise than on presenting any factual account of his life or deeds. Certainly that is in keeping with his often controversial and ambiguous religious and political status. Indeed, the only biographical reference of note at all is mention of his efforts to protect Tibetans during the Cultural Revolution. Instead, the report conveys the sense of incredulity that pervaded Dharamsala when the news broke on the BBC and Radio Beijing, with both the Dalai Lama and the Kashag reported as finding it "suddenly for a moment in the realm of the unbelievable" (*lam sang yud tsam thugs yid ma ches pa lta bur gyur*).[6] An article putting forward a poisoning hypothesis followed in a later issue, discussed below.

Language and structure

The formal terminology employed in these articles is that of the classical language of Tibetan Buddhist texts, refined over centuries. Indeed, modern literary forms tend to lack the technical precision required to describe the activities of such august beings. The contemporary title 'obituary notice' (*'das brda*) is never employed; instead the more formal and honorific 'saddening news' (*yid skyo'i gnas tshul*) serves as a heading, though use of this term is limited to the laity and lesser luminaries amongst the ordained, such as the adept Tenpai Gyentsen; higher levels of honorific terminology are utilised, according to the deceased's reputation and spiritual status within the Tibetan community. Strictly religious biographical treatment prefers an abstract and philosophical bent: the genre is termed "aspects of liberation"[7] while some obituaries prefer the honorific heading "deeds" (*mdzad*).[8] Articles on the passing of senior lamas can rapidly become an encomium, with the use of honorific forms expanding according to the subject's stature in the hierarchy. Whereas Gyalsay Tulku effects a "sudden passing away",[9] the Panchen Lama "enacts dissolution into the sphere of emptiness"[10] and Dilgo Khyentsé Rimpoché "departs with the aspiration that seeks others' welfare" (*gzhan don du gshegs pa*). This technical vocabulary is often cryptic, if not obscure, and its use assumes a familiarity on the part of the reader with the philosophical concepts underpinning the system. Without that background many reports cannot be easily understood. The high-flown phraseology of classical biography, the constant use of elegant metaphor and similar descriptive figures of speech are other key features of such material. This follows from the fact that many such notices are provided by the lama's household, so are likely to be the work of relatively well-educated monks or scholars. Hence the stylised structure of these various elements consistently follows that of the *namtar*.

Biographical elements

The wholesale transfer of the *namtar* structure and its specialised technical language will be apparent from the following examination of the components of these obituaries.

Honorific titles

Sheja's standard introduction comprises up to several lines of honorific appellations or courtesy and religious titles, in part reflecting the subject's standing in Tibetan society. Material is often prefaced as being "a mere drop from the ocean-like biography" of the subject, as in the case of Pangnang Rimpoché (*rnam par thar pa rgya mtsho lta bu las chu thig tsam*).[11] This is, however, no mere panegyric as most of the terms have precise technical significance in the literature of sutra and tantra; as an introduction – echoing the Western tradition of presenting a summary or abstract at the head of an academic paper – they guide the informed reader through the deceased's spiritual credentials and attainments. In the case of Kongtrül Rimpoché this extends to over four lines of text:

> The incomparable lion, Lödrö Chökyi Senge, the third Jamgön Kongtrül Rimpoché, our most excellent leader, a wondrous practitioner of supermundane compassion and spiritual works with regard to, in this degenerate age, the doctrine generally and the precious teachings of accomplishment and transmission in particular.[12]

In an equally imposing, if not grandiose, vein, the report on the Panchen Lama's passing commences with sweeping praise, which highlights his tantric connection with Amitābha Buddha, the Dhyānī Buddha of the Western Paradise:

> The incomparable glorious protector of the teachings and sentient beings, the protector of the western Buddhafield of joy, the Omniscient Panchen, knower of all, the tenth incarnation, the venerable Tenzin Trinlé Jigmé Chökyi Wangchug, the supreme majestic one.[13]

Biography by Instalment

Causes of death

Next follows details of the circumstances, usually illness, leading to death. The majority of obituaries repeat Tibetan stock phrases, undoubtedly simplifying the editorial work involved; such reliance suggests that *Sheja*'s editors readily achieve the desired nuance by selecting from a set of standard form precedents. The usual pattern is of the onset of a sudden illness for which Tibetan and Western/Indian/Chinese medicine (depending on the place of demise) proves of little or no assistance, as do religious rituals or the entreaties of the faithful. For the more senior lamas, the implication is always of a conscious decision on their part that their earthly presence has served its intended purpose – for that particular lifetime. In Buddhist terms theirs is the choice to leave a particular body and move on to another incarnation to serve sentient beings elsewhere. For Ratö Rimpoché, who was requested by the Dalai Lama in person to remain here longer, the following text appears:

> Although he had consulted successive Tibetan and Indian doctors and taken courses of treatment, he did not fully recover ... to remedy the condition, he performed successive rituals, [involving] taking medicine; foremost, the Supreme Protector [ie Ratö Rimpoché] was entreated by everyone individually in his presence to remain for a long time. Yet on the one hand his body had grown old; on the other, although he was manifesting illness, [the pain] was extremely intense. So, having ripened disciples in this realm, it was as if his mind was set on departing to another pure realm.[14]

The act of passing away is always referred to as being the lama's final demonstration of the impermanence of conditioned phenomena and as stressing the need for spiritual practice. The standard phraseology used time and again appears, for example, in Dilgo Khyentsé Rimpoché's obituary: "in order to exhort wordly-minded disciples to practise the doctrine" (*gdul bya rtag 'dzin can rnams chos la bskul phyir*).[15] In the case of Khenchen Sanggyé Tenzin Rimpoché, a very detailed report from the intriguingly-named "Remains Service Committee" (*sku gdung zhabs zhu tshogs chung*)[16] notes that he had never been seriously ill in his 87 years, ceasing daily teachings but a fortnight before his passing and was seen to manifest fatigue only the day before he entered the meditative absorption period. Indeed, those around him were unsure whether or not he was just continuing with an unusually long daily prayer session as, the report notes, an hour before death his face remained radiant and his breathing had only slowed imperceptibly. In fact, it proved necessary to call another meditation master to confirm that the Khenchen was entering the 'clear light meditative absorption' (*thugs dam 'od gsal*) in which he then remained for over eight days. Three days before his passing, it continues, there had been earth tremors in the locale (Darjeeling), which the report attributes to the strength of his compassion, thus implying an ability on the part of the lama to influence natural phenomena. Similarly with the unusually clear and warm weather experienced in the area during that November period, which is portrayed as no mere coincidence.

Signs and portents at and after death

Tibetans attach considerable significance to the appearance of para-normal phenomena in relation to a lama's birth, death or cremation. Such indications are taken as signs of great attainment in a lama's spiritual practice and also as portending future events, such as the likely direction of the lama's next rebirth. In relation to the latter, the most celebrated instance concerns the search for the present Dalai Lama, who, in his book *ngos kyi yul dang ngos kyi mi mang* (*My Land and My People*), refers to the period following the death of his predecessor (the Thirteenth Dalai Lama) in 1933 as follows:

> At that time there were many unusual cloud formations to the northeast of Lhasa. The body of the Supreme Lord of the Conquerors was seated on a throne in the Norbulingka, with his face looking south. Thereafter his face was seen to be facing to the east. Later, a star-shaped white fungus suddenly appeared on the side of a tall pillar on the northeast side of the shrine room . . .[17]

Even the brief notice for the adept Tenpai Gyentsen devotes several lines to the day of his death, referring to "the appearance of a rainbow in the middle of a clear blue sky and of a 'rainbow tent' (*'ja' gur*) around his room, which was seen by all".[18] After the passing of the previous Tara Geshé incarnation, Tara Rimpoché's mother is recorded as having dreamt of his coming with a golden rosary into a Buddhist household in her village.[19] Some control over physical forces is again suggested in the description of Khenzur Ngawang Nyima's departure. He:

> . . . entered a meditative equipoise within the clear light of emptiness; after dissolution of the movement of breath, his body's radiance became greater than before. At that moment the gross movement of wind outside completely ceased and the leaves on the trees in the immediate area were still – this was perceived by all.[20]

Weather patterns receive particular attention. *Sheja* notes that at Gyalsay Tulku's cremation, morning cloud cleared and the sun shone as his body was brought out for the ceremony. A little rain during the preliminary

Biography by Instalment

rituals was followed by bright sunlight as the pyre was lit. At that moment a rainbow appeared and three vultures and two crows circled overhead; the Tibetan tradition considers circumstances like the arrival of such birds as significant signs, frequently terming them 'auspicious'; they are referred to in the obituaries as the "unobstructed hallmarks of a distinguished lineage" (*gdung rabs khyad par can gyi mngon rtags 'gog med*).[21] Science and sceptical rationalism may, of course, explain these events very differently. Still, references to unusual optical or atmospheric effects are legion. When Pangnang Rimpoché's pyre was lit in Tibet, the report notes that more than a thousand people witnessed the descent on to the pyre of a brilliantly banded pavilion of rainbow light. His obituary also mentions that, around the time of his birth, a white vulture had stayed for many days on the roof of the house in which he was born, at which time peas in the kitchen stove there had sprouted.[22] A similar love of such detail appears in the report on Zong Rimpoché's cremation in the south of India. Five vultures are described as endlessly circling high above the crematorium. That two of them flew off to the east was taken as an indication of the direction in which the reincarnation would be found.[23] Cloud formations appearing during the ceremony were interpreted in terms of Buddhist auspicious emblems, particularly the precious parasol and the white conch shell. A rainbow pavilion of light is again mentioned, appearing just before the pyre was lit; the unexpected arrival of an elephant as the burning began was also taken by all present as a peerless sign.[24]

The meditative absorption period

Following what is usually regarded as the conventional point of death, at least to Western thinking, the lama's mindstream enters and remains in a state of meditative equipoise (*thugs dam*), often for a considerable period, without any deterioration in the state of the body taking place. The *namtar* texts also view this ability as conclusive evidence of advanced spiritual attainment. For Tibetan Buddhists, the point of death is at the conclusion of this period. The number of days that a lama remains in such absorption, usually seated upright in meditational full lotus posture, is invariably recorded. For those listed at Table 2, some two to six days was, on average, spent in this state. Ling Rimpoché is exceptional in remaining two weeks "in the sphere of the profound immovable meditative stabilization" (*gyo med ting 'dzin zab mo'i dbyings*). Zepug Rimpoché's body is described as taking on a brilliance throughout the three days of his absorption period. *Sheja* notes that his emergence from that state coincided with a soft drizzle and a variegated rainbow, which again are taken as auspicious signs.[25] Similar emphasis is laid on the earth tremors and rainbows which marked Khenchen Sanggyé Tenzin Rimpoché's emergence from the state of absorption.

Kevin Garratt

Disposal of the body

A more mundane sign of the mindstream's emergence from absorption is the commencement of the body's physical deterioration. With the mindstream by then on its way to another incarnation, disposal of the corpse can safely begin. Despite the lack of ready fuel on the Tibet plateau (and increasingly so in India), cremation is the usual means of disposal reserved for the precious remains (*sku gdung rin po che*) of a lama, whereas the fate of most ordinary Tibetans' remains (at least on the Tibet plateau) is to become food for the birds. The process normally involves construction of a purpose-built enclosed, often whitewashed, crematorium (*pur khang*), usually in the shape of a Buddhist reliquary stupa, with a chimney structure replacing the normal, elaborate finial. Idiosyncratic design certainly occurs: the Khenchen Sanggyé Tenzin Rimpoché line – so notes his obituary – has, over lifetimes, developed a stylised exterior for their stupa-shaped crematoria which, symbolising liberation from cyclic existence (*myang 'das mchod rten*), are decorated with representations of the five sense objects and other symbolic offerings, thus suggesting the involvement of tantric ritual in these rites. In that regard, the tantric adept Tenpai Gyentsen's obituary is notable in reporting that when his body was consigned to the flames it shrank away to nothing, departing in the form of a rainbow body (*'ja' lus*), a very advanced Tibetan tantric practice. The exceptional regard, if not awe, in which Ling Rimpoché was held may be gauged by the fact that his remains were embalmed rather than burnt. His abbreviated biography supplies very little detail on the embalming processes involved, referred to in Tibetan as preparing 'the casket for the remains' (*sku gdung za ma tog*), instead it reported the sculpting of his likeness, based on a death mask, by an American sculptress working in Dharamsala – an unusual departure given that such work has traditionally been the province of Tibetans.

Two of the lamas listed in Table 2 died outside Asia: Wöntrül Rimpoché in Belgium (1987)[26] and Gyalsay Tulku in Australia (1993). It would appear that cremation outside Tibet or the Indian sub-continent does not readily meet with Tibetan favour, as in both these cases the body was returned to India expressly for that purpose. Indeed, the request for such removal had come from very senior figures in the respective religious lineages: Tai Situ Rimpoché, one of the Kagyu Regents and Wöntrül's student in the former case and Sakya Trinzin, head of the Sakya order to which Gyalsay belonged in the latter. Justification for such removal may in part have been (at least in Wöntrül's case) that it would enable a long list of notables and dignitaries to attend the cremation in Himachal Pradesh: eight reincarnate lamas and many Tibetan government and lay figures are mentioned by name. Further attention to detail appears in the description of the ceremony itself – the body being cremated within four maṇḍalas, made by the lamas present, at which time more than a hundred mourners present witnessed rainbows appearing simultaneously from the four cardinal directions. Post-mortem incisions made

Biography by Instalment

by Australian doctors on Gyalsay's body in Canberra before appropriate Buddhist rituals had been carried out distressed many Tibetans and vividly exposed the inadequacies of Australian law in dealing with cultural and spiritual beliefs about dying that differ from those of mainstream Christianity. At least, those circumstances led the Australian Capital Territory to review its laws on post-mortem examinations.

Reports of cremation ceremonies also focus on the presence of particular birds circling over the crematorium, their number, colour and direction of flight, the direction of the smoke and details of rainbows and any paranormal phenomena. All of these occurrences are interpreted in relation to the lama's spiritual attainments or reincarnation prospects. Details from the report on the passing of the yogi Yeshé Gyentsen (aged over ninety)[27] are typical in demonstrating *Sheja*'s reportage of such events: a rain of flowers fell on the day of his death and, at the cremation, smoke from the crematorium became a five coloured rainbow in which images of the sacred syllables *om ah hum* and of tantric ritual hand implements (*vajras* and bells) were seen by all present. Reopening the sealed crematorium occurs on a day determined as propitious, usually by the lama in charge of the cremation, which could be days or weeks after the burning; reports sometimes detail the metamorphosed relics (*ring bsrel*) found, their size and number. On occasion, it is recorded that certain organs remained untouched by the fire, which Tibetans again tend to ascribe to the power of the lama's religious practice.

Reviewing milestones

Next comes a chronological record of significant events in a lama's life. The order of such material follows a conventional pattern while the language employed is rather stylised, perhaps reflecting the fact that many of the achievements recorded date from the relative tranquility of a lost theocratic age. References to birth may include the mother's significant dreams, referred to below. Material on the search for, finding, recognition and enthronement of a reincarnate usually details the involvement of noted senior lamas. Thus Jamgön Kongtrül Rimpoché, a Karma Kagyu lama, was recognised at seventeen months old by the head of that lineage, the sixteenth Karmapa. Similarly, the ninth Jetsun Dampa Rimpoché, an important Mongolian lama reborn in Lhasa in 1932 who had been subsequently identified by the then Regent of Tibet, Reting Rimpoché, was not formally recognised by the Dalai Lama until 1991, at the age of fifty-nine.[28] Though born in a Tibetan milieu, the Jetsun is credited with having spoken Mongolian at a very early age, which was taken at the time as a sign of his antecedents. Notably, his two-page biography is the only one of a living reincarnate published during the decade.[29]

A plethora of detail follows: the monastery first entered, ages at which novice and fully ordained monk's vows were taken and the identity of the ordaining lamas. Particular prominence is given to the receipt of vows from the Thirteenth Dalai Lama, or indeed to any contact with him. Indeed, the obituaries of those lamas born early this century are peppered with references to their meetings and teacher/student relationships with famous Tibetan spiritual masters of the day. Covering more recent times, there is a mutual exchange of teacher/student roles between Dilgo Khyentsé and the present Dalai Lama; also, the Taglüng Shabdrung's obituary indicates that, once he had settled in Sikkim after twenty years in Chinese prisons, he passed on a host of unbroken initiations, oral transmissions and precepts from his lineage to seven other lamas including the Dalai Lama and Dilgo Khyentsé. The line of Ling Rimpochés is recorded as having been tutor to four Dalai Lamas.[30]

These reports quickly become a mine of biographical data, with details of journeys to central Tibet and its monastic universities, sutra texts studied and names of teachers, the level of geshé lharampa (the highest academic level of non-tantric monastic qualification) obtained, retreats undertaken, pilgrimages to the holy sites in India, oral transmissions of the entire Buddhist canon given (the Kanjur and Tanjur texts) and volumes of works composed. For polymaths like Dilgo Khyentsé and Ling Rimpoché, the catalogue of accomplishments in all these areas becomes breathtaking. Narrative proceeds to tantric studies and the ranks attained in the monastic hierarchy – tantric chanting-master (*dbu mdzad*), disciplinarian (*dge skos*), abbot (*mkhan po*) and ex-abbot (*mkhan zur*), reaching the pinnacle, in the case of Ling Rimpoché, of being the ninety-seventh holder of the throne of Ganden in Drepung monastery (and thus head of the Gelug tradition).[31]

The chronology then moves to activities following the 1959 exodus from Tibet. For many that has included travel beyond South Asia and involved the foundation of many monasteries and religious centres, all duly recorded. Jamgön Kongtrül Rimpoché, for example, bestowed the novice or fully ordained monk's vows on over 3000 people in India, Nepal, Tibet and the West during his short thirty-nine year lifespan. Some reincarnates have visited Tibet to initiate the rebuilding of monasteries. In 1985 Dilgo Khyentsé went via Bhutan to commence the restoration of Samyé (the first Buddhist monastery founded in Tibet, 775 C.E.),[32] with description of the attendant consecration rites. For some, academia beckoned: at sixty years of age, the ex-abbot Ngawang Nyima Rimpoché, after teaching at Banaras Hindu University for seven years, became an Associate Professor at the University of Leiden in Holland, later publishing in India some six volumes of his written works.

Entreaties for a quick return

Obituaries and biographies conclude with a customary entreaty for the speedy return of a 'supreme emanation' (ie reincarnation) of the lama (*mchog sprul myur du byon pa*). In the case of the most exalted, that extends to publication

Biography by Instalment

of a prayer for recitation by the faithful. The one for the Panchen Lama – entitled "The Song of a True Sage, an Entreaty Petitioning a Speedy Return" – was composed by the Dalai Lama himself. It follows a traditional structure and metre: nine verses, each of four lines, each containing nine syllables.[33]

A record of more worldly formalities is not overlooked. Official messages of condolence are mentioned; for instance, the death of the Panchen Lama's father in Xining in 1992 prompted the Kashag to send condolences to the deceased's wife in Lhasa and to other members of his family. Closure of Tibetan government offices for a half day or more as a mark of respect is accorded to some; indeed, Dharamsala decreed three days official mourning on the death of the Panchen Lama. Tibetan-owned shops and restaurants in Darjeeling closed on the day of Khenchen Sanggyé Tenzin Rimpoché's cremation, the shopkeepers no doubt joining the "several thousand" (*stong phrag 'ga' shas*) mourners recorded as gathering to pay their final respects.

Obituaries of secular figures

Sheja does not, of course, restrict its coverage of the deceased to religious notables alone, yet the dividing line between religious and secular status can become blurred in the case of blood relations of exalted religious figures. Tibetan society tends to treat those like the Panchen Lama's father and the Dalai Lama's elder brother, Lozang Samten, with an almost religious veneration. That tone is adopted in the presentation of their obituary notices (hence their inclusion in Table 2). On the other side of a very fine dividing line is, arguably, the Dalai Lama's personal physician, Jamyang Tashi.[34] While in his case the use of language and detail recorded remains very close to that discussed above, the style and presentation is more matter of fact, suggesting that the *dam pa* (the excellent one) is to be viewed in a secular light.

The remaining spectrum of Tibetan secular obituaries becomes progressively easier to categorise. That of Lozang Dolma (Ama Lozang), a skilled doctor practising in the traditional Tibetan medicine system, recounts how she maintained a very busy practice in Dharamsala until her unexpected death in 1989, aged fifty-five.[35] Notably, hers is one of only two obituaries of women appearing in *Sheja* during the decade. Amongst the laity generally, obituaries of Tibetan politicians and government officials of both pre-1959 Tibet and the refugee era tend to predominate but, more colourfully, we have Pon Lha Gé, a sometime guerilla leader in Tibet and publisher in India of the Gesar of Ling folk epic cycle.[36] A wealth of pious and philanthropic works within the refugee community is enumerated in a half page obituary for Jinpa Gyatso (September 1994), including monastery building in Simla, sponsoring a Kalachakra initiation given by the Dalai Lama and providing generally for the sick and needy. On a wider canvas, reportage on non-Tibetan figures covers both prominent Indians, possibly to bolster Indo-Tibetan relations, and world figures too. Thus a whole page is devoted to Khan Abdul Ghaffar (otherwise the [North-West] 'Frontier Gandhi'), aged ninety-eight and deeply respected by all Indians,[37] yet the February 1989 funeral of Emperor Hirohito of Japan merits only five lines in 'News in Brief'.[38] Untimely deaths, such as apparent suicides and assassinations, are always newsworthy and so receive considerable coverage – Rikha Lozang Tenzin, a former Cultural Office secretary in the Dharamsala government's administration,[39] Petra Kelly, leader of the German Green Party and a strong supporter of Tibet,[40] and Rajiv Gandhi, former prime minister of India.[41]

Significant events concerning a reincarnation

Discovery and recognition

Tibetan Buddhist belief in a cycle of lives accepts that mental development to a certain level enables a person's stream of consciousness to choose the time and place of rebirth. That ability is usually ascribed, in part at least, to a reincarnate's motivation of seeking to serve all other sentient beings, rather than merely being propelled into a particular rebirth through the force of previously accumulated karmic imprints, as is the case for those less advanced on the path to enlightenment. Tibetans tend to perceive their reincarnate lamas as manifestations of this ideal. Thus the brief biography of the twenty-first Ling Rimpoché records his lives as including that of the great Arhat Charka, a contemporary of the historical Buddha Śākyamuni in India and, more than a millennium later in Tibet, as a great practitioner of the Vajrabhairava tantra, the famous translator Ra Lotsawa Dorjé Dragpa. In the same way, the stature in Tibet of the twelfth Künling Tatsag Hutuktu results in the thirteenth's ordination, haircutting and naming ceremonies, held on 13 April 1993, receiving detailed treatment. The fact that those rituals were carried out by the Dalai Lama personally in Dharamsala's main temple may have added to the event's newsworthiness. *Sheja* in fact reproduces the text of the Dalai Lama's recognition statement. Although the article gives Lhasa as the site of the Hutuktu's discovery, no birthdate or more precise indication of his birthplace appear and the text glosses over his move to India; those omissions tend to suggest an effort by Dharamsala to limit Chinese knowledge about how young reincarnates are smuggled out of the PRC, given the likelihood of repercussions for any Tibetans in the PRC found to have been involved in such activities.

The correct identification of a reincarnate may occur within a framework of competing claimants and so is a serious and significant undertaking in Tibetan society, often attracting considerable community attention and corresponding column space in *Sheja*. It can also carry considerable political weight, both within Tibetan society and even internationally, given

Biography by Instalment

the influence a reincarnation can wield over a constituency of the faithful. A recent instance is that of the Gyalwa Karmapa, head of the Karma Kagyu lineage; concern and speculation mounted over the years between the passing of his sixteenth incarnation, Rolpai Dorjé, in Chicago in 1981 and the recognition of the seventeenth in the PRC in 1992. The long delay in identification of the reincarnation had led to many rumours among Tibetans, including considerable criticism of the Kagyu regents' apparent inability to find a successor. That culminated in a spate of articles in 1992 (four in six months) with repeated publication of the Dalai Lama's statement recognising Ügyen Trinlé, a seven year old nomads' son from eastern Tibet, as the seventeenth reincarnation. The tenor of *Sheja*'s journalism sought to defuse the situation,[42] yet the controversy appears far from resolved, as discussed below.

Interest inevitably focuses on those lamas whose attainments were exceptional in their immediately preceding life, so the finding of a true incarnation and his recognition by the Tibetan establishment are crucial events not just in religious terms but in the political and social dimension too. No reports of female reincarnates appeared during the decade, possibly reflecting the relatively limited opportunities for Tibetan nuns to study and practise their religion. News reports focusing on the recognition of reincarnations are only seven in number over the decade. Such treatment, therefore, seems to be reserved for very senior lamas.

Table 3 *Announcements of the recognition of reincarnations*

Issue	Name	Previous incarnation
85.4	Trichang Rimpoché[43]	Dalai Lama's junior tutor (d. 1981)
87.9	Ling Rimpoché[44]	Dalai Lama's senior tutor (d. 1983)
88.11	Serkong Rimpoché[45]	Dalai Lama's debating partner (d. 1981)
90.8	Zong Rimpoché[46]	Senior Gelugpa lama (d. 1984)
92.7	Gyalwa Karmapa[47]	Head of Karma Kagyu lineage (d. 1981)
92.8	Ratö Dongkong (Junior, b.1982)[48]	Gelugpa lama, died in Chinese detention
93.4	13th Tatsag Jedrung Hutuktu[49]	Renowned scholar, found in Lhasa, recognised after move to India

In the case of the two tutors and the Karmapa, the full text of the Dalai Lama's official note and seal authenticating the recognition was also reproduced in *Sheja*. Moreover, the long article on the twenty-second Ling Rimpoché's recognition goes into great detail on the processes involved in the search for a reincarnation. Curiously though, three and a half pages of information does not mention his date of birth. Still, we learn of the various divinations undertaken by the Dalai Lama at the outset of the search which, as it narrowed, involved him performing them before the embalmed relics of the twenty-first incarnation at the Ling residence (*bla brang*) in Dharamsala. To Tibetans, the sanctity and inherent power of such relics, deriving from the deceased lama's spiritual attainments, would exert a positive influence in determining an accurate outcome from the divination. Search parties were then sent to various parts of India and 690 names investigated before the focus eventually settled on the Delhi and Bir areas in northern India. The final field of the four most promising Bir candidates was subjected to time-honoured tests using rosaries and other ritual implements belonging to the previous incarnation; further divinations and other unspecified rituals led to the eventual choice, which was duly confirmed by the Dalai Lama.

The longstanding practice of seeking divination from the Dalai Lama in the search for reincarnations has now been officially discouraged. A Kashag announcement in *Sheja* (January 1994) pointed to ever-growing demands on both his time and health as the key reasons for the break with tradition.[50] Other alternatives remain, with dreams accorded considerable significance though the following account suggests that their utility may sometimes be underestimated. When an official party carrying the Dalai Lama's letter of recognition to the reincarnation of Zong Rimpoché arrived at the latter's birthplace in the Kulu region of the Indian Himalayas, a close Western female student of the previous incarnation is recorded as having immediately recognised the area, his house and the forested valley from a dream of two or three years earlier. Although she had at that time described the dream to the previous Rimpoché's steward, it had evinced little interest and the lead had not been pursued. Yet, when the present Rimpoché's mother had moved to Kulu (prior to the birth), she too was able to identify those very same features, seen previously by her in a vivid dream as well.[51]

Offering the robes

By no means does the biographical continuum end with a successor's discovery and recognition. The next rite of passage is that of offering and putting on the robes of an ordainee (*na bza' sgron 'bul*). Few Tibetan Buddhist ordainees would encounter the elaborate ceremonial involved in this process, as described in a two-part report charting the progress of the very young Ling Rimpoché.[52] However, *Sheja* records only one other robing ceremony *per se*, that of Tugsé Rimpoché. If column space reasonably reflects status, he is accorded a much lower station, as his 1986 rebirth at Chushul village on the Indo-Tibet border and 1987 robing ceremony conducted by Drugchen Rimpoché in Ladakh fifteen months later are but briefly noted. *Sheja*'s only commentary is that the ceremony took place following his recognition by the Dalai Lama as the true reincarnate.[53]

Biography by Instalment

Entering the doctrine

For a young reincarnate, the fourth event of significance is the "entering the doctrine ceremony" (*chos zhugs mdzad sgo*), often referred to as "enthronement". It covers the reincarnate's formal entry into the monastery with which he had been connected in the preceding lifetime and also denotes commencement of religious studies. *Sheja* devoted some four pages to details of events for the three-year-old Trichang Rimpoché, held in the south of India monasteries in February 1988.[54] Two pages meticulously catalogue the main day's ceremonial at Ganden monastery: starting with an early morning tea offering through to a list of rituals performed, such as maṇḍalas, and offerings made by religious and lay officials and devotees. Even a list of prayers recited appears. The scale of offerings received by the lama's household (*bla brang*) – and hence the importance of this reincarnation to the Tibetans – can be gauged by the sheer number and size of donations made by the household over a nearly three-week marathon. A curious but noteworthy feature of Tibetan exiles' life is that the dire poverty facing many of them in South Asia does not appear to constrain their ability, as a community, to shower important lamas with offerings. Indeed, tradition demands that a lama's household makes sizeable donations to various monasteries, their colleges and even to individual monks at each institution on such significant occasions. The report notes that some 100,101 rupees (roughly 7000 Australian dollars in 1987 terms) had already gone to the construction of a new assembly hall at Ganden. After the main day's events, a further ten days activity, spread over nearly three weeks, was spent in equally impressive ceremonial at the other main monasteries in the south – Drepung, Sera and Tashilhunpo – with the household disbursing 10,000 rupees to some colleges, five or ten rupees to each monk, and in some cases a Tibetan coin too. The whole operation must surely have been quite a gruelling schedule for a three-year-old child, to say nothing of the finance required for such a prodigious undertaking.

A similar burst of activity in the south of India is briefly reported in relation to the nine-year-old Junior Ratö Dongkong. This time, though, all costs were borne by his parents – presumably a not inconsiderable financial feat either.[55] He had been brought to India from Tibet in 1984, aged two, after oracles there had pronounced him to be a reincarnate; formal recognition from Dharamsala came in 1991. Similar events for the two-year-old Serkong Tugsé Rimpoché and the three-year-old Ling Rimpoché were announced in *Sheja*'s pages (September and October 1990); however no reports of the actual events – held in November and December 1990 respectively – ever appeared.[56] Brief accounts cover the enthronements in India of the eighth Taglüng Tulku and of Jagzam Tulku. That of the former occurred in 1986 (no location given), under the aegis of the Sharmapa,[57] while Jagzam (born in Paro, Bhutan) was brought to India under the auspices of Dilgo Khyentsé Rimpoché for the enthronement, held in Simla in 1989.[58] The haircutting ceremony is the focus of an article only once: a seven-line entry devoted to Zhépa Rimpoché. Even then the bulk of the text instead covers the Dalai Lama's prediction of the parents' names and of the Dalai's subsequent recognition of the boy in Manali, Himachal Pradesh.[59]

One report stands out for its wealth of detail. A 1985 article from the Dharamsala religious affairs office on the enthronement of the Khunu Lama Rimpoché reincarnation[60] compresses a mass of valuable information on his discovery, recognition, robe offering and enthronement into just over a page of text – surely a triumph of condensation. The previous Khunu Lama, Tenzin Gyentsen, was an unusual and revered figure in Tibetan society, being an Indian layman who had become a teacher of the present Dalai Lama. His passing in India in 1977 (by then in his eighties) was deeply mourned. While the article identifies the reincarnate's father and the father's monastery (Gonjo Dodzong) at Markham in the PRC,[61] there is no indication of the child's date or place of birth or even his name or age at any stage of the chronology. Repeated references to the Kham region of Tibet may suggest a birthplace there but the report fails to provide any dates for the many events it describes. If he was born in Tibet, there is no indication of how or when he reached India; such silence on facts routinely appearing in other articles again suggests something more than slipshod reporting. No doubt the PRC authorities would be looking for any clue on how such an important reincarnate could have been spirited across the border, with the attendant loss to China of political leverage over non-PRC Tibetans. The child, while small, was announced by Dujom Rimpoché's son, Trinlé Norbu, as the Khunu reincarnation; that prediction was endorsed by the head of the Sakya school, the Sakya Trinzin, who apparently urged enthronement. Once the recognition had been confirmed by the Dalai Lama, the installation ceremony was held in the Ögyen Heruka throne room of Tsopema monastery,[62] a favourite residence of the previous Khunu Lama. The report concludes with a paragraph on the child's subsequent (undated) audience in Dharamsala with the Dalai Lama, who indicated that the direction of the boy's education should be written Tibetan and dialectics, even identifying the teaching institutions of his choice.

Religious biography in Trunggö Böjong 1993–94

Coverage

As noted earlier, this periodical's coverage differs markedly from *Sheja*'s in many respects – the quantity of relevant material is proportionately far less and its focus and analysis differ as well. Accordingly, a review of its 1993 and 1994 issues serves as a representative indication of the publication's contribution in the field. In line with the PRC's unswerving political position on Tibet, virtually every article in that period is devoted to some facet of Tibetan's economic, social or cultural life. With religion perhaps still regarded by Beijing as the opiate of the people and Tibetan Buddhism more likely viewed as a rallying point for Tibetan nationalism, any element of religious biography features only to the extent that it presumably serves Beijing's policy agenda on Tibet. Indeed, only five articles appear of any relevance at all to this discussion. Two of them provide a Tibetan name as author but significantly state that those articles are translations; the source language in question is not indicated in the coy notes naming the Tibetan or Chinese translator at the foot of those articles. Nonetheless, the appearance of transliterated Chinese names as author, co-author or translator suggest little room for speculation and emphasises the increasing dominance of Mandarin in the PRC as a channel of communication on Tibetan religious affairs.

Nonetheless, it is a welcome sign that vocabulary mostly shuns transliterated Chinese loan words; syntax and grammar maintain a Tibetan pedigree, albeit somewhat divergent from non-PRC writings. The appearance in 1993 of two pages of Sakya Pandita's writings may be a token acknowledgement of Tibetan religious creativity in the bad old days before 'liberation'.

Enthronement of the seventeenth Karmapa

In the spring 1993 issue the enthronement of the seventeenth Karmapa not unexpectedly takes pride of place. It seems unlikely that its broad coverage can be fully ascribed to an act of faith or religious zeal on the part of the editor (or censors) concerned. A more likely reason is the carefully calculated political and diplomatic mileage anticipated from investing in a high profile, but controlled, reportage of the event. Still, the material's very publication at least sheds an unprecedented PRC perspective on valuable biographical material concerning an illustrious line of reincarnates and so cannot be dismissed lightly.

This was the only religious event covered by both *Sheja* and *Trunggö Böjong* and so presents the sole opportunity to contrast their respective approaches to the same biographical material. The Karmapa, it may be recalled, is head of the Karma Kagyu lineage within Tibetan Buddhism. In exile, the sixteenth incarnation had resided at Rumteg monastery in Sikkim after moving from Tsurphu in Tibet in 1959. He had always been regarded as one of Tibet's more formidable lamas – something that has remained a hallmark of the Karmapa line. During the long interregnum following the Sixteenth's death in 1981, administration of that Kagyu lineage and of Rumteg lay with four regent lamas, including the highly respected and popular Jamgön Kongtrül Rimpoché (whose *Sheja* obituary reflects that stature). The latter's untimely death in 1992, soon after his entrustment with the search for the Karmapa reincarnation, only seemed to heighten controversy. The Dalai Lama's recognition of Ügyen Trinlé, living in the PRC, as the true reincarnation inevitably resulted in Beijing's sudden involvement in the saga, bringing the first PRC recognition of a reincarnation since the turbulent events of 1959.

The PRC view

The lead story in the spring 1993 issue is on the enthronement of the seventeenth Karmapa at Tsurphu, west of Lhasa, on 27 September 1992.[63] The event's significance went far beyond the confines of religion, with Chinese officialdom and Tibetan Autonomous Region dignitaries flocking to hear read out the first Chinese Government instrument of approval (*chog mchan bkod yig*) of a reincarnation since the 'Tibetan democratic reforms of 1959'. Accordingly, the magazine's cover comprised a colour picture of the boy (wearing a junior replica of the Karmapa's famous black hat) with the caption "the new incumbent of Tsurphu monastery" (*mtshur phu dgon pa'i dgon bdag gsar pa*); a further page of colour pictures appeared inside as well as black and white photos of the event. A four-page article described the history of the Karmapa incarnations (dating back to 1204 C.E., long before the commencement of those of the Dalai and Panchen Lamas which run from the fifteenth century) and also detailed the identification process of the present reincarnation (see below) and the three days of ceremonies at Tsurphu.

Intriguingly, while the identical colour picture was used for the cover of the English language spring issue, appearing in a China International Book Trading Corporation advertising leaflet in 1994, its caption ("17th Garmaba officially installed") bears no relation at all to that in the Tibetan edition and in no way can be taken as a translation. The English version also employs the Chinese romanised form of the lama's name ("Garmaba"), rather than the "Karmapa" found in English language material published by Tibetans outside the PRC and in publications in the West; the sinicisation may simply reflect a transliteration policy or could have a more political connotation. In the absence of a complete English language edition of that issue, the tantalising question of whether the English edition is a direct, or even approximate, translation of the Tibetan (and the allied relationship between the Tibetan and Mandarin versions) must remain unconfirmed. In 1995, however, *Sheja* presented a withering six-page indictment of the content and substance of *Trunggö Böjong*:

> The periodical entitled 'China's Tibet' is a black propaganda publication. Up till now it has appeared in three languages, English, Chinese and Tibetan. Most of its contents are just fabrications and distortions incompatible with the reality of events. Moreover, contrasting

the readings of some articles presenting a political slant on history or current affairs in the respective language editions shows time and again that what is written in the English is not in the Chinese and what appears in the Chinese is not in the Tibetan. Anyone can understand that approach.[64]

Political constraints

While *Sheja*, through a dry, factual coverage of events, seeks to avoid hinting at any notion of discord within the Kagyu hierarchy, *Trunggö Böjong* prefers to maximise the impact of Ügyen Trinlé's enthronement, with constant emphasis on official Chinese involvement in the recognition process. Thus, the central, not regional, religious affairs bureaucracy is credited with conducting the successful search – certainly not the monks of Tsurphu. To validate proceedings, PRC authentication naturally requires a formal document from the Chinese authorities. Indeed, the actual proclamation by a high official from Beijing is almost given pride of place in the report. However, even Beijing's political agenda seems to require a token, if brief, allusion to the history of the lineage; yet the emphasis is on a spontaneous outpouring of faith by the tens of thousands present – on the basis of the government-sanctioned recognition. Therefore, eliciting accurate and objective biographical data from this source (or indeed from *Sheja*) requires some circumspection, since material is presented selectively, usually to suit a wider political agenda. Thus its accommodation within a biographical framework requires corroboration from other written sources, if available, both in and outside the PRC as well as reliance on anecdotal evidence, usually from within the Tibetan community.

Dharamsala's approach

In contrast, *Sheja*'s minimalist reportage devotes less than a column and a half to the event. The bald facts of the enthronement are quickly – and tersely – stated. This low-key approach reflects the impact of the continuing controversy within the Kagyu hierarchy and the wider political dimension to the succession, as Dharamsala would not at that stage have wished to prejudice requests to the PRC – which proved futile – about the boy being allowed to visit or be educated at the Sixteenth's monastery across the Indian border in Sikkim. Most of the space in *Sheja* is devoted to a history of the Karmapa line, emphasising recent (1992) developments in the search made by regents Tai Situ and Gyentsab (Rimpochés) and the obtaining of the Dalai Lama's approval of the boy.[65] The only real common ground between the two reports remains the bald and incontrovertible fact of the child's birth and of the presence of tens of thousands of devotees at Tsurphu for the event. The PRC material prefers to play down the role of lamas "from abroad", merely noting the presence of the two abovementioned regents at Tsurphu whom, it states, had come specially from India to officiate at the haircutting and naming ceremonies. Moreover, hints of the controversy – following Jamgön Kongtrül's demise – between those two regents and the fourth one, the Sharmapa, over the identity of the correct reincarnation appear in two earlier issues of *Sheja* that year.[66]

That argument continued unabated into 1994 with the *Far Eastern Economic Review* noting the Sharmapa's intention to produce the "correct" incarnation,[67] while Dharamsala continues to support the Dalai Lama's position, with statements to that effect appearing even in the Indian national press. Of direct biographical concern is the Kashag's call for general acceptance of the Dalai Lama's approval of Ügyen Trinlé, in the interests of "peace and harmony in the [Tibetan] community at the present critical juncture".[68] Hence this biographical strand appeared to be far from complete (with the controversy still unresolved at the time of going to press).

Other material

Comparatively, the other material from 1993 is miniscule by comparison and so of more limited value. "Pictorial News" (*gsar 'gyur 'dra par*) in the summer 1993 issue covers the enthronement of the eighth incarnation of the Lugyal abbot held at Thung monastery in the Pari (Tianzhu) Tibetan Autonomous County of Gansu Province[69] and is little more than a footnote. Coverage comprises just two small captioned black and white photos, one of which prominently features a camera-wielding male figure clad in the regulation-issue raincoat of Chinese officialdom, perhaps suggesting the presence of plain-clothes police rather than that of the press. Issue 3 profiles the venerable Jigme Tenpai Wangchug, the sixth (and present) Gungthang Tulku (b.1926)[70] and offers considerable biographical information spread over a six-page article, including a limited chronology of his activities in the 1940s and 1950s; nothing is said of his whereabouts during the bleak thirty years that followed. The long interview presents a wealth of somewhat random biographical data in a breezy interview style but relegates his religious activities to passing reference only. He is pictured seated aboard a plane with the late Panchen Lama, perhaps to emphasise his Buddhist credentials. However, the Tibetan author chooses to dwell more on the benefits the lama's powdered milk plants have brought to Tibetans in his Aba region of Sichuan – with even a joint venture with the republic of Kazakhstan in the offing. Still, he is lauded as the first to have given the Kālachakra initiation twice in one year (1991), thus attempting to suggest a degree of religious toleration. Certainly, his view that "education is the crux for improvement in livelihood and economic

Biography by Instalment

progress" (*dpal byor 'phel rgyas su gtong rgyu dang 'tsho ba legs bcos bya rgyu'i gnad gag thug sa ni slob gso red*) accords with similar statements by the Dalai Lama (in *Sheja*'s many reports of his speeches) on the Tibetan people's right to education. Although there is no analysis of Tibetans' rights in that or any other field, at least the article does contain biographical material on a notable reincarnate, despite the suspicion of considerable selectivity in the choice of material used.

Relevant material in 1994 is in a similar vein. An article in Issue 1 on the reconstruction of the Gungthang stupa, destroyed during the Cultural Revolution, covers a variety of religious and administrative positions held by Gungthang Tulku yet his comments are limited to praising the freedom of religion currently enjoyed in the PRC and condemning the ultra-leftist excesses which led to the stupa's destruction. The wealth of detail on the restoration itself concludes with him endorsing "our well-settled national policy of freedom of genuine religion [which] is very stable".[71] In Issue 2, a five-page article (and also in 'Tibetan News in Brief') on a January conference in Beijing marking the fifth anniversary of the Panchen Lama's passing, devotes over a page to an interview with Chöshé Rimpoché, from Kumbum monastery in Qinghai and principal of the China Tibetan Language High Institute of Buddhism in Beijing. The only other information given which is of assistance is that he had met the Panchen many times and received numerous teachings from him.

Conclusion

The discussion has revealed a diversification of the textual biographical tradition in recent years. Formal biographical material as well as that with obvious potential in the field – once its veracity is beyond dispute – has now spread beyond the confines of a religious textual tradition into the realm of hitherto non-existent Tibetan newspapers and magazines. Yet there remains a sharp contrast and divergence between the way *Sheja* and *Trunggö Böjong* present their material. From the PRC's apparent position of strength in the Tibetan equation, *Trunggö Böjong* can undoubtedly afford to be selective in tailoring its subject-matter to suit the PRC's current policies on Tibet; by contrast, *Sheja* must cover all aspects of Tibet-related issues from around the world in an attempt, no doubt, to bolster the position of Tibetans outside Tibet as well as seeking to discredit Beijing at every turn.

Coverage of religious figures and events in *Trunggö Böjong* remains sparse, seemingly reflecting ideological, political and censorial constraints. Both its 1993 and 1994 editions exemplify a piecemeal coverage in the field with emphasis placed on the activities of living religious figures on whom potentially biographical material is presented primarily for the purpose of justifying Chinese political claims concerning freedom of religious belief and practice in Tibet. The tenor of each report suggests that political, not religious, dictates remain the predominant concern of those controlling the publication.

A decade of *Sheja* retains a strong sense of the Tibetan biographical tradition relating to reincarnate lamas – utilising discrete news reports, detailed obituary notices and condensed formal biographies, while maintaining the traditional emphasis on the spiritual dimension, especially Tibetans' love of para-normal phenomena. For literate Tibetans outside Tibet, who are increasing in number with Dharamsala's emphasis on education, a distinct and useful biographical and historical record has developed by way of occasional instalment, charting the life and lives of both celebrated lineages and lesser-known figures too. These developments in part respond to a need in Tibetan society as a whole for information and updates on a social group who still remain of fundamental importance to the survival of a unique culture. This trend is to be welcomed as it brings such material to a far wider audience than would be able to access formal religious texts, with their reliance on an abstruse classical Tibetan language. Even the few formal obituaries in *Sheja* retaining that approach have veered towards the use of simplified terminology.

While the quantity of relevant material in *Sheja* far outweighs that appearing in *Trunggö Böjong*, it is important to remember that the political interests governing the latter publication's content are strongly secular, if not anti-religious, and that Tibetan lamas are seen by Beijing as rallying points and foci for Tibetans' nationalistic and independence-oriented aspirations. Hence, relevant material that can be reasonably expected to appear in a publication in Tibetan which is subject to tight PRC government control must be limited in terms of both subject-matter and quantity. The biographical strand is purely a happy but coincidental outcome. Seemingly, fewer restraints inhibit editorial freedom in *Sheja*, except in cases of politically sensitive matters such as the Karmapa succession.

Although the diametrically opposed political interests of the two camps inevitably affect the flow of material into these publications to differing degrees, the serial nature of material on a subject-matter as specialised as reincarnate lamas is sufficient in aggregate to form a sound basis from which the reader may, over time, construct a biographical framework. Thus continues the evolution of a burgeoning tradition of biography by instalment.

Biography by Instalment

Glossary

TIBETAN SPELLING OF NAMES – RELIGIOUS AND SECULAR FIGURES

[N.B. Tibetan entries cover courtesy titles and principal names, as appearing in the Tibetan periodical concerned]

Sheja (38 entries)

English	*Tibetan*
Achen Rimpoché	nang chen a chen rin po che
Wöntrül Rimpoché	dpal spungs dbon sprul rin po che
Dilgo Khyentsé Rimpoché	skyabs rje dil mgo mkhyen rtse rdo rje 'chang chen po mchog
Gonpo Tseten	yab chen mgon po tshe brtan
Gyalsay Tulku	gling tshang rgyal sras sku gzhon bshad sgrub bstan 'phel mchog
Hirohito	gnam bskos gong ma hi ro'o hi kro
Jagzam Tulku	lcags zam sprul sku
Jamyang Tashi	sku'i bla sman 'jam dbyangs bkris
Jetsun Dampa	khal kha rje btsun dam pa
Khan Abdul Ghaffar	ded dpon kha'n ab dul ghaphar kha'n
Khunu Lama Rimpoché	khu nu bla ma rin po che
Kongtrül Rimpoché	'jam mgon kong sprul rin po che sku phreng gsum pa blo gros chos kyi seng ge mchog
Ling Rimpoché (21st)	skyabs rje yongs 'dzin dga' khri gling sprul rdo rje 'chang rje btsun thub bstan lung rtogs rnam rgyal 'phrin las dpal bzang po mchog
Lozang Dolma (Ama Lozang)	sman pa blo bzang sgrol ma
Lozang Samten	sku'i gcen po blo bzang bsam gtan
Ngawang Nyima	mkhan zur ngag dbang nyi ma rin po che
Panchen Lama	kun gzigs pan chen thams cad mkhyen pa sku phreng bcu pa rje btsun bstan 'dzin 'phrin las 'jigs med chos kyi dbang phyug dpal bzang po mchog
Pangnang Rimpoché	khyab bdag bka' 'gyur ba chen po 'bras tre hor spang nang rin po che mchog
Pema Gyentsen	rje btsun padma rgyal mtshan dpal bzang po mchog
Pon Lha Gé	dpon lha dge (bdud 'dul rnam rgyal)

Petra Kelly	lcam sku pi krar ke li
Rajiv Gandhi	sku zhabs ra jib ghan rdi mchog
Ratö Chuwar Rimpoché	skyabs rje brag gyab rva stod chu dbar rin po che ngag dbang tshul khrims bstan 'dzin rgya mtsho dpal bzang po mchog
Ratö Dongkong (Junior)	rwa stod gdong kong sku chung
Rikha Lozang Tenzin	ri kha blo bzang bstan 'dzin lags
Sanggyé Tenzin Rimpoché	mkhan chen sangs rgyas bstan 'dzin rin po che
Serkong (Tugsé) Rimpoché	skyabs rje mtshan zhabs ser kong thugs sras rin po che
Taglüng Tulku	ri che stag lung dgon gyi sprul sku
Tara Rimpoché	shar pa chos rje ta' ra rin po che mchog
Tatsag Rimpoché	kun gling rta tshag rje drung ho thog thu
Tenpai Gyentsen	drang srong brtson 'grus bstan pa'i rgyal mtshan mchog
Thubten Ngodrub	thub bstan dngos grub
Tugsé Rimpoché	skyabs rje thugs sras rin po che
Trichang Rimpoché	skyabs rje yongs 'dzin khri byang rdo rje 'chang mchog
Yeshé Gyentsen	rig 'dzin rnal 'byor ba ye shes rgyal mtshan
Zepug Rimpoché	ze phug rin po che blo bzang bstan 'dzin chos kyi dbang phyug dpal bzang po mchog
Zhépa Rimpoché	bzhad pa rin po che
Zong Rimpoché	skyabs rje zong sprul rdo rje 'chang rje btsun blo bzang brtson 'drus thub bstan rgyal mtshan dpal bzang po mchog

Trunggö Böjong (4 entries)

Chöshé Rimpoché	chos shes rin po che
Gungthang Tulku	gung thang sku phreng drug pa stan pa'i dbang phyug (a lags gung thang tshang)
Karmapa Ügyen Trinlé	karma pa sku phreng bcu bdun pa'i yang srid ao rgyan dgra 'dul 'phrin las rdo rje mchog
Lugyal abbot	sprul sku klu rgyal mkhan po sku phreng brgyad pa

Biography by Instalment

Notes

1 See, for example, *Report of the Australian Human Rights Delegation to China, 14–26 July 1991* (Canberra: AGPS, September 1991), 31–32.
2 Content of the 1994 issues, however, goes a little way to reversing this apparent editorial policy.
3 Melvyn C. Goldstein, *Modern Literary Tibetan* (New Delhi: Goldstein, 1977), 429–503.
4 R. Conlan, "Gyalsay Tulku Rinpoche – A Tribute," *Australia Tibet Council News* (February–March 1994), 11. See also, "Dispute over Lama's body," *Canberra Times* (22 November 1993), 1. The latter report notes his age as 41.
5 *"nang chen a chen rin po che sku gshegs pa* (Passing of Nangchen Achen Rimpoché)," *Sheja* (October 1990), 26.
6 *Sheja* (February 1989), 5.
7 *rnam mthar.* See *"zhing gshegs 'bras blo gling mkhan zur rin po che padma rgyal mtshan mchog gi rnam par thar pa mdo tsam brjod pa* (A short expression of the biography of the late precious ex-abbot of Drepung Loseling, the supreme Pema Gyentsen)," *Sheja* (October 1985), 18.
8 See *"skyabs rje bde bar gshegs pa yongs 'dzin dga' khri gling rin po che mchog gi mdzad rnam mdor bsdus . . .* , (A summary of the deeds of the Protector Buddha, the Tutor, the Throne Holder of Ganden, the precious Ling Rimpoché)," *Sheja* (January 1987), 17.
9 *"gling tshang rgyal sras glo bur sku gshegs pa* (The sudden passing away of Lingtsang Gyalsay)," *Sheja* (December 1993), 24.
10 *"kun gzigs pan chen rin po che mchog re shig gzugs sku'i bkod pa chos dbyings su thim tshul bstan par mya ngan gus 'dud zhu* (Respectful mourning at the enactment of dissolution into the sphere of emptiness of the Omniscient Panchen Rimpoché's manifest supreme form body)," *Sheja* (February 1989), 3.
11 *Sheja* (October 1993), 24.
12 *"snyigs dus kyi skabs 'dir bstan pa spyi dang bye brag sgrub bsgyud kyi bstan pa rin po che 'dir thun min gyi thugs bskyed dang mdzad 'phrin phyag rjes rmad du byung ba bdag cag rnams kyi 'dren mchog 'jam mgon kong sprul rin po che sku phreng gsum pa blo gros chos kyi seng ge mchog,"* *Sheja* (May 1992), 23.
13 *"bstan 'gro'i dpal mgon mtshungs med nub phyogs bde ldan zhing gi mgon po kun gzigs pan chen thams cad mkhyen pa sku phreng bcu pa rje btzun bstan 'dzin 'phrin las 'jigs med chos kyi dbang phyug dpal bzang po mchog,"* *Sheja* (December 1989), 3.
14 "[A]lthough he was manifesting illness" refers to the Tibetan belief that spiritually advanced beings such as high lamas are able, according to their level of mental attainment, to exert some degree of control over physical phenomena such as the weather or their own bodies. Thus they are held able to manifest sickness in themselves as a means of demonstrating to others the transitoriness of life and the consequent need for immediate spiritual practice. Tibetan text: *"rgya bod em rje rim pas brtag dpyad zhus te gsol sman 'phrad bzhes rim mdzad lags kyang bsnyun khams sel gdang ma byung mur . . . rkyen sel zhabs brtan rim pa sgrub thog gsol sman 'phrod bzhes gtzo bor skyabs rje mchog la spyi sger so sos zhabs pad yun du brtan pa'i gsol 'debs rim zhus bcas de ltar yang phyogs gcig nas sku na smin pa dang gnyis nas tshul bstan bsnyun bab kyang ha cang lci zhing lhag par zhing 'di'i gdul bya rdzogs nas dag pa'i zhing gzhan du gshegs rgyu'i dgongs pa gtad grub pa lta bus,"* *Sheja* (September 1992), 28.
15 *Sheja* (October 1991), 11.

16 The Committee, most likely composed of ordained and laity who were students of the Khenchen, would supervise the wealth of administrative and practical tasks associated with the receipt of offerings from the faithful, the use of relics from the cremation and preparation and distribution of *tsha tsha*, make decisions about the construction of a reliquary stupa to house relics and assist in decision making relating to the possible search for the Khenchen's successor. "*dad ldan dang ba 'dren pa'i rna rgyan*, (Ear ornament inducing devotion in the faithful)," *Sheja* (January 1991), 25–26. *Tsha tsha* refers to a funerary memorial for a high lama in the shape of a miniature figure, made in quantity (up to 100,000) from clay mixed with a small amount of the lama's ashes, impressed with (or sometimes moulded into) a lama, tantric deity or stupa motif. Taken by Tibetan Buddhists as thus imbued with the spiritual power of the deceased, they are usually distributed, as an act of piety, as keepsakes for devotees or at spiritually significant sites such as stupas or at shrines along circumambulation paths.

17 "*de'i skabs lha sa nas byang shar la sprin pa chags stangs mi 'dra ba mang po byung ba dang rgyal dbang mchog gi sku pur de 'nor bu gling gar' bzhugs khri'i steng zhal lhor bstas te bzhugs pa nas zhal shar ngos su gzigs pa'i snang ba dang rjes su mchod sdong gi byang shar ka ring gi ldebs la glo bur du skar ma 'dra ba'i dkar sha zhig skyes pa*," The Dalai Lama, *Ngos kyi yul dang ngos kyi mi mang* (*My Land and My People*) (Darjeeling: Freedom Press, 1963), 13–14.

18 "*nam mkha' sngo bsang dvangs ba'i klong du 'ja' sprin dang gzim chung thog 'ja' gur shar ba ser skya kun gyis mjal,*" *Sheja* (May 1985), 27.

19 "*rin po che sku gong ma ta' ra dge bshes dgong pa rdzogs pa'i rjes ser spreng dang bcas te phu rdza nang pa'i nang du phebs pa rmi lam byung don ltar,*" *Sheja* (July 1991), 17.

20 "*stong pa 'od gsal gyi ngang la thugs dam bzhugs ljags dbyugs kyi rgyu ba nang du thim pa'i rjes su sku'i gzi gdangs snar bzhin rgyas par gyur pa dang de ma thag phyi'i rlung gi rgyu ba rags pas yongs su 'gag bar gyur pa kun gyi mthong snang du gyur,*" *Sheja* (April 1990), 25.

21 *Sheja* (December 1993), 23.

22 *Sheja* (October 1993), 24.

23 Kulu, the birthplace of the reincarnation (in the Indian Himalayan state of Himachal Pradesh), lies more to the north than the east of the cremation site.

24 *Sheja* (December 1984), 23.

25 *Sheja* (September 1993), 26.

26 "*dpal spungs dbon sprul rin po che zhi bar gshegs pa* (Death of Pälpung Wöntrül Rimpoché)," *Sheja* (November 1987), 24–25.

27 "'*rnal 'byor pa ye shes rgyal mtshan sku gshegs pa* (Passing of the yogi Yeshé Gyentsen)," *Sheja* (January 1987), 28.

28 "*gong sa skyabs mgon chen po mchog nas sog yul gyi bla ma che ba rje btzun dam pa'i yang srid ngos 'dzin mdzad pa* (Recognition of the incarnation of the important Mongolian lama, the Jetsun Dampa, by the Dalai Lama, the supreme great Protector)," *Sheja* (October 1991), 8–10.

29 The short biography of the present medium for the Nechung State Oracle, Thubten Ngödrub (b.1957), included in an article confirming him thus, is different. The medium is merely the Oracle's chosen mouthpiece of the time. Reincarnation is not a criterion for receiving the office. The monastery's reincarnate is its head, the Nechung Rimpoché. See *Sheja* (September 1987), 24–25.

30 The sixth, Tsangyang Gyatso; the eleventh, Khedrub Gyatso; the thirteenth, Thubten Gyatso and the fourteenth, Tenzin Gyatso, *Sheja* (January 1987), 17.

31 A misconception common to many non-Tibetans is assuming that the Dalai Lama, rather than the Ganden Tripa, is head of the Gelug (Virtuous Way)

tradition, perhaps as it is the largest (numerically) of the four traditions: Gelug, Kagyu, Sakya and Nyingma.
32 C.E. (Common Era) is used in this paper instead of the more familiar A.D., as more appropriate to a study where the use of a dating scale of Christian origin is solely a matter of convenience.
33 *myur byon smon tshig tu gsol ba drang srong bden pa'i sgra dbyangs, Sheja* (February 1989), 16.
34 *Sheja* (April 1986), 24–25.
35 *Sheja* (January 1990), 26.
36 *Sheja* (June 1990), 24–26.
37 *Sheja* (February 1988), 19.
38 *Sheja* (February 1989), 28.
39 *Sheja* (May 1993), 10.
40 *Sheja* (October 1992), 28.
41 *Sheja* (May 1991), 17.
42 *Sheja* (July 1992), 6.
43 *Sheja* (April 1985), 14.
44 *Sheja* (September 1987), 14–16, 25–26.
45 *Sheja* (November 1988), 20–21.
46 *Sheja* (August 1990), 23–25.
47 *Sheja* (July 1992), 6.
48 *Sheja* (August 1992), 26–27.
49 "*kun gling rta tsag rje drung sku phreng bcu gnyis pa'i mchog sprul yang srid nges rnyed byung ba* (Recognition of the supreme emanation reincarnation of the twelfth Kunling Tatsag Jedrung)," *Sheja* (April 1993), 8–9.
50 "*kod gzhung bka' shag gi gsal bsgrags* (Tibetan Government Cabinet Announcement: ... [divination] should be sought from the high lamas of each religious tradition rather than from the Dalai Lama when searching for reincarnations of lamas ...)," *Sheja* (February 1994), 23.
51 *Sheja* (August 1990), 23–25.
52 "*skyabs rjes gling mchog sprul rin po che na bza' sgron 'bul dang gdan zhu nang ba* (Inviting and offering of robes to the Protector Ling, the supreme emanation Rimpoché)," *Sheja* (October 1987), 18, 25 and (November 1987), 19.
53 "*thugs sras rin po che'i yang srid gdan zhu* (Inviting the Tugsé Rimpoché reincarnation)," *Sheja* (November 1987), 22.
54 "*skyabs rjes khri byang mchog sprul rin po che gdan sar chos zhugs mdzad sgo gnang ba* (The ceremony for the Protector Trichang, the supreme emanation Rimpoché, entering the doctrine at the new seat)," *Sheja* (April 1988), 12–16.
55 "*rva stod gdong kong sku chung gi yang srid nges rnyed* (Reincarnation of the Junior Ratö Dongkong confirmed)," *Sheja* (August 1992), 26.
56 "*ser kong thugs sras rin po che chos zhugs gnang gtan 'khel ba* (Serkong Tugsé Rimpoché entering the doctrine is settled)," *Sheja* (September 1990), 21; "*skyabs rjes gling mchog sprul rin po che chos zhugs mdzad sgo'i sngon brda* (Advance notice of the Protector Ling, the supreme emanation Rimpoché, entering the doctrine)," *Sheja* (October 1990), 25.
57 "*ri che stag lung dgon gyi sprul sku mna' gsol* (Enthronement of the reincarnation of Riché Taglüng monastery)," *Sheja* (October 1986), 22. The location may have been in Sikkim, as his 1994 obituaries (Tibetan and English) note that he had settled there in 1980 after 20 years in Chinese prisons. See "*skyabs rjes stag lung zhabs drung rin po che dgongs pa gzhan don gshegs pa'i skyo gnas* (Sad news of the selfless passing of the Protector Taglüng Shabdrung Rimpoché)," *Sheja* (September 1994), 19–20, 32 and "Kagyu Lama passes away," *Tibetan Bulletin*

(September–October 1994), 18. The latter report records his birthplace as Lhasa (1915) and death in Calcutta, 4 September 1994.
58 "*lcags zam sprul sku chos zhugs gnang ba* (Jagzam Tulku enters the doctrine)," *Sheja* (May 1989), 25.
59 "*bzhad pa rin po che'i gtzug phud 'bul bzhes* (Haircutting ceremony of Zhépa Rimpoché)," *Sheja* (September 1986), 23.
60 "*khu nu bla ma rin po che'i yang srid gong ma'i gdan khrir mnga' gsol ba* (Installation of the reincarnation of Khunu Lama Rimpoché on the predecessor's throne)," *Sheja* (May 1985), 8–9.
61 Located in the eastern part of the Tibetan Autonomous Region.
62 Zahor Tsopema (*za hor mtsho padma*; Hindi: *Rewalsar*), near Mandi, is approximately half a day's road journey east of Dharamsala. This important pilgrimage site (for Buddhists, Hindus and Sikhs alike) is closely associated with Padmasambhava who, with consort, is said to have meditated there – in a cave high above the sacred lake.
63 "*mtshur phu dgon pa'i dgon bdag gsar pa* (The new incumbent of Tsurphu monastery)," *krung go'i bod ljongs* 1 (1993), 19–22.
64 "*krung go'i bod ljongs" zer ba'i dus deb ni de'i khongs kyi dril bsgrags yig cha nag po zhig yin zhing/ da bar dbyin yig dang/ rgya yig/ bod yig bcas snga rjes su yig rigs gsum thog bton pa dang/ nang don phal che ba dngos yod gnas tshul dang mi mthun pa'i rdzun gtam 'khyog bshad sha stag red/ lhag par lo rgyus kyi gnas tshul dang 'brel ba'i chab srid gnad don skor 'khod pa'i rtzom yig 'ga' zhig yig rigs so so'i klog pa po'i gnas tshul la gzhigs te dbyin yig la 'khod pa rgya yig la mi 'khod pa dang/ rgya yig la 'khod pa bod yig la mi 'khod pa'i gnas tshul yang yang yong gi yod pa de'i rgyu rkyen ni mi rnams kyis go ba len thub pa zhig red*. *Shes bya* (May 1995), *rgya'i rtsom yig la dpyad pa'i gtam btsan 'dzul par mdun lam med pa* (Lack of perspective in aggressive analytical rhetoric in Chinese publication), 12–18.
65 "*mtshungs med karma pa'i mchog sprul rin po che mtshur phur sku gong ma'i gdan khrir 'khod pa* (The supreme emanation Rimpoché of the incomparable Karmapa ascends the throne of the previous presence at Tsurphu)," *Sheja* (October 1992), 7–8.
66 "*dpal karma pa bcu drug pa chen po'i yang srid kyi skor dang 'jam mgon rin po che'i dgongs rdzogs kyi skor* (Concerning the reincarnation of the great sixteenth illustrious Karmapa and concerning the demise of Jamgön Kongtrül Rimpoché)," *Sheja* (June 1992), 10–11. See also "*rgyal ba karma pa'i yang srid 'khrungs zin pa* (Birth of the reincarnation of the victorious Karmapa)," *Sheja* (April 1992), 20.
67 L. Terhune, "Divided House, Tibet's Kagyu Buddhists face a leadership battle," *Far Eastern Economic Review* (24 March 1994), 36–8.
68 "*da lta'i dus skabs gnyan 'phrang can 'dir spyi tshogs nang lhing 'jags bag phebs*," *Sheja* (April 1994), 9–10.
69 *gsar 'gyur 'dra par* (Pictorial News), *Krung go'i Bod ljongs* (1993 No. 2), 45.
70 "*a lags gung thang tshang la bcar 'dri theng gsum zhus pa* (Three interviews with Ala Gungthang Tsang)," *Krung go'i Bod ljongs* 3 (1993), 9–14.
71 "*rang re'i rgyal khab kyi yang dag pa'i chos lugs dad mos rang dbang gi srid jus dngos 'bebs byung yod pa dang ha cang brtan brling yin pa.*" *Krung go'i Bod ljongs* 1 (1994), 41.

9
The Factor of Fate in Religious Biography

Scott Davis

The Ethnological Setting

In the course of more than a year of ethnographic fieldwork in Taiwan, I was once obliged to interview a shady kind of fellow whose real job was "Gangster," but who was thinking of taking on a second job as a spirit-medium. This fellow operated a gambling den, and some people who were on close terms with him – people whose job description was "doing a little of this and a little of that" – disappeared for longish periods, and then re-surfaced after a while looking very thin and nervous. I had to go to this man's home and interview him because as a child he had known the spirit-medium at the shrine where I was doing my fieldwork, and probably this early childhood experience influenced some of his later occupational choices. Eventually, he would go on officially to open his own shrine and in effect go into competition with the shrine of his childhood mentor. When I went to interview him, it turned out that he had already placed statues of the possessing gods on his household altar; this stated that the gods were ready to take control of him, whenever any of the neighbours wanted to come by and have him take care of any problems or business they had. For some reason, at that time very few of the neighbours had availed themselves of the opportunity.

From time to time the fellow would drop by the shrine where I was doing field observations, and would bore us with quite insipid "god-tricks": for example, he would go into a questionable trance, put chopsticks in a tall glass, pour in uncooked rice, and then laboriously attempt to lift the glass with the chopsticks. Or he would brush a couple of dozen burning incense sticks against his bare chest the way possessed mediums are supposed to do in Taiwan. In a similar way, the interview I had with this petty gangster was so very uninspired, that it leads me to relate it as a "zero-degree" limit of religious biography; and that is a minimum I am aiming for in this essay.

His narrative was primitively concocted: it turns out that he often felt dizzy at night and was awakened as if by jostling. He was unable to understand the trouble until he finally realized that he was being possessed and, after a period of indecision, had the whole thing explained and legitimated by a trusted shaman in a well-known temple in another district. Now he can be possessed by three or four different gods, to become their proud avatar.

Now the life-history I obtained from the spirit-medium I worked with most carefully was far richer, just as her possessions were far more profound and her healing sessions more inspired. Nonetheless, the outline of the narrative is insistent: from an early age, she was in dangerously close contact with the *yin* world of the spirits and, consequently, her health was affected. She exhibited many symptoms of instability which everybody, including herself, took to be psychiatric. However, the ghosts which took control of her (such as the spirit of her dead infant, and of the uncle of her husband) imparted enough information to the family to validate partially her special knowledge of the *yin* world. After bearing seven children, she had to have a complete hysterectomy. Two hours after surgery she was possessed by a little god named the Third Prince and ran around the hospital room threatening to jump from the window. The operation served a symbolic purpose of purifying her female body to prepare it for service as a spirit-medium. However, her status as a deranged working mother continued for several more years while she and her husband resisted her vocation of shamanism. Finally, some very powerful possessions occurred, and the neighbourhood people started coming by for guidance. Eventually, the front wall of the living room had to be torn out to accommodate all the clients each night. Thus, a spirit shrine was born.

The narrative elements of initial illness, gradual awakening to the spiritual calling, prolonged resistance, and final compulsion to the fate of being a medium are a consistent basis of shamanism, not only in Taiwan, but as Mircea Eliade has documented, in cultures throughout the world. As Carmen Blacker remarked:

> These notable characters ... exhibit in their personal histories a curiously uniform pattern. Nearly all of them in their early life betray symptoms of what could be called 'arctic hysteria'. They are sickly, neurotic, hysterical, odd, until a moment comes when, exacerbated by suffering, these symptoms rise to a climactic interior experience of a mystical kind. A deity, by means of a dream or a possession, seizes them and claims them for his service. Thenceforward they are changed characters. Their former oddity and sickliness give way to a remarkable strength and magnetism of personality, which is conferred on them, together with various supernormal powers, by the deity who has possessed them and who henceforth governs their lightest move.[1]

All that is variable about the pattern is contingent: from case to case, the locus of the disorder shifts from one part of the organism to another, but

The Factor of Fate in Religious Biography

the point of the account is always the recovery of health by accepting the fate of being a shaman. The monotony with which the narrative is presented, it seems to me, justifies Lévi-Strauss's observation that "The poverty of religious thought can never be over-estimated."[2]

Now, it may very well be pointed out that this discussion was unfairly set up to reach this conclusion, selecting the pathetic attempt of my petty gangster at articulating this universal religious archetype. It is true that the extensive biographical account of *The Life and Hard Times of a Korean Shaman*, given us by Laurel Kendall, for example, does not use the idiom of ill-health and recovery to narrate the pathway the shaman took to reach her vocation. Instead, it focuses much more on the social and political hardships which the prospective *mudang* had to overcome: the torturous marriage, the escape from the Communist army, etc. Nonetheless, even in this alternative idiom, the implicit message is that at each crisis was revealed a further connection between the gods and the shaman. All in all, what is at question here is whether, at least as far as the amorphous practice of "shamanism" – trance, change of consciousness, possession, spiritual journey – is concerned, the concept of religious biography is not something of an oxymoron: to the extent it is religious, the biographical details seem contingent and of secondary significance, to be subsumed in the framework of fate, which has a specifically religious dimension, but which excludes difference[3]. Or, in deistic terms, "The religious impulse is the arch-enemy of biography, for 'a deep belief in a personal deity destroys all deep belief in the unconquerable personality of man'"[4]. In the present anthology, we can see similar problems emerge in contrasts between the highly structured "sacred songs" and the "narrative events," "cultural or textual pattern" and "individual life." It behooves us to examine how these supposed contradictions between structure and process work out in some philosophical material.

At first approximation, a biography is a text of a life[5], but this opening definition would be false under too narrow a construal of "text"; oral biographies, of the sort just touched upon, are also texts of human lives. It is the *narrative* quality of the account which maintains the textual sense of biography. Narrative involves the inter-relations of beginning, middle and end of a textual series, implying special temporalities and intra-referential devices. Keeping in mind these oral biographies of spirit mediums (*tang-ki*) such as one can elicit in Taiwan, I want to concentrate on these aspects of narrative, while looking at some native ideas concerning fate such as are discussed in the classical tradition. There are some characteristics of religious biography which are particularly clear when we focus on the life-career of a person the distinctive feature of whom is that her personality becomes elided by possessions and trances; the specifically religious aspect of her vocation means that the construction of her life's continuity is periodically cancelled by her contacts with the sacred. By considering the structural peculiarities of this kind of situation, understood as a kind of fate, I hope to throw some light upon some deeper moments of this sort of religious life and its attendant symbolism.

Anthropologists sometimes are of a fairly cynical turn of mind in treating religious themes, and they often leap to pursue functional understandings of the claim of the shamans to have acquiesced to their fate. Naturally, the idea of fate serves certain general psychological functions of consolation and theodicy. In terms of the shaman's social role as healer, there are transparent motivations for disclaiming personal interest by claiming the operation of fate. These explanations are undeniable. However, I would be pleased to hint at the existence of some more comprehensive configurations which come into play in this entire problematic. To do so, we turn to the concepts brought to bear on the phenomena I observed in the field, namely those deployed in the Chinese languages in use in sites where I worked.

A review of some key statements about fate in Chinese philosophical tradition will demonstrate that in general the tradition deals with the problem in a reflexive way, in terms of the way fate is established as a narrative, rather than a brute fact, and that this conceptual or semiotic reading of the problematic of fate motivates an internal splitting or torsion introduced into the framework of the discussion. Next, some comparative points from Western philosophical traditions will be examined, to bolster the argument made here that the Chinese approach has always tended towards the constitution of a philosophical anthropology. Finally, in the conclusion we will return to the specific problems of the factor of fate in religious biography, to show that although contact with the sacred does impose its archetypes on the individual careers of its vehicles, still the active fulfilment of such models of fate does provide an ample arena for the unfolding of personal biography in Asian religious contexts.

Some Chinese Philosophical Perspectives

A central point to understand in this paper is that the basic Chinese term for fate, that is to say, *ming*, has the great advantage of preserving the connection with language which the English word "fate" shows only etymologically[6]. *Ming*, of course, has a double function, both verb and object, both, "to order" and "order"; reminiscent of similarly doubled words like "lightning" (an action-phenomenon). There could hardly be a better model of an event than this. The grammar of *ming* as fate can be demonstrated using a Song dynasty model: "Without *qi* heaven has no way to order people, without *qi* people have no way to receive the order of heaven." In this way (through the counterfactual argument), *qi* is asserted to be the medium of transmission, and humans are the indirect object; heaven "orders" (verb) the "orders" (direct object), which *qi* transmits to humans and humans receive in the form of their fate.

The Factor of Fate in Religious Biography

But how does this work? On the face of it, this talk of fate presents us with the picture of the future already in existence, like looking down an extended tube containing the ineluctable that is to come, traversed internally by the series of presents which just actualize these fated events, as if they were a rolling sphere which simply brought about repeated contacts with the walls of the container. Is it inevitable that this model of destined events taking place must end up by reifying a causal object, pre-existent in linear, physical time, which pre-determines its effects on lives and renders volition absurd? Must we see in these ideas a dead (because inalterable) teleology, which Buddhists call *suminglun*, of a causal influence which travels backwards in time to have its consequence in what is earlier? Or is it perhaps a matter here of a logical determinism, which holds that if a proposition is true at all, then it is timelessly true, equally so whether it happens to be referred to events which are past or future to the present? In this way, if X became a shaman in 1980, then the simple constative utterance, "X becomes a shaman in 1980" is just as true in the Zhou dynasty as it is in 1997, which thereby is taken to demonstrate (logically) the inexorability of fate.

In this paper I argue that the narrative connection of *ming* with the surface of language events forestalls the impulse which divides the field of concern into an objectifying, causal construal, and a logical, atemporal construal. Rather, the doubled internal structure of these concepts has been exploited to elucidate, embody or reveal some critical features in the nature of narrative knowledge. It would be unwise to insist that a causal picture of fate has never been held in China, or that none of the other determinisms have ever emerged. However, I want to indicate some contextual patterns in the operation of such a concept in Chinese culture which bias its interpretative outcome in such a fashion that talk of fate is more likely to be useful and informative (in a reflexive way) in delineating and acting upon features of human life from a general point of view, than would be expected in the case of a fatalism based on causality.

The considerations I have in mind go something like this. Rather than join a metaphysical debate on the issue of individual free-will defended on ethical grounds, one can productively remain on the level of a philosophical anthropology when dealing with Chinese sources, and look to treat the problems in general terms as distinctive features of a human form of life. In such a way, the most interesting aspects of the concept of fate turn out to involve its use in displaying these anthropological markers, and this, in turn, amounts to treating fate in terms of its contribution to a narrative account, or a discursive framework, for anthropological understanding of organic and human temporality. Human temporality and intentionality share deep parallels in their existential organization, so that understanding the former in narrative terms helps us treat issues of the latter, such as the way fateful limitation impinges on it. It will be argued here that for human beings, the inevitability ongoing events acquire in the stream of time stems less from history as determined, causal fate, than from the narrative nature of the process – that, for instance, by the time it becomes clear what significance our actions have taken on in the overall story, it is already too late to have them changed. Such factors index limits of our "control over our own destinies".[7] Biography, as revelation of fate, and fate, as the deferred, absent trace of meaning, are tools with which we direct our understanding of human temporality and its deconstructive and narrative-generating interplay with intentionality. There are clues that this position is also readily expressed in Chinese terms.

Accordingly, we turn to some formulations about *ming* which elaborate its internal structure. First, two passages from *Mencius* which doubtless are to be read together[8]:

> *Mencius 7A:1*: Mengzi said: For someone to give full realization to their heart is for them to understand their own nature, and someone who knows their own nature will know heaven. By conserving their heart/mind and nurturing their nature, they are serving heaven. Whether they are going to die young or to live to a ripe old age makes no difference to their steadfastness of purpose. It is through awaiting whatever is to befall them with perfected character that they stand firm on their proper destiny.

> *Mencius 7A:2*: Mengzi said: Though nothing happens that is not due to destiny, one goes along willingly only with what is one's proper destiny. That is why someone who understands destiny does not stand under a wall on the verge of collapse. Someone who dies after having done their best in following the *Dao* dies according to their proper destiny. It is never anyone's proper fate to die in penal restraints.

There are two issues to point out within these passages. First, the predominant aspect of the problem of fate addressed here has to do with the decreed death, the fated end of life. Fate manifests here in terms of whether the subject experiences "the good death."[9] Thus, the second issue is that fate undergoes a differentiation into "proper" and "improper" fate, closely associated with the circumstances of death. On the one hand, fate is acknowledged as all-inclusive, thereby leaving no domain for voluntary action. On the other, though, a torsion is re-introduced by the distinction of "proper" and "improper" fates, and the corresponding directive concerning which sort of fate one should "go along with." Clearly, some free space is reserved for the play of volition in this scheme. And from just this minute difference in the ways fate manifests, a whole cosmological ethics issues – of waiting, cultivating, conserving, and plumbing the depths of one's spiritual resources.

The Factor of Fate in Religious Biography

A second selection from *Mencius* shows another kind of tension, while shifting the concern clearly away from the issue of the fated "Hour of Our Death" to the manner of the functioning life in relation to fate.

Mencius 7B:24: Mengzi said: The way the mouth is disposed towards tastes, the eye towards colours, the ear towards sounds, the nose towards smells, and the four limbs towards pleasant relaxation is nature. But there is fate involved, so the lordly person does not speak of nature here.

The way human-heartedness pertains to the father-son relation, the way rightness pertains to the lord-subject relationship, the way ritual propriety pertains to the guest-host relationship, the way wisdom pertains to the wise, the way the sage pertains to the heavenly *Dao*: this is fate. But there is nature involved, so the lordly person does not speak of fate here.

Here, one finds the issue of fate laid out, in the typical monumental style of this philosophy, against the interplay of what we might call biological and social dimensions. The torsion in the argument is set up in many respects: in the first place, in the alternating between the two dimensions, where the summary labels themselves undergo alternation, from fate to nature, then from nature to fate. The primary opposition, the domain of nature (bodily senses) versus the domain of fate (value relations), has no claim to be an exclusive or privative contrast (as between a proposition and its negation) because within each primary domain lies a singularity from the opposite domain: that is, there is at least some point or some aspect which expresses the opposite. Moreover, this secondary alternation, fate-which-is-still-nature, or nature-which-is-still-fate, contains a further tension, inasmuch as its statements can be construed, superficially, as flat contradictions, between the statements: "it is fate" and "we do not say it is fate" (or "it is nature" and "we do not say it is nature"). In this passage, the fine discrimination and distribution of primary dichotomies take place not in the modality of death-fate, but in the modality of speech. It may be that our biological apparatus reveals our nature, but we do not *say* it is so; fate may unfold within our social relations, but we do not form this proposition (unless it be formed only to negate itself). The whole passage begins to seem more about what can be performed under the conditions of the state of affairs, and less about the state of affairs itself; it takes on the semblance of a conceptual analysis or reflexive ruling about the idea of fate.

We will return to this second Mencian paradigm of fate, to fill in its contours under the guidance of the Song philosopher Zhu Xi. First, though, I want to reiterate that the apparently rhetorical function of the phrases concerning what is to be said or not said (which are ubiquitous in Chinese philosophy) is more than just as sequencing devices in the explication: in fact, they indicate the proper nature of the discourse of such philosophy, namely its conceptual or linguistic focus. An example from Zhu Xi is helpful. The Master was once asked whether heaven produced sages "accidentally and not with any intention." He replied:

> Does heaven-and-earth really say, 'I especially want to give birth to a sage'? It's just that the courses of *qi* converge at this point and time, and thus a sage emerges; once he's emerged, then it is just as if heaven had intended it, that's all.[10]

Naturally, heaven-and-earth do not voice their intentions. Yet the operation of this cosmos is far from mechanical, and the outcomes seem to bespeak intentionality. In particular, biological processes at some point have given rise to intentional behaviour, to projects which are related to mental events and external objects. The human form of life is our prime exemplar of intentionality and intelligibility. Was this form and were these behaviours fated to come into existence teleologically in the evolution of the world? Zhu Xi sketches for us the configuration of a world in which intentionality arises from a pre-intentional condition.[11]

Were the intention there, perhaps heaven-and-earth would speak of it; failing the verbal report of the intention, which naturally heaven-and-earth are in no position to give, the status of the intention is neither fully negated nor affirmed. Consequently, the world he describes features a characteristic sort of temporality, in the aspect of the "future perfect." The fate which will seem to have been in effect is not yet in the world, but is present in the modality of the Not-Yet: it exists ahead of itself, grounding our present anticipatory behaviour. When the sage will be produced, then there will be a retrospective recognition of the factor of fate in his or her emergence. It is a kind of temporality in which life lives ahead of itself.[12] We know it because it is a feature of human lives. As Whitehead observed, "Cut away the future, and the present collapses, emptied of its proper content".[13]

This complex temporal attitude is also documented in early Chinese sources. In 621 BCE, Duke Mu of Qin died and was buried; according to his own instructions, three human victims were sacrificed at the grave. The biographers' judgement was severe: Duke Mu's failure to command great power outside his own country during his life was fitting, because the circumstances of his death were cruelly arranged. In this example, we see the way the present depends upon the future: not in a causal way, but through founding the present on what is ahead of it, so that the totality resonates as a whole. And nonetheless, in spite of this example, we know from the chronicles that rites of bloody sacrifices accompanying dramatic banishments, including human sacrifices, could be the key to prestige in the feudal circumstances of ancient China. As Granet put it: "It's a speculation upon destiny . . . the future will decide who would pay".[14] I am suggesting here that

The Factor of Fate in Religious Biography

the kinds of temporalities involved in the Song formulation of fated events have evolved from a long, long meditation on modelling the dimensions, the risks, the relevancies of human action, largely in ritual frameworks. Here is an example from the *Zuozhuan* (*Cheng* 13, 578 BCE):

> Liuzi said: "I have heard it stated: In order to live, the people receive that which is in the middle of heaven and earth. This is what is called 'orders'. It is this to which we have recourse to move and create the principles of Ceremony, Rightness, and Awesome outer appearance. This is how we fix solidly our 'orders'. Those who are capable nourish this [acquisition] and achieve blessing thereby; those who are incapable are defeated by drawing catastrophe from it. For this reason, the Lordly Person works hard at Ceremony and the inferior people exert themselves to the utmost. There is nothing more important than respect, for working hard at Ceremony, and for utmost exertion there is nothing more important than great-hearted sincerity. The source of respect is in nourishing the spirits. The source of sincerity is in conserving to one's function. The important affairs of state are sacrificial ceremony and warfare. Sacrificial ceremony has its offering of roasted meat. Warfare has its receiving of raw meat. This is the great articulation of spirit."

This passage is a clear rendition of ancient views on the social and spiritual form and function of sacrificial ceremony in relation to human fate. Note that "nourish" finds its way into the exposition twice, with opposing kinds of objects for each usage; this is a key to understanding the import of these words for the topic of sacrifice. The doubled character of sacrificial nourishment in this passage is paralleled in the structure of the discussion on fate, where on the one hand, one *receives* fate (nourishes what heaven and earth have bestowed on one and thus achieves blessing), but on the other hand, one *sets up* one's fate (nourishes the spirits). There is no point in working with a concept of fate unless it can be parsed and finessed in some such way as this. When it can be, then it indexes features of human action which constitute its narrative quality: it articulates an essentially paradoxical configuration for concepts such as intentionality and destiny.

Now, returning to the *Mencius* passage on "fated nature" and "natural fate," a quick review of Zhu Xi's treatment[15] of this classic source may help to unpack the internal positions which the earlier work condenses. We saw that the modulation and distribution of difference in the classical text took place at several levels. Zhu Xi adds to the complexity by introducing his own key distinction, which of course is not a dualism of *li* and *qi*, pattern-principle and material energy or whatever, but actually a difference between *li* and *li*-and-*qi*[16]. Zhu Xi's distinction translates into two sorts of *ming*: "one kind, spoken of in terms of what is received" in the allotment of resources from the cosmos; "one kind, spoken of in terms of its values, in terms of what it is worth." The latter is also considered "heaven's *ming*." As we will now see, these two modes of *ming* might be given the labels: *ming* as distributive outcome, and *ming* as limiting function.

The biological functions which ground the individual's sensory awareness are the domain of one's nature; "in speaking this way, one is taking the body together with materially based desires." Attributing this domain to nature is "said from the point of view of *qi*." From the point of view of pattern and principle, though, the domain involves *ming*, in its function of "limiting the human heart/mind." "You cannot say, 'Because it is my nature to have these [sensory resources], therefore I must demand to get them'; you also cannot say, 'It's my lot to have them, and I must take my desires to their extreme.'" Thus, the limiting function of heavenly *ming* prevents an excess of the human heart/mind. These bio-sensory functions "are certainly natural. But they are decrees that have been issued to and received by those in a subordinate position."

On the other hand, the social matrix of relationships would seem to be the theatre of fate; "speaking in terms of what has been received, there are thick or thin allotments of *qi*." People are born in all types of favourable and unfavourable physical and social circumstances, which act as their fates. This "is said from the point of view of *qi*." However, "speaking from the point of view of pattern and principle," the domain also involves one's nature, which is "the heart/mind of the Dao." One should not overemphasize the fated aspect of this circumstance, to avoid discouraging individuals making full recourse to their heart/mind. "Certainly, this is fate. But just as well it is each individual getting the principle he or she is to receive; hence it is nature."

As it all works out – and one cannot fail to sense the central role that "speaking from a certain point of view" plays in constructing the various facades of the model – Zhu Xi's construal of the Mencian paradigm resolves to an expression of two kinds of *ming*. There is active, heavenly *ming* and there is the passive *ming* of what one receives from the heavenly dispensation. This latter category can also be called one's nature. Each time, from the point of view of *qi*, it seems as though we are dealing with dual domains; but the viewpoint from the aspect of pattern-and-principle always makes this previous clause into a concessive: *li* always brings out the fused values, or the singularity from the opposite side, in each domain.

In this sort of thinking, a temporal distinction is hidden which is reminiscent of the temporalities modelled in structural linguistics, such as the "paradox of speech" indicated by Deleuze, Merleau-Ponty and others. Thus, as Zhu Xi writes, the heavenly *ming* is like the bureaucratic office; therefore, it gives us the hierarchical positionality, it is synchronic or even atemporal for any particular case of action. In the speech act, it is the aspect of *langue*, the matrix of differential form. Nature, or the receptive *ming*, paradoxically is like the performance of duties in the office. It is time-sensitive, carried out diachronically, like *parole*.

The Factor of Fate in Religious Biography

> What is called *ming* is like the emperor ordering me to become a certain official. As to the duties of that office – whether they are easy or difficult, what can be done and what cannot be done – all that, is fate *at that moment*. All one can do is proceed ...[17]

In this way, Zhu Xi ends up using the same term for a concept which applies to the centre (in the direction of the vertical, the command voiced from on high), and to the periphery (contingent, coming from the outside, in the thick of things, actualized in the encounter with circumstances during performance). In the result, peculiarly, the performative dimension turns out to be the same as the passive aspect (one's nature) while the active dimension (from above) is characterized by its negative, limiting role, in its contribution to difference. One might wonder if any successful account of fate can avoid this fate of differentiation and repetition in itself.

Some Western Philosophical Perspectives

In order to reach a better understanding of the factors which dictate and articulate this necessary internal refraction of fate, we begin by reading to the end of the quote from Deleuze cited in note three:

> What brings destiny about at the level of events, what brings an event to repeat another in spite of all its difference, what makes it possible that a life is composed of one and the same Event, despite the variety of what might happen, that it be traversed by a single and same fissure, that it play one and the same air over all possible tunes and all possible worlds – all these are not due to relations between cause and effect; it is rather an aggregate of noncausal correspondences which form a system of echoes, of resumptions and resonances, a system of signs – in short, an expressive quasi-causality, and not at all a necessitating causality.[18]

As Deleuze demonstrated for the case of fate in Stoic and Epicurean philosophies, "In either case, one begins by splitting the causal relation, instead of distinguishing types of causality as Aristotle had done and Kant would do. And this split always refers us back to language, either to the existence of a *declension* of causes, or ... to the existence of a *conjugation* of effects".[19] We have also seen that traditional Chinese considerations of fate proceed on the plane of language, modelling what can or cannot be said about it. In short, the philosophy of fate in Chinese culture aims squarely at bringing out the *narrative nature* of the operation of fate in human life. At most, we find what Deleuze calls "an expressive quasi-causality," such as governs relations between the incorporeal events taking place on the surface of thought:

for example, regularities between mental states, constitutive reasons, conventional behaviour, signification, or grammatical properties. It would be an erroneous interpretation which concentrated on identifying the strictly causal dimensions of *ming*.

The linguistic basis of fate is clearest when we consider the aspect of the problem dealing with the manifestation of *ming* through the functioning life; this problem in turn contrasts with the manifestation of *ming* in the modality of death. I submit that these two aspects, though related, are not on the same level of being. It is true, Heidegger's version of *ek-stasis* would allow a collapsing of these levels; discourse, for Heidegger, is the way the "thrown project" is lived through the interpenetration of understanding possibilities of the project and finding oneself in states of mind, of thrownness. The entire framework is motivated by care, subsuming the course of a life in its "Being-towards-death," the resolute anticipation of the possibility of the impossibility of all possibilities. The resulting philosophy of *Being and Time* takes on a rather heroic stance at the expense of a kind of fatedness towards death which we share with all living beings.[20] There is a sense, after all, in which an animal which comes to a violent end has not lived out the fullness of the potentiality which it embodies (as a limiting case, biographies of animals might be framed in these terms). For this reason, I prefer the formulation of Helmuth Plessner, in a book published a year after *Sein und Zeit*, that all life involves the feature of being lived ahead of itself, over the anthropocentric Heideggerian version of the *ek-static* temporality. In his philosophical anthropology, Plessner attempted to do a conceptual or semiotic analysis of *what we mean* when we attribute life to a thing; thus, it was an analysis posited on an anthropic principle in the life sciences (exploiting the special reflexive logic of the attribution of life to living objects). To this end, Plessner developed a structural framework of relations across a boundary, so as to posit an organism over beyond itself and back into itself. These essentially doubled directions build level after level of opposed features which we know from our ordinary experience with the life world, as a world known to (human) organisms which correspond to it. In effect, Plessner sketches the conditions for understanding the way the organism claims its natural place and natural time, as distinct from the spatial and temporal properties of purely physical things. Thus, in their time-having aspect, all living things live in advance of themselves, and have possibilities which they select for realization or neglect. This gives a sense for saying that a certain level of the problem of *ming* has to do with the destiny of death, and this is a destiny that we share at a certain level of being, across the spectrum of the organic worlds.[21]

And yet it is true that the really complex problems having to do with fate arise from another level of being, from the plane of thought made possible by what Plessner calls eccentric positionality, the way of organization of the body, and of the world, characteristic of the human form of life. Language, significance, culture, as well as the foreknowledge of impending death, are entailments of this organizational form. A few aspects of Plessner's theoretical framework will be mentioned in conclusion, which have important bearing on the problems this paper has been considering.

By the term "eccentric," Plessner referred to the characteristic of human positionality which is distinct from the "centric" animal form.

> The animal lives out beyond its centre, inside its centre; however, it does not live as centre. In the surrounding field, it experiences contents, alien and proper; it is also able to acquire mastery over its own living-centred body; it forms a system related back reflectively to itself, a Self. However, it does not experience – its self.[22]

For human beings, on the other hand, there is available an organizing point, or a self, which stands over beyond the body, or rather which is not grounded on any spatiotemporal locus at all.

> As "I," which makes possible the full back-reference of the living system to itself, the human stands no longer in Here-Now, but rather "behind" it, behind himself, placeless, in Nothing; he is absorbed in Nothing, in space-time-having Nowhere-Never. Placeless-timeless, he makes possible the experience of himself, and at the same time the experience of his Place- and Timelessness as the standing outside of himself, because the human is a living thing which no longer stands only in himself, but rather whose "standing in himself" means the ground of his standing. He is posited in his boundaries – which bound him, the living thing – and thereby over beyond them. He not only lives and experiences, but rather he experiences his experience. However, the fact that he experiences himself as something which can no longer be experienced, which no longer manifests in objective positing – as pure "I" (in distinction to the psychophysical individuality identical to the experienceable "me") – has its ground uniquely and only in the special boundary-positedness of the things called human. More acutely stated: it brings this directly to expression.[23]

In this way, Plessner developed a philosophical anthropology which shares certain vital features with the Chinese traditions examined earlier. In the first place, both systems are fundamentally anthropic; they work within a cosmos which has given rise to human beings, and which is being observed precisely in light of that "fact" (it is as much an external fact as a precondition of the investigation, certainly). Moreover, both types of philosophy acknowledge the relativity of organism and world, such that the "world" under study here is specifically a human world. Finally, insofar as Plessner concludes with the development of the eccentric variant of positionality, and in doing so points out the importance of the "empty centre" as the basis for human reflexivity, his thinking coincides with a good deal of religious thought, such as has been expressed in China in terms of "non-ego" in a variety of Chinese traditions, Daoist, Ru, Buddhist, etc. And in terms of the present paper, eccentricity provides a congenial basis for interpretation of the phenomena of trance, possession, magic journey, and so forth, which are associated with shamanism and spirit-mediumship. In this view, the experiences of change of state of consciousness such that one's personality is no longer co-referred to one's bodily locus, dissociation, depersonalization, etc., are variations of the eccentric reflexivity between the subject and the body. In this way we can understand the regularity with which religious practitioners claim to transform their relational attitudes towards their mundane bodies, to stand outside of themselves, to undergo disruptions in the continuity of their personal identities, and so forth, as being expressions of the typical forms of organization of the human being.

For the human case, Plessner's scheme features three "worlds," each of which arises from the structures of directed pathways mediating double-directional relationships at the boundaries of the human body: thus, there are the external world, the inner world, and the mutual world. Each of these planes of existence bears the traces of eccentric positionality. The eccentric organization of the mutual world humans inhabit can be seen, for instance, in the proposition that one comes to know of oneself, and thus of the world, only indirectly through the inputs of others, through the symbolic resources imparted from others: "The existence of the mutual world is the condition of the possibility that a living creature can comprehend itself in its setting, namely, as a link of this mutual world".[24] As well, there is a kind of openness and transparency in the mutual world – to be sure, a characteristic that is countered by hiddenness and opacity, but is there nonetheless – inasmuch as human beings realize their radical contingency and interchangeability, that anyone could have been anyone else, had the circumstances of birth and subsequent life been different.

> The formation and expression of solidary feeling and behaviour present in concrete society are built on top of the substitutability and replaceability of each individual with another, in the form of "We"; this forms the background from which singularity peels away as individuality. Fundamentally, the individual is the same as the other; he stands where the other stands, and the other occupies his place. Therefore, the other can hold a position in the reality of the world without and of the world within, a position which each human possesses in his absolute Here, or – "he could also have been the other." In his real replaceability and substitutability, the single human has the guarantee and the certainty of the contingency of his being, or his individuality.
>
> This is the ground of his pride and of his modesty. Not even the factual irreplaceability of his own living substance, in which he is

different from everyone else, outweighs the replacement in the "We," the replaceability through every other with whom he comes together. Therefore, humans must be ashamed, in all their preciousness. The ground of modesty is formed by the nothingness of their existence, their complete permeatedness and the knowledge that we are all fundamentally the same, because we are individuals, each for ourselves, and so, different from one another (the ground of modesty is only secondarily formed by the object of a metaphysical shaming and the beginnings of humility). Granted, thus formed it is indirect and mediated through the inner reality of mental being. Thereby is awakened in them that ambiguity, which tears humans back and forth between the urge to openness and value, and the urge to suppression and restraint. This ambiguity is one of the ground-motifs of social organization.[25]

Biography, of course, also takes its cogency from such a background. So it turns out that biography teaches us about fate in many ways, but particularly insofar as it shows the cluster of fate around one life. However, the eccentric character of the human form of life gives a peculiar opposing proposition equal value: the cluster of factors which are the individual's fate show as well that this could have been anyone's life, had they been visited with such factors. Thus this highly unique individual life is also no one's life; or more accurately phrased: it shows the way this individual is grounded in factors which are neutral to subjects, objects, first, second or third persons. In Deleuze's terms, a biography may reveal the ambit of the "fourth person singular," the pre-personal singularity, which organizes the life in question, and expresses the paradoxical structures of fate and contingency, sacred structure and narrative event, or cultural pattern and individual pattern, that have been brought to light in the course of many of the essays collected here.

Conclusion

"A fatalist ... thinks of the future in the manner in which we all think of the past."[26] Although, superficially considered, biography and the idea of fate both happen to suggest in different ways a view of the past as irrevocably determined, the situation as depicted here is not that of the temporal continuum as just dead and closed. The constitution of the individual subject through history should not be thought of as the mechanical accretion of external influences. The past and present are constantly subject to revisions stemming from what belongs to their future, and so, within a certain range, are open and changing. Since the significance of what one intends to accomplish is subject to reinterpretation by future history, intention cannot be taken in any straightforward manner as simply radiating out to its fulfilment in reality. There are several senses in which it is true that one never reaches what one intends; but on the other hand this is not to say, with tragic pessimism, that our efforts are intrinsically doomed to failure. Rather, the fragmentation of the intention, and the satisfaction of the impulse, often are the same event. Due to the eccentric positionality of the human form of life, or the expressivity of the human frontal stance to the world, human intentionality is already broken by the character of the human place in the world, which itself is correspondingly broken in its objects and their immanence, simultaneously hidden and revealed in one. In this way, the operation of essentially refracted intentionality can comprise the fulfilment of the intention. Although the paradoxical equivalences of realism and idealism, of transcendentalism and immanence in consciousness, are awkward for those who attempt to frame them in a rigorous, logical way, the anthropological description of the actual situation could scarcely be otherwise.[27] So, freedom of will and fated outcomes co-exist and are even structurally equivalent, and even though this constitutes an unthinkable situation, it seems to be a more faithful account of the human condition than strictly philosophical versions.

Clearly, "narrative" as used in this essay is not only another word for storytelling, but rather is a typical dimension of every present human action in the life-world. Narrative knowledge is to be taken in a far broader sense than merely the ability to keep track of characters in a work of literary fiction. Indeed, narrative temporality is the crucial feature by which human beings find their place in the mutual world and in the extended objective world of calculable relationships – a place which, we have just said, is also outside of any place. For the point of the attribution of a narrative character of fate is not simply that humans become what they are fated to become; nor is it that human beings become what they will themselves to become. Rather, human beings must make themselves into what they already are becoming:

> As eccentrically organized being, he [viz. the human being] must *first make* himself into what *he already is*. Only in this way does he fulfil the way, compelled by his vital form of existence – not simply to be absorbed in the centre of his positionality, like the animal which lives from out of its centre, relates to everything from its centre, but rather to stand in the centre of his positionality, and so at the same time to know of his positedness. This mode of being of standing in his positedness is possible only as *execution* from the centre of positedness outwards. Such a way of being is executable only as realization. Humans live only insofar as they lead a life. To be human is the "lifting away" of the living being from being, and the accomplishment of this lifting away, due to which the stratum of vitality appears as a quasi-autonomous sphere. . . . In consequence, humans neither simply live to the end of what they are – they do not live themselves out (radically understanding the terms in their directness) – nor do they just make themselves into what they are. Their existence is of such a

kind that it does indeed compel this differentiation in itself, but at the same time it lies beyond it. For philosophy, this "breech-birth" of humans is explained by eccentric positionality; but it is not helped by that. Whoever is in it, stands in the aspect of an absolute antinomy: to have to first make oneself into what one already is, to lead the life which one lives.[28]

This configuration from philosophical anthropology confirms and helps explicate the meaning of the doubling of active and passive fates, the topological identification of centre and periphery, which we have reviewed in the Chinese teachings. As Plessner put it: "Artificiality in behaviour, thinking and dreaming is the inner means whereby humans as living, natural beings stand in agreement with themselves... Therefore, humans *live* only when they *lead* a life".[29] The doubled locus of action motivates a type of cut, twist and re-joining, like a Möbius strip, which gives an excellent image for the paradoxical, eccentric form of the human position.[30] Fate is always what one is engaged in willing and doing.

When a shaman acquiesces to her fate, she is acknowledging that this future is, and always has been, "there" for her. And yet, being an artificial role, it is not *simply there*: the acquiescence and subsequent, on-going dramatic elaboration are necessary and constitutive in the development of the shamanistic career.[31] One's *ming* is not a straightforward determinant, just as the past is not "simply there," either; rather, one must make one's *ming* by recognizing, enacting and intensifying it, even as it is being "solidified" through the actions taken in the present. The narrative preconditioning, the transitional relations of earlier and later situations, which are effected in such a way, follow their own rather stringent logic, but this is not simply framed in the functional factors of a sociological role; or rather, the concept of sociological role is clearly subsumed into the wider narrative organization. We cannot expect to arrive at a physics of the social system. The social system, we have known since Durkheim and Mauss, is susceptible to totalizing events or symbols; this marks its basically semiotic nature. Such totalizing is one kind of generality in the social realm; needless to say, such totalizing processes, such as occur as an individual yields to fate, really cannot be thought of nomothetically, as are law-like statements in physics: in terms of traditional differences in inferential levels, such as specific referents at times t to t_n, falling under timeless, general laws conceived causally or functionally. Instead, such dramatizations of fate mean acceding to a *totalizing particularization* of one's individual life. Against the world-horizon which is thus given recognition, there arises an array of possibilities for selection; for human beings, the narrative element comes into play synonymously with the work of selection and elimination of possibilities. But if we can speak of narrative here, to whom should we attribute authorship? To make a life make sense, seen in such a way, its singularity – or rather its series of singularities –

activating the selection recedes, in the totalizing moment, to the pre-personal or "fourth person singular."

Therefore, the operation of fate in these biographical expressions which we have been considering is not simply the cancellation of the contingent by the timeless, and it does not present an insurmountable contradiction in discussing religious biography, the stories of the religious lives of its subjects. Since Eliade,[32] we have been accustomed to thinking of history, in its religious interpretation, as requiring periodic renewals through the intervention of the sacred, or its redemption through the assumption of historical time in the Christian doctrines. A concept such as *ming*, as well, is like an "instrument for the obliteration of time".[33] However, as in the teaching of the historical incarnation of Christ, the idea of *ming* tacitly acknowledges that "only through time time is conquered".[34] Expanding to the proper world-horizons of the human actor, fragmented and flexible in order to match its field of application, the operation of a well-crafted concept of fate advances its adherents towards a cosmological setting in which – as we have seen in other papers in this collection as well – the domain of the mundane becomes less distinguishable from the domain of the miraculous.

Notes

1. C. Blacker, *The Catalpa Bow: A Study of Shamanistic Practices in Japan*. (New York: Mandala, 1975), 129.
2. C. Lévi-Strauss, *The Savage Mind* (Chicago: University of Chicago Press, 1966), 95.
3. In investigating fate, of course, we are looking for, as Deleuze describes it: "What brings destiny about at the level of events, what brings an event to repeat another in spite of all its difference, what makes it possible that a life is composed of one and the same Event, despite the variety of what might happen, that it be traversed by a single and same fissure, that it play one and the same air over all possible tunes and all possible worlds." *The Logic of Sense* (New York: Columbia University Press, 1990), 170.
4. David Novarr, *The Lines of Life: Theories of Biography, 1880–1970*, quoting Harold Nicolson, (West Lafayette, Indiana: Purdue University Press, 1986), 47.
5. We can presently defer consideration here of some interesting questions whether there is any real sense to a biography of an animal life (in a non-derivative sense, so as to leave aside stories such as *Black Beauty*).
6. "Fate" stems from the PIE root *bha-, "to speak," from which we get such words as "phonics," "prophet," "banish," and "infant".
7. A.C. Danto, *Narration and Knowledge* (New York: Columbia University Press, 1985), 284.
8. All translations from *Mencius* are very loosely based on those of D.C. Lao (Harmondsworth: Penguin Classics, 1970), 182, 198–99.
9. The dying possibly found themselves in surroundings and family circumstances roughly comparable to those conditions described by Philippe Aries as "the tame death."
10. *Zhuzi yulei* (Taipei: Hanjing wenhua shiye youxian gongsi, 1980), 33.

The Factor of Fate in Religious Biography

11 This world contains what Deleuze calls the "paradox of speech," that is,

"Speech begins: ... *when the formative elements of language are extracted at the surface from the current of voice which comes from above*. On the one hand, it refers to language as to something withdrawn which preexists in the voice from above; on the other hand, it refers to language as to something which must result, but which shall come to pass only with formed units. Speech is never equal to language. It still awaits the result, that is, the event which will make the formation effective. It masters the formative elements but without purpose ..." (*The Logic of Sense*, 232–33).

Of course, the problematic of this relationship between speech and language has been treated by many scholars in various ways – for instance, Saussure, *Course in General Linguistics* (New York: Philosophical Library, 1959), Wittgenstein [*PI §§138–42*], Benveniste, *Problems in General Linguistics* (Coral Gables: University of Miami Press, 1971), 47, 110, 206–11, etc. Deleuze's observations about this paradoxical quality of the performance of the speech event are quite comparable to those of Merleau-Ponty, which address the issue in terms of a "ruse" of "incarnate intentionality":

"Speech ... is that moment when the significative intention (still silent and wholly in act) proves itself capable of incorporating itself into my culture and the culture of others – of shaping me and others by transforming the meaning of cultural instruments. It becomes "available" in turn because *in retrospect* it gives us the illusion that it was contained in the already available significations, whereas by a sort of *ruse* it espoused them only in order to infuse them with a new life." ("On the phenomenology of language," in *Signs* (Evanston, Illinois: Northwestern University Press, 1964), 92, first emphasis added).

In such systems as express an anthropic principle, there is the phenomenon of a sort of "leap" taken by any language-like system – "a finite system of signs which claimed to be capable in principle of winning by a sort of ruse any being which might present itself" – and for which "the place of truth would ... be that of anticipation (*Vorhabe*)" (Merleau-Ponty, "On the phenomenology of language," 95). In this type of human-inhabited world (and this is a redundant phrase, since "*man* is a being of the same type as *the world*" (J.-P. Sartre, *The Emotions: Outline of a Theory* (New York: Philosophical Library, 1948), 6), speech is a hinge, a central switch, which blocks dualistic or direct trajectories from realms putatively opposed by privative criteria. Fate is one way intentionality is refracted in this breach, to cast its patterns from the future backwards towards the past.

12 Or *ek-statically* (in Heidegger's terminology); its culture resolves to a "thrown project" (*Geworfen Entwurf*).

13 A.N. Whitehead, *Adventures of Ideas* (Cambridge: Cambridge University Press, 1947), 46.

14 M. Granet, *Danses et Légendes de la Chine Ancienne*. (Paris: Felix Alcan, 1926), 169–70.

15 *Zhuzi yulei*, 580–82.

16 For our purposes, we could even take this distinction in Deleuzean terms, as referring to the depth of corporeal bodies, and the surface of thought and incorporeal events which arises out of it but is independent of it.

17 Translation in W.T. Chan, *Chu Hsi: New Studies* (Honolulu: University of Hawaii Press, 1989), 217, emphasis added.

18 Deleuze, *The Logic of Sense*, 170.
19 Deleuze, *The Logic of Sense*, 6.
20 Compare J. Derrida, *Of Spirit*. (Chicago: University of Chicago Press, 1989), 57.
21 "Youth, maturity and aging are the forms of destiny of life, because they are essential for the developmental process. Forms of destiny are not forms of being, rather for being; being appears under them and bears them. Next to the regularities of "what" [there is] (essentiality) and the regularities of process (causality), as a third kind there appears the necessity of destiny. According to the first kind, everything which is something is determined. According to the second kind, everything which runs off in time is determined. According to the third kind, all, and only, living things are determined." H. Plessner, *Die Stufen des Organischen und der Mensch: Einleitung in die philosophische Anthropologie* (Berlin: Walter de Gruyter and Company, 1928), 154.
22 Plessner, *Die Stufen des Organischen und der Mensch*, 288.
23 Plessner, *Die Stufen des Organischen und der Mensch*, 292.
24 Plessner, *Die Stufen des Organischen und der Mensch*, 302–03.
25 Plessner, *Die Stufen des Organischen und der Mensch*, 344.
26 R. Taylor, "Fatalism," *Philosophical Review* 71:1 (1962), 56.
27 Plessner, *Die Stufen des Organischen und der Mensch*, 321–41.
28 Plessner, *Die Stufen des Organischen und der Mensch*, 309–10.
29 Plessner, *Die Stufen des Organischen und der Mensch*, 309–10, emphasis added.
30 Compare Deleuze, *The Logic of Sense*.
31 Writing about the local poetics of life in West Virginia, Kathleen Stewart describes, "Where other women threaten to go *crazy*, Eva Mae enacts the threat and fashions herself in its image to make herself a walking allegory. [. . .] You could say that Eva Mae performs a transgression that transforms her otherness and marginality into the disruptive power of excess and social abandon. [. . .] It is not a way out of the oppression, danger, and contingency of the hills but a way in through mimetic excess. It pushes into the matter of things, intensifies latent forces to the point of their visibility, and makes countervailing possibilities tangible by playing them out." *A Space on the Side of the Road: Cultural Poetics in an "Other" America* (Princeton, NJ: Princeton University Press, 1996), 60–61. Stewart's vision well expresses the counter-intuitive, performative nature of one's fate which the present paper aims to elucidate in connection with possession religion in the spirit shrines. Fate is work one is compelled to undertake on oneself, the way one transforms oneself. Shamanism involves enacting the excesses of such fated contact with the sacred.
32 M. Eliade, *Cosmos and History: The Myth of the Eternal Return* (New York: Harper and Row, 1959).
33 C. Lévi-Strauss, *The Raw and the Cooked* (New York: Harper and Row, 1969), 16.
34 T.S. Eliot, *Four Quartets* (London, Faber and Faber, 1944), I:2, l. 44.

Contributors

T.H. Barrett
T.H. Barrett was educated in the United Kingdom, graduating in Chinese Studies from Cambridge University in 1971, before studying East Asian Religion at Yale and in Tokyo. He returned to Cambridge in 1975 to teach Chinese Studies, gaining his Yale doctorate in 1978 which formed the basis for *Li Ao: Buddhist, Taoist or Neo-Confucian?* (1992). He left Cambridge in 1986 to take up the Chair of East Asian History in the School of Oriental and African Studies in the University of London, moving in 1997 to the Department of the Study of Religions. His publications, including *Taoism Under the T'ang*, (1996), have mainly concerned medieval Chinese religion. In addition to a large number of book reviews in the *London Review of Books* and elsewhere, he has also published on a number of other topics, including the Western understanding of China and aspects of Chinese historiography. He is currently working on a study of the religious background to the introduction of printing in China.

Benjamin Penny
Benjamin Penny's research is concerned with medieval Daoism, in particular on religious biography and behavioural precepts for monks. He is currently completing a monograph on the biographies of the founder of Daoism, Zhang Daoling as well as editing papers for a volume on the history of Daoism. He is also beginning a project concerned with the discovery of Chinese religions by western missionaries in the nineteenth century. He works in the Humanities Research Centre at the Australian National University as Executive Officer of the Herbert and Valmae Freilich Foundation.

Barbara Hendrischke
Barbara Hendrischke did a textual analysis of the *Wenzi* for her doctoral dissertation at Würzburg University. She has also worked on the *Taiping jing* and other issues in the history of Daoist thought and Daoist religion.

Contributors

A.J. Prince
After completing a Ph.D in modern Chinese literature at the University of Sydney, Tony Prince spent three years teaching at the College of Chinese Culture (now the Chinese Culture University) outside Taipei, Taiwan, and working in the Institute for the Study of Buddhist Culture attached to the college. Following a further two years in Japan, he returned to the University of Sydney in 1977, where he taught courses in Chinese literature and thought until his retirement last year. His research is mainly concerned with the Huayen School of Chinese Buddhism, and he has published a couple of articles and (with Adrian Buzo) a book on this subject.

John Jorgensen
John Jorgensen completed his Ph.D 1990 on Ch'an and Chinese theories of poetry at the Australian National University having also studied in Japan and South Korea. A visiting lecturer at UCLA in 1985 and 1986, he has been teaching modern Japanese history, culture and society at Griffith University since 1990. His research interests are Chinese Buddhism, with a specific focus on Ch'an; Korean Buddhism in general and Korean new religions; and Buddhism and the environment. He is preparing a book on the sixth patriarch of Ch'an, Huineng, and a history of Korean new religions.

David Templeman
David Templeman has worked for many years on the translation of Tibetan hagiographical works focussing on the writings of Tāranātha, the Tibetan 17th century polymath. He has had published his small works on *The Origin of the Tara Tantra* (1981), *The Seven Instruction Lineages* (1983) and his *Life of Kṛṣṇācārya/Kāṇha* (1989) as well as many articles deriving from their study. Nearing completion are translations of Tāranātha's *Wanderings of the 16th-17th Century Buddhist Yogin Buddhaguptanātha* and Kün-da Dröchog's version of Kṛṣṇācārya's life. In a recent departure from hagiography he has been studying the links between the Iranian cultural world and that of Tibet in its formative period from the 2nd to the 9th centuries. This study has explored themes such as cosmogony, dualism and artistic expression, as well as burial customs in Tibet's formative period. He has taught history at Collingwood College in Melbourne for over twenty years.

Colin Jeffcott
Colin Jeffcott was taught History and Philosophy at Victoria University in New Zealand, and Chinese and Sinology at Oxford and the Australian National University. He has been trying since then to combine these fields to some good purpose. He presently teaches in the Faculty of Asian Studies at the Australian National University.

Contributors

Geoffrey Samuel
Geoffrey Samuel was awarded a Ph.D in social anthropology from the University of Cambridge in 1975 for research on religion in Tibetan societies. He is currently Professor of Anthropology at the University of Newcastle, NSW, Australia, and has written extensively on issues relating to Tibetan society, religion and music, and anthropological theory. He is the author of *Mind, Body and Culture* (1990) and *Civilized Shamans: Buddhism in Tibetan Societies* (1993), and co-editor of *Tantra and Popular Religion in Tibet* (1994), *Nature Religion Today* (1998), *Healing Powers and Modernity* (in press) and *The Daughters of Hariti* (forthcoming).

Kevin Garratt
Kevin Garratt is a lawyer and independent scholar, holding an LLM in International Law and a Litt.B in Sanskrit and Tibetan studies from the Australian National University. Between 1975 and 1984, he studied in Dharamsala, India, at the Library of Tibetan Works and Archives and the then Buddhist School of Dialectics. He was a member of the Australian Government Human Rights Delegations to China, 1991 and 1992. His research interests also cover the fields of human rights, refugees and minority populations. He is the author of several articles on those subjects and has contributed various book reviews dealing with those areas to a number of scholarly journals.

Scott Davis
Scott Davis is an Assistant Professor in Anthropology at Miyazaki International College on the island of Kyushu in Japan. His field work experience includes study of the idiom of spirit possession, as a focus of medical and religious anthropology. Besides shamanism and folk religion in China and Japan, other research interests include comparative mythology and folklore; philosophical anthropology; and the study of Chinese antiquities and its classical tradition, particularly focussing on the structural analysis of the *Yijing*, and on the culture or intertextuality of *Yijing*, *Zuozhuan*, and *LunYu* in archaic China. A long time resident of Taiwan and other Pacific Rim countries, this author enjoys playing stringed instruments such as the guitar, gu-zheng, and shamisen.

Chinese Character Glossary

Characters presented in this glossary are listed according to the reading of them given in the essay in which they occur.

Abidamo fazhilun	阿毗達磨發智論	Cheng weishi lun yingchao	成唯識論應抄
An Lushan	安祿山	Cheng weishi lun	成唯識論
Anding	安定	Cheng weishi lunshu	成唯識論疏
Baibo	白波	Cheng	成
Baiyuchan	白玉蟾	Chengdu	成都
Ban Gu	班固	Chewang nyŏndae yŏk	諸王年代歷
Baopuzi	抱朴子		
Beimang	北邙	Chimu	尺木
Bi Wan	畢萬	Chinp'yŏng	真平
Biezhuan	別傳	Chiri	智異
Boruo xin jing	般若心經	Chiyi Zipi	夷子皮
Bozhen	薄塵	Cho Myŏnggi	趙明基
bu (ke) siyi	不(可)思議	Chŏmt'ak	漸涿
Cao Cao	曹操	Chosŏn	朝鮮
Ch'oe Ch'iwŏn	崔致遠	Chu	楚
Chajang	慈藏	Chuan deng lu	傳燈錄
Chan	禪	Chuigong	垂拱
Changan	長安	Chukji-rang	竹旨郎
Chanlin miaozhi	禪林妙記	Chunqiu	春秋
Chaoxian	朝鮮	Ci'en	慈恩
chen (trigram)	震	Cishan	慈善
Chen Baoguang	陳葆光	Crazy Ji	濟顛
Chen Shou	陳壽	Cui Shi	崔湜
Cheng weishi lun biezhang	成唯識論別章	Dai Zhen	戴震
		Dao	道
Cheng weishi lun guangchao	成唯識論光抄	Dao Ying	道膺
		Daoshi	道世
Cheng weishi lun liaoyi deng	成唯識論了義燈	Daoxuan	道宣

Chinese Character Glossary

Daoyin	道氤	Guandi	關帝
Daozang	道藏	Guang hongming ji	廣弘明集
Dasheng Ji	大乘基	Guangshiyin	光世音
Dasheng miyan jing	大乘密嚴經	Guangyin	光音
Dasheng xianshi jing	大乘顯識經	Guangyue	廣越
Daxue	大學	Guankong	觀空
Dayang	大陽	Guanshiyin	觀世音
Dazhu	大珠	Guanyin	觀音
Deqing	德清	Guanzhong	關中
Dianlüe	典略	Guanzizai	觀自在
Dilun	地論	Guiben	歸本
Ding Lingwei	丁令威	Guo Pu	郭璞
Dong Jing	董經	Guochao Songxue yuanyuan ji	國朝宋學淵源記
Dongfang Shuo	東方朔	Guoyu	國語
Donglin si	東林寺	Haein	海印
Dongshan Liang Jie	洞山良价	Han Sui	韓遂
Dongxian zhuan	洞仙傳	Han Wudi neizhuan	漢武帝內傳
Du Shu	杜恕	Han Yu	韓愈
Dunhuang	燉煌	Han	漢
Ennin	圓仁	Hanlin	翰林
Fa Zang	法藏	Hanshu	漢書
Fabao	法寶	Hatani Ryōtai	羽溪了諦
Facheng	法成	He Zhizhang	賀知章
Fajie	法界	Hedong	河東
Fan Li	范蠡	Hong lou meng	紅樓夢
Fan Ye	范曄	Hongming ji	弘明集
Fangbian	方便	Hossō	法相
Fangwai	方外	Hou Hanshu	後漢書
Faxiang	法相	Hou Jing	侯景
Fazang	法藏	Hou Wuyang	侯武陽
Feisheng	飛生	Hu Ting	胡珽
Fengde	豐德	Hua	化
Foshouji	佛授記	Huabiao	華表
Gan Ji	干吉	Huainan	淮南
Gao Panlong	高攀龍	Huangbo	黃檗
Gaoseng zhuan	高僧傳	Huangfu Mi	皇甫謐
Gaoshi zhuan	高士傳	Huanyuan	還源
Gaozong	高宗	Huayan jing	華嚴經
Gatha(ji)	偈	Huayan lun	華嚴論
Ge Hong	葛洪	Huayan nian Fo sanmei lun	華嚴念佛三昧論
Ge Zhanggeng	葛長庚		
Gou Jian	勾踐	Huayan	華嚴
Gouyi Furen	鉤翼夫人	Huayanjing chuanji	華嚴經傳記
Guan suoyuan lun	觀所緣論	Hui Wu	慧悟
Guan suoyuan lunshu	觀所緣論疏	Huijiao	慧皎
Guan Yü	關羽	Huizhao	慧沼

Chinese Character Glossary

Hŭngnyŭn	興輪	Kyunyŏ	均如
Hwang	黃	Langye	瑯邪
Hwangbok	皇福	Lanling	蘭陵
Hwaom sa sajŏk	華嚴寺事蹟	Laozi	老子
Hwaŏm	華嚴	li	理
Hyeso	慧昭	Li Bai	李白
Hyŏnjun	賢俊 (雋/儁)	Li Boji	李伯紀
Hyoso	孝昭	Li Gang	李綱
Ik-sŏn	益宣	Li Hong	李弘
Iryŏn	一然	Li Hongdu	李宏度
Jia Mu	賈穆	Li Hongjing	李宏慶
Jia Yi	賈誼	Li Shaojun	李少君
Jian'an	建安	Li Shimin	李世民
Jianfen	見分	Li Tongxuan	李通玄
Jiang Fan	江藩	Li Yi	李義
Jiangbiao zhuan	江表傳	Li Yong	李邕
Jiangnan	江南	Liang Wudi	梁武帝
Jiangxi	江西	Liangshu	梁書
Jiao Xian	焦先	Liaodong	遼東
Jiaozhi	交趾	Liexian zhuan	列仙傳
Jiashang	嘉尚	Liezhuan	例傳
Jie shenmi jingshu	解深密經疏	Liezi	列子
Jin	晉	Lingbian	靈辯
Jingang boruo	金剛般若	Lingzhao	靈照
Jingmao	靖邁	Linji Yi Xuan	臨濟義玄
Jingtu sheng xian lu	淨土聖賢錄	Liqixiang	歷谿鄉
Jinhuo	金貨	Lishi zhenxian tidao tongjian	歷世真仙體道通鑑
Jinling	金陵	Liu An	劉安
jinshi	進士	Liu Ke	劉軻
Jinshi cuibian	金石粹編	Liu Qianzhi	劉謙之
Jinshu	晉書	Liu Xiang	劉向
Jinzhou	金州	Liu Yimin	劉遺民
juren	舉人	Liuzi	劉子
Jushi zhuan	居士傳	Longmen	龍門
Kamata Shigeo	鎌田戊雄	Longxing	龍興
Kim Poksun	金福順	Lu Deming	陸德明
Kim Sanghyŏn	金相鉉	Lu Dunxin	陸敦信
King Wu	武王	Lü Guan	盧綰
Koguryŏ	高句麗	Lu Jing	陸景
Kong Anguo	孔安國	Lu Qi	盧杞
Kongkongzi	空空子	Lü Shang	呂尚
Kuiji	會基	Lu Xiangshan	陸象山
Kŭmgangsammei gyŏng	金剛三昧經	Lü Zangyong	盧藏用
Kyerim	雞林	Lujiang	盧江
Kyŏl'ŏn	決言	Luo Yao	駱曜
Kyŏngju	慶州	Luo Yougao	羅有高

Chinese Character Glossary

Lushan	廬山	Renmin Ribao	人民日報
Lüzong	律宗	Renwang jingshu	仁王經疏
Ma Chao	馬超	Renwang	仁王
Ma Zhi	馬支	ruyizu	如意足
Mei Fu	梅福	Samguk yusa	三國遺事
Mengzi	孟子	Sandong qunxian lu	三洞群仙錄
Ming (emperor)	明	Sanguo zhi	三國志
Ming	命	Sanmenxia	三門峽
Mo(r)yang	牟梁	Sat'ak	沙涿
Mu	穆	Sengbian	僧辨
Mun'a	文雅	Shabo	少伯
Muyŏm	無染	Shan	陝
Nanshi	南史	Shandong	山東
Northern Qi	北齊	Shang (dynasty)	商
Northern Wei	北魏	Shang	尚
O Hyŏnggŭn	吳亨根	Shanxi tongzhi	陝西通志
Ouyang Xiu	歐陽修	Shanxi	山西
P'ung	馮	Shelun	攝論
Paekche	百濟	shentong bianhua	神通變化
Pak	朴	Shentong	神通
Pang Yun	龐蘊	Shenxian zhuan	神仙傳
Pei Songzhi	裴松之	Shenzu	神足
Peng Jiqing	彭際清	shi (apparent reality)	事
Peng Qifeng	彭啟豐	shi (S.vijñana and S.vijñapti)	識
Peng Shaosheng	彭紹升		
Peng	彭	Shiji	史記
Pengzhou ershisi hua zhi	彭州二十四化志	Shijie	尸解
		Shijing	詩經
Pŏpsang	法相	Shiyi mian shenchou xin jing	十一面神呪心經
Pu Songling	浦松齡		
Puguang	普光	Shouqian	守千
Pulguk Sa kogŭm ch'anggi	佛國寺古今創記	Shu	蜀
		Sichuan	四川
Pulguk Sa sajŏk	佛國寺事蹟	Silla	新羅
Pulguk	佛國	Sima Qian	司馬遷
qi	氣	Sima Tan	司馬談
Qi	齊	Sinmun	神文
Qi Song	契嵩	Sŏn	禪
Qianlong	乾隆	Song	宋
Qiao	譙	Song Fu	宋復
Qidan	契丹	Song Gaoseng zhuan	宋高僧傳
qin (instrument)	琴	Suminglun	宿命論
Qin	秦	Sun Ce	孫策
qing (color)	青	Sun En	孫恩
Qing	清	Sun'gyŏng	順璟
Qinglong	青龍	Sŭngjang	勝莊
Qingshi lie zhuan	清史列傳	Suzong	肅宗

Chinese Character Glossary

T'ak	涿	Wutai Shan	五台山
Taehyŏn	太賢	Xiahou Zhan	夏侯湛
Tai	太	Xiajiang	峽江
Taigong Wang	太公望	Xiangfen	相分
Taihe	太和	Xiangguo	相國
Taiping	太平	Xiangshan	香山
Taiping jing	太平經	Xianyuan bianzhu	仙苑編珠
Taiyang	太陽	Xiao Ziyun	蕭子雲
Taizong	太宗	Xiao	孝
Tan Xun	曇訓	Xie	謝
Tan Yi	曇義	Xie An	謝安
Tang	唐	Ximing	西明
tang-ki	童乩	xin	心
Tankuang	曇曠	xing	性
Tao	陶	Xingjiao	興教
Tao Qian	陶潛	xingzhuang	行狀
Tojŭng	道證	Xiong Shili	熊十力
Tongguan	潼關	Xiwangmu	西王母
Tongzi	童子	Xu gaoseng zhuan	續高僧傳
Toyun	道倫	Xu	徐
Tuoba	拓跋	Xuan	宣
Ŭich'in	義天	Xuanpin lu	玄品錄
Ŭisang	義相	Xuanzang	玄奘
upasaka	優婆塞	Xuanze	玄則
Wang Bi	王弼	Xue Huaiyi	薛懷義
Wang Chang	王昶	Xue Qifeng	薛起鳳
Wang Dun	王敦	Yan Shigu	顏師古
Wang Jin	汪縉	Yan Zhenqing	顏真卿
Wang Yangming	王陽明	Yan	燕
Wansui tongtian	萬歲通天	Yancong	彥琮
Wei Man	衛滿	Yang Xiong	揚雄
Wei	魏	Yangzhou	揚州
Weilüe	魏略	Yi	夷
weishi	唯識	Yijing	義淨
Weishi shuchao	唯識疏鈔	Yingchuan	潁川
Wen Qiao	溫嶠	Yisheng jueyi lun	一乘決疑論
Wi Man	衛滿/魏滿	Yu Di	于頔
Wŏnch'ŭk	圓測	Yu Huan	魚豢
Wu	武	Yu Ji	于吉
Wu Bei	伍被	Yu Liang	庾亮
Wu Pingyi	吳平一	Yuan Hongdao	袁宏道
Wu Yue chunqi	吳越春秋	Yuance	圓測
Wu Zhuzhi	吳豬芝	Yuanfasi	元法寺
Wu(state)	吳	Yuankang	元康
Wuliangyi jing	無量義經	Yue jueshu	越絕書
Wuliu xiansheng zhuan	五柳先生傳	Yue	越
		Yuefu	樂府

Chinese Character Glossary

Yuga	瑜伽	Zhenke	真可
Yuhuasi	玉華寺	zhi	芝
Yujia shidi lunji	瑜伽師地論集	Zhi Ning	志寧
Yuki Reimon	結城令聞	Zhi Yan	智儼
Yulu	語錄	Zhiguai	志怪
Yunjisi	雲際寺	Zhiguizi zhuan	知歸子傳
Yunju	雲居	Zhiguizi	知歸子
Yunqi qiqian	雲笈七籤	Zhixu	智旭
Yusi	玉筍	zhong tong fen	眾同分
Yuyi	嵎夷/嵎夷	Zhongguo Xizang	中國西藏
Zanning	贊寧	Zhongnan Shan	終南山
Zenju	善珠	Zhongnan	終南
Zhang Jue	張角	Zhongping	中平
Zhang Ling	張陵	Zhongzong	中宗
Zhang Tianyu	張天雨	Zhou	周
Zhang Weiping	張維屏	Zhu Nan	朱南
Zhang Xiu	張修	Zhu Shaosun	朱紹蓀
Zhang Zhidong	張之洞	Zhu Xi	朱熹
Zhao Daoyi	趙道一	Zhu Zishe	朱子奢
Zhao Dazhou	趙大洲	Zhu	朱
Zhao Zhenji	趙貞吉	Zhuangzi	莊子
Zhao	昭	Zhuhong	袾宏
Zhao(state)	趙	Zhunü	祝衄
Zhending	真定	Zizhi tongjian	資治通鑑
Zhenghe	政和	Zudaopin	助道品
Zhengshi	正史	Zuo Wu	左吳
Zhenguan	貞觀	Zuozhuan	左傳

Tibetan Glossary

Except where words are well known in an alternative transcription (e.g. tashi) the system for transliterating Tibetan used here corresponds with the pronunciations given in Melvyn Goldstein's *A Tibetan English Dictionary of Modern Tibetan* (Kathmandu, Ratna Pustak Bhandar, 1975), with minor modifications.

Aba	rnga ba
Achen Rimpoché	a chen rin po che
Amdo	a mdo
Amdowa	a mdo ba
babdrung	'babs sgrung
Butön	bu ston
Changchub Gyentsen	byang chub rgyal mtshan
Chenrezig	spyan ras gzigs
chö-yön	mchod yon
Chödrub	chos grub
Chöshé Rimpoché	chos shes rin po che
Chushul	chu shul
Dalai Lama	ta la'i bla ma
Dartsedo	dar rtse mdo
Dergé	sde dge
Dilgo Khyentsé Rimpoché	dil mgo mkhyen rtse rin po che
Dodzong	rdo rdzong
Drepung	'bras spungs
Drepung Loseling	'bras spungs blo gsal gling
Drugchen Rimpoché	'brug chen rin po che
Drugpa Kagyupa	'brug pa bka' brgyud pa
Drugu Chögyé Rimpoché	gru gu chos rgyal rin po che
Drugu	gru gu
Dujom Rimpoché	bdud 'joms rin po che

Tibetan Glossary

dzong	rdzong
Ganden	dga ldan
Ganden Shartsé	dga ldan shar rtse
Ganden Tripa	dga' ldan khri pa
Geleg Rimpoché	dge legs rin po che
Gelugpa	dge lugs pa
Gendzo	ge 'dzo
Gesar	ge sar
geshé lharampa	dge bshes lha ram pa
Gum Sakya	gum sa skya
Gomang	sgo mang
Gonjo Dodzong	go 'jo rdo rdzong
Gonjo	go 'jo
Gonpo Tseten	mgon po tshe brtan
Gungthang Tulku	gung thang sprul sku
Guru Chöwang	gu ru chos dbang
Guru Rimpoché	gu ru rin po che
Güüshi Khan	gu shrvi khang
Gyalsay Tulku	rgyal sras sprul sku
Gyalwa Karmapa	rgyal ba karma pa
Gyandé	rgya sde
Gyentsab	rgyal tshab
gyepo	rgyal po
hutuktu	ho thog thu
Jagzam Tulku	lcags zam sprul sku
Jamgön Kongtrül Rimpoché	'jam mgon kong sprul rin po che
Jampeyang	'jam dpal dbyangs
Jamyang Zhépa	'jam dbyangs bzhad pa
Jang	'jang
Jetsun Dampa	rje btsun dam pa
Jigmé Tenpai Wangchuk	'jigs med bstan pa'i dbang phyug
Jinpa Gyatso	sbyin pa rgya mtsho
Ju Mipam	'ju mi pham
Jyekundo	khyer dgun mdo
Kagyupa	bka' brgyud pa
Kandzé	dkar mdzes
Kanjur	bka' 'gyur
Karma Kagyupa	kar ma bka' brgyud pa
Karmapa	kar ma pa
Kashag	bka' shag
Khaché	kha che
Kham	khams
Khampa	khams pa
Khedrub Gyatso	mkhas grub rgya mtsho

251

Tibetan Glossary

Khenchen	mkhan chen
Khenzur	mkhan zur
Khunu	khu nu
Kongtrül Rimpoché	kong sprul rin po che
Kumbum	sku 'bum
kün khyen	kun mkhyen
Kün-ga Dröchog	kun dga' grol mchog
Kün-ga Nyingpo	kun dga' snying po
Künling Tatsag Hutuktu	kun gling rta tsag ho thog thu
Lekshé nyingpo	legs bshad snying po
Lhasa	lha sa
Lhomon	lho mon
Ling	gling
Ling Rimpoché	gling rin po che
Lingtshang	gling tshang
Lödrö Chökyi Senge	blo gros chos kyi seng ge
Loyul	lo yul
Lozang Dolma	blo bzang sgrol ma
Lozang Samten	blo bzang bsam gtan
Lugyal	klu rgyal
Machen pomra	rma chen spom ra
Manéné	ma ne ne
Markham	rmar khams
Marpa	mar pa
Milarepa	mi la ras pa
namtar	rnam thar
Nangchen	nang chen
Nechung	gnas chung
Ngawang Nyima	ngag dbang nyi ma
Norbulingka	nor bu gling ka
Nyingmapa	rnying ma pa
Öpagmé	'od dpag med
Ögyen Heruka	o rgyan he ru ka
Panchen	pan chen
Pangnang Rimpoché	spang nang rin po che
Pari	dpa ris
Paro	spa to
Pawo Tsug (Tsuglag)	dpa' bo gtsug (gtsug lag)
Pema Gyentsen	padma rgyal mtshan
Pon Lha Gé	dpon lha dge
Potala	po ta la
Powo	spo bo
Ra Lotsawa Dorjé Dragpa	rva lo tsva ba rdo rje grags pa
Ratö Dongkong	rva stod gdong kong

Tibetan Glossary

Ratö Rimpoché	rva stod rin po che
Rechungpa	ras chung pa
Reting Rimpoché	rva sgreng rin po che
Rigsum Gönpo	rigs gsum mgon po
Rikha Lozang Tenzin	ri kha blo bzang bstan 'dzin
Rimé	ris med
rimpoché	rin po che
Rolpai Dorjé	rol pa'i rdo rje
rü	rus
Rumteg	rum bteg
rüpa	rus pa
Sakya	sa skya
Sakya Trinzin	sa skya khri 'dzin
Samyé	bsam yas
Sanggyé Tenzin Rimpoché	sangs rgyas bstan 'dzin rin po che
Sera Mé	se ra smad
Sera	se ra
Serkong (Tugsé) Rimpoché	ser kong (thugs sras) rin po che
Shabdrung	zhabs drung
Sharmapa	zhva dmar pa
Sharpa Chöjé	shar pa chos rje
Sheja	shes bya
Sogpo	sog po
Sumpa Khenpo	sum pa mkhan po
Taglüng	stag lung
Tai Situ	ta'i si tu
Tanjur	bstan 'gyur
Tara Geshé	ta' ra dge bshes
Tara Rimpoché	ta' ra rin po che
Tāranātha	tva ra na tha
Tashi jong	bkra shis ljongs
Tashilhunpo	bkra shis lhun po
Tatsag Jedrung Hutuktu	rta tsag rje drung ho thog thu
Tenpai Gyentsen	bstan pa'i rgyal mtshan
Tenzin Gyatso	bstan 'dzin rgya mtsho
Tenzin Trinlé Jigmé Chökyi Wangchug	bstan 'dzin 'phrin las 'jigs med chos kyi dbang phyug
Thubten Gyatso	thub bstan rgya mtsho
Thubten Ngödrub	thub bstan dngos grub
Thung	thung
Tichang Rimpoché	khri byang rin po che
Trisong Detsen	khri srong lde brtsan
Trunggö Böjong	krung go'i bod ljongs
Tsang	gtsang

Tibetan Glossary

Tsangyang Gyatso	tshangs dbyangs rgya mtsho
tsempo	btsan po
Tsongkhapa	tsong kha pa
Tsopema	mtsho padma
Tsurphu	mtshur phu
Tugsé Rimpoché	thugs sras rin po che
tulku	sprul sku
Ügyen Trinlé	ao rgyan 'phrin las
Wöntrül Rimpoché	dbon sprul rin po che
Yarlha Shampo	yar lha sham po
Yarlung	yar lung
Yeshé Gyentsen	ye shes rgyal mtshan
Zepug Rimpoché	ze phug rin po che
Zong Rimpoché	zong rin po che

Bibliography

DZ refers to works in *Zhentong Daozang*, with the text number as recorded in K.M. Schipper, *Concordance du Tao-Tsang* (Paris: École francaise d'Extrême-Orient, 1975).
T refers to works in *Taishō shinshū daizōkyō*, with the text number followed by the volume.
Z refers to works in the Hong Kong reprint of the *Zoku zōkyō*, with the volume followed by page numbers.

Pre-modern Chinese and Tibetan Works

Beitang shuchao, Tianjin: Tianjin guji chubanshe, 1988.
Bowu zhi jiaozheng, Fan Ning ed., Beijing: Zhonghua shuju, 1980.
Chuxue ji, Beijing: Zhonghua shuju, 1962.
DaTang Daci'ensi Sanzang Fashi zhuan, T.2053 (50).
DaTang Daxianfusi gu Dade Kangzang Fashi zhi bei, T.2054 (50).
DaTang gu Sanzang Xuanzang Fashi xingzhuang, T.2052 (50).
Gaoshi zhuan, Siku quanshu ed.
Guochao qixian leizheng chubian, 1890, reprinted Taibei: Wenhai chubanshe 1965.
Guoyu, Shanghai: Guji chubanshe, 1978.
Hanshu, Beijing: Zhonghua shuju, 1975.
Hanyu dacidian, Shanghai: Hanyu dacidian chubanshe, 1986.
Hou Hanshu, Beijing: Zhonghua shuju, 1973.
Jingtu sheng xian lu, xubian, Z.135:194–232.
Jinshu, Beijing: Zhonghua shuju, 1974.
Jiu Tangshu, Beijing: Zhonghua shuju, 1972, reprinted Shanghai: Zhonghua shuju, 1975.
Jushi zhuan, Z.149:396–506.
Kaiyuan shijiao lu, T.2154 (55).
Kun dga' grol mchog, *The Autobiographies of Jo-nan Kun dga' grol- mchog and His Previous Embodiments*, 2 vols, New Delhi: Tibet House, 1982.
Liexian zhuan, DZ 294.
Lishi zhenxian tidao tongjian, DZ 296.
Meixian guanji, DZ 600.
Mengzi ziyi shu zheng, Dai Zhen, He Wenguang, ed., Beijing: Zhonghua shuju, 1961.
Nanshi, Beijing: Zhonghua shuju, 1973.

Bibliography

Ouyang Xiu xuanji, Chen Xin and Du Weimo, eds., Shanghai: Guji chuban she, 1986.
Peng Shaosheng, *Erlin juji*, 1881 edition.
Qingshi liezhuan, Beijing: Zhonghua shuju, 1987.
Quan shanggu sandai QinHan Sanguo Liuchao wen, Beijing: Zhonghua shuju, 1958.
Renwang boruo jingshu, T.1707 (33).
Sandong qunxian lu, DZ 1248.
Sandong zhunang DZ.1139.
Sanguo zhi, Beijing: Zhonghua shuju, 1973, reprinted 1985.
Sanguo zhi jijie, Lu Bi ed., Beijing: Zhonghua shuju, 1982.
Shenxian zhuan, Longwei mishu edition.
Shiji, Beijing: Zhonghua shuju, 1959.
Song Gaoseng zhuan, T.2061 (50).
Songxue yuanyuan ji, Guangzhou: Yueya tang, 1822.
Sui Tiantai Zhizhe Dashi biezhuan, T.2050 (50).
Taiping guangji, Beijing: Zhonghua shuju, 1961.
Taiping guangji, Saoye shanfang yinhang edition.
Taiping yulan, Beijing: Zhonghua shuju, 1985.
Tang Dajianfusi gusizhu fanjing dade Fazang heshang zhuan, T.2054 (50).
Tang hufa shamen Falin biezhuan, T.2051 (50).
Tang wushijia shiji, Shanghai: Guji chubanshe, 1989.
Tanjiao wenji T.2115 (52).
Tāranātha, Jo-Nan rJe btsun, *The Collected Works of Jo-Nan rJe btsun Tāranātha*, Leh, Ladakh: Smanrtsis Shesrig Dpemzod Series, 1985.
Wei shu Beijing: Zhonghua shuju, 1974.
Wu Yue chunqiu, Gujin yishi edition.
Xianyuan bianzhu, DZ 596.
Xin Tangshu, Shanghai: Zhonghua shuju, 1975.
Xu Gaoseng zhuan, T.2060 (50).
Xuanpin lu, DZ 781.
Yi sheng jue yi lun Z.104:75–84.
Yiwen leiju, Shanghai: Shanghai guji chubanshe, 1965.
Yue jueshu, Shanghai: Shangwu yinshuguan, 1956.
Yunqi qiqian, Daozang jinghua ed.
Zhuangzi jishi, Guo Qingfan, ed., Beijing: Zhonghua shuju, 1985.
Zhuzi Yulei, Taipei: Hanjing Wenhua Shiye Youxian Gongsi, 1980.

Modern Works in Asian Languages

An Zhenghui, *Dai Zhen zhexue zhuzuo xuanzhu*, Beijing: Zhonghua shuju, 1979.
Araki Kengo, "Hō Shōshō o meguru futari no jinbutsu," in his *Yōmeigaku no kaiten to bukkyō*, Tokyo: Kenbun shuppan, 1984.
Cao Shibang (Tso Sze-bong), "Guanyu Fojiaodi 'yizhang'" *Hsien-tai tsa-chih*, offprint (n.d.).
Cao Shibang, "Zhongguo Fojiao shizhuan yu mulu yuanchu lüxue shamen zhi tantao: shang," *Xinya xuebao* 6:1 (1964).
Cao Shibang, "Zhongguo Fojiao shizhuan yu mulu yuanchu lüxue shamen zhi tantao: xia," *Xinya xuebao* 7:2 (1966).
Cao Shibang, "Zhongguo Fojiao shizhuan yu mulu yuanchu lüxue shamen zhi tantao: zhong," *Xinya xuebao* 7:1 (1965).

Bibliography

Ch'ae T'aeksu (Inhwan), "Shiragi Daiken to *kosekki* ni tsuite," in Kim Chigyŏn and Ch'ae Inhwan, eds, *Shiragi bukkyō kenkyū*, Tokyo: Sankibo busshorin, 1973.
Ch'oe Chun'ok, comp., *Kug'yŏk Koun Sŏnsaeng munjip*, 2 vols, Seoul: Poryŏnkak, 1982.
Ch'oe Yŏngsŏng, trans. and annotator, *Chuhae sasan pimyŏng*, Seoul: Asea munhwa sa, 1987.
Chi Paesŏn, "Puk-Yŏn e taehayŏ I," *Tongbang Hakji* 54.55.56 (1987).
Cho Myŏnggi, *Silla Pulgyo ŭi i'nyŏm kwa yŏksa*, Seoul: Sin t'aeyang chulbansa, 1962.
Eda Toshio, "Shiragi no Tonrin to 'rinki' so'in no Tōdai shoka," in *Chōsen bukkyōshi no kenkyū*, Tokyo: Kokusho kankōkai, 1977.
Fukaura Seibun, *Yuishikigaku kenkyū*, 2 vols, Tokyo: Nagata bunshōdō, 1954.
Guo Peng, *Song Yuan Fojiao*, Fuzhou: Fuzhou renmin chubanshe, 1981.
Han'guk Pulgyo yŏn'guwŏn, *Silla ŭi p'yesa I*, Han'guk ŭi sach'al series 3, Seoul: Iljisa, 1974.
Hatani Ryōtai, "Yuishikishū no iha – Chōsenkei no Yuishikishū," in *Hatani hakushi bukkyō ronsetsu senshū*, 1916; Tokyo: Daitōshuppansha, 1971.
Hayashi Tadayoshi, *Chūgoku Bukkyō shiseki yōsetsu*, Kyoto: Nagata bun shōdō, 1979.
He Longxiang, ed., *Nüdan hebian*, Chengdu: Erxianan, 1906.
Hibino Takeo, *Kareinaru Zui-Tō teikoku: Zusetsu Chūgoku no rekishi 4*, Tokyo: Kodansha, 1977.
Hwang Sŏnggi, "Wŏnch'ŭk ŭi yusikhakgwan e kwanhan yŏn'gu," *Pulgyo hakbo* 9 (1972).
Imanishi Ryū, "Chōsen Chi'isan Kegonji jiseki ki ni tsuite," in Hwang Suyong, *Pulguk Sa Hwaŏm Sa sajŏk*, Kogo misul charyŏ 7 (Seoul: Kogo misul tong'in hoe, 1975).
Inaba Shōju, "Chōsen shusshin-sō Enjiki hosshi ni tsuite," *Chōsen gakuhō* 2 (1952).
Inaba Shōju, *Enjiki-sen Gejinmikkyōsho sanitsububun no kambun'yaku*, Kyoto: Hōzōkan, 1949.
Inoue Hideo, *Kodai Chōsen*, Tokyo: NHK Bukkusu, 1972.
Ishii Kōsei, *Kegon shisō no kenkyū*, Tokyo: Shunjūsha, 1996.
Kamata Shigeo, *Chōsen bukkyō no tera to rekishi*, Tokyo: Daihōrinkaku, 1980.
Kamata Shigeo, *Chūgoku Kegonshisōshi no kenkyū*, Tokyo: Tokyo Daigaku shuppankai, 1965.
Kim Ch'ŏljun, *Han'guk kodae sahoe yŏn'gu*, Seoul: Chisik san'ŏpsa, 1976.
Kim Poksun, *Silla Hwaŏmjong yŏn'gu*, Seoul: Minjoksa, 1990.
Kim Sanghyŏn, *Silla Hwaŏm sasangsa yŏn'gu*, Seoul: Minjoksa, 1991.
Kim Tongju, *Yuance zhi weishixue guan*, Taibei: Huiwen tang, 1987.
Kim Tujin, *Ŭisang: kŭ ŭi saeng'ae wa Hwa'ŏm sasang*, Seoul: Min'ŭmsa, 1995.
Kim Yŏngt'ae, "Haeoe munhŏn chung ŭi Han'guk pulgyo saryo," *Pulgyo hakbo* 13 (1976).
Kim Yŏngt'ae, "Pulguksa ŭi Hwaŏm Pŏpsa Wŏnch'ŭk e taehayŏ," *Han'guk Pulgyohak* 19 (1994).
Kim Yŏngt'ae, *Han'guk Pulgyo kojŏn myŏngcho ŭi se'gye*, Seoul: Minjoksa, 1994.
Kitsukawa Tomoaki, "Enjiki Yuishikigaku ni okeru *Jō yuishikiron* no shiryoteki mondai," *Indogaku bukkyōgaku kenkyū* 42:2 (1994).
Ko Ikjin, "Sŏmyŏng yusik ŭi kibon ipjang," *Tongguk sasang* 10:11 (1978).
Lü Cheng, *Zhongguo foxue yuanliu luejiang*, Taibei: Liren shuju, 1985.
Maejima Shinji, *Genjō Sanzō*, Tokyo: Iwanami shinsho, 1952.
Makita Shigeo, *Chūgoku kinsei Bukkyōshi kenkyū*, Kyoto: Heirakuji shoten, 1957.
Meng Guofang, ed., *Huang Zhengqing yu Wushi Jiamuxiang*, Gansu wenshi ziliao xuanbian, vol. 30; Lanzhou: Gansu renmin chubanshe, 1989.
Mishina Akihide et al., *Sankoku iji kōshō*, vol. 2, Tokyo: Hanawa shobō, 1979.

Bibliography

Mishina Akihide, *Shiragi Karo no kenkyū*, republished in *Mishina Akihide rombunshū*, vol. 6, 1943; Tokyo: Heibonsha, 1974.
Miura Shūichi, "Hō Shōshō no shisō," *Tōhō gakuhō* 60 (March 1988).
Mizuno Kōgen, ed., *Shin Butten kaidai jiten*, Tokyo: Shunjusha, 1966.
Mochizuki Shinkō, *Bukkyō Daijiten*, 10 vols, Tokyo: Sekai seiten kankō kyōkai, 1933–36; reprinted Taibei: Diping xian chuban she, 1979.
Morohashi Tetsuji, *Dai Kan-Wa jiten*, 13 vols, Tokyo: Daishukan shoten, 1966.
Nakamura Kaoru, *Kegon no jōdo*, Kyoto: Hōzokan, 1991.
Nogami Shunjō et al., *Bukkyō shi gaisetsu – Chūgoku hen*, Kyoto: Heirakuji shoten, 1968.
O Hyŏnggŭn, "Silla Wŏnch'ŭk Pŏpsa ŭi yusik sasang yŏn'gu," *Pulgyo hakbo* 25 (1988).
O Hyŏnggŭn, "Silla yusik sasang ŭi t'ŭksŏng kwa kŭ yŏksajŏk chŏn'gae," in Han'guk ch'ŏlhak hoe, ed., *Han'guk ch'ŏlhak yŏn'gu*, 3 vols, Seoul: Tongmyŏngsa, 1977.
O Hyŏnggŭn, "Wŏnch'ŭk Pŏpsa ŭi sinsiksŏl e taehayŏ," *Pulgyo hakbo* 13 (1976).
O Hyŏnggŭn, "Wŏnch'ŭk Pŏpsa wa Ilsŭng sasang," *Han'guk pulgyohak* 2 (1976).
Pak Chonghong, "Han'guk ch'ŏlhaksa – kodae p'yŏn," in Han'guk sasang yŏn'gu hoe, comp., *Han'guk sasangsa – kodae p'yŏn*, Seoul: Pŏmmunsa, 1966.
Sakade Yoshinobu, ed., *Dōkyō no daijiten*, Tokyo: Shin jinbutsu orai sha, 1994.
Shōtarō Iida, "Wŏnch'ŭk (613–696) ŭi saeng'ae wa chŏsŏ yŏn'gu: t'ŭk'i Han'guk'inuroso Chungguk Pulgyo wa T'ibet'an Pulgyo ui paljon e ibajihan ŏpjŏk ul chungsim hayŏ," in *Kwangbok 30 chu'nyon chonghap haksul hoeŭi nonmunjip*, Seoul: Haksulwon, 1975.
Sin Hyŏngsik, "Sug'wi haksaeng ko: Namal Yŏch'o ŭi chisikin ŭi tonghyang e taehan ilgu," in Yŏksahakhoe, ed., *Han'guk sa nonmun sŏnjip (Kodae p'yŏn) II*, Seoul: Ilchogak, 1976.
Sin Hyŏnsuk, "Shiragi yuishikigaku no tenseki shōsō," in Kim Chigyŏn and Ch'ae Inhwan, eds, *Shiragi bukkyō kenkyū*, Tokyo: Sankibo busshorin, 1973.
Sin Hyŏnsuk, "Tang Kyugi wa Silla Wŏnch'ŭk ŭi sangwisŏl yon'gu I," *Han'guk pulgyohak* 4 (1979).
Tongguk Taehakkyo Han'guk Pulgyo ch'ŏnsŏ p'yŏnch'an wiwŏnhoe, comps, *Han'guk Pulgyo ch'onso*, 12 vols, Seoul: Tongguk Taehakkyo, 1992.
Tongguk Taehakkyo Pulgyo munhwa yŏn'guso, comp., *Han'guk Pulgyo ch'ansul munhŏn ch'ongnok*, Seoul: Tongguk Taehakkyo, 1976.
Tsukamoto Zenryū, *Tō chūki no Jōdokyō*, Kyoto: Hōzōkan, 1975.
Ueyama Daishun, "Tonkō to Tonkō no bukkyōgaku," *Tōhō gakuhō* 35 (1964).
Wŏn Ŭibŏm, "Wŏnch'ŭk ŭi yusik sasang," in Sungsan Pak Kiljin paksa hwagap ki'nyŏm saŏphoe, ed., *Han'guk pulgyo sasangsa*, Iri: Wŏn pulgyo sasang yŏn'guwŏn, 1975.
Wu Jiyu, "Daibankoku Daitoku Sanzōshi Hōsei denkō," in Makita Tairyō and Fukui Fumimasa, eds., *Tonkō to Chūgoku Bukkyō*, Kōza Tonkō, 7, Tokyo: Daitō shuppansha, 1984.
Yamazaki Hiroshi, *Zui-Tō Bukkyōshi no kenkyū*, Kyoto: Hōzōkan, 1967.
Yanagida Seizan, *Zen no goroku I: Daruma no goroku*, Tokyo: Chikuma shobō, 1969.
Yi Man'yŏl, "Samguk ŭi hangjaeng," in Kuksa p'yŏnch'an wiwŏnhoe, comp., *Han'guk sa*, 24 vols, Seoul: Taehan min'guk mungyobu Kuksa p'yŏnch'an wiwŏnhoe, 1981.
Yi Man, "Silla'in ch'ansul ŭi *Sŏng Yusiknon* so san'ibon pug'wŏn," *Pulgyo hakbo* 30 (1993).
Yi Nŭnghwa, *Chosŏn Pulgyo t'ongsa*, 3 vols, Keijō: Sinmunguan 1918, reprinted in 2 vols, Tokyo: Kokusho kankōkai, 1974.

Bibliography

Yi Pyŏngdo, comp. and trans., *Samguk yusa*, Seoul: Kwangjo ch'ulpansa, 1980.
Yokoyama Kōitsu, *Yuishiki no tetsugaku*, Kyoto: Heirakuji shoten, 1979.
Zhu Baojiong and Xie Peilin, *MingQing jinshi timing beilu suoyin*, Shanghai: Shanghai guji, 1980.

Modern Works in European Languages

Alheit, P. and B. Dausien, "Biographie," in H.J. Sandkuhler, ed., *Europaische Enzyklopadie zu Philosophie und Wissenschaften*, vol. 1, Hamburg: Meiner, 1990.
Balazs, Étienne, "Nihilistic Revolt or Mystical Escapism," in *Chinese Civilization and Bureaucracy: Variations on a Theme*, New Haven: Yale University Press, 1964.
Balazs, Étienne, "Political Philosophy and Social Crisis at the End of the Han Dynasty," in *Chinese Civilization and Bureaucracy: Variations on a Theme*, New Haven: Yale University Press, 1964.
Barrett, T.H., "History Writing and Spirit Writing in Seventeenth-Century China", *Modern Asian Studies* 23.3 (1989).
Bauer, Wolfgang, "The Hermit's Temptation: Aspects of Eremitism in China and the West in the Third and Early Fourth Century A.D.," in *Guoji Hanxue huiyi lunwenji* 9:1 (1981).
Bauer, Wolfgang, "The Hidden Hero: Creation and Disintegration of the Ideal of Eremitism," in Donald Munro, ed., *Individualism and Holism in Chinese Values*, Ann Arbor: Centre for Chinese Studies, University of Michigan, 1985.
Beckwith, Christopher I., "Tibet and the Early Medieval *florissance* in Eurasia," *Central Asiatic Journal* 21:2 (1977).
Beckwith, Christopher I., *The Tibetan Empire in Central Asia*, New York: Princeton University Press, 1987.
Benveniste, Emile, trans. Mary Elizabeth Meek, *Problems in general linguistics*, Coral Gables: University of Miami Press, 1971.
Berkowitz, A., Patterns of Reclusion in Early Medieval China: A Study of the Formulation of the Practice of Reclusion in China and its Portrayal, unpublished PhD thesis, University of Washington, 1989.
Birnbaum, Raoul, "The manifestation of a Monastery: Shen-ying's Experiences on Mount Wu-t'ai in T'ang Context," *Journal of the American Oriental Society* 106.1 (1986).
Birrell, A., *Popular Songs and Ballads of Han China*, London, Sydney & Wellington: Unwin Hyman, 1988.
Blacker, C., *The Catalpa Bow: A Study of Shamanistic Practices in Japan*, New York: Mandala, 1975.
Bokenkamp, Stephen R., "Taoist Literature, Part 1: Through the T'ang Dynasty," in W.H. Nienhauser, ed., *The Indiana Companion to Traditional Chinese Literature*, Bloomington: Indiana University Press, 1986.
Bokenkamp, Stephen R., *Early Daoist Scriptures*, Berkeley: University of California Press, 1997.
Boltz, J.M., "Taoist Literature Part 2: Five Dynasties to the Ming," in W.H. Nienhauser, ed., *The Indiana Companion to Traditional Chinese Literature*, Bloomington: Indiana University Press, 1986.
Boltz, J.M., "Taoist Literature," in M. Eliade, *The Encyclopedia of Religion*, vol. 14, New York: Macmillan 1987.

Bibliography

Boyer, Régis, "An Attempt to Define the Typology of Medieval Hagiography," in Hans Bekker-Nielsen, Peter Foote, Jørgen Højgaard Jørgensen, and Tore Nyberg, eds, *Hagiography and Medieval Literature: A Symposium*, Odense: Odense University Press, 1981.

Brown, Peter, *The Cult of the Saints: Its Rise and Function in Latin Christianity*, Chicago: University of Chicago Press, 1981.

Ch'en Chi-yun, "Confucian, Legalist and Taoist Thought in Later Han," in Michael Loewe and Edward L. Shaughnessy, eds., *The Cambridge History of China*, vol. 1, *The Ch'in and Han Empires 221 B.C.-A.D. 220*, Cambridge: Cambridge University Press, 1986.

Chan, W.T., *Chu Hsi: New Studies*, Honolulu: University of Hawaii Press, 1989.

Chavannes, Édouard, "Les pays d'Occident d'après le Wei lio," *T'oung Pao* 6 (1905).

Chavannes, Édouard, *Les Memoires Historiques*, Paris: Adrien-Masonneuve, 1967.

Chaves, Jonathan, *Pilgrim of the Clouds*, New York: Weatherhill, 1992.

Conlan, R., "Gyalsay Tulku Rinpoche – A Tribute," *Australia Tibet Council News*, February–March 1994.

Cosgrove, Denis and Domosh, Moria, "Author and Authority: Writing the New Cultural Geography," in James Duncan and David Ley, eds., *Place/Culture/Representation*, London: Routledge, 1993.

Craig, Mary, *Kundun: A biography of the Family of the Dalai Lama*, London: HarperCollins, 1997.

Dalai Lama, *Ngos kyi yul dang ngos kyi mi mang (My Land and My People)*, Darjeeling: Freedom Press, 1963.

Dalia, Albert A., "The 'Political Career' of the Buddhist Historian Tsan-ning," in David W. Chappell, ed., *Buddhist and Taoist Practice in Medieval Chinese Society: Buddhist and Taoist Studies II*, Honolulu: University of Hawaii Press, 1987.

Danto, A.C., *Narration and Knowledge*, New York: Columbia University Press, 1985.

Daud Ali, "Technologies of the Self: Courtly Artifice and Monastic Discipline in Early India," *Journal of the Economic and Social History of the Orient* 41.2 (1998).

Davidson, R.M., "Reflections on the Maheśvara Subjugation Myth: Indic Materials, Sa-skya-pa Apologetics, and the Birth of Heruka," *The Journal of the International Association of Buddhist Studies* 14:2 (1991).

Davis, A.R., "The Narrow Lane: Some Observations on the Recluse in Traditional Chinese Society", *The Twelfth George Ernest Morrison Lecture in Ethnology*, Canberra: Australian National University, 1959.

De Bary, Wm. T., ed., *Self and Society in Ming Thought*, New York: Columbia University Press, 1970.

De Certeau, Michel, *The Mystic Fable, volume 1: The Sixteenth and Seventeenth Centuries*, Michael B. Smith, trans., Chicago: University of Chicago Press, 1992.

De Crespigny, Rafe, *Northern Frontier: The Policies and Strategies of the Later Han Empire*, Canberra: Faculty of Asian Studies, 1984.

De Crespigny, Rafe, *The Records of the Three Kingdoms*, Canberra: Faculty of Asian Studies, 1970.

De Jong, J.W., review of *Passionate Enlightenment* in *Indo-Iranian Journal* 19.2 (1996).

De Jong, J.W., "Buddha's word in China," *The Twenty-Eighth George Ernest Morrison Lecture*, Canberra: Australian National University, 1968.

Deleuze, G., trans. Mark Lester with Charles Stivale, *The Logic of Sense*, New York: Columbia University Press, 1990.

Demiéville, Paul, "Philosophy and religion from Han to Sui", in Michael Loewe and Edward L. Shaughnessy, eds., *The Cambridge History of China*, vol. 1, *The Ch'in*

Bibliography

and Han Empires 221 B.C.-A.D. 220, Cambridge: Cambridge University Press, 1986.
Demiéville, Paul, "Récents travaux sur Touen-Houang." T'oung Pao, 56 (1970).
Derrida, J., trans. Geoffrey Bennington and Rachel Bowlby, *Of Spirit*, Chicago: University of Chicago Press, 1989.
Despeux, Catherine, *Immortelles de la Chine ancienne. Taoïsme et alchimie féminine*, Puiseaux: Pardes, 1990.
Deuchler, Martina, *The Confucian Transformation of Korea: A Study of Society and Ideology*, Cambridge Ma.: Harvard University Press, 1992.
Dowman, K., trans., *Grub thob brgyad cu rtsa bzhi'i lo rgyus* [*Masters of Mahāmudrā*], New York: State University of New York Press, 1985.
Duara, Prasenjit, *Culture, Power, and the State: Rural North China, 1900-1942*, Stanford: Stanford University Press, 1988.
Duara, Prasenjit, "Superscribing Symbols: The Myth of Guandi, Chinese God of War", *Journal of Asian Studies*, 47.4 (1988).
Dudbridge, Glen, *The Hsi-yu chi: A Study of Antecedents to the Sixteenth-Century Chinese Novel*, Cambridge: Cambridge University Press, 1970.
Duncan, James and David Ley, "Introduction: Representing the Place of Culture," in James Duncan and David Ley, eds., *Place/Culture/Representation*, London: Routledge, 1993.
Eagle, Dorothy and Hilary Carnell, *The Oxford Literary Guide to the British Isles*, Oxford: Oxford University Press, 1977.
Eckel, Malcom David, *To See the Buddha: A Philosopher's Quest for the Meaning of Emptiness*, Princeton: Princeton University Press, 1992.
Eichhorn, W., "Description of the rebellion of Sun En and earlier Taoist Rebellions," *Mitteilungen des Institüts für Orientkunde*, 2 (1954).
Eichhorn, W., *Heldensagen aus dem unteren Yangtse-Tal*, Wiesbaden: Steiner, 1969.
Eliade, M., *Cosmos and History: The Myth of the Eternal Return*, New York: Harper and Row, 1959.
Eliot, T.S., *Four Quartets*, London, Faber and Faber, 1944.
Eskildsen, Stephen, *Asceticism in Early Taoist Religion*, Albany: State University of New York Press, 1998.
Fang, Achilles, *The Chronicle of the Three Kingdoms (220-265), Chapters 67-78 from the Tzu Chih T'ung Chien of Ssu-ma Kuang*, Cambridge, Ma.: Harvard University Press, 1965.
Farrell, Frank B., *Subjectivity, Realism and Postmodernism: The Recovery of the World in Recent Philosophy*, Cambridge: Cambridge University Press, 1994.
Faure, Bernard, "Bodhidharma as Textual and Religious Paradigm," *History of Religions* 25:3 (1986).
Faure, Bernard, "Random Thoughts: Wonhyo's 'Life' as Thought," *Bulgyo Yongu* 11/12 (1995).
Feuchtwang, Stephan, *The Imperial Metaphor*, London: Routledge, 1992.
Frauwallner, Erik, *The Earliest Buddhist Vinaya and the Beginnings of Buddhist Literature*, Serie Orientale Roma VIII, Rome, 1956.
Fu Chi-Ying and Ven. Master Hsing Yun, *Handing Down the Light: The Biography of Venerable Master Hsing Yun*, Taipei: Commonwealth Publishing, 1995.
Funk, Robert W. and The Jesus Seminar, *The Acts of Jesus: The search for the authentic deeds of Jesus*, San Francisco: HarperSanFrancisco, 1998.
Funk, Robert W., Roy W. Hoover and the Jesus Seminar, *The Five Gospels: The search for the authentic words of Jesus*, New York: Macmillan, 1993.
Gardiner, K.H.J., *The Early History of Korea*, Oriental Monograph Series 8, Canberra: Australian National University Press, 1969.

Bibliography

Gellner, Ernest, *Plough, Sword, and Book*, Harmondsworth: Penguin, 1988.
Gellner, Ernest, *Saints of the Atlas*, London: Weidenfeld and Nicolson, 1969.
Gernet, Jacques, trans. Janet Lloyd, *China and the Christian Impact*, Cambridge: Cambridge University Press, 1985.
Goldstein, Melvyn C., *Modern Literary Tibetan*, New Delhi: Goldstein, 1977.
Goodrich, Michael, *Vita Perfecta: The Ideal of Sainthood in the Thirteenth Century*, Monographien zur Geschichte des Mittelalters, vol. 25, Stuttgart: Anton Hiersemann, 1982.
Graham, A.C., *The Book of Lieh-tzu*, London: John Murray, 1960.
Granet, M., *Danses et Légendes de la Chine Ancienne*, Paris: Felix Alcan, 1926.
Grant, Beata, "Who is This I? Who is That other? The Poetry of an Eighteenth Century Buddhist Laywoman", *Late Imperial China* 15.1 (1994).
Guntsch, G., *Das Shen-hsien chuan und das Erscheinungsbild eines Hsien*, Frankfurt a. M.: Lang, 1988.
Gyatso, Janet, "Autobiography in Tibetan Religious Literature: Reflections on its Modes of Self-Presentation," in S. Ihara and Z. Yamaguchi, eds., *Tibetan Studies: Proceedings of the 5th Seminar of the International Association for Tibetan Studies, Narita, 1989*, Narita: Naritasan Shinshoji, 1992.
Haarh, Erik, *The Yar-luṅ Dynasty*, Copenhagen: G.N.O.Gad's Forlag, 1969.
Hamashita, Takeshi, "The Tribute Trade System and Modern Asia," *Memoirs of the Tōyō Bunko* 46 (1988).
Hamilton, Clarence H., trans., *Wei Er Shih Lun*, American Oriental Series, vol. 13, New Haven: American Oriental Society, 1938.
Hanan, Patrick, *The Chinese Vernacular Story*, Cambridge, Ma.: Harvard University Press, 1981.
Haraway, Donna, "The Promises of Monsters: A Regenerative Politics for Inappropriate/d Others," in Lawrence Grossberg, Cary Nelson and Paula A. Treichler, eds., *Cultural Studies*, New York: Routledge, 1992.
Havnevik, Hanna, *Tibetan Buddhist Nuns: History, Cultural Norms and Social Reality*, Oslo: Norwegian University Press and Institute for Comparative Research in Human Culture, 1989.
Heissig, Walther, *The Religions of Mongolia*, London: Routledge & Kegan Paul, 1980.
Holmgren, Jennifer, "Social Mobility in the Northern Dynasties: A Case Study of the Feng of Northern Yen," *Monumenta Serica* 35 (1981–1983).
Horton, John and Mendus, Susan, eds., *After MacIntyre: Critical Perspectives on the work of Alisdair MacIntyre*, Cambridge: Polity Press, 1994.
Jan Yün-hua, "Portrait and Self-portrait: A Case Study of Biographical and Autobiographical Records of Tsung-mi," in Phyllis Granoff and Koichi Shinohara, eds., *Monks and Magicians: Religious Biographies in Asia*, Oakville, Ontario: Mosaic Press, 1988.
Jiacuo, Jiangbian [= Vjam-dpal rgya-mtsho], "Gesar and Religion," *Tibet Studies: Journal of the Tibetan Academy of Social Sciences* 1 (1989).
Jiacuo, Jiangbian, "Gesar and the Tibetan Culture," paper for the 5th Seminar of the International Association for Tibetan Studies, Narita, Japan, 1989.
Johnston, David, "Communication, Class and Consciousness," in David Johnston et al., eds., *Popular Culture in Late Imperial China*, Berkeley: University of California Press, 1985.
Jones, David, *Epoch and Artist*, London: Faber and Faber, 1959.
Junjirō Takakusu, *The Essentials of Buddhist Philosophy*, Wing Tsit Chan and Charles A. Moore, eds., 3rd ed. Honolulu: Office Appliance Co., 1956.
Kaltenmark, M., *Le Lie-sien Tchouan*, Paris: College de France, Institut des Hautes Etudes Chinoises, 1987.

Bibliography

Kalupahana, David J., *Buddhist Philosophy: A Historical Analysis*, Honolulu: University Press of Hawaii, 1976.
Kandel, B., "Der Versuch einer politischen Restauration – Liu An, der Konig von Huai-nan," *Nachrichten der Gesellschaft für Natur- und Volkerkunde Ostasiens* 113 (1973).
Kapstein, Matthew, "The Purificatory Gem and its Cleansing: A Late Tibetan Polemical Discussion of Apocryphal Texts," *History of Religions* 28:3 (1989).
Karmay, Samten, "The Social Organization of Ling and the Term *Phu-nu* in the Gesar Epic," *Bulletin of the School of Oriental and African Studies* 58 (1995).
Karmay, Samten, "The Theoretical Basis of the Tibetan Epic, with Reference to a 'Chronological Order' of the Various Episodes in the Gesar Epic," *Bulletin of the School of Oriental and African Studies* 56 (1993).
Kieschnick, John, *The Eminent Monk: Buddhist Ideals in Medieval Chinese Hagiography*, Honolulu: University of Hawai'i Press, 1997.
Kirkland, J. Russell, "The Spirit of the Mountain: Myth and State in Pre-Buddhist Tibet," *History of Religions* 21 (1982).
Kirkland, J. Russell, Taoists of the High T'ang: An Inquiry into the Perceived Significance of Eminent Taoists in Medieval Chinese Society, unpublished Ph.D dissertation, University of Indiana, 1986.
Koichi Shinohara, "Two sources of Chinese Buddhist Biographies: Stupa Inscriptions and Miracle Stories," in Phyllis Granoff and Koichi Shinohara, eds, *Monks and Magicians: Religious Biographies in Asia*, Oakville, Ontario: Mosaic Press, 1988.
Korean Buddhist Research Institute, *Buddhist Thought in Korea*, Seoul: Dongguk University Press, 1994.
Kvaerne, P., *An Anthology of Buddhist Tantric Songs: A Study of the Caryagiti*, Oslo, Bergen & Tromso: Det Norske Videnskaps-Akademi, Universitetsforlaget, 1977.
La Vallée Poussin, Louis de, *Vijñaptimatratasiddhi: La Siddhi de Hiuan-Tsang*, 2 vols, Paris: Paul Guenther, 1928–29.
LaFleur, W., "Biography," in M. Eliade, ed., *The Encyclopedia of Religion*, vol. 2, New York: Macmillan 1987.
Lao, D.C., *Mencius*, Harmondsworth: Penguin Classics, 1970.
Lee, Peter H., *Lives of Eminent Korean Monks: The Haedong Kosŭng chŏn*, Cambridge, Ma.: Harvard University Press, 1969.
Legge, James, *Shijing* vol. 4 of *The Chinese Classics*, 1865, reprinted Taibei: Wenshizhe chuban she, 1972.
Levi, Jean, *Les fonctionnaires divins: politique, despotisme et mystique en Chine ancienne*, Paris: Seuil, 1989.
Lévi-Strauss, C., *The Savage Mind*, Chicago: University of Chicago Press, 1966.
Lévi-Strauss, C., trans. J. and D. Weightman, *The Raw and the Cooked*, New York: Harper and Row, 1969.
Levine, Nancy E., "The Theory of *rü* Kinship, Descent and Status in a Tibetan Society," in C. von Fürer-Haimendorf, ed., *Asian Highland Societies in Anthropological Perspective*, New Delhi: Sterling, 1981.
Lieu, Samuel N.C., "The Holy Men and their Biographers in Early Byzantium and Medieval China," in Ann Moffat, ed, *Maistor: Classical Byzantine and Renaissance Studies for Robert Browning*, Canberra: The Australian Association for Byzantine Studies, 1984.
Liu, James T.C., *Ou-yang Hsiu: An Eleventh-Century Neo-Confucianist*, Stanford: Stanford University Press, 1967.
Lopez, Donald S. Jr, ed., *Religions of Tibet in Practice*, Princeton: Princeton University Press, 1997.

Bibliography

Lopez, Donald S., Jr, "On the Interpretation of the Mahāyāna sūtras," in Donald S. Lopez, Jr, ed., *Buddhist Hermeneutics*, Honolulu: University of Hawaii Press, 1988.
Lynn, Richard John, *The Classic of Changes: A New Translation of the I Ching as Interpreted by Wang Bi*, New York: Columbia University Press, 1994.
MacIntyre, Alisdair, *After Virtue: A Study in Moral Theory*, 2nd edition, London: Duckworth, 1985.
Mansvelt-Beck, B.J., "The Fall of Han", in Denis Twitchett and Michael Loewe, eds., *The Cambridge History of China*, vol. 1, *The Ch'in and Han Empires 221 B.C.-A.D. 220*, Cambridge: Cambridge University Press, 1986.
Martin, Helmut, "Literature of the Ming and Ch'ing," in Gilbert Rozman, ed., *Soviet Studies of Premodern China*, Ann Arbor; Center for Chinese Studies, The University of Michigan, 1984.
McKay, Alex, *Pilgrimage in Tibet*, Richmond, Surrey: Curzon, 1998.
McMullen, David, "Historical and Literary Theory in the Mid-Eighth Century," in A.F. Wright and D. Twitchett, ed., *Perspectives on the Tang*, New Haven: Yale University Press, 1973.
Morris, Mark, "Desire and the Prince: New Work on Genji monogatari – A Review Article", *Journal of Asian Studies* 49.2 (May, 1990).
Nagao, Gadjin M., *Mādhyamika and Yogācāra: A Study of Mahāyāna Philosophy*, trans. Leslie S. Kawamura, Albany: State University of New York Press, 1991.
Naquin, Susan and Chün-fang Yü, *Pilgrims and Sacred Sites in China*, Berkeley: University of California Press, 1992.
Nattier, Jan, *Once Upon a Future Time*, Berkeley: Asian Humanities Press, 1991.
Nattier, Jan, "The *Heart Sutra*: A Chinese Apocryphal Text," *Journal of the International Association of Buddhist Studies* 15:2 (1992).
Nienhauser, W.H., *The Indiana Companion to Traditional Chinese Literature*, Bloomington: Indiana University Press, 1986.
Novarr, David, *The Lines of Life: Theories of Biography, 1880–1970*, West Lafayette, Indiana: Purdue University Press, 1986.
Obermiller, E., *History of Buddhism (Chos-hbyung) by Bu-ston*, part 1, *The Jewelry of Scripture*, Leipzig: Harrassowitz, 1931.
Pachow, Werner, "A study of the Twenty-Two Dialogues on Mahāyāna Buddhism," *The Chinese Culture* 20:1 (1979).
Pachow, Werner, *A Study of the Twenty-two Dialogues on Mahāyāna Buddhism*, Taipei: Tungchu Publishing, 1992.
Paper, Jordan C., *The Fu-tzu: A Post-Han Confucian Text*, Monographies du T'oung Pao 63, Leiden: E.J. Brill, 1987.
Pelliot, P., "La théorie des quatre fils du Ciel," *T'oung Pao* 22 (1923).
Penny, Benjamin, "Immortality and Transcendence" in Livia Kohn, ed., *Handbook of Taoism*, Leiden: E.J. Brill, 2000.
Penny, Benjamin, Early Daoist Biography: A Study of the Shenxian zhuan, unpublished Ph.D thesis, Australian National University, 1993.
Penny, Benjamin, Historicising Immortality, paper presented at the Australian Association for Asian Studies conference, Perth, 1994.
Plessner, H., *Die Stufen des Organischen und der Mensch: Einleitung in die philosophische Anthropologie*, Berlin: Walter de Gruyter and Company, 1928.
Poo, Mu-chou, "The Images of Immortals and Eminent Monks: Religious Mentality in Early Medieval China," *Numen* 42 (1995).
Potter, Beatrix, *The Tale of Squirrel Nutkin*, London: Frederick Warne, 1903.
Pye, Michael, *Skilful Means: A Concept in Mahayana Buddhism*, London: Duckworth, 1978.

Bibliography

Radin, Paul, *The Trickster: A Study in American Indian Mythology*, London: Routledge & Kegan Paul, 1955.
Report of the Australian Human Rights Delegation to China, 14–26 July 1991, Canberra: Department of Foreign Affairs and Trade, September 1991.
Robinet, Isabelle, *Histoire du Taoisme des Origines au XIVe Siecle*, Paris: Les Editions du Cerf, 1991.
Robinson, Richard H., *The Buddhist Religion: A Historical Introduction*, Belmont: Dickenson Publishing, 1970.
Said, Edward W., *Orientalism: Western Concepts of the Orient*, first published 1978; Harmondsworth: Penguin, 1991.
Samuel, Geoffrey, "Gesar of Ling: The Origins and Meaning of the East Tibetan Epic," in S. Ihara and Z. Yamaguchi, ed., *Tibetan Studies: Proceedings of the 5th Seminar of the International Association for Tibetan Studies, Narita, 1989*, Narita: Naritasan Shinshoji, 1992.
Samuel, Geoffrey, "Music and Shamanic Power in the Gesar Epic," in Jamie Kassler, ed., *Metaphor: A Musical Dimension*, Sydney: Currency Press, 1991.
Samuel, Geoffrey, "Some Tibetan Ritual Texts about King Gesar," paper for the 2nd International Conference on Gesar Epic Studies, Lhasa, Tibet, August 1991.
Samuel, Geoffrey, "Tibet as a Stateless Society and Some Islamic Parallels," *Journal of Asian Studies* 41:2 (1982).
Samuel, Geoffrey, *Civilized Shamans: Buddhism in Tibetan Societies*, Washington DC: Smithsonian Institution Press, 1993.
Samuel, Geoffrey, *Mind, Body and Culture: Anthropology and the Biological Interface*, London and New York: Cambridge University Press, 1990.
Sartre, J.-P., trans. B. Frechtman, *The Emotions: Outline of a Theory*, New York: Philosophical Library, 1948.
Saussure, Ferdinand de, trans. W. Baskin, *Course in General Linguistics*, New York: Philosophical Library, 1959.
Schipper, K., *L'Empereur Wou des Han dans la Legende Taoiste*, Paris: Ecole Francaise D'Extrême-Orient, 1965.
Seidel, A., "Image of the Perfect Ruler in Early Taoist Messianism," *History of Religions* 9 (1969).
Shahar, Meir, *Crazy Ji: Chinese Religion and Popular Literature*, Cambridge, Mass.: Harvard University Asia Center, 1998.
Shaw, Miranda, *Passionate Enlightenment*, Princeton: Princeton University Press, 1994.
Shek, Richard, "Testimony to the Resilience of the Mind: The Life and Thought of Peng Shao-sheng (1740–1796)," in Richard J. Smith and D.W.Y. Kwok, eds., *Cosmology, Ontology, and Human Efficacy: Essays in Chinese Thought*, Honolulu: University of Hawaii Press, 1993.
Shōju Inaba, "On Chos-grub's Translation of the *Chieh-shen-mi-ching-shu*," in Leslie S. Kawamura and Keith Scott, eds., *Buddhist Thought and Asian Civilization*, Emeryville: Dharma Publishing, 1977.
Shōtarō Iida, "A MuKung-hwa in Changan: A Study of the Life and Works of Wŏnch'ŭk (613–696), with special interest in the Korean contributions to the development of Chinese and Tibetan Buddhism," *Proceedings of the International Symposium Commemorating the 30th Anniversary of Korean Liberation*, Seoul: National Academy of Sciences, 1975.
Shōtarō Iida, "The Three Stupas of Ch'ang An," *Papers of the 1st International Conference on Korean Studies*, Seoul: The Academy of Korean Studies, 1980.
Shōtarō Iida, "Who Best Can *Return* the Dharma-cakra?," *Indogaku bukkyōgaku kenkyū* 34:2 (1986).

Bibliography

Sivin, Nathan, "On the Word 'Taoist' as a Source of Perplexity", *History of Religions* 17:3&4 (1969).
Smith, T.E., Ritual and the Shaping of Narrative: The Legend of the Han Emperor Wu, unpublished Ph.D dissertation, University of Michigan, 1992.
Smith, Warren, *Tibetan Nation: A History of Tibetan Nationalism and Sino-Tibetan Relations*, Boulder, Colorado: Westview, 1996.
Stauffer, Donald A., *English Biography before 1700*, New York: Russell and Russell, 1964.
Stcherbatsky, Theodore, *Buddhist Logic*, 2 vols, 1930, New York: Dover reprint, 1962.
Stein, R.A., "La Soumission de Rudra et Autres Contes Tantriques," *Journal Asiatique* 283:1 (1995).
Stein, R.A., *Tibetan Civilisation*, Stanford: Stanford University Press, 1972.
Steiner, George, *After Babel: Aspects of Language and Translation*, Oxford: Oxford University Press, 1975.
Stewart, Kathleen, *A Space on the Side of the Road: Cultural Poetics in an "Other" America*, Princeton: Princeton University Press, 1996.
Suzuki, D.T., *Laṅkāvatāra Sūtra*, London: Routledge & Kegan Paul, 1932.
Swann, N., *Food and Money in Ancient China*, Princeton: Princeton University Press, 1950.
Tambiah, S.J., "The Galactic Polity in Southeast Asia," in S.J. Tambiah, *Culture, Thought and Social Action: An Anthropological Perspective*, Cambridge, Ma. & London: Harvard University Press, 1985.
Tambiah, S.J., *The Buddhist Saints of the Forest and the Cult of Amulets: A Study in Charisma, Hagiography, Sectarianism and Millennial Buddhism*, Cambridge: Cambridge University Press, 1984.
Taylor, Charles, *Sources of the Self: The Making of the Modern Identity*, Cambridge, Ma: Harvard University Press, 1989.
Taylor, R., "Fatalism," *Philosophical Review* 71:1 (1962).
Templeman, David, "A Narrative Account of a Ganacakra and the fulfilment of Guhyasamāja through Cakrasaṃvara," *Studies in Central and East Asian Religions*, vols 5/6 (1992/1993).
Templeman, David, "Reflexive Criticism – The Case Of Kun dga' grol mchog and Tāranātha," in P. Kvaerne, ed., *Tibetan Studies, Proceedings of the 6th Seminar of the International Association for Tibetan Studies, Fagernes, 1992* (Oslo: Institute for Comparative Research in Human Culture, 1994).
Templeman, David, "The Account of the Prince Rāmagopāla," *The Tibet Journal* 17:4 (Winter, 1992).
Templeman, David, *Tāranātha's Life of Kṛṣṇācārya/Kāṇha*, Dharamsala: Library of Tibetan Works and Archives, 1989.
Templeman, David, *The Seven Instruction Lineages*, Dharamsala: Library of Tibetan Works and Archives, 1983.
Terhune, L., "Divided House, Tibet's Kagyu Buddhists face a leadership battle," *Far Eastern Economic Review*, 24 March 1994.
Thomas, Edward, *A Literary Pilgrim in England*, Oxford: Oxford University Press, 1980.
Track, Norman S., *Song of a Water Dragon*, Jamaica Plains: YMAA Publication Center, 1996.
Tsai, Kathryn Ann, *Lives of the Nuns: Biographies of Chinese Buddhist Nuns from the Fourth to Sixth Centuries*, Honolulu: University of Hawaii Press, 1994.
Tucci, Giuseppe, "The Secret Characters [=Sacral Character] of the Kings of Ancient Tibet," *East and West* 6:2 (1955).

Bibliography

Tucker, Charles O., *A Dictionary of Official Titles in Imperial China*, Stanford: Stanford University Press, 1985.
Twitchett, Denis and Wechsler, Howard J., "Kao-tsung (reign 649–83) and the Empress Wu: the inheritor and the usurper," in Denis Twitchett, *The Cambridge History of China, Sui and T'ang China, 589–906*, part 1, Cambridge: Cambridge University Press, 1979.
Twitchett, Denis and Arthur F. Wright, "Introduction" in Denis Twitchett and Arthur Wright, eds., *Perspectives on the T'ang*, New Haven: Yale University Press, 1973.
Twitchett, Denis, "Chinese Biographical Writing," in E.G. Pulleyblank and W.G. Beasley, eds., *Historians of China and Japan*, New York: Oxford University Press, 1961.
Twitchett, Denis, "Hsüan-tsung (reign 712–756)," in Denis Twitchett, ed., *The Cambridge History of China*, vol. 3, *Sui and T'ang China, 589–906*, part 1, Cambridge: Cambridge University Press, 1979.
Twitchett, Denis, "Problems of Chinese Biography," in Arthur F. Wright and Denis Twitchett, eds, *Confucian Personalities*, Stanford: Stanford University Press, 1962.
Vaihinger, H., *The philosophy of 'As If'*, trans. C.K. Ogden, 2nd ed., London: Routledge & Kegan Paul, 1935.
van Gulik, Robert H., *Siddham: An Essay on the History of Sanskrit Studies in China and Japan*, Nagpur: Chandra, 1956.
Verellen, Franciscus, ed., *Culte des sites et culte des saints en Chine, Cahiers d'Extrême-Asie* 10 (1998).
Vervoorn, Aat, *Men of the Cliffs and Caves: The Development of the Chinese Eremitic Tradition to the End of the Han Dynasty*, Hong Kong: The Chinese University Press, 1990.
Waley, Arthur, *Monkey: Folk Novel of China*, New York: Grove Press, 1958.
Wallacker, B., "Liu An, Second King of Huai-nan (180?–122? B.C.)," *Journal of the American Oriental Society* 92:1 (1972).
Wang Yinuan, "Incomplete Statistics of Sections and Lines in the Tibetan *King Gesar*" [in Chinese] *Gesar Yanjiu [Gesar Research]* 1 (1985).
Warder, A.K., *An Introduction to Indian Historiography*, Bombay: Popular Prakashan, 1972.
Watanabe Hiroshi, *Confucianisme et societés asiatiques*, Yuzo Mizoguchi and Léon Vandermeersch, eds., Paris: Harmattan, 1991.
Watson, B., *Courtier and Commoner in Ancient China*, New York & London: Columbia University Press, 1974.
Watson, Burton, trans., *The Complete Works of Chuang Tzu*, New York: Columbia University Press, 1968.
Wei Tat, *Ch'eng Wei-shih Lun: Doctrine of Mere-Consciousness*, Hong Kong: Ch'eng Wei-Shih Lun Publication Committee, 1973.
Weightman, Simon, "Symbolism and Symmetry", forthcoming in Leonard Lewisohn, ed., *Proceedings of the Conference on Sufism in Safavid and Mughal Times* (provisional title).
Weinstein, Donald and Rudolph M. Bell, *Saints and Society: The Two Worlds of Western Christendom, 1000–1700*, Chicago: University of Chicago Press, 1982.
Weinstein, Stanley, "A Biographical Study of Tz'u-ên," *Monumenta Nipponica* 15 (1959–60).
Weinstein, Stanley, *Buddhism under the T'ang*, Cambridge: Cambridge University Press, 1987.
Weinstein, Stanley, "Imperial Patronage in the Formation of T'ang Buddhism", in Arthur F. Wright and D.C. Twitchett, *Perspectives on the T'ang*, New Haven: Yale University Press, 1973.

Bibliography

Welch, Holmes, *The Buddhist Revival in China*, Cambridge, Ma.: Harvard University Press, 1969.
Welter, Albert, "The Contextual Study of Chinese Buddhist Biographies: The Example of Yung-ming Yen-shou (904-975)," in Phyllis Granoff and Koichi Shinohara, eds., *Monks and Magicians: Religious Biographies in Asia*, Oakville, Ontario: Mosaic Press, 1988.
Whitehead, A.N., *Adventures of Ideas*, Cambridge: Cambridge University Press, 1947.
Wilhelm, Hellmut, "From Myth to Myth: The case of Yueh Fei's Biography", in A.F. Wright, and D.C. Twitchett, *Confucian Personalities*, Stanford: Stanford University Press, 1962.
Wilson, George M., *Patriots and Redeemers in Japan: Motives in the Meiji Restoration*, Chicago: University of Chicago Press, 1992.
Wright, Arthur F., "Biography and Hagiography. Hui-chiao's Lives of Eminent Monks," in *Silver Jubilee Volume of the Jimbun-Kagaku-Kenkyūshō*, Kyoto: Jimbun Kagaku Kenkyujo, 1954, reprinted in *Studies in Chinese Buddhism*, Robert M. Somers, ed., New Haven: Yale University Press, 1990.
Wright, Arthur F., "Values, Roles and Personalities," in Arthur F. Wright and D.C. Twitchett, eds., *Confucian Persuasion* (Stanford: Stanford University Press, 1962).
Wright, Dale S., "Historical Understanding: The Ch'an Buddhist Transmission Narratives and Modern Historiography," *History and Theory* 31:1 (1992).
Wu P'ei-yi, *The Confucian's Progress*, Princeton: Princeton University Press, 1990.
Yang Lien-sheng, "The Organization of Chinese Official Historiography," in E.G. Pulleyblank and W.G. Beasley, eds., *Historians of China and Japan*, New York: Oxford University Press, 1961.
Young, Robert, *White Mythologies: Writing History and the West*, London: Routledge, 1990.
Zürcher, E., *The Buddhist Conquest of China*, Leiden: E.J. Brill, 1958, reprinted 1972.

Index

Abhayadatta 134
Agotra 78
Atīśa 51–52
Avataṃsaka Sūtra 7, 57–67, 71, 94, 109, 122

Balazs, Étienne 2
Beckwith, Christopher 180
Berkowitz, Alan 2
Biographies for the Qing History see *Qingshi liezhuan*
Biographies of Buddhist Laymen see *Jushi zhuan*
Biographies of Lofty Men see *Gaoshi zhuan*
Biography,
  administrative 17–21
  and hagiography 87–91
  and representation 85–87
  and saṃsāra 153–154
  as "confessional" 150–151
  genre 14, 15, 25–26
  historically verifiable 14
  narrative qualities of 223–223, 236–238
  of immortals 15–17, 30–45
  of Lofty Men 21–24
  rewriting of 14, 30–45
  traditional Chinese 16, 89–90, 152, 161; influence on Buddhist 83
  as "life-and-times" 148–151
Blacker, Carmen 222
Bodhiruci 109
Boltz, Judith 30–31
Bowu zhi 25

Brief History of the Wei Dynasty see *Weilüe*
Buddha,
  intention of 81
  miracles of 54–56
Buddhabhadra 56–57, 59
Buddhism,
  Chan 66–69; *Recorded Sayings* (*yulu*) 66–67; Sixth Patriarch 5
  Faxiang 74–82
  Gelugpa order 179, 182
  Hossō (*see* Buddhism, Faxiang)
  Huayan 53, 56–66
  Karma Kagyupa order 183
  Mādhyamika 81
  Pure Land 158
  Sakya order 183
  syncretic 157
  Vajrayāna 179
  Vijñānavāda 74–81, 85–86, 91–92, 96, 104, 110
  Vinaya 82
  Yogācāra 76, 79, 81, 83
Butön Rinpoché 135

Cakravartin 182
Candrakīrti 81
Caryā Songs *see* Caryāgīti
Caryāgīti 134, 137–138
Chen Shou 19
Cheng weishi lun 75, 80, 92, 94, 106, 110, 118
Chenrezig 182–183
China's Tibet see *Trunggö Böjong*
Chödrub 76, 111

Index

Ch'oe Ch'iwŏn 53, 75, 82–85, 87, 90–91, 97–102, 106, 109–113
Chuan deng lu 162
Ci'en Ji *see* Dasheng Ji
Commentary on the Avataṃsaka Sūtra 59
Confessions (St Augustine) 150–152
Confucianism 154–157, 159–161, 164, 168–170
Continuation of the Lives of the Eminent Monks see *Xu Gaoseng zhuan*
Crazy Ji 8

Dai Zhen 166, 171, 174, 177
Ḍākinī Songs 138–140
Dalai Lama 1, 182–183, 189–190, 198, 202
Dante 52
Daoism 15–17, 30–45, 155, 159
Daoxuan 82
Dasheng Ji 74–75, 77, 79, 90–93, 96–97, 106, 108–111
Deleuze, Gilles 231–232, 235, 238–239
Deqing 157
Dharmapāla 74–75, 77, 80, 92, 106, 110, 120–121
Dharmarāja 182–183
Divākara 107, 109
Dong Jing 15, 17, 19, 21, 22
Dongfang Shuo 38–40
Dongshan Liang Jie 66
Dongxian zhuan 40
Drugu Chögyé Rinpoché 179
Durrant, Stephen 31

Eliade, Mircea 222, 238
Emperor Wu 35–36, 39
Erikson, Erik 78

Fachang 94, 103–104
Fan Li 32–35
Fate,
  in Chinese philosophy 224–231
  in western philosophy 231–235
Fazang 53, 56–58, 61, 71, 83–84, 97
Five Commandments (Buddhist) 160
Five Virtues (Confucian) 160
Fu Xi 24
Fu Xuan 24

Gaṇḍavyūha Sūtra 65
Gaoseng zhuan 151, 159

Gaoshi zhuan 21–26
Garmaba *see* Karmapa
Ge Hong 16
Gellner, Ernest 180
Geng Fu 24
Gernet, Jacques 3
Gesar of Ling 178–188
  as Bodhisattva emanation 185
  as folk-religion figure 185
  in the People's Republic of China 186–187
Gou Jian 32–33
Granet, Marcel 228
Guandi 4, 185
Guankong 76
Guṇabhadra 58
Guo Pu 41–42
Guochao Songxue yuanyuan ji 168–170
Guoyi Furen 45
Gyatso, Janet 133

Hagiography *see* Religious biography
Hamilton, Clarence 80
Han Wudi neizhuan 31, 35, 39
Han Wudi *see* Emperor Wu
Hanshu 36–40
Hatani Ryōtai 76
He Zhizhang 43–44
Heidegger, Martin 232
History of the Three Kingdoms see *Sanguo zhi*
Huangbo 67
Huangfu Mi 21–23
Huayan jing see *Avataṃska Sūtra*
Huayan lun see *Commentary on the Avataṃsaka Sūtra*
Huayanjing chuanji see *Transmission of the Avataṃsaka Sūtra*
Hui Wu 61
Huijiao 90, 151–152, 159
Huizhao 92, 96, 106
Hyŏnch'ŭk (Wŏnch'ŭk) 105, 129
Hyŏnjun, 83

Ibn al-'Arabī 54
Inaba Shōju 76
Iryŏn 101, 112

Jia Mu 18, 21
Jiang Fan 168–170, 172
Jingtu shengxian lu 161, 166–167
Jinshu 41–43

Index

Journey to the West 8
Ju Mipam 185
Jushi zhuan 154, 158–159, 162
Just King *see* Dharmaraja

Kaltenmark, Max 33
Kamata Shigeo 76
Karmapa, Seventeenth 209–212
Karmay, Samten 184
Kendall, Laura 223
Kevaddha Sutta 51
Kham, and the Gesar epic 178–179, 181
Khenchen Sanggyé Tenzin Rimpoché 197–198
King Arthur (parallels with Gesar) 4, 179
King of Huainan *see* Liu An
Kongtrül Rimpoché 196
Kṛṣṇācārya 132–142
Kün-ga Dröchog 132–133, 135–142

Laṅkāvatāra Sūtra 81
Laozi 6
Lévi-Strauss, Claude 223
Li Tongxuan 59–62, 64–65, 69, 71
Li Yong 24
Liangshu 43
Liexian zhuan 7, 31, 33–35, 39
Liezhuan *see* Biography, traditional Chinese
Liezi 6
Lineage, Tibetan 133
Ling Rimpoché 195
Lingtshang 184
Linji Yi Xuan 69
Lishi zhenxian tidao tongjian 34, 39–41, 43–44
Liu An 36–38
Liu Xiang 33, 35
Lives of Eminent Monks see *Gaoseng zhuan*
Lu Shang 7
Lu Xiangshan 156
Luo Yao 6
Luther, Martin 78

Ma Zhi 60
Machen Pomra 184
MacIntyre, Alisdair 173
Madhyānta-vibhāṅga 79
Manéné 184

Marpa 52
Marx, Groucho 6
Meditation 78–79
Mei Fu 32
Mencius 226–227
Merleau-Ponty, Maurice 239
Milarepa 52, 62, 190
Ming *see* Fate
Mohammed 78
Monkey King 8
Montaigne, Michel de 150

Namtar *see* Religious biography, traditional Tibetan
Nanshi 43

O Hyŏnggŭn 75
Obituaries 203–204
Öpagmé 183
Ouyang Xiu 165, 175–176

Panchen Lama 195–196
Penny, Benjamin 30, 34
Plessner, Helmut 232–237
Pu Songling 8

Qingshi liezhuan 167

Ratö Rimpoché 197
Recorded Sayings of Pang Yun 67–68
Reincarnate,
  discovery and recognition of 204–206
  entering the doctrine 207–208
  offering robes 206
Religious biography,
  as teachings themselves 141–142
  immortals 15–17, 30–45
  levels of meaning 136–137, 140–142
  modern Tibetan, causes of death in 197–198; disposal of the body in 200–201; entreaties for a quick return in 202–203; honorific titles in 196; meditative absorption period in 199; political considerations in 213–214; reviewing significant events in 201–202; signs at death in 198–199
  spirit-mediums 221–223
  traditional Tibetan 132, 189–190, 192–193, 196

Index

Representation 79–87
 and biography 85–87
 and Chinese Buddhist biography 81–85
Resolving Doubts about the One Vehicle of Truth see *Yisheng jueyi lun*
Rodinson, Maxime 78
Rousseau, Jean-Jacques 150, 153

Saṃdhinirmocana Sūtra 76, 78–81
Sandong qunxian lu 41
Sanguo zhi, Pei Songzhi's commentary to 14, 19, 23
Seidel, Anna 2, 41
Sengbian 94, 103–104
Shahar, Meir 8
Shan nüren zhuan 7
Sheja 189–216
Shenxian zhuan 14–17, 19–21, 24, 25–26, 30, 33–38, 41
Shiji 31–34, 36–39
Skilful means 51
Smith, Thomas 35
Song Fu 74, 84–85, 90–91, 97, 100, 102, 105, 113
Song Gaoseng zhuan 74–75, 82–84, 90, 96–97, 99
Spirit-mediums 221–223
Squirrel Nutkin 10
Stewart, Kathleen 240
Su Wu 25
Sun Ce 40–41
Sun Wukong *see* Monkey King

Taehyŏn 110
Tai Situ Changchub Gyentsen 181–182
Taiping jing 40
Tambiah, Stanley 181
Tankuang 5, 110–111
Tantra,
 Cakrasaṃvara 133–134, 136, 138–139, 143–144
 Guhyasamāja 138–139, 143–144
 Hevajra 133–134
 Kālacakra 135
 Nātha Abhyudaya 135
 Vasantatilaka 134
Tao Qian 164–165, 175–176
Tāranātha 132–133, 135–136, 141
The Life and Hard Times of a Korean Shaman 223

The Lives of Eminent Monks Compiled in the Song Dynasty see *Song Gaoseng zhuan*
The Rhapsody on Snow see *Xuefu*
The Springs and Autumns of Mr Wei see *Weishi chunqiu*
Tibet,
 Lhasa state 181
 Mongol rule 181
 Yarlung dynasty 180, 183
Tibetan Bulletin 190
Tibetan periodical literature 189–216
Tojŭng 110
Toyun 96
Transmission of the Avataṃsaka Sūtra 56, 58, 61
Trunggö Böjong 189–216
Tsongkhapa 76
Twitchett, Denis 2

Ŭich'ŏn 96–97, 113
Universal monarch *see* Cakravartin

Vaihinger, Hans 87, 115
Vasubandhu 80
Vervoorn, Aat 2
Vimalakīrti-nirdeśa Sūtra 62–64
Viṃśatikā 80

Wang Yangming 156, 171–172
Weilüe 17–21, 23, 25–26
Weinstein, Stanley 2
Weishi chunqiu 24
Whitehead, A.N. 228
Wright, Arthur 151–152
Wu Bei 38
Wuliu xiansheng zhuan 164–165

Xiao Ziyun 42–43
Xu Gaoseng zhuan 82
Xuanpin lu 34, 40
Xuanzang 74–77, 80, 90–97, 103–111
Xuanze (Wŏnch'ŭk) 105–107
Xuefu 24–25

Yan Zhenqing 44
Yisheng jueyi lun 164, 166
Yu Ji 40–41
Yuan Hongdao 6
Yuance (Wŏnch'uk) 107
Yuki Reimon 93
Yunju 67

Index

Zanning 74–77, 82–84, 88, 90–93, 97, 100, 106, 108, 111, 117
Zenju 74
Zhang Hua 25
Zhang Jue 6
Zhang Weiping 172–173
Zhang Xiu 6
Zhao Daoyi 34
Zhenke 157
Zhiguizi 154
Zhiguizi, Biography of 162–164
Zhixu 157
Zhongguo Xizang see *Trunggö Böjong*
Zhu Xi 156, 171, 227–231
Zhuangzi 2, 39
Zhuhong 157
Zuozhuan 229

For Product Safety Concerns and Information please contact our EU representative GPSR@taylorandfrancis.com
Taylor & Francis Verlag GmbH, Kaufingerstraße 24, 80331 München, Germany

www.ingramcontent.com/pod-product-compliance
Lightning Source LLC
Chambersburg PA
CBHW070555300426
44113CB00010B/1267